A History of Cant and Slang Dictionaries

Volume II 1785–1858

For Margaret Coleman and Evelyn Sheppard: two fine rum mollishers.

A History of Cant and Slang Dictionaries

Volume II 1785–1858

JULIE COLEMAN

By the same author

A History of Cant and Slang Dictionaries
Volume I: 1567–1785

OXFORD
UNIVERSITY PRESS

OXFORD

UNIVERSITY PRESS

Great Clarendon Street, Oxford OX2 6DP

Oxford University Press is a department of the University of Oxford.
It furthers the University's objective of excellence in research, scholarship,
and education by publishing worldwide in

Oxford New York

Auckland Bangkok Buenos Aires Cape Town Chennai
Dar es Salaam Delhi Hong Kong Istanbul Karachi Kolkata
Kuala Lumpur Madrid Melbourne Mexico City Mumbai Nairobi
São Paulo Shanghai Taipei Tokyo Toronto

Oxford is a registered trade mark of Oxford University Press
in the UK and in certain other countries

Published in the United States
by Oxford University Press Inc., New York

© Julie Coleman, 2004

British Library Cataloguing in Publication Data

Data available

Library of Congress Cataloging in Publication Data

Data available

ISBN 0-19-925470-2

1 3 5 7 9 10 8 6 4 2

Typeset by Newgen Imaging Systems (P) Ltd., Chennai, India
Printed in Great Britain
on acid-free paper by
Biddles Ltd., King's Lynn

Contents

vi   Contents

Preface

> HALF-FLASH AND HALF-FOOLISH, this character is applied
> sarcastically to a person, who has a smattering of the cant language,
> and having associated a little with *family* people, pretends to a knowl-
> edge of *life* which he really does not possess, and by this conduct
> becomes an object of ridicule among his acquaintance. (Vaux)

In 1567, when he published the *Caveat or Warening for Commen
Cursetors*, Thomas Harman launched a profitable and long-lived
branch of publishing: the cant list.[1] Purporting to provide a tantaliz-
ing insight into the secret language of thieves and vagabonds, these
lists pandered to and fed a titillating fear of crime. Although B. E.
included slang and colloquial language in his *New Dictionary of the
Terms Ancient and Modern of the Canting Crew*, published in *c*.1698, it
was not until the late eighteenth century that broader based slang
dictionaries began to appear. While continuing to appeal to a
nervous fascination with crime, these volumes also gloried in the
base language of the working people and offered the possibility of
entry into the fashionable demi-monde.

This volume considers slang and cant lists first published between
1785 and 1858 and some later derivative works. Volume I in this
series looked at the earlier word-lists.[2] Later volumes will consider
slang and cant dictionaries published from 1859 onwards.

The University of Leicester, the British Academy, and the Arts
and Humanities Research Board all provided financial support for
this research. I am very grateful to them, and also to the staff of the
libraries I have visited and corresponded with: the British Library,
the Bodleian, the National Library of Scotland, the London Library,
the Library of Congress, the Chicago Newberry Library, the New
York Public Library, the Beinecke Rare Book and Manuscript
Library at Yale university, and the university libraries of Leicester,
Cambridge, London, Newcastle, and Edinburgh. I am especially

---

[1] Thomas Harman, *Caveat or Warening for Commen Cursetors* (London: William Griffith, 1567).
[2] Julie Coleman, *A History of Cant and Slang Dictionaries: Volume I 1567–1784* (Oxford: Oxford University Press, 2004).

indebted to the inter-library loan staff at Leicester. Robert Bruce of the Bodleian Music Library and Max Tyler of the British Music Hall Society were kind enough to help me to locate the earliest published version of a song, cited under **uncle** in a number of these dictionaries. I am also very grateful to Elaine Treharne, the best head of department there ever was, for her support and understanding. Julie and Robert, Keith and Tom, were kind enough to put me up and put up with me while I was working in the British Library. Martin Halliwell kindly gave me useful advice on part of chapter two. I owe a great debt to Janet Bately, Jane Roberts, Christian Kay, John Simpson, and Joan Beal, for all of their support. I have had some interesting discussions with Christopher Stray and Jesse Sheidlaner since the publication of volume one of this series—all, alas, too late to be reflected here. John Davey, Stuart Fowkes, and Henry Miller have eased this volume through the press at OUP. Most of all, I am grateful to my family, for helping me through what has not been an easy time.

J.C.

Acknowledgements

All illustrations are reproduced by permission of the British Library, except Figure 3.2, which is reproduced by permission of the Bodleian Library, Oxford.

List of Illustrations

Abbreviations and Conventions

Abbreviations

a	ante (before) e.g. *a*1700. In the *OED*, *a* is used for *adjective*
adv	adverb
Aus	Australian
c.	circa (about) e.g. *c.*1698. In B. E.'s dictionary, *c.* is employed to mark cant terms
d	pence (pre-decimal)
DAB	*Dictionary of American Biography*
dial	dialect
DNB	*Dictionary of National Biography*
n	note. In the *OED*, *n* is used for *noun*
OED	*Oxford English Dictionary*
$p = 0.01$	probability of less than 1 per cent of something happening by chance
$p = 0.05$	probability of less than 5 per cent of something happening by chance
pl	plural
r	recto (right): the right-hand page of an open book; the front of a leaf of paper
s	shilling
Sc	Scottish
US	American
v	verso (turned): the left-hand page of an open book; the back of a leaf of paper. In the *OED*, *v* is used for *verb*

Typographical conventions

italics	cited terms
bold italics	dictionary headwords
SMALL CAPITALS	semantic fields
'single inverted commas'	quotations, including quoted definitions
"speech marks"	my own definitions

[square brackets]   restored readings; editorial insertions.
                                     Square brackets around *OED* citations
                                     and dates indicate doubtful usage
                                     evidence

\<chevrons\>   orthographical notation (exact spell-
                                     ing, letter-forms, capitalization, and
                                     punctuation)

Introduction

This volume provides an account of cant and slang dictionaries first published between 1785 and 1858. Although literary authors and historians of the Georgian and Victorian periods have made extensive use of them, these dictionaries have, until now, received little scholarly attention in their own right. Even Eric Partridge, thorough and knowledgeable as he was, used the dictionaries as resources rather than studying them in any detail.

There are three possible reasons for the neglect of this fascinating field. First, the contents of the dictionaries undermine their authority. As well as recording countless slang and colloquial expressions, some of the editors delighted in the inclusion of profanities, obscene jokes, and smutty anecdotes. Secondly, the dictionaries are too recent for time to have rendered their contents quaint and harmless. Thirdly, few of these lists are entirely original, which undermines their credibility as genuine witnesses to contemporary speech.

What scholars have studied is the cant and slang dictionaries of the sixteenth and seventeenth centuries, which are validated by their debt to the European rogue-book tradition and by contemporary playwrights' use of their glossaries. Gotti's study of early cant and slang lists includes the first edition of Grose's *Classical Dictionary of the Vulgar Tongue*.[1] It is fitting that Grose should be both Gotti's cut-off and my starting point for this volume, because his work marks the fullest realization of the old cant dictionary tradition, as well as the beginning of a new tradition of slang dictionaries. Grose based his work on many of the dictionaries that preceded it; his influence is apparent in most that followed.

It is useful to distinguish between the labels I have used for various types of non-standard language. *Colloquial* language is the language of conversation. *Dialect* terms are restricted to a geographical region. Although both colloquial and dialect terms find their way into the dictionaries studied here, they remain peripheral. *Slang* is usually short-lived, and often belongs to a specific age group or social clique. It is used, like fashion, to define in-groups and out-groups. *Jargon* is

---

[1] Maurizio Gotti, *The Language of Thieves and Vagabonds* (Tübingen: Max Niemeyer Verlag, 1999).

the specialized language of an occupational or interest group, and functions as often to exclude as to include. *Cant* is the secret language of thieves and beggars, and is used for deception and concealment. *Flash* is used with specific reference to the fashionable slang of London's eighteenth- and nineteenth-century demi-monde. The boundaries between these types of language cannot be clearly defined, and individual terms move easily between categories as they are adopted by new sets of speakers. The lexicographers discussed do not all use them with the meanings outlined here. *Cant* and *slang* both sometimes means "jargon", and *flash* sometimes means "slang", sometimes "cant". Some lexicographers join them all together and make little distinction between them. The link between all of these language types is that they do not belong to what is now known as standard English. All are found in the dictionaries studied here.[2]

This is not a history of cant and slang. The emphasis throughout is on the dictionaries themselves rather than the terms they list. My intention is to discuss these dictionaries in the context of the general and specialized dictionaries available at the time. I shall demonstrate how the dictionaries are related to each other and not only which earlier glossaries they used, but also how they used them. I shall also identify distinctive features of content and methodology. By reference to each dictionary's sources and to the *Oxford English Dictionary*,[3] it is possible to determine how reliable they are as witnesses of contemporary cant and slang. Reference to historical and social contexts is another useful way of appreciating the dictionaries' topicality and understanding their role. After all, publishers would not have continued to produce such works if there had not been a market for them.

Without rehearsing the whole history of the English dictionary, it is worth putting these word-lists into their lexicographic context.[4] The two main general dictionaries in circulation in the 1780s were Nathan Bailey's *Universal Etymological Dictionary*, first published in

---

[2] For a fuller discussion, see Coleman, *Cant and Slang Dictionaries* i.3–5.

[3] *Oxford English Dictionary* (*OED*), 3rd edn., ed. John Simpson. *OED Online*. (Oxford: Oxford University Press, 2000–) [http://dictionary.oed.com/cgi/entry/00299451]

[4] Sidney I. Landau, *Dictionaries. The Art and Craft of Lexicography* (1984) (Cambridge: Cambridge University Press, 1993), 35–75, provides a useful summary of the history of English lexicography. For a more detailed account, see De Witt T. Starnes and Gertrude E. Noyes, *The English Dictionary from Cawdrey to Johnson, 1604–1755* (Chapel Hill: University of North Carolina Press, 1946). I am heavily dependent on both here.

1721 (revised as *Dictionarium Britannicum* in 1730 and as *A New Universal English Dictionary* in 1755), and Samuel Johnson's *Dictionary of the English Language* (1755). Both of these works fulfil many of our modern expectations of what a general dictionary of English ought to be. For example, they attempt to include the whole vocabulary of English, including common terms as well as the 'hard words' found in their seventeenth-century forebears. Unlike Johnson, who largely omitted them, Bailey includes tabooed and vulgar terms, treating them like any other except for his tendency towards Latin definitions:

CUNT [cunnus, L. cþið [sic], *Sax.* kutte, *Belg. con*, F.] *pudendum muliebre*, L.

To FUCK [probably of **fupcken**, *Du.* to thrust or knock, *Dr. T.H.* others of **foḃer**, *Du.* to beget; others of *futico*, L. of φυτάω, *Gr.* to plant] a term used of a goat; also *subagitare fœminam*.

A PRICK [price, *Sax.* **prick**, *Du*] a Man's Yard.[5]

Both dictionaries are fully alphabetized, instead of merely grouping their contents to the first or second letter as some earlier lists had. Each treats *i/j* and *u/v* as single letters, and alphabetizes accordingly. Both give some indication of word stress, but not consistently. Each provides etymologies, which are frequently speculative. Although both Bailey and Johnson demonstrate a commendable knowledge of Latin, Greek, and French, there is little evidence of the study of Old or Middle English.

   These dictionaries have much in common with each other, but Johnson's is the more modern of the two, in that it excludes some of the proverbial and encyclopaedic information found in Bailey. Johnson also includes illustrative citations, largely from literary sources. He includes more usage labels than Bailey, and occasionally indicates pronunciation by comparison with other words. Although he cannot take credit for regularizing the spelling of English, Johnson did provide an authoritative account of a reasonably modern system. His was the first to become the definitive authority that we now expect dictionaries to be.

   In his *Plan of a Dictionary of the English Language* and in the preface to the *Dictionary* itself, Johnson discussed the principles behind his work. In the eight years between the *Plan* and the *Dictionary*, his ideas were to change on some important matters, particularly the question

---

[5] Nathan Bailey, *Dictionarium Britannicum* (London: T. Cox, 1730).

of whether a language could be fixed and preserved from future alteration. Although, he decided, change could not be prevented, it could be delayed:

> Life may be lengthened by care, though death cannot be ultimately defeated: tongues, like governments, have a natural tendency to degeneration; we have long preserved our constitution, let us make some struggles for our language.[6]

Although he came to believe that it was impossible to stop language changing, Johnson did guide his readers on matters of questionable usage:

> To BAMBOOZLE. *v.a.* [a cant word not used in pure or in grave writings.] To deceive; to impose upon; to confound . . .
> To QUOB. *v.n.* [a low word.] To move as the embrio does in the womb; to move as the heart does when throbbing.
> To SCONCE. *v.a.* . . . To mulct; to fine. A low word which ought not to be retained.
> WO'NDERFUL. *adv.* To a wonderful degree. Improperly used . . .[7]

It was into this tradition that Grose's dictionary was published, and it is against these dictionaries that he should be judged. By compiling his dictionary from numerous earlier word-lists, Grose aimed to be definitive. He cites both Bailey and Johnson within the body of his dictionary, but it is Johnson's influence that shapes the work itself.

Grose's opinions on language change are in direct opposition to Johnson's. While Johnson viewed change as regrettable but unavoidable, Grose saw the mutability of language not only as essential, but also as something to be celebrated. Johnson avoided listing short-lived terms and those not dignified by tradition. For Grose, the more novel, the more transient terms are, the more reason there was for recording them:

> The many vulgar allusions and cant expressions that so frequently occur in our common conversation and periodical publications, make a work of this kind extremely useful, if not absolutely necessary, not only to foreigners, but even to natives resident at a distance from the metropolis, or who do not mix in the busy world; without some such help, they might hunt through all the ordinary Dictionaries, from Alpha to Omega, in search of the words, 'black legs, lame duck, a plumb, malingeror, nip cheese, darbies, and the new drop,' although these are all terms of well-known import, at New-market, Exchange-alley, the City, the Parade, Wapping, and Newgate. The fashionable words, or favourite expressions of the

---

[6] Samuel Johnson, *A Dictionary of the English Language* (London: W. Stratham for J. & P. Knapton, etc., 1755; repr. Hildesheim: Georg Olms Verlagsbuchhandlung, 1968), Preface, C2v.

[7] Johnson, *Dictionary*.

day, also find their way into our political and theatrical compositions; these, as they generally originate from some trifling event, or temporary circumstance, on falling into disuse, or being superseded by new ones, vanish without leaving a trace behind, such were the late fashionable words, a Bore and a Twaddle, among the great vulgar, Maccaroni and the Barber, among the small; these too are here carefully registered.[8]

Even the *OED* had to restrict its coverage of slang and tabooed terms, not only for practical reasons, but also because the publishers and public were not ready for them. Grose was, in this respect, ahead of his time.

Johnson's dictionary fulfilled a nationalistic need. The French Academy had completed a dictionary of French in 1694, and English dictionaries were felt to be lacking in comparison. Johnson's publication was met with jingoistic acclaim, and in his preface, he remarked that a prescriptive dictionary like that of the French Academy was incompatible with the English spirit of liberty. Not one to miss a trick, Grose appealed to a similar sentiment:

The great Approbation, with which so polite a nation as France has received the Satyrical and Burlesque Dictionary of Monsieur Le Roux, testified by the several editions it has gone through, will, it is hoped, apologise for an attempt to compile an English Dictionary on a similar plan, our language being at least as copious as the French, and as capable of the witty equivoque, besides which, the freedom of thought and speech, arising from, and privileged by our constitution, gives a force and poignancy to the expressions of our common people, not to be found under arbitrary governments, where the ebullitions of vulgar wit are checked by the fear of the bastinado, or of a lodging during pleasure in some gaol or castle.[9]

What might seem mere vulgarity, we are told, should be valued and preserved as an expression of English liberty.

Grose's *Classical Dictionary* is in some ways an antidote to Johnson's: its contents are neither uplifting nor educational; its purpose is to amuse and entertain. Grose's skills as a lexicographer should not be overstated. His was not, by the standards of the time, a well-written dictionary.[10] Nor were its contents entirely new or reliable. It is, however, an invaluable source of information about slang and colloquial language in the late eighteenth century. Testament to this is that the *OED* cites Grose's dictionary hundreds of times.

---

[8] Francis Grose, *A Classical Dictionary of the Vulgar Tongue* (London: S. Hooper, 1785), ii.

[9] Grose, *Classical Dictionary* (1785), i.

[10] See Gotti, *The Language of Thieves*, 105–7, for examples of Grose's failings.

It provides the earliest and sometimes the only citation for dozens of terms.

Although he has been described as 'a pioneer of the lexicography of slang',[11] Grose was by no means the first to publish a dictionary of non-standard English. Dialect dictionaries date back to John Ray's *Collection of English Words* (1674),[12] and accounts of dialect had been published at the beginning of the seventeenth century. Dictionaries of cant, the language of thieves and beggars, also have a venerable history. Cant terms were used in the text of several sixteenth-century publications,[13] but the first significant cant list was published in 1567: Thomas Harman's *Caveat or Warening for Commen Cursetors*. Harman's word-list was adapted by Thomas Dekker, and contributed to the success of his *Belman of London* pamphlets, in which a night-watchman wandered through the capital, exposing its vices.[14] Samuel Rowlands exposed Dekker's plagiarism, and added a few terms and a little commentary of his own.[15]

Harman's word-list was expanded by Richard Head, first in his *English Rogue* and then in the *Canting Academy* in the 1660s and 70s.[16] There are two lists in the *Canting Academy*, one arranged by the English term, and the other presenting cant term first. These lists were reprinted under various names and titles during the seventeenth and eighteenth centuries, sometimes together, but more often separately. Perhaps their most significant use was by Elisha Coles in the general word-list of his *English Dictionary*.[17]

B. E.'s *New Dictionary of the Terms Ancient and Modern of the Canting Crew* was the first slang dictionary, covering a wider range of non-standard language than the earlier lists.[18] In its compilation, B. E. used several sources including Coles's *English Dictionary* and a short glossary published with Thomas Shadwell's play, *The Squire of Alsatia* (1688).[19] B. E.'s dictionary, in its turn, spawned many other word-lists. These

[11] Ian Ousby (ed.), *The Cambridge Guide to Literature in English* (Cambridge and New York: Cambridge University Press, 1993), 395.

[12] John Ray, *A Collection of English Words not Generally used . . .* (London: H. Bruges for Tho. Burrell, 1674).

[13] Most notably, John Awdelay's *The Fraternitie of Vacabondes* (1561) (London: I. Awdeley, 1575) and Gilbert Walker's *A Manifest Detection of the Most Vyle and Detestable Use of Diceplay . . .* (London: Abraham Uele, 1552).   [14] For example, *The Belman of London* (London: Nathaniel Butter, 1608).

[15] S[amuel] R[owlands], *Martin Mark-all, Beadle of Bridewell* (London: John Budge & Richard Bonian, 1610).

[16] Richard Head, *The English Rogue described in the Life of Meriton Latroon* (London: Henry Marsh, 1665); *The Canting Academy, or the Devils Cabinet Opened* (London: F. Leach for Mat. Drew, 1673).

[17] Elisha Coles, *An English Dictionary* (London: Samuel Crouch, 1676).

[18] B. E., *A New Dictionary of the Terms Ancient and Modern of the Canting Crew* (London: W. Hawes, c.1698).   [19] Thomas Shadwell, *The Squire of Alsatia* (London: James Knapton, 1688).

each took a different selection from the thousands included in B. E.'s influential work, but tended to concentrate on those marked as 'cant'. *The New Canting Dictionary* made a few additions and was subsequently used as a source by, among others, Bailey.[20] A glossary derived from the *New Canting Dictionary* is also found in about fifty editions of the life of Bampfylde-Moore Carew. These range in size from thirty headwords to over 750, though most contain around 300.

The dictionaries belonging to the main Harman–Head–B. E. tradition all share a common core of vocabulary, but there are many early word-lists not belonging to this tradition. A generation after Harman, Robert Greene's cony-catching pamphlets (1591–2) included short lists of the terminology of various con-tricks.[21] The little glossary to Shadwell's *Squire of Alsatia* is a foretaste of the newfound interest in recording contemporary slang and cant that characterized the eighteenth century. These lists, largely unrelated to any that had gone before, confirm the continued use of some of the terms found in the main tradition, and add many others, some of which find their way into later dictionaries.

By the 1780s, editions of cant and slang word-lists were being published at a rate of two each year, which is four times the rate of the previous decade. Whether Grose was shrewdly responding to this growing interest in the language of the underworld, or whether he was himself carried along by it, can only be a matter for conjecture. What is certain is that Grose was living in a period and in a city that found the subject of crime and punishment both fascinating and entertaining.

It is easy to appreciate why a folk-criminologist in late eighteenth-century London might have looked to the past with nostalgia.[22] Even the prisons of a few decades before could be seen through a rosy haze as places of conviviality, diversion, and (for those who could afford it) relative comfort. The drinking clubs of Newgate and other prisons were abolished in 1784. Prison reformers and missionaries were beginning to replace the throng of guests and sightseers. Not only were the sins of gambling, idleness, and drunkenness suppressed, but also those arising from free association between the

---

[20] *New Canting Dictionary* (London: The Booksellers of London and Westminster, 1725).

[21] For example, Robert Greene, *A Notable Discoverie of Coosnage* (London: John Wolfe for T.N., 1591).

[22] Very little of what follows is original. It is a simplified digest from many sources. Where there seems to be general agreement, I have not cited a source. I have provided notes only for contentious opinions, quoted words, and cited figures. All books and articles consulted are listed in the bibliography.

sexes. Prisons were commercial ventures, whose jailers recouped the cost of purchasing their position by charging for essential services, like locking and unlocking doors. Denied the opportunity to raise money by selling alcohol and facilitating gambling, jailers lost a dependable source of income, and many concentrated instead on extortion. It was not until 1813 that jailers were paid a salary, and the payment of fees for release was abolished.

As conditions in prisons became harsher, public sympathy for some of their inmates increased. By the late 1770s, about half of incarcerated prisoners were debtors. If they could not rely on the help of family and friends, they had little hope of ever leaving prison. They were dependent for support upon the creditors who had imprisoned them. These costs, along with prison dues, were added to the debt whose repayment was their only chance of release. While such treatment of debtors was not new, it was beginning to be viewed as a national disgrace.

There were, on the other hand, few who argued that felons should be treated with more compassion. Their numbers had risen beyond the penal system's ability to cope with them, and harsh measures seemed the only solution. Transportation had fallen into temporary abeyance after America stopped receiving British convicts in 1775. Although the decision to end transportation had been forced upon the British authorities, the punishment had already fallen into some disrepute, because many convicts fared well in the New World, and for those who did not, it was easy enough to return. As a temporary solution, ships moored on the Thames, known as the *hulks*, were used to house prisoners from 1776, and the Penitentiary Act of 1779 introduced hard labour for these and other convicts. The hulks were already becoming a national scandal by the time Grose published his dictionary, and when transportation to Australia began in 1787, the disadvantages of the practice were gratefully ignored. The 1779 Act had also allowed the building of prisons that would use humiliating conditions and solitary confinement to bring about repentance and reformation, though none were built before 1812. It was all a far cry from the free movement and lively conviviality that had once punctuated the misery of life in Newgate.

The first professional police force was not established until 1798, but the efforts of the Bow Street magistrates had demonstrated that professional thief-takers need not be villains, like Jonathan Wild, or political spies, like the feared Parisian force. Nevertheless, Pitt's bill, which would have allowed the setting up of a professional force to police the whole of London, failed in 1785. When Grose published his dictionary, London was still largely policed by parish constables, who were widely regarded as at best ineffective, and at worst corrupt. *Charlies*, who were paid to patrol London's streets at night, 'were often old, in poor health, inadequately armed, and lax in the performance of their duties.'[23] Appointment as a parish constable, which had once conferred considerable dignity, had become so burdensome and unattractive that parish councils had been known to fill the office with their most unpopular neighbour out of spite.[24]

Although attempts to reform prisons and the police did not meet with unqualified success, some improvements in the legal process had been achieved. The 1720s and 1730s saw the appearance at the Old Bailey of lawyers for the prosecution and defence. They were viewed with suspicion and distrust from the first, but by the end of the century lawyers were commonly engaged by any defendant who could afford them. By the middle of the eighteenth century, the law was beginning to distinguish between child and adult criminals. Moreover, instead of having to pay the full costs of prosecution themselves, poor prosecutors were beginning to be compensated by the courts. The unseemly speed at which trials were conducted had also become cause for concern: at the assizes, the average case took half an hour, including the jury's deliberation. By the end of the eighteenth century, it had been established that judges had the power to adjourn overnight if necessary. The awesome majesty of the assize judge, pronouncing speedy justice with the full authority of God, the king, and the local community, was thus replaced by a clash between quibbling lawyers that might easily outlast spectators' interest.

Even executions had lost some of their pageantry. The procession of condemned criminals from Newgate to Tyburn in open carts, with nooses around their necks, caused so much disorder and disruption to normal business that it had been abolished in 1783:

If we take a view of the supposed solemnity from the time at which the criminal leaves the prison to the last moment of his existence, it will be found to be a period full of the most shocking and disgraceful circumstances. If the only defect were the want of ceremony the minds of the spectators might be supposed to be left in a state

---

[23] John L. McMullan, *The Canting Crew. London's Criminal Underworld 1550–1700* (New Brunswick, NJ: Rutgers University Press, 1984), 82.

[24] Clive Emsley, *Policing and its Context 1750–1870* (London: Macmillan, 1983), 23–4.

of indifference; but when they view the meanness of the apparatus, the dirty cart and ragged harness, surrounded by a sordid assemblage of the lowest among the vulgar, their sentiments are inclined more to ridicule than pity. The whole progress is attended with the same effect. Numbers soon thicken into a crowd of followers, and then an indecent levity is heard . . . till on reaching the fatal tree [the crowd] became a riotous mob, and their wantonness of speech broke forth in profane jokes, swearing and blasphemy . . . Thus are all the ends of public justice defeated; all the effects of example, the terrors of death, the shame of punishment, are all lost.[25]

From December 1783, executions took place outside Newgate itself, and although disorder and even deaths among the crowd occurred, public execution was not abolished in England until 1874.

Although the number of crimes punishable by death continued to rise until the last decades of the eighteenth century, largely to protect property, the proportion of convictions that ended in execution fell. Transportation, and then the hulks and hard labour, were seen as merciful alternatives to execution, and pardons conferring these lesser punishments were the eventual lot of many of the felons who were initially sentenced to death. Thus the law could be both terrible and merciful: giving up a handful of criminals to the gallows as an example, but not diminishing the spectacle by executing too many. By the 1780s several other European nations had abolished the death penalty altogether as 'needlessly cruel and socially useless'.[26] The deterrent effect was beginning to lose its credibility, and mercy appeared to depend more on influence and whim than justice.

Despite these apparent moves towards liberality, of thought, if not always in deed, the 1780s were characterized by 'an alarming sense of increasing crime'.[27] This was fuelled in part by the Gordon riots in 1780, during which the Bank of England came under attack and Fleet Street prison was burnt down. The Revolution in America and incipient rumblings of unrest in France further shook the confidence of England's rulers.

The eighteenth century was a period of surplus labour. Large numbers of the rural poor left behind the familiarity of the 'fear and gratitude' of provincial justice when they moved to London.[28]

[25] Arthur Griffiths, *The Chronicles of Newgate* (London: Chapman and Hall Ltd, 1896), 72–3, quoting a contemporary pamphlet.

[26] Ted Robert Gurr, *Rogues, Rebels, and Reformers. A Political History of Urban Crime and Conflict* (Beverly Hills/London: Sage Publications, 1976), 150–1.

[27] J. E. Thomas, *House of Care. Prisons and Prisoners in England 1500–1800* (Nottingham: University of Nottingham, Dept of Adult Education, 1988), 112.

[28] Douglas Hay, 'Property, Authority and the Criminal Law', 17–63, in Douglas Hay et al., *Albion's Fatal Tree. Crime and Society in Eighteenth Century England* (London: Penguin, 1975), 54–5.

As mechanization was introduced into traditional industries, the poor grew ever poorer. Attitudes towards poverty were also changing. The virtue of charity was now overshadowed by the doctrine of self-help: poverty was caused by failure rather than misfortune. As work moved from the home to the factory, the children of labouring parents were increasingly left unsupervised. Declining attendance at school added to the hoard of idle children amusing themselves by petty theft. Government response to the increase in minor and major lawlessness was to deny pardons to criminals guilty of robbery, burglary, or housebreaking. In the year that Grose's dictionary was published, about 65 per cent of condemned criminals were hanged, as opposed to an average of 29 per cent for the years from 1756 to 1781. By 1787 this had risen to 80 per cent.[29]

Hanging had not only become more common and less entertaining, it had also grown more reliably deadly. At the beginning of the eighteenth century, hanging was still a rather amateur business. Ropes often broke and necks sometimes did not. The condemned were left to dangle until they died through asphyxiation, sometimes hastened by the merciful aid of friends pulling on their legs. By the end of the century, the technology of execution had improved, and convicts stood on a trapdoor whose opening brought a relatively swift release. Although this was clearly a more humane death, it must have been anti-climactic for the bloodthirsty crowds who remembered the jerking struggles of the hanging man, performing his last dance: the *Paddington frisk*. It brought to an end the romantic possibility of executed criminals being whisked away and revived. All excitement was not suppressed by cold-hearted precision and efficiency, however. Execution-goers could still enjoy the spectacle of burning at the stake, which was a punishment reserved for women guilty of treason, and used until 1788. Only the year after the *Classical Dictionary* was published, a crowd 20,000 strong watched the strangulation and burning of husband-murderer Phoebe Harris.

In 1785, then, when Grose published the first edition of his dictionary, executions were being performed at an unprecedented rate, but without the pageantry they had once involved. They no longer fulfilled the requirements of those who wanted felons to suffer painfully before an impressionable crowd. They no longer entertained and

---

[29] Philip Rawlings, *Crime and Power. A History of Criminal Justice 1688–1998* (London and New York: Longman, 1999), 39.

thrilled the baying mob. Those who felt that the death penalty had never been an effective deterrent were confirmed in their opinion. Instead of pardoned felons being transported to an exciting new life in America, where conditions and prospects were probably better than at home, they were instead incarcerated in the rotten, overcrowded, and insanitary hulks. Prisons threatened to become places of isolation, discomfort, and hard work.

Criminals themselves were also less appealing. Who could live up to the example set by Jack Sheppard, escaping from prison four times before he was finally executed in 1724? What modern criminal could aspire to the romance of the highwayman, performing acts of gallantry as he dispensed social justice? Who could achieve the success of Jonathan Wild, who had his thieves steal to order, and then charged the owners for the return of stolen goods? The condemned man, dressed as if for his wedding, cheered by the crowds lining the route to Tyburn, and making his final glorious defiant farewells at the gallows, had become a thing of the past.

In literature, too, criminals lost some of their glory. The eighteenth century had adored rogue biographies, which detailed the entertaining criminal careers of the likes of Bampfylde Moore-Carew and Moll Flanders, and readers had delighted in their successes in eluding capture. Villains continued to receive their just desserts in the end, but when the reader stopped identifying with them, the rogue biography lost its value as a moral lesson. Instead, towards the end of the century, we see the first signs of an interest in detectives. From unpromising beginnings as 'at worst, a villain, and, at best, a suspect and ambiguous character',[30] the fictional sleuth was metamorphosizing into the amateur genius epitomized by Sherlock Holmes. With its protagonist motivated by the intellectual challenge rather than financial reward, the detective novel is the story of the investigation not the crime: from centre-stage the criminal is relegated to the status of supporting cast.[31]

Like the outlaws of the Wild West, criminals had once been able to gain notoriety by outwitting the law. As the law became more effective, or at least less merciful, its breakers' exploits necessarily became less bold and more brutal, and their ends came more swiftly.

[30] Ian Ousby, *Bloodhounds of Heaven. The Detective in English Fiction from Godwin to Doyle* (Cambridge, MA/London: Harvard University Press, 1976), 18.
[31] Dennis Porter, *The Pursuit of Crime. Art and Ideology in Detective Fiction* (New Haven/London: Yale University Press, 1981), 25.

But it was not just the penal and legal systems that were changing: roads were improving, trade was increasing, London and other cities were expanding. In short, the industrial age was altering the social and geographical landscape forever.

One effect, among many, of industrialization, was that there was no longer a perfect match between wealth and social status. Men of relatively humble origins who had made their fortune in business could now afford to mix in polite society. This made it essential to find some way of distinguishing between old and new money. In part as a by-product of industrialization, therefore, the eighteenth century saw an increasing interest in social distinctions in language use.[32] The development of the notion of 'standard English' demarcated non-standard Englishes by their exclusion.

In the period covered by this volume, language was felt to be changing as rapidly as society. The working classes were leaving behind rural pursuits and dialects in their migration to the industrial towns and cities. Concerned gentlemen throughout the country rushed into cornfields and cowsheds, notebook in hand, to preserve time-honoured dialects before the wave of change washed them away forever.[33]

Clubs provided opportunities for discussing such social and linguistic change in a convivial and sometimes educated atmosphere. These discussions were continued in numerous periodical publications. *The Gentleman's Magazine*, for example, includes pieces on the history of vagabonds, and the etymologies of some of the terms included in contemporary slang dictionaries.[34] The world was certainly ready for an authoritative lexicon of slang, which would provide welcome relief from the puritanical earnestness that seemed to be taking over:

At Hooper's, the bookseller, in High Holborn, who was publisher of Captain Grose's Works, a room was set apart, where a *conversationé* was held between the literary characters of that period. It is asserted that the Captain was a most prominent feature in those meetings, and that the company were delighted with the peculiar felicity with which he related his various facetious stories and interesting anecdotes.[35]

---

[32] See Lynda Mugglestone, *'Talking Proper'. The Rise of Accent as Social Symbol* (Oxford: Clarendon, 1995).

[33] It was not until later in the nineteenth century that dialectology was professionalized. See Helmut Gneuss, *English Language Scholarship: A Survey and Bibliography to the End of the Nineteenth Century* (Binghampton, NY: Medieval and Renaissance Texts and Studies, 1996), 62–3.

[34] The relevant editions are cited in the bibliography.

[35] Pierce Egan, *Grose's Classical Dictionary of the Vulgar Tongue. Revised and Corrected* (London: Printed for the Editor, 1823), xxxii–xxxiiix.

1 Francis Grose's *Classical Dictionary of the Vulgar Tongue*

Francis Grose was born in about 1731 in Greenford, Middlesex.[1] His father, a Swiss jeweller, provided him with a classical education and a place in the College of Arms as Herald for Richmond. He also left young Francis an independent fortune 'which he was not of a disposition to add to or even to preserve'.[2]

Grose clearly did not like the position his father had provided for him, with its responsibility for proving and recording pedigrees. He resigned in 1763 to pursue two careers: one military and the other artistic. He became adjutant and paymaster first in the Hampshire and then in the Surrey militia. In the fulfilment of these roles, he had apparently learnt little from his own financial mismanagement. He had:

(as he used pleasantly to tell) only two books of accounts, viz. his right and left hand pockets. In the one he received, and from the other paid; and this, too, with a want of circumspection which may be readily supposed from such a mode of book-keeping.[3]

Although he is frequently referred to by his military title, Grose was far more successful in his artistic career. He had been a Fellow of the Society of Antiquaries since 1757, and by 1766 he had also become a member of the Incorporated Society of Artists. From 1769 he exhibited his works, mostly of architectural remains, at the Royal Academy. These were published as a dry, much footnoted, account of notable ancient monuments, county by county.[4] The emphasis is largely historical and architectural: little of Grose's character can be seen in these volumes. He published similar works on military antiquities.[5]

It was probably his interest in antiquities that persuaded Grose to publish, in 1785, what is now his most influential work. Grose, 'a sort

---

[1] Biographical information is from the *Dictionary of National Biography* (*DNB*) (London: Smith, Elder & Co., 1885–1903) xxiii.272–3, unless otherwise stated.   [2] Egan, *Grose's Classical Dictionary*, xxix.

[3] Egan, *Grose's Classical Dictionary*, xxx.

[4] *The Antiquities of England and Wales* (London: Hooper & Wigstead, 1773–87).

[5] *A Treatise on Ancient Armour and Weapons* (London: S. Hooper, 1785–9) and *Military Antiquities respecting a History of the English Army, from the Conquest to the Present Time* (London: S. Hooper, 1786).

of antiquarian Falstaff',[6] made regular trips into the slums of St Giles's with Batch, his servant and companion:

It was from these nocturnal sallies, and the *slang* expressions which continually assailed his ears, that Captain Grose was first induced to compile a CLASSICAL DICTIONARY OF THE VULGAR TONGUE, intended for the amusement, if not for the benefit, of the public.[7]

This antiquarian interest in language gave rise, only two years later, to Grose's *Provincial Glossary*, a collection of dialect terms, proverbs, and local superstitions. Second editions of the *Classical Dictionary* and the *Provincial Glossary* came out in 1788 and 1790. In 1789 he toured Scotland, and began publishing his drawings of its antiquities. Before the publication of this work was complete, he set out for a similar tour of Ireland, in 1791, during which he died. *The Antiquities of Ireland* was completed and published by his friend Dr Edward Ledwich.[8]

Such a bald account of Grose's life and work gives us little indication of his character and figure, which every commentator treats as intertwined. Egan records that:

When he went to Ireland, his curiosity led him to see every thing in the capital worthy of notice: in the course of his perambulations, he one evening strolled into the principal meat-market of Dublin, when the butchers, as usual, set up their cry of 'what do you buy? what do you buy, master?' Grose parried this for some time, by saying 'he wanted nothing;' at last, a butcher starts from his stall, and, eyeing Grose's figure from top to bottom, which was something like Doctor Slop's in Tristram Shandy, exclaimed, 'Well, sir, though you don't want any thing at present, only say you buy your meat of me; and by G—you'll make my fortune'.[9]

More notable men than butchers commented on Grose's girth. During his tour of Scotland he met Robert Burns, and served as his muse three times:

If in your bounds ye chance to light
Upon a fine, fat, fodgel wight*   plump creature
O' stature short, but genius bright,
That's he, mark weel—

---

[6] *DNB*, xxiii.273.   [7] Egan, *Grose's Classical Dictionary*, xxxvii.
[8] *A Provincial Glossary* (London: S. Hooper, 1787); *The Antiquities of Ireland* (London: S. Hooper, 1791–5); *The Antiquities of Scotland* (London: Hooper & Wigstead, 1797).
[9] Egan, *Grose's Classical Dictionary*, xxxix. Compare this with the entry for *beef* in the second edition of Grose's dictionary, published three years before:
. . . Say you bought your beef of me; a jocular request from a butcher to a fat man, implying that he credits the butcher who serves him.

And wow! he has an unco slight*   skill
    O' cauk and keel*.   sketching
. . .
It's tauld he was a sodger bred,
And ane wad rather fa'n* than fled: fallen
But now he's quat the spurtle-blade*,   sword
    And dog-skin wallet,
And taen the—*Antiquarian trade*,
    I think they call it. . . .[10]

'Ken ye ought o' Captain Grose?' is a brief note sent by Burns to Grose via his publisher.[11] The third verse on Grose is an epigram written in anticipation of his death:

> The Devil got notice that GROSE was a-dying,
> So whip! at the summons, old Satan came flying:
> But when he approach'd where poor FRANCIS lay moaning,
> And saw each bed-post with its burden a-groaning
> Astonished! confounded, cry'd Satan, By G-d,
> I'll want 'im, ere I take such a d—ble load.[12]

It is clear that Grose was also happy to laugh at himself. When his military uniform was changed to a style that did not suit his figure, he wrote 'A Verse to the Right Hon Lord On—w' complaining that the costume would bring the military into disrepute, and enclosed a caricature of himself looking ridiculous (see Figure 1.1). The poem is signed 'Your Gross and faithful Adjutant'.[13]

Grose's loves of food and conversation may well have caused his death, which was by 'an apoplectic fit', presumably through choking, at table. An obituary published in *The Gentleman's Magazine* lists his works with respect and praise until it reaches the *Classical Dictionary*: 'which it would have been for his credit to have suppressed.'[14]

The Classical Dictionary of the Vulgar Tongue (1785)

> The much sought after FIRST EDITION, but containing nothing, as far as I have examined, which is not to be found in the *second* and *third* editions.

---

[10] 'On the Late Captain Grose's Perigrinations thro' Scotland, collecting the Antiquities of that Kingdom', in James Kinsley (ed.), *The Poems and Songs of Robert Burns* (Oxford: Clarendon, 1968), 494–6.   [11] Kinsley, *Poems and Songs of Robert Burns*, 564–5.

[12] 'Epigram on Capt. Grose, The Celebrated Antiquarian', in Kinsley, *Poems and Songs of Robert Burns*, 566.   [13] Francis Grose, *The Olio* (London: S. Hooper, 1792), 96–100.

[14] *The Gentleman's Magazine*, May 1791, 493.

Figure 1.1. 'Your Gross and Faithful Adjutant', Francis Grose, *The Olio* (1792), 96 [BL 012230.g.52]

> As respects indecency, I find all the editions equally disgraceful. . . . Excepting the obscenities, it is really an extraordinary book, and displays great industry if we cannot speak much of its morality.[15]

Grose's dictionary was a shrewd appeal to the concerns of its time. The out-of-towner coming to London, as so many did during this period, needed to understand the language used there. Customers wanted to be alert to tradesmen's tricks. Property-holders could be encouraged to fear the plottings of the menacingly large underclass. Justices of the Peace had to keep track of criminal ingenuity. People of conservative tastes, alarmed by the rapid changes taking place in society, wanted to preserve what was being lost. On the other hand, those enjoying the dynamic fast-moving world liked to be up-to-date in their speech and manners as well as their clothes. The disreputable of all social classes enjoyed a dirty story and a good joke. In short, this work fulfilled many contemporary needs, and did so more comprehensively than any that had gone before. Although criminals and sinners do figure largely (see Appendix, Table 1.2), Grose's interests were much wider than this. He does include cant, but this is a dictionary of non-standard English in general.

Unlike many of his predecessors in canting lexicography, Grose gives credit to his sources. Instead of claiming originality, he parades his scholarly credentials:

[the canting] terms have been collected from the following Treatises:
The Bellman of London, . . .—1608 . . .
Thieves falling out, true men come by their goods.—1615
English Villainies, . . .—London 1638.
Bailey's, and the new canting dictionary, have also been consulted, with the History of Bamfield More Carew [sic], the Sessions Papers, and other modern authorities; as many of these terms are still professionally used by our present race of free-booters of different denominations, who seem to have established a systematical manner of carrying on their business; a knowledge of them may therefore be useful to gentlemen in the commission of the peace.[16]

These sources are not quite as extensive as they appear. Dekker's *Bellman of London* and *English Villainies* contain essentially the same word-list. Moreover, the cant-lists in Bailey's dictionary and in the life of Bampfylde-Moore Carew are both derived from the *New Canting Dictionary*. Conversely, Grose appears to have used both B. E.'s

---

[15] John Camden Hotten, *A Dictionary of Modern Slang, Cant, and Vulgar Words* (London: John Camden Hotten, 1859), 154.   [16] Grose, *Classical Dictionary* (1785), iv–v.

New Dictionary and the *New Canting Dictionary*, though he does not distinguish between them in his introduction.

Between them, these word-lists account for 2,127 of Grose's 3,893 entries (55 per cent), and 1,725 of his 3,041 headwords (57 per cent). The degree of overlap (see Appendix, Table 1.1) not only demonstrates their indebtedness to each other, but also suggests that Grose may have given preference to terms found in more than one of his sources. Since the compiler of the *New Canting Dictionary* selected predominantly terms labelled 'cant' from B. E.'s dictionary, and since the Carew and Bailey lists are both derived from that selection of cant terms, the overlap between cant terms is particularly large.

Grose's use of B. E.'s *New Dictionary* is extensive enough to make some statistical analysis possible. He included 1,904 of B. E.'s 4,052 entries (47 per cent), and 1,555 of his 2,872 headwords (54 per cent); 722 (39 per cent) of these entries and 610 (37 per cent) of the headwords are labelled 'cant' in B. E.'s dictionary ($p = 0.01$). Cant terms were chosen for inclusion regardless of meaning.

Meaning does appear to have been a selection factor for terms not labelled as 'cant', however.[17] The fields of PLEASURE, ANIMALS, and GEOGRAPHY & TRAVEL are significantly smaller in Grose's selection of terms from B. E. than can be explained by chance (all $p = 0.01$). Significantly larger are CRIME & DISHONESTY, BODY & HEALTH, SEX (all $p = 0.01$), and POVERTY ($p = 0.05$).

Like B. E., Grose included more than just cant terms in his dictionary. He aimed to provide a much broader account of non-standard language use:

The Vulgar Tongue consists of two parts; the first is the Cant Language, called some-times Pedlar's French, or St. Giles's Greek: the second, those Burlesque Phrases, Quaint Allusions, and Nick-names for persons, things and places, which from long uninterrupted usage are made classical by prescription.[18]

One way of assessing the content of Grose's dictionary is by his own categorization. About a sixth of the dictionary's entries include usage labels, with 'cant' being by far the most common (see Appendix, Tables 1.3 and 1.3.1). This is a relatively small proportion, but some cant and slang lists, like the *New Canting Dictionary*, provide no usage labels at all. No usage labels are actually necessary, because we can assume that everything included is cant. A similar assumption

[17] Coleman, *Cant and Slang Dictionaries* i.200 (Appendix A, Table 4.4).
[18] Grose, *Classical Dictionary* (1785), ii–iii.

might be made with respect to Grose's dictionary: that everything not otherwise labelled is non-standard.

Of the terms that Grose labels 'cant', 350 (88.8 per cent) are from the dictionaries considered above. Grose labels as 'cant' thirty-nine entries that B. E. does not. These are all found in one or other of his other dictionary sources, where they are either labelled as cant, or their very inclusion is an implicit 'cant' label.

Forty-four of the entries that Grose labels as cant are not in his main dictionary sources. For twenty-nine entries (0.7 per cent), he cites his source, with Shakespeare being most commonly cited:

BILBOA, (*cant*) a sword. Bilboa in Spain was once famous for well tempered blades: these are quoted by Falstaff, where he described the manner in which he lay in the buck basket.

PICKT HATCH, to go to the manor of pickt hatch, a cant name for some part of the town noted for bawdy houses in Shakespeare's time, and used by him in that sense.

Shakespeare and Ben Jonson are cited many times for terms that are not labelled as cant, for example:

COKES, the fool in the play or [sic] Bartholomew fair, and hence (perhaps) the word coxcomb.

FULHAMS, loaded dice are called high and low men, or high and low fulhams, by Ben Johnson and other writers of his time, either because they were made at Fulham, or from that place being the resort of sharpers.

JEW'S EYE, that's worth a Jew's eye, a pleasant or agreeable sight, a saying taken from Shakespeare.

SIR JOHN, the old title for a country parson, as Sir John of Wrotham, mentioned by Shakespear [sic].

Dekker is cited within the dictionary as well as in the introduction:

RENDEZVOUS, a place of meeting; the rendezvous of the beggars were about the year 1638, according to the bellman . . .

Samuel Butler's *Hudibras* is also cited several times:

LOB'S POUND, a prison. Dr. Grey in his notes on Hudibras, explains it to allude to one Doctor Lob, a dissenting preacher, who used to hold forth when conventicles were prohibited, and had made himself a retreat by means of a trap door at the bottom of his pulpit. Once being pursued by the officers of justice, they followed him through diverse subterraneous passages, till they got into a dark cell, from whence they could not find their way out, but calling to some of their companions, swore they had got into Lob's pound.

RIDING SKIMMINGTON, a ludicrous cavalcade in ridicule of a man beaten by his wife. It consists of a man riding behind a woman with his face to the horse's tail, holding a distaff in his hand, at which he seems to work, the woman all the while beating him with a ladle, a smock displayed on a staff is carried before them as an emblematical standard, denoting female superiority, they are accompanied by what is called the *rough music*, that is frying pans, bulls horns, marrow bones and cleavers, &c. a procession of this kind is admirably described by Butler in his Hudibras.

Jonathan Swift is a more modern source:

SAD DOG, a wicked debauched fellow, one of the ancient family of the sad dogs, Swift translates it into Latin by the words, *tristis canis*.

As might be expected, Grose also refers to other dictionaries:

HUM DRUM . . . also a set of gentlemen, who (Bailey says) used to meet near the charter house, or at the King's Head, in St. John's Street, who had more of pleasantry, and less of mystery than the free masons.

By far the most frequent sources of Grose's entries, though, are popular literature and proverbial wisdom:

CAT'S PAW, to be made a cat's paw of, to be made a tool, or instrument to accomplish the purpose of another. An allusion to the story of a monkey, who made use of a cat's paw, to scratch a roasted chesnut [sic] out of the fire.
CRISPIN, a shoe maker, from a romance, wherein a prince of that name is said to have exercised the art and mystery of a shoe maker, thence called the gentle craft; or rather from the saints Crispinus and Crispianus, who, according to the legend, were brethren born at Rome . . .
DOG . . . dog in a manger, one who would prevent another from enjoying, what he himself does not want, an allusion to the well known fable . . .
LONG MEG, a jeering name for a very tall woman, from one famous in story, called Long Meg of Westminster.
PIG . . . boil'd pig, he can have boil'd pig at home, a mark of being master of his own house, an allusion to a well known poem and story.

In all, 448 entries (11.5 per cent) contain illustrative citations, many with no authority given (see Appendix, Table 1.4). For example:

BITCH . . . the most offensive appellation that can be given to an English woman, even more provoking than that of whore, as may be gathered from the regular Billingsgate [sic] or St. Giles's answers, 'I may be a whore, but can't be a bitch.'
CHITTERLINS, the bowels; there is a rumpus among my chitterlins, i.e. I have the cholick.

Grose's inclusion of citations is significantly higher than B. E.'s ($p = 0.01$). This is largely because he gave preference to entries illustrated by citation from his sources. In selecting entries from B. E., Grose was significantly more likely to choose those illustrated by citation ($p = 0.01$). This preference for entries including citations was secondary to the preference for 'cant' terms: the selection of terms labelled as 'cant' is not influenced by the presence of citations, but the selection of other terms is ($p = 0.01$).

Grose does not mention one of his written sources at all:

Parker[19]	Classical Dictionary
THESE are Journeymen Plumbers and Glaziers who repair houses, and Running Dustmen. To *fly the Blue Pigeon* is cutting off lead from what they call a Prayer Book up to a Bible: they wrap it round their body, and pass the most attentive eye without suspicion. (ii.63–4)	BLUE PIDGEON FLIERS, thieves who steal lead off houses and churches. (*cant*)
crapped—hanged (ii.30)	CRAPPED, hanged, (*cant*).

To cite an antiquarian source is to demonstrate one's scholarship; to cite a more modern source reveals plagiarism.

The terms discussed so far were largely drawn from written authorities, but documents were not Grose's only sources:

The second part or burlesque terms, have been drawn from the most classical authorities; such as soldiers on the long march, seamen at the cap-stern, ladies disposing of their fish, and the colloquies of a Gravesend-boat; many heroic sentences, expressing and inculcating a contempt of death, have been caught from the mouths of the applauding populace, attending those triumphant processions up Holborn-hill, with which many an unfortunate hero, till lately finished his course, and various choice flowers have been collected at executions, as well those authorized by the sentence of the law, and performed under the direction of the sheriff, as those inflicted under the authority and inspection of that impartial and summary tribunal, called the Mob, upon the pick-pockets, informers, or other unpopular criminals.[20]

Unfortunately, such sources are unidentifiable and unverifiable. Perhaps the best place to search for their influence in the dictionary is among Grose's citations, of which there are almost 200 entries that cannot be traced to the sources mentioned above. Some are unconvincing because they smack more of careful consideration than spontaneous speech:

BEGGARS BULLETS, stones; the beggar's bullets began to fly, i.e. they began to throw stones.
CANDLESTICKS, bad, small, or untuneable bells. Hark! how the candlesticks rattle.

[19] George Parker, *A View of Society and Manners in High and Low Life* (London: Printed for the Author, 1781).   [20] Grose, *Classical Dictionary* (1785), v–vi.

PAY . . . also to beat; I will pay you as Paul paid the Ephesians, over face and eyes,
   and all your d—d jaws . . .
WORM . . . he is gone to the diet of worms, he is dead and buried, or gone to
   Rot-his-bone.

But others really do represent new colloquial idioms, and often
provide the first or an early citation in the *OED*:

KINGDOM COME, he is gone to kingdom come, he is dead.
KIT . . . is used also to express the whole of different commodities; here, take the
   whole kit, i.e. take all.
POTATO TRAP, the mouth; shut your potato trap, and give your tongue a holiday,
   i.e. be silent.
TANTRUMS, pet, or passion; madam was in her tantrums.

One unfortunate obstacle to any assessment of Grose's importance
as a recorder of contemporary speech is that later writers attempting
to represent the language of the lower orders frequently made use of
his dictionary and of others derived from it. This undermines much
apparently independent verification of the words and phrases that
Grose documents.

   After cant terms, the register best represented is jargon. Seventy-
five terms, almost 2 per cent of all the entries in Grose's dictionary,
are marked as jargon (see Appendix, Tables 1.3 and 1.3.1). The largest
group is naval and nautical terms, several of which are derived, label
and all, from B. E.'s dictionary:

B. E.

Adrift, loose. *I'll turn ye adrift*, a
   Tar-phrase; I'll prevent ye doing
   me any harm.
Painter, the Rope that lies in the Ship's
   Longboat, or Barge, alwaies ready
   to Fasten her, or Hale her on Shoar.
   I'll Cut your Painter for ye, I'll prevent
   ye doing me any Mischief; the
   Tar-Cant, when they Quarrel one
   with another . . .

Classical Dictionary

ADRIFT, (*sea phrase*) loose, turned
   adrift, discharged.

PAINTER, I'll cut your painter for you,
   I'll send you off, the painter being
   the rope that holds the boat fast
   to the ship, (*sea term*).

Many other nautical and naval terms are listed which are not from
B. E.'s dictionary, including:

ABEL-WACKETS, blows given on the palm of the hand with a twisted handkerchief,
   instead of a ferula; a jocular punishment among seamen, who sometimes play
   at cards for wackets, the loser suffering as many strokes as he has lost games.

BOGY, ask bogy, i.e. ask mine a—se (*sea wit*).

LUBBER, an aukward fellow, a name given by sailors to landsmen.

SHIFTING BALLAST, a term used by sailors, to signify soldiers, passengers, or any landsmen on board.

SHIP SHAPE, proper, as it ought to be, (*sea phrase*).

Trade and craft vocabularies were first published during the eighteenth century, but dictionaries of English nautical terminology appeared towards the end of the seventeenth. Sailors were also one of the earliest occupational groups to be given a distinctive speech-style in literature.[21]

Perhaps from a more personal acquaintance, Grose's next largest type of jargon is military. Of these, only one is found in B. E.'s dictionary, though defined in different terms:

B. E.	*Classical Dictionary*
Sconce, to build a large Sconce, to run deep upon Tick, or Trust.	SCONCE . . . to build a sconce, a military term for bilking one's quarters . . .

Others could be derived from Grose's own experience, including:

BUTCHER, a jocular exclamation used at sea, or by soldiers on a march, when one of their comrades falls down, and means, butcher! butcher! where are you? here is a calf that has the staggers, and wants bleeding.

MOHAIR, a man in the civil line, a townsman, or tradesman, a military term, from the mohair buttons worn by persons of those descriptions, or any others not in the army; the buttons of military men being always of metal; this is generally used as a term of contempt, meaning a bourgeois, tradesman, or mechanick.

USED UP, killed; a military saying, originating from a message sent by the late General Guise, on the expedition at Carthagena, where he desired the commander in chief, to order him some more grenadiers, for those he had were all used up.

The rest of Grose's jargon belongs to a wide variety of occupations and pastimes, ranging from prostitutes, boxers, and cock-fighters to surveyors, stock-merchants, and booksellers. A few are found in his sources, including the following, which are all from B. E.'s dictionary:

CONGER, to conger, the agreement of a set or knot of booksellers of London, that whosoever of them shall buy a good copy, the rest shall take off such a particular number in quires at a stated price; also booksellers joining to buy either a considerable or dangerous copy.

MILCH COW, one who is easily tricked out of his property; a term used by gaolers, for prisoners who have money and bleed freely

UPRIGHT MEN . . . Go upright, a word used by shoemakers, taylors, and their servants, when any money is given to make them drink, and signifies, bring it

---

[21] N. F. Blake, *Non-standard Language in English Literature* (London: Andre Deutsch, 1981), 114–15.

all out in liquor, though the donor intended less, and expects change, or some of his money to be returned

But several remain for which Grose is not indebted to his predecessors:

TO BUG, a cant word among journeymen hatters, signifying the exchanging some of the dearest materials of which a hat is made for others of less value . . .

CINDER GARBLER, a servant maid, from her business of sifting the ashes from the cinders, (*Custom-house wit*)

DEVIL'S GUTS, a surveyor's chain, so called by farmers, who do not like their land should be measured by their landlords.

SPANISH WORM, a nail, so called by carpenters when they meet one in a board they are sawing.

TOP . . . Top, the signal among taylors for snuffing the candles, he who last pronounces that word, is obliged to get up and perform the operation.

YELLOW CAT, the golden lion, a noted brothel in the Strand, so named by the ladies who frequented it.

Also featuring largely among Grose's labelled terms are those restricted in use by region, country, or race. For southern counties, English dialect terms are labelled with more specificity than was normal in contemporary general dictionaries:[22]

CHURCH WARDEN, a Sussex name for a shag, or cormorant, probably from their voracity.

GOTCH GUTTED, pot bellied; a gotch in Norfolk, signifying a pitcher, or large round jug.

NATION, an abbreviation of damnation, a vulgar term used in Kent, Sussex, and the adjacent countries, for very; nation good, very good; a nation long way, a very long way.

WEDDING, emptying a necessary house in and about London.

while northern counties tend to be grouped together:

CROWDY, oatmeal and water, or milk, a mess much eaten in the north.

GIB CAT, a northern name for a he cat; there commonly called Gilbert; as melancholy as a gib cat; as melancholy as a he cat who has been catterwauling, whence they always return scratched, hungry, and out of spirits.

Some Welsh and Scots terms are also included. Most are common enough to be listed by the *OED*, which confirms many of Grose's labels:

GILLY GAUPUS, a Scotch term for a tall awkward fellow.

KEFFEL, a horse, (*Welch*).

---

[22] N. E. Osselton, 'Dialect Words in General Dictionaries,' 34–45 in N. E. Osselton, *Chosen Words. Past and Present Problems for Dictionary Makers* (Exeter: University of Exeter Press, 1995), 38–9.

Mow, to mow, a Scotch word for the act of copulation.
Odds plut and her nails, a Welch oath, frequently mentioned in a jocular
    manner, by persons (it his [sic] hoped) ignorant of its meaning, which is, by
    God's blood, and the nails with which he was nailed to the cross.[23]
Shanks naggy, to ride shanks naggy, to travel on foot, (*Scotch*)

Far more common that either Scots or Welsh, though, is the dialect
most frequently represented on the stage and in novels at this
period:[24]

Bog Latin, (*Irish*) barbarous latin. See dog latin and apothecaries latin.
Bud sallogh, shitten p—ck; an Irish appellation for a sodomite.
Munster plumbs, potatoes, (*Irish*).
Six and tips, whisky and small beer, (*Irish*).

Early commentators on American English, no matter which side
of the Atlantic they were on, were all in agreement that it was incorrect.[25] This alone would have justified to Grose's contemporaries the
inclusion of American terms. He lists very few, however:

Calibogus, rum and spruce beer, an American beverage.
Stewed quaker, burned rum with a piece of butter, an American remedy for a cold.
Yankey, or yankey doodle, a booby or country lout, a name given to the New
    England men in North America.

Following the American War of Independence, there was 'a considerable influx of black immigrants' into England during the 1780s.[26]
They joined the African communities of the major slaving ports,
including London, who had largely been imported as novelty servants. By the end of the eighteenth century, there was a fluctuating
population of between 10,000 and 20,000 Black people in England
and Wales, so Grose need not have travelled far to record Black
English:[27]

Bumbo . . . also the negroe name for the private parts of a woman.
Kickerapoo, dead, (*negroe word*).
Pickaniny, a young child, an infant, negroe term.
Scavey, sense, knowledge; 'massa, me no scavey,' master, I don't know, (*negroe
    language*) perhaps from the French scavoir.

[23] This use of /p/ for /b/ is characteristic of stage-Welsh from Fluellen's appearance in *Henry V*
(Blake, *Non-Standard Language*, 84–5).   [24] Blake, *Non-Standard Language*, 121, 134–6.
[25] H. L. Mencken, *The American Language. An Inquiry into the Development of English in the United States*
(1919), 4th edn. (New York: Alfred A. Knopf, 1937), 12–66.
[26] Douglas Lorimer, *Colour, Class and the Victorians* (Leicester: Leicester University Press, 1978), 29.
[27] Peter Fryer, *Staying Power. The History of Black People in Britain* (1984) (London: Pluto Press, 1992),
68, 72; David Killingray (ed.), *Africans in Britain* (Ilford: Frank Cass, 1994), 3.

Representing the language of the lower classes and marginal groups was not Grose's only intention. His work also has an encyclopedic dimension:

In the course of this work many ludicrous games and customs are explained, which are not to be met with in any other book . . .[28]

The 'ludicrous games and customs' that Grose includes are largely elaborate practical jokes, which tend to result in the butt of the joke being ducked or drenched:

AMBASSADOR, a trick to duck some ignorant fellow or landsman, frequently plaied on board ships in the warm latitudes, it is thus managed: a large tub is filled with water, and two stools placed on each side of it, over the whole is thrown a tarpawlin or old sail, this is kept tight by two persons, who are to represent the king and queen of a foreign country, and are seated on the stools. The person intended to be ducked plays the ambassador, and after repeating a ridiculous speech dictated to him, is led in great form up to the throne, and seated between the king and queen, who rising suddenly as soon as he is seated, he falls backward into the tub of water.

CAT-WHIPPING, or WHIPPING THE CAT, a trick often practised on ignorant country fellows, vain of their strength; by laying a wager with them, that they may be pulled through a pond by a cat; the bet being made, a rope is fixed round the waist of the party to be catted, and the end thrown across the pond, to which the cat is also fastened by a packthread, and three or four sturdy fellows are appointed to lead and whip the cat, these on a signal given, seize the end of the cord, and pretending to whip the cat, haul the astonished booby through the water.

while others involve distinctly unpleasant forfeits, and some outright physical violence:

GALLEY, building the galley, a game formerly used at sea in order to put a trick upon a landsman, or fresh water sailor; it being agreed to play at that game, one sailor personates the builder, and another the merchant or contractor; the builder first begins by laying the keel, which consists of a number of men laid all along on their backs one after another, that is head to foot; he next puts in the ribs or knees by making a number of men sit feet to feet at right angles to and on each side of the keel, he now fixing on the person intended to be the object of the joke, observes he is a fierce looking fellow, and fit for the lion, he accordingly places him at the head, his arms being held or locked in, by the two persons next to him, representing the ribs. After several other dispositions, the builder delivers over the galley to the contractor as compleat, but he among other faults and objections observes the lion is not gilt, on which the builder or one of his assistants runs to the head, and dipping a mop in the excrement, thrusts it into the face of the lion.

---

[28] Grose, *Classical Dictionary* (1785), vi.

HOOP, to run the hoop, an ancient maritime custom, four or more boys having their left hands tied fast to an iron hoop, and each of them a rope, called a nettle, in their right, being naked to the waist, wait the signal to begin, this being made by a stroke with a cat of nine tails, given by the boatswain to one of the boys, he strikes the boy before him, and every one does the same; at first the blows are but gently administered, but each irritated by the strokes from the boy behind him, at length lays it on in earnest; this was anciently practised when a ship was wind bound.

Not all of the games involve physical triumphs, however:

DOWDYING, a local joke practised at Salisbury, on large companies, or persons boasting of their courage. It was performed by one Pearce, who had the knack of personating madness, and who by the direction of some of the company, would burst into a a [sic] room, in a most furious manner, as if just broke loose from his keeper, to the great terror of those not in the secret. Dowdying became so much the fashion of the place, that it was exhibited before his Royal Highness the Prince of Wales, father of our present sovereign. Pearce obtained the name of Dowdy, from a song he used to sing, which had for burthen the words dow de dow.

KITTLE PITCHERING, a jocular method of hobbling or bothering a troublesome teller of long stories: this is done by contradicting some very immaterial circumstance at the beginning of the narration, the objections to which being settled, others are immediately started to some new particular of like consequence, thus impeding, or rather not suffering him to enter into the main story. Kittle pitchering is often practised in confederacy, one relieving the other, by which the design is rendered less obvious.

Other customs include games played at country fairs, often involving cruelty to animals, and already being suppressed by changes in popular sentiment:

GOOSE RIDING, a goose whose neck is greased being suspended by the legs to a cord tied to two trees or high posts, a number of men on horseback riding full speed attempt to pull off the head, which if they effect, the goose is their prize. This has been practised in Derbyshire within the memory of persons now living.

MUMBLE A SPARROW, a gambol practised at wakes and fairs, in the following manner: a cock sparrow whose wings are clipped, is put into the crown of a hat, a man having his arms tied behind him, attempts to bite off the sparrow's head, but is generally obliged to desist, by the many pecks and pinches he receives from the enraged bird.

PIG RUNNING, a piece of game frequently practised at fairs, wakes, &c. a large pig, whose tail is cut short, and both soaped and greased, being turned out, is hunted by the young men and boys, and becomes the property of him who can catch and hold him by the tail, above the height of his head.

A few of Grose's games are still familiar:

BLINDMAN'S BUFF, a play used by children, where one being blinded by a
handkerchief bound over his eyes, attempts to seize any one of the company,
who all endeavour to avoid him; the person caught must be blinded in his stead.
HIDE AND SEEK, a childish game . . .
TITTER TATTER . . . also the childish amusement of riding upon the two ends of
a plank, poised upon a prop put underneath its center, called also see saw;
perhaps tatter is a rustic pronunciation of totter.
TRAY TRIP, an ancient game like Scotch hop, played on a pavement, marked out
with chalk into different compartments.

Other games play a social function, by mocking the pomposity of
those in authority:

GARRET ELECTION, a ludicrous ceremony practised every new parliament, it
consists of a mock election of two members to represent the borough of
Garrat (a few straggling cottages near Wandsworth in Surry [sic]) the
qualification of voter [sic] is having enjoyed a woman in the open air within
that district; the candidates are commonly fellows of low humour, who dress
themselves up in a ridiculous manner, as this brings a prodigious concourse of
people to Wandsworth, the publicans of that place jointly contribute to the
expence, which is sometimes considerable.
HIGHGATE, sworn at Highgate, a ridiculous custom formerly prevailed at the
public houses in Highgate, to administer a ludicrous oath to all travellers of the
middling rank who stopped there. The party was sworn on a pair of horns,
fastened on a stick, the substance of the oath was never to kiss the maid, when
he could kiss the mistress, never to drink small beer, when he could get strong,
with many other injunctions of the like kind, to all which was added the saving
cause of 'unless you like it best.' The person administering the oath was always
to be called father, by the juror, and he, in return, was to stile him son, under
the penalty of a bottle.

or preserving for the less privileged their small areas of influence:

DISHCLOUT . . . to pin a dishclout to a man's tail, a punishment often threatened
by the female servants in a kitchen, to a man who prys too minutely into the
secrets of that place.

In most of the practical jokes, the butt of the joke would not become
a victim if he did not suffer from excessive pride in his courage, physical strength, or verbal abilities. Jokes played upon people with lower
social status than the instigator long remained an accepted part of
indenture into an apprenticeship. Jokes whose humour is at the
expense of those of a higher social status belong to a long tradition of
humorous and carefully contained role reversal, often as part of the

May Day festivities. They can all be seen as forms of social control, in that they serve as harmless outlets for resentment and rebellion.[29]

As well as promising entertaining information about games and customs, Grose sets out a more sombre aim in his preface:

> the succession of the finishers of the law, the abolition of the triumph or ovation of Holborn-hill, with the introduction of the present mode of execution at Newgate, are chronologically ascertained; points of great importance to both the present and future compilers of the Tyburne Chronicle.[30]

These claims are, however, nothing more than cunning advertising, based largely upon information scattered between entries, including:

> DERICK, the name of the finisher of the law, or hangman, about the year 1608 . . .
> DUN . . . Dun was also the general name for the hangman, before that of jack ketch.
> KETCH, Jack Ketch, a general name for the finishers of the law, or hangmen, ever since the year 1682, when the office was filled by a famous practitioner of that name, of whom his wife said, that any bungler might put a man to death, but only her husband knew how to make a gentleman die sweetly. . . .

Grose's claim to trace the development of customs surrounding execution is similarly fulfilled. The information is there, but only for those who are able to find it:

> HOLBORN HILL, to ride backwards up Holborn hill, to go to the gallows; the way to Tyburn, the place of execution for criminals condemned in London, was up that hill. Criminals going to suffer always ride backwards, as some conceive to encrease the ignominy, but more probably to prevent their being shocked with a distant view of the gallows; as in amputations, surgeons conceal the instruments with which they are going to operate. The last execution at Tyburn, and consequently of this procession, was in the year 1784, since which the criminals have been executed near Newgate.

Although Grose lists numerous disparaging terms used by and with reference to various trades and professions, including:

> BURN CRUST, jocular name for a baker.
> CABBAGE, cloth, stuff, or silk purloined by taylors from their employers, which they deposit in a place called *hell*, or their *eye*: from the first, when taxed with their knavery, they equivocally swear, that if they have taken any, they wish they may find it in *hell*; or alluding to the second protest, that what they have over and above is not more than they could put in their *eye*.
> FINGER POST, a parson, so called, because like the finger post, he points out a way he has never been and probably will never go, i.e. the way to heaven.

---

[29] Joan Lane, *Apprenticeship in England 1600–1914* (London: University College London Press, 1996), 108, 112–13.   [30] Grose, *Classical Dictionary* (1785), vi.

MIX-METTLE, a silver smith.
SMEAR, a plaisterer.
SPOIL IRON, the nick name for a smith.

he carefully disowns the opinions expressed:

The Editor likewise begs leave to add, that if he has had the misfortune to run foul of the dignity of any body of men, profession, or trade, it is totally contrary to his intention; and he hopes the interpretations given to any particular terms that may seem to bear hard upon them, will not be considered as his sentiments, but as the sentiments of the persons by whom such terms were first invented, or those by whom they are used.[31]

This modern descriptive approach is not carried over into Grose's treatment of obscenity, however:

To prevent any charge of immorality being brought against this work, the Editor begs leave to observe, that when an indelicate or immodest word has obtruded itself for explanation, he has endeavoured to get rid of it in the most decent manner possible; and none have been admitted but such, as either could not be left out, without rendering the work incomplete, or, in some measure, compensate by their wit, for the trespass committed on decorum. Indeed respecting this matter, he can with great truth make the same defence that Falstaff ludicrously urges in behalf of one engaged in rebellion, viz. that he did not seek them, but that, like rebellion in the case instanced, they lay in his way, and he found them.[32]

We have already seen that Grose's protestations in this matter are ingenuous, because he chose more SEX words from his sources than can be explained by chance. A selection of Grose's obscene entries follows, as a sample of his decency and wit:

CLAP, a venereal taint. He went out by Had'em, and came round by Clapham home; i.e. he went out a wenching, and got a clap.
DILDO, an implement, resembling the virile member, for which it is said to be subsituted, by nuns, boarding school misses, and others obliged to celibacy, or fearful of pregnancy. Dildoes are made of wax, horn, leather, and diverse other substances, and if fame does not lie more than usually, are to be had at many of our great toy shops and nick nackatories.
SAL, an abbreviation of salivation; in a high sal, in the pickling tub, or under a salivation.[33]
WINDWARD PASSAGE, one who uses, or navigates the windward passage, a sodomite.
WOMAN OF THE TOWN, OR WOMAN OF PLEASURE, a prostitute.

[31] Grose, *Classical Dictionary* (1785), vii.   [32] Grose, *Classical Dictionary* (1785), vi–vii.
[33] The treatment of syphilis with mercury caused excessive salivation.

Defecation also features to a far greater extent than we have seen in earlier cant and slang dictionaries:

FARTLEBERRIES, excrement hanging to the hairs about the anus, &c. of a man or woman.
FIZZLE, an escape backward, more obvious to the nose than ears.
PLUCK . . . to pluck a rose, an expression said to be used by women, for going to the necessary house, which in the country usually stands in the garden.

In these entries we can see that Grose sometimes does use euphemisms in his definitions. Occasionally the terms listed are so obscene that he refuses to define them at all:

BAGPIPE, TO BAGPIPE, a lascivious practice too indecent for explanation.
HUFFLE, to huffle, a piece of beastiality too filthy for explanation.
LARKING, a lascivious practice that will not bear explanation.

In other entries he censors individual terms. Sometimes single letters are obscured or omitted:

CLOSE, as close as God's curse to a whore's a—se; close as shirt and shitten a—se.

with an increasing proportion of letters obscured according to the obscenity of the word:

ARMOUR, in his armour, pot valiant; to fight in armour, to make use of Mrs. Philip's ware. See c—d—m.
CODS, nick name for a curate. A rude fellow meeting a curate, mistook him for a rector; and accosted him with the vulgar appellation of, Bol—ks the rector, No, Sir, answered he, only Cods the curate, at your service.
F—K, to copulate.
GOBBLE P—K, a rampant lustful woman.
QUANDARY . . . also one so overgorged as to be doubtful which he should do first, sh—e or spew . . .
SIRREVERENCE, human excrement, a t—d.

For the truly unprintable terms, we are guided by asterisk-counting and context alone:

BENISON, the beggar's benison, may your ***** and purse never fail you.
COFFEE HOUSE, to make a coffee-house of a woman's ****, to go in and out and spend nothing.

This censorship is not entirely consistent. *Prick* is presented both as p—k and *****, for example, and *cunt* both as c**t and ****. However, the level of obscuration accorded to individual terms does give some indication of relative obscenity.

A total of 485 of Grose's entries (12.5 per cent) contain etymologies, which are spread fairly evenly through the alphabet. Almost 40 per cent give figurative, metonymic, or metaphorical origins (see Appendix, Tables 1.4 and 1.5). For example:

ADMIRAL OF THE BLUE, who carries his flag on his mainmast, a landlord or publican wearing a blue apron, as was formerly the custom among gentlemen of that vocation.

WEEZLE FACED, thin meagre faced; weezle gutted, thin bodied. A weasel is a thin long slender animal with a sharp face.

Proper names account for a further 20 per cent of Grose's etymologies. Some of these are correct:

TAWDRY, garish, gawdy, with lace, or staring and discordant colours; a term said to be derived from the shrine and altar of St. Audrey, (an Isle of Ely saintess) which for finery exceeded all others thereabouts, so as to become proverbial, whence any fine dressed man or woman was said to be all St. Audrey, and by contraction, all tawdry.

while many narrative etymologies can be at best described as speculative:

DAVID'S SOW, as drunk as David's sow, a common saying, which took its rise from the following circumstance: One David Lloyd, a Welchman, who kept an alehouse at Hereford, had a living sow with six legs, which was greatly resorted to by the curious; he also had a wife much addicted to drunkenness, for which he used sometimes to give her due correction. One day David's wife having taken a cup too much, and being fearful of the consequences, turned out the sow, and lay down to sleep herself sober, in the stye. A company coming in to see the sow, David ushered them into the stye, exclaiming there is a sow for you! did any of you ever see such another? all the while supposing the sow had really been there; to which some of the company, seeing the state the woman was in, replied, it was the drunkenest sow they had ever beheld; whence the woman was ever after called David's sow.

Grose makes reference to languages other than English in less than an eighth of his etymologies. In some cases he gives both word and language source:

FOOTY DESPICABLE [sic], a footy fellow, a despicable fellow, from the French foutüe.

KICKSHAWS, French dishes, corruption of *quelque chose*.

STIVER CRAMPED, needy, wanting money; a stiver is a Dutch coin, worth somewhat more than a penny sterling.

but often only one or the other:

To CAROUSE, to drink freely or deep, from the German word expressing all out.

MORGLAG, a brown bill, or kind of halbert, formerly carried by watchmen,
   corruption of *more*, great, or broad, and *glave* blade.[34]

SPADO, a sword, (*Spanish*).

In one case, Grose translates the headword into English, but assumes enough knowledge of Latin that his audience will understand the implicit etymology:

TANDEM, a two wheeled chaise, buggy, or noddy, drawn by two horses, one
   before the other, that is *at length*.

The miscellaneous category (see Appendix, Table 1.5) is largely sense-extension of English terms, in this case implied rather than stated:

SATYR, a libidinous fellow, those imaginary beings are by poets reported to be
   extremely salacious.

It also includes some lengthy narrative etymologies:

BASKET, an exclamation frequently made use of in cock pits, at cock fightings,
   where persons refusing or unable to pay their losings, are adjudged by that
   respectable assembly to be put into a basket suspended over the pit, there to
   remain during that day's diversion. On the least demur to pay a bet, basket is
   vociferated in terrorem.

One hundred and forty four of Grose's entries (3.7 per cent) include a total of 155 cross-references (see Appendix, Table 1.4). For example:

ALTAMEL, vide Dutch reckoning, a verbal or lump account, without particulars,
   such as is commonly produced at bawdy houses, spunging houses, &c.

To KNOCK ANTHONY, said of an inkneed person, or one whose knees knock
   together. See to cuff Jonas.

The distribution of cross-references through the alphabet is fairly even. However, over a fifth of all cross-references are to entries beginning with the same letter: over a third to the same or the two adjacent letters. What this suggests is that the insertion of cross-references depended on memory: that Grose flicked backwards and forwards through the alphabet to include cross-references to the terms freshest in his mind.

---

[34] *Morglay* is Welsh (or Breton or Cornish), and was originally the name of Sir Bevis's sword, which was later used allusively for any sword (*OED*).

One of the tests of careful lexicography is how successfully cross-references are followed through; 16.8 per cent of Grose's cross-references are to entries that are spelt differently, included under a different headword or, rarely, excluded altogether. For example:

A BAM, a jocular imposition, the same as a humbug. See humbug.
HUM, to hum, or humbug, to deceive, or impose on one by some story or device.

BECK, a beadle. See hermanbeck.
HARMAN BECK, a beadle, (*cant*).

BILL OF SALE, a widow's weeds. See house to let.
SIGN OF A HOUSE TO LET, a widow's weeds.

Unsuccessful cross-references are evenly distributed through the alphabet.

This edition of Grose's dictionary also includes a few addenda and corrigenda. The additions include:

JAPANNED, ordained; to be japanned, to enter into holy orders, to become a clergyman; from the colour of the Japan ware, which is black.
TWADDLE, perplexity, a confusion, or any thing else, a fashionable term that succeeded a bore.
WHITE SWELLING, a woman with child is said to have a white swelling.

The corrections include:

Main text	Additions and corrections
ALSASIA THE HIGHER, White Fryers . . .	For *Alsasia* read *Alsatia*
ALSASIA THE LOWER, the Mint in Southwark.	
GREGORIAN TREE, so named from Gregory Brandon, a famous finisher of the law . . .	After *Gregorian tree* insert the *gallows*

The inclusion of these additions and corrections indicates that, in keeping with the protestations of his preface, Grose cared enough about the contents of the dictionary to proofread and, as the later editions also demonstrate, to supplement it.

A measure of the influence of Grose's dictionary is that the *OED* cites the first edition 487 times, often through Farmer and Henley's *Slang and its Analogues*.[35] There are another seventy-three entries for which the *OED* could have predated its existing citations from the

[35] John Stephen Farmer and William Ernest Henley, *Slang and Its Analogues Past and Present* (London/Edinburgh: Privately published for subscribers only, 1890–4).

first edition of Grose's dictionary.[36] *OED* first citation dates, along with differences in spelling or definition, are given in brackets (see *larking*). Definitions within quotation marks are my own (see *puffing*); those contained within single inverted commas are Grose's or the *OED*'s, as indicated (see *pickle, rattle-trap*). Grose's headwords are enclosed within square brackets where necessary (see *King Arthur*). Where the relevant definition may be difficult to locate, I have included the *OED* reference code (see *gig*):

all nations "a drink made from slops at a bar" (1823)
[***Arthur***] *King Arthur* [a game played at sea] (1847–52)
babes in the wood "criminals in the stocks" (1795: "inexperienced or guileless persons")[37]
to badger "to confuse or tease" (1794)
to beat Banaghan "to tell incredible stories" (1830: *to beat (or bang) Banagher* "to surpass everything")
blarney "lying or flattery" ([1766] 1796)
to bolt "to eat greedily" (1794)
bore "a dull person" (1812)
bouncer "a great lie" (1805)
bubbly-jock "a turkey cock" (1814)
buckeen "a bully" (1793: 'A young man belonging to the 'second-rate gentry' of Ireland, or a younger son of the poorer aristocracy, having no profession, and aping the habits of the wealthier classes.')
cauliflower "the female genitals" (1803: 'A thing which resembles a cauliflower in shape')[38]
click "a blow" (1847–78)
to come over "to cheat" (1822)
crab-shell "a shoe" (1807)[39]
damper "a snack" (1804)
devil's taptoo "drumming the foot on the ground" (1803: *tattoo* "drumming the fingers")
dew-beater "a foot" (1811)
dilly "a public stagecoach" (1786)
dumbfounded "silenced" (1815)
German duck "half a sheep's head boiled with onions" (1796)
gig "a one-horse carriage" (1791: n^2)
ginger-hackled "red haired" (1839)
to gouge "to squeeze out someone's eye" (1800)

---

[36] Now that *OED3* is being updated quarterly online, it is a moving target. I have checked against *OED3* for the letter *m* and for *n* up to *necessity*. In those sections, many of the antedatings I had found in cant and slang dictionaries had been picked up and included. Where a number of dictionaries in this volume include the same usage, I have listed only the earliest antedating.

[37] Grose's sense is a play on the *OED* meaning, and is therefore evidence for its earlier use.

[38] Grose's definition makes it clear that similarity of appearance underlies this use of *cauliflower*.

[39] The *OED* definition read 'the carapace of a crab; *slang* a shoe', but it is not clear which of the two senses the single citation supports.

[**gunner's daughter**] *to kiss the gunner's daughter* "to be whipped" (1821)

to hop the twig "to run away" (1797)

knowledge-box "the head" (1796)

larking "a lascivious practice" (1813: "fun")

a lick of the tar brush [**blue-skin**] [with reference to someone of mixed race] (1796)

lickspittle "a parasite, a sycophant" ([1629] 1825)

to lump the lighter "to be transported" (1890: *to lump* "to load")

to mumble a sparrow "to try to get a sparrow's head into one's mouth without using the hands" (1852: *sparrow-mumbling*)

to nab the rust "(of a horse) to be restive" (1801)

niffy-naffy fellow "a trifler" (1796)

Norfolk capon "a red herring" (1836)

Norway neckcloth "the pillory" (a1790)

to nurse "to cheat" (1796)

odd's plut "God's blood" (1856: *Od's blood*)

old ewe dressed lamb-fashion [**ewe**] "a woman dressed in clothes inappropriate to her age" (1810: *lamb-fashion*)

paddy whack [**whack**] "a brawny Irishman" (1811)

peppery "passionate" (1826 with reference to speech or writing; 1861 with reference to people)

pickle "a waggish man" (1788: 'a troublesome or mischievous person')

pillaloo "a cry expressing grief or anger" (1796)

piper "a broken-winded horse" (1831)

to plant "to bury (someone)" (1855)

puffing "bidding at an auction to raise the price" (1858)

pug "a type of dog" (1789)

puzzle-text "one who does not understand a passage in the Bible" (1837)

rattle-trap "any portable piece of machinery" (1822: 'A rattling, rickety coach or other vehicle')

red lane "the throat" (1821)

roister "a hound that follows the wrong scent" (1796)

scaly fish "a sailor" (1796)

scandal-broth "tea" (1795)

scapegallows "one who deserves to be hanged" (1799)

scapegrace "a dissolute man" (1809)

[**scarce**] *to make oneself scarce* "to slip away" (1809)

scran "food" (1808)

scull-thatcher "a wig-maker" (1859: *skull-*)

shallow [a type of hat] (1795)

sharp "a sharper, a cheat" (1797)

on the shelf [**laid on the shelf**] "pawned" (1859)

shoulder-tapper [**tap**] "a bailiff" (1842: *shoulder-tapping* adj; 1881: *shoulder-tap* n)

[**suck**] *to suck the monkey* "to drink wine, beer, or spirits by inserting a straw into the barrel" (1797)

swipes "weak beer" (1796)

[*tabby*] *to drive tab* "to go out with one's wife and family" (1909: *tab* "an elderly woman; a young woman")

thorough-go-nimble "an attack of diarrhoea" (1825)

toad-in-a-hole "meat baked in a crust" (1787: *toad in the (a) hole*)

to touch "to arrest" (1791)

[*tucked up*] *tucker-up* "a mistress" (1796: *tucker*)

wooden surtout "a coffin" (1865)

woolbird "a sheep" (1825)

[*yoked*] *yoke* "a spell of work at a plough" (1796)

The types of texts that these citations predate give us some measure of the reliability of Grose's word-list as a witness of contemporary cant and slang, and may also indicate the range of his influence. Many of them predate first citations from later slang dictionaries, including eight from the third edition of Grose's dictionary (1796), and two from the edition published as *Lexicon Balatronicum* in 1811. Two predate citations from Potter's dictionary (dated a1790), and two predate citations from Hotten's dictionary (1859). This edition of Grose's dictionary also provides earlier citations for terms first cited from dialect dictionaries, including Halliwell, Jamieson, Brockett, and Grose's own *Provincial Glossary*. Of the other authors that this edition predates, Scott occurs four times; O'Keeffe, Edgeworth, and Malkin twice each. No other author or work is predated more than once, though newspapers and magazines provide the first *OED* citations for *bore*, *to nab the rust*, *pillaloo*, *to plant*, and *shallow*. It is these non-dictionary sources that best demonstrate that Grose really was representing terms found in contemporary speech.

In addition to these, there are a number of terms for which, although Grose does not provide the earliest citation, the *OED* has cited the third edition (1796) instead of the first: *old Harry* "the devil", *japan* "to ordain", *rough music* "a noisy outcry against a neighbour", *rusher* "a thief who forces his way into a house when the door is opened", *scrip* "subscription", *trapsticks* "thin legs", and *to tip the traveller* "to tell wonderful stories".

There are several entries in which this dictionary is cited for terms that occur only in later editions. For example, *bastardly gullion* "a bastard's bastard" (1788), *dummee* "a wallet" (1811), *hen* "a woman" (1811), and *slapbang shop* [a type of restaurent] (1788). The *OED* entry for *gammy* "the cant language" suggests the source of these errors:

1893 Farmer *Slang* s.v., citing (in error) Grose *Dict. Vulg. Tongue* (1785), Do you stoll the gammy? Do you understand cant? (*OED*)

In fact, the misdating of all but *hen* is attributable to Farmer and Henley's *Slang and its Analogues*.

Grose's Working Copy

The Museum copy of the *First Edition* is, I suspect, Grose's own copy, as it contains numerous manuscript additions which afterwards went to form the second edition.[40]

In the British Library's collections there are several copies of the first edition of Grose's dictionary. One is described in the catalogue as 'interleaved and copiously annotated' (see Figure 1.2), but other than this brief note, and Hotten's remark, quoted above, it has received little attention.[41]

There are a number of reasons for believing that this is Grose's own working copy. First, before the title page, written in ink, are the publication details of Harman's *Caveat*, Head's *Canting Academy*, and *Hell upon Earth*, which are listed, in this order, as new sources in the second edition of the dictionary, where they are joined by the *Scoundrel's Dictionary*.[42] Secondly, written in hand on the interleaved pages are some of the entries added in the second edition:

Annotations	1788
<u>Anodyne Necklace</u>. a Halter.	ANODYNE NECKLACE. A halter.
<u>Cagg Maggs</u>. Old Lincolnshire Geese, which having been ~~picked~~ pluck'd ten or twelve years, are sent up to London to feast the Cockneys.	CAG MAGGS. Old Lincolnshire geese, which having been plucked ten or twelve years, are sent up to London to feast the cockneys.
<u>Whore Monger</u> One who keeps several Mistresses. A Country gentleman who kept a female friend, being reproved by the parson of the Parish & stiled a Whoremonger asked the parson whether he had a Cheese in his house, & being answered in the Affirmative, pray said he & does that one Cheese make you a Cheesemonger.	WHORE-MONGER. A man that keeps more than one mistress. A country gentleman, who kept a female friend, being reproved by the parson of the parish, and styled a whore-monger, asked the parson whether he had a cheese in his house; and being answered in the affirmative, 'Pray,' says he, 'does that one cheese make you a cheese-monger?'

---

[40] Hotten, *Dictionary*, 154.

[41] The volume is shelved at 440.g.25.

[42] *Hell upon Earth: or the most Pleasant and Delectable History of Whittington's Colledge, Otherwise (vulgarly) called Newgate* (London: no publisher's details, 1703); *Scoundrel's Dictionary* (London: J. Brownnell, 1754).

B L U

alehouse, lane or alley; an obscure, or little known or frequented alehouse, lane or alley.

BLIND HARPERS, beggars counterfeiting blindness, playing on fiddles, &c.

BLINDMAN'S BUFF, a play used by children, where one being blinded by a handkerchief bound over his eyes, attempts to seize any one of the company, who all endeavour to avoid him; the person caught must be blinded in his stead.

BLINDMAN'S HOLIDAY, night, darkness.

BLOCK HOUSES, prisons, houses of correction, &c.

BLOODY BACK, a jeering appellation for a soldier, alluding to his scarlet coat.

BLOOD, a riotous disorderly fellow.

BLOSS, (cant) the pretended wife of a bully, or shop lifter.

TO BLOT THE SKRIP AND JARK IT, (cant) i.e. to stand engaged, or bound for any one.

BLOW, (cant) he has bit the blow, i.e. he has stolen the goods. *who steals the place.*

BLOWER, a mistress or whore.

TO BLOW THE GROUNDSILS, (cant) to lie with a woman on the floor.

TO BLOW THE GAB, (cant) to confess, or impeach a confederate.

A BLOWSE, OR BLOWSABELLA, a woman whose hair is dishevelled and hanging about her face, a slattern.

BLUBBER, the mouth, (cant) I have stopped the cull's blubber, I have stopped the fellow's mouth, meant either by gagging or murdering him.

TO BLUBBER, to cry.

BLUE, to look blue, to be confounded, terrified, or disappointed.

BLUE DEVILS, low spirits.

BLUE PIDGEON FLIERS, thieves who steal lead off houses and churches. (cant)

C   BLUE

Blue as a Razor perhaps Blue as Azure

Blubber to shot Blubber said of a large Coarse woman who exposes her Bosom.

Blubbering throwing about the Saliva, Crying

Blubber Cheek, Large flaccid Cheek, hanging like the feat or Blubber of a whale

Blue Boar The Vulgar term for a Venereal Bubo.

Blower the Mistress of a gentleman of the Scamp. Cant.

Blunt. Money. Cant.

Figure 1.2. Grose's working copy, Francis Grose, *The Classical Dictionary of the Vulgar Tongue* (1785), B7v & C [BL 440.g.25]

Thirdly, the handwritten versions of these entries were polished and improved for the published edition, both orthographically and stylistically, thus indicating that they were not copied from the second edition (the other possible explanation for the similarity):

Annotations	1788
Admiral of the Narrow Seas One who from Drunkenness vomits into the lap of his opposite companion. Sea phrase.	ADMIRAL OF THE NARROW SEAS. One who from drunkenness vomits into the lap of the person sitting opposite to him. *Sea phrase.*
Pursers Pump a Basson [sic], Sea Wit from the resemblance that instrument bears to a Crane [sic] or Syphon, frequently used by the Purers [sic] in drawing off Liquors	PURSER'S PUMP. A bassoon: from its likeness to a syphon, called a purser's pump.
Whittington's College. Newgate, built or repaird by the famous Lord Mayor of that name.	WHITTINGTON'S COLLEGE. Newgate: built or repaired by the famous Lord Mayor of that name.

The published edition tends to expand final <d> to <ed> (see *repaired* in the entry for **Whittington's College**), to insert apostrophes to show possession (see **Purser's Pump**), and to insert full stops between headwords and definitions. The punctuation of the published entries is also more sophisticated than the handwritten ones, in that colons and semi-colons replace commas and missing punctuation marks to show relationships between different parts of the definition (see **Purser's Pump**, **Whittington's College**, **Whoremonger**).

Fourthly, some entries are radically different, which confirms that these are not copied from the second edition:

Annotations	1788
Bargain a Hum bug. To sell a bargain, because the buyer seldom gives more than the words, What for or Why for it. Ex the Seller comes into a Room with a very grave face & says that Mr A, the barber is just taken into Custody, one of the Company who (as the phrase is) is not up to the Rig very naturally asks „what for." The Answer is, for shaving his wifes xxxx with a wooden razor. Another mode	BARGAIN. To sell a bargain; a species of wit, much in vogue about the latter end of the reign of Queen Anne, and frequently alluded to by Dean Swift, who says the maids of honour often amused themselves with it. It consisted in the seller naming his or her hinder parts, in answer to the question, What? which the buyer was artfully led to ask. As a specimen, take the following

of selling a bargain consisted in the seller naming his hinder parts to the buyer. this was a Species of wit in vogue even at Court, in the reign of K. Ge[o]rge the first & is much alluded to by Swift, as a Specimen take the following Instance. A Lady would come into a Room apparently in a great fright. crying it is white, & follows me, on any of the Company asking what. the Lady sold him [or her] a bargain by saying Mine A—e.[43]

instance: A lady would come into a room full of company, apparently in a fright, crying out, It is white, and follows me! On any of the company asking, What? she sold him the bargain, by saying, Mine a—e.

Five Shillings The Sign of five Shillings. the Sign of the Crown. the Sign of fifteen Shillings. The three Crowns.

FIVE SHILLINGS. The sign of the five shillings; i.e. the crown. Fifteen shillings; the sign of the three crowns.

Another indication that these annotations were not copied from the second edition is the fact that a few entries in the working copy are not found in the published text:

Bitch pye the sting of a droll blackguard made use of upon the batter as follows—go to hell where you ought to be & you will find your sister there helping the Devil to make your mother into a bitch pye
Flag of distress the Cockade of a half pay Officer.
Moll's three Misfortunes. i.e. Broke the pot. bes—t the bed & Cut her A-s-e.

Further evidence that these entries were copied for rather than from the second edition is found in a single entry in the working copy containing a date:

Annotations

1788

Nyp or Nip Half a Pint, a Nyp of Ale, whence Nypperkin a small Vissil [sic] or pot. The Peacock in Grays Inn Lane is now. 1786 called the Nyp-Shop because Burton Ale is there sold in Nyps

NYP, OR NIP. A half pint, a nyp of ale: whence the nipperkin, a small vessel.
NYP SHOP. The Peacock in Gray's Inn Lane, where Burton ale is sold in nyps.

Since the second edition was not published until 1788, these annotations cannot have been copied from it. The similarities between them and the changes made in the second edition indicate that they are Grose's own notes. Comparison between these notes and known

[43] The additions in square brackets were added later, apparently in the same hand.

examples of Grose's handwriting confirms that as well as compiling these notes he also copied them into the annotated edition himself.[44]

There are 188 new entries in total, largely in the earlier part of the alphabet. In fact, only thirty-eight new entries (20.2 per cent) are in the letters N–Z ($p = 0.01$).[45] This suggests that Grose began with good intentions, but ran out of patience before he finished the task.

In comparison with the first edition, the working copy has significantly more citations ($p = 0.01$) and more authorities ($p = 0.05$). The proportion of entries containing both etymologies and cross-references is slightly lower than we might expect, but not significantly so (see Appendix, Tables 1.4 and 1.4.1).

Forty-two of the additional entries include usage labels. The proportion of entries containing usage labels is in keeping with the practice of the first edition (see Appendix, Tables 1.3–1.3.2.1). Significantly more terms are labelled as 'naval'/'nautical' or 'vulgar' than we would expect in comparison with the first edition ($p = 0.01$). Grose appears to have gathered types of entries together, perhaps from a single source.

Among the new entries noted on this working copy, there are significantly more terms for FOOD ($p = 0.01$) and for BODY & HEALTH ($p = 0.05$) than we would expect in comparison with the first edition, and significantly fewer for EMOTION & TEMPERAMENT ($p = 0.05$) (see Appendix, Table 1.2.1). This indicates that Grose was by no means consistent in his collection of new entries. Although he was influenced by meaning, he kept changing his mind about what subject matter he wanted to include.

Annotations to existing entries are also revealing, in that they show Grose at work not just as a compiler, but also as an editor of his own work. Some of these thirty-three annotations appear more or less as they were to appear in the published second edition:

1785	Annotations	1788
AQUA POMPAGINIS, pump water, (*apothecaries Latin.*)	/U AQUA POMPAGINIS	AQUA PUMPAGINIS. Pump water. *Apothecaries Latin.*
BRUISER, a boxer, one skilled in the art of boxing.	+ also an inferior Workman among Chasers.	BRUISER. A boxer, one skilled in the art of boxing; also an inferior workman among chasers.

[44] Compare with British Library Add MS 17398.
[45] This is significant to $p = 0.01$ whether the comparison is with the first edition or with the additions made in the second edition.

44   Francis Grose

1785	Annotations	1788
MARTINET, a military term for a strict disciplinarian, from the name of a French general, famous for restoring military discipline to the French army.	(+) he first disciplined the french Infantry & regulated the method of Encampment he was killed at the Siege of Doesbourg A.D. 1672.	MARTINET. A military term for a strict disciplinarian: from the name of a French general, famous for restoring military discipline to the French army. He first disciplined the French infantry, and regulated their method of encampment: he was killed at the siege of Doesbourg in the year 1672.
TESTER, a sixpence.	+ from Teston, a coin with a head on it.	TESTER. A sixpence: from *teston*, a coin with a head on it.

some are rewritten:

1785	Annotations	1788
BALLUM RANCUM, a hop or dance, where the women are all prostitutes, a dance at a brothel.	where the partys dance naked.	BALLUM RANCUM. A hop or dance, where the women are all prostitutes. N.B. The company dance in their birthday suits.
BOOTS, the youngest officer in a regimental mess, whose duty it is to skink, that is to stir the fire, snuff the candles, and ring the bell. See skink.	+ to ride in any one's old boots. To marry or keep a Cast off Mistress.	BOOTS. The youngest officer in a regimental mess, whose duty it is to skink, that is, to stir the fire, snuff the candles, and ring the bell. See SKINK.—To ride in any one's old boots; to marry or keep his cast-off mistress.

and some are rejected altogether:

1785	Annotations	1788
BLOW, (*cant*) he has bit the blow, i.e. he has stolen the goods.	he has done the deed.	BLOW. He has bit the blow, i.e. he has stolen the goods. *Cant.*

PARSON, a guide post, hand or finger post by the road side for directing travellers; compared to a parson, because, like him it sets people in the right way. See guide post.

[. . . in the right way] tho it never travels it. [See . . .]

PARSON. A guide post, hand or finger post by the road side for directing travellers: compared to a parson, because, like him, it sets people in the right way. See GUIDE POST . . .

Like the new entries, annotations to existing entries are concentrated in the first half of the alphabet. Only six (18.2 per cent) are found in the letters N–Z. Because there are so few in total, however, this is not statistically significant.

Having established that this copy does represent Grose's own preliminary notes for the second edition, we can observe a number of features of his working practice. It seems that he continued taking notes after the publication of the first edition instead of waiting until a second edition was due. Changes in ink colour and thickness demonstrate that the annotations were written into this copy in sequence, working through the alphabet. There is a change of ink at *Gentleman of the Three Ins* and in the entry for *Grog*, but other than that the variations in ink colour are consistent with continuous writing and pen dipping. This indicates that Grose had already collected his new entries, perhaps on separate sheets or slips of paper, and had sorted them alphabetically for insertion.

He paid relatively little attention to the task of rewriting existing entries, however: where they are altered it is largely by addition rather than revision. Neither does the printed form add anything to the new entries found here: Grose revised some of them, but he did not work his way through the dictionary systematically adding, for example, etymologies or usage labels. This indicates that he was not a methodical worker, and that he had little interest in uniformity of style or content. The new entries noted in this copy are largely as they are found in the published second edition. However, as far as this working copy indicates, questions of spelling, punctuation, and typesetting were addressed at press rather than in manuscript.

It appears that Grose collected his word-list at least partially by type. Of the erroneous pronunciations eventually added to the second edition, only *foxes paw* and *dowser* are listed here (see below). Of the gentlemen's clubs, only *swizzle club* is (see below). No jokes are among the annotations (see below). This suggests that Grose added types of entries en masse: that he decided to include names of gentlemen's clubs, for instance, and then sought examples, or that he found all of these entries in a single source. It is also apparent that Grose was not a patient worker: he began the task of noting his additional entries with enthusiasm, but by half-way through the alphabet his interest was waning.

The Second Edition (1788)

> The favourable reception with which this Book was honoured by the Public, has encouraged the Editor to present a second edition, more correctly arranged, and very considerably enlarged.[46]

Only three years after the publication of *The Classical Dictionary*, Grose issued a second edition with the same publisher. It contains 4,999 entries for 3,975 headwords, as opposed to 3,895 entries for 3,040 headwords in the first edition: an increase of 28 per cent in the number of entries and of 31 per cent in the number of headwords. This is certainly enough to justify the claim that the dictionary had been 'very considerably enlarged', though the use of a smaller typeface obscures its growth.

The other claim, that the dictionary is now 'more correctly arranged', cannot be substantiated, in that the order of existing entries has not been altered. Here, for example, are a run of entries for the letter 'a' from the first edition:

APRIL FOOL; APRON STRING HOLD; AQUA POMPAGINIS; AN ARCH ROGUE, or DIMBER DAMBER UPRIGHT MAN; AN ARCH DELL, or ARCH DOXY; ARISTIPPUS; ARMOUR; ARK; ARK RUFFIANS; ARS MUSICA; ARSE; ARSY VARSEY; ARTHUR, KING ARTHUR; ASSIG

The second edition has:

APRIL FOOL; APRON STRING HOLD; AQUA PUMPAGINIS; ARRBOR VITAE; ARCH DUKE; ARCH ROGUE, or DIMBER DAMBER UPRIGHT MAN; ARCH DELL, or ARCH DOXY; ARD; ARISTIPPUS; ARMOUR; ARK; ARK RUFFIANS; ARRAH NOW; ARS MUSICA; ARSE; ARSY VARSEY; ARTHUR, KING ARTHUR; ARTICLES; ASSIG; ASK, OR AX MY A–E

---

[46] Francis Grose, *A Classical Dictionary of the Vulgar Tongue* (London: S. Hooper, 1788), i.

This selection also demonstrates a minor feature of the editing that has taken place in the production of the second edition, which is that all the main words in the headword now have large initial capitals, instead of just the first.

A few other editorial changes are followed through in the second edition almost consistently. For example, headwords for verbs now more regularly include 'to' to indicate their grammatical function. The first edition divides headword and definition with a comma, often beginning definitions in lower case, while the second uses a full-stop followed by a capital letter. In the first edition, usage labels, normally italicized and within brackets, followed the definition; in the second edition, all usage labels are capitalized and follow a full-stop at the end of the entry. Illustrative citations are generally also preceded by a full-stop in the second edition, rather than by a semi-colon or comma as in the first. For example:

1785	1788
KATE, a picklock; (*cant*), 'tis a rum kate, it is a clever picklock.	KATE. A picklock. 'Tis a rum kate; it is a clever picklock. *Cant.*
KEN, a house; (*cant*) a bob ken, or a bowman ken, a well furnished house, also a house that harbours thieves; biting the ken, robbing the house.	KEN. A house. A bob ken, or a bowman ken; a well-furnished house, also a house that harbours thieves. Biting the ken; robbing the house. *Cant.*
KEN MILLER, or KEN CRACKER, a housebreaker, (*cant*).	KEN MILLER, or KEN CRACKER. A housebreaker. *Cant.*

In the preface to the second edition of the *Classical Dictionary*, Grose listed some additional sources. These were Harman's *Caveat*, the second edition of Head's *Canting Academy* (1674), *Hell upon Earth* (1703), and *The Scoundrel's Dictionary* (1754).[47] As with the sources listed in the preface to the first edition, this promises more than it delivers. *The Scoundrel's Dictionary* merely contains one of the word-lists from *The Canting Academy*. It also is difficult to demonstrate that Harman's *Caveat* provides any new entries, because practically all of Harman's terms were already listed in the first edition, via Dekker's glossary and B. E.'s dictionary. Although a few terms from Harman's list were added to the second edition, it is not the only possible source for any of them.[48]

---

[47] Grose, *Classical Dictionary* (1788), iv–vii.
[48] The new entry *queer-ken* "a prison" is clearly derived from the identical entry in Head's *Canting Academy*, rather than from "quyerkin a pryson house" in the *Caveat*, and the spelling of *nab-cheat* "a hat" also suggests that Head or B. E.'s dictionary is Grose's source for this entry rather than Harman's *nab-chet*.

Neither does the *Canting Academy* make a great contribution to Grose's word-list, largely because much of its contents were included in B. E.'s dictionary, which Grose had already used. Fourteen of the new entries in the second edition are from the *Canting Academy*. Nine of these are in B. E.'s dictionary as well as Head's. Forty-six new entries come from *Hell upon Earth*. One of these, *band-log*, defined as "a band-box" in *Hell Upon Earth* is subsumed in the entry for *band-dog* in the *Classical Dictionary*.

These are clearly not the only sources to provide new entries, however. Grose appears to have consulted both B. E.'s dictionary and the *New Canting Dictionary* again. Between them, these account for fifty-three new entries (excluding the nine that may be from the *Canting Academy*). Other authorities that Grose has returned to for the second edition of his dictionary include Shakespeare and Bailey's dictionary:

Source	*Classical Dictionary* (1788)
It is like a barber's chair that fits all buttocks . . .[49]	BARBER'S CHAIR. She is as common as a barber's chair, in which a whole parish sit to be trimmed; said of a prostitute.
So they were bleeding new my lord, there's no meat like 'em . . .[50]	BLEEDING NEW. A metaphor borrowed from fish, which will not bleed when stale.
BLUE *as a razor*, corrupt for *blue as azure*.[51]	BLUE . . . Blue as a razor; perhaps, blue as azure.

It is possible that Grose also incorporated new material from the work of more recent writers, though rarely verbatim:

Source	*Classical Dictionary* (1788)
Lookee . . . if you come athwart me, 'ware your gingerbread-work; I'll be foul of your quarter, d—n me.[52]	GINGERBREAD WORK. Gilding and carving: these terms are particularly applied by seamen on board Newcastle colliers, to the decorations of the sterns and quarters of West-India-men, which they have the greatest joy in defacing.
Lady Smart . . . You stand in your own Light . . . *Ld. Sparkish*. I'm sure he	GLAZIER . . . Is your father a glazier? a question asked to a lad or young

---

[49] *All's Well that Ends Well*, II.ii.16.   [50] *Timon of Athens*, I.ii.77–9.

[51] Bailey, *Dictionarium Britannicum*.

[52] Tobias Smollett, *The Adventures of Roderick Random*, ed. Paul-Gabriel Boucé (Oxford: Oxford University Press, 1979), 9 (ch. 3).

sits in mine: Prythee, *Tom*, sit a little farther: I believe your Father was no Glasier.[53]

man, who stands between the speaker and the candle, or fire. If it is answered in the negative, the rejoinder is—I wish he was, that he might make a window through your body, to enable us to see the fire or light.

Miss Nancy was, in vulgar language, soon made an honest woman.[54]

HONEST WOMAN. To marry a woman with whom one has cohabited as a mistress, is termed, making an honest woman of her.

In fact, Swift's *Polite Conversation*, a dialogue satirizing fashionable slang, accounts for forty-eight (4.2 per cent) of Grose's new entries. Fielding and Swift are both cited by name in entries new to the second edition:

CROSS BUTTOCK. A particular lock or fall in the Broughtonian art, which, as Mr. Fielding observes, conveyed more pleasant sensations to the spectators than the patient.

KISS MINE A-SE. An offer, as Fielding observes, very frequently made, but never, as he could learn, literally accepted . . .

LILIPUTIAN. A diminutive man or woman: from Gulliver's Travels, written by Dean Swift, where an imaginary kingdom of dwarfs of that name is described.

A source that Grose does not identify, which may possibly account for about a dozen entries, is *The Whole Art of Thieving*.[55] For example:

Whole Art

. . . two or three of us hold him up whilst some prads or rattlers come by: if they nap the bit, they cry pike; then we go and fisk the bit, and ding the empty bit, for fear it should be found, and fisk the blunt and gee if none is quare; to prevent a rapp, it is a bit or [sic] rige or wage: Come, let us pike to glee for a pitter or leather: there is a cull that has a rum loag, gammon: then we

Classical Dictionary (1788)

TO FRIZ, OR FRISK. Used by thieves to signify searching a person whom they have robbed. Blast his eyes! friz, or frisk him.

DING . . . Also to throw away or hide: thus a highwayman who throws away or hides any thing with which he robbed, to prevent being known or detected, is, in the canting lingo, styled a Dinger.

---

[53] Jonathon Swift, *Polite Conversation* (1738), ed. Herbert Davis with Louis Landa, *A Proposal for Correcting the English Tongue, Polite Conversation, &c.* (Oxford: Basil Blackwell, 1957), i. 13.

[54] Henry Fielding, *The History of Tom Jones. A Foundling*, ed. Martin C. Ballestin and Fredson Bowers (Oxford: Clarendon, 1974), ii, 815 (Book 15, ch. 8).

[55] *The Whole Art of Thieving and Defrauding Discovered* (London: Printed for the Booksellers, 1786).

jostle him up, and one knocks his kelp off, and while he lifts his hand up, his loag is napp'd, and after the gaff it is christen'd and fenc'd. (6–7)

CHRISTENING. Erasing the name of the true maker from a stolen watch, and engraving a fictitious one in its place.

Grose also recycled, though rather more briefly, some terms and phrases listed in his *Provincial Glossary*. A few are from the glossary:

Provincial Glossary (1787)

HAVY-CAVY. Undetermined, wavering, (habe cave) doubtful whether to accept or reject a thing. Nottingham.

VESSEL OF PAPER. Half a quarter of a sheet.

Classical Dictionary (1788)

HAVY CAVY. Wavering, doubtful, shilly shally

VESSEL OF PAPER. Half a quarter of a sheet

but most are from the selection of local proverbs, listed county by county. For example:

Provincial Glossary (1787)

He is a representative of Barkshire.
  A vulgar joke on any one afflicted with a cough, which is here termed barking. [L2r]
Wiltshire moon-rakers.
  Some Wiltshire rusticks, as the story goes, seeing the figure of the moon in a pond, attemped to rake it out. [R7v]
Yellow bellies.
  This is an appellation given to persons born in the Fens, who, it is jocularly said, have yellow bellies, like their eels. [O6v]

Classical Dictionary (1788)

BARKSHIRE. A member or candidate for Barkshire; said of one troubled with a cough, vulgarly styled barking

MOON RAKERS. Wiltshire men: because it is said that some men of that country, seeing the reflection of the moon in a pond, endeavoured to pull it out with a rake
YELLOW BELLY. A native of the Fens of Lincolnshire: an allusion to the eels caught there

In the *Provincial Glossary* these were presented as dialect or as proverbial references to regions and their inhabitants. In the *Classical Dictionary* we interpret them as cant or slang. It appears that for Grose it was more important to supplement his word-list than to be too precise about register. He is similarly willing to reuse material from his essays:

The Olio

A jolly Bacchanalian, reproaching a sober man for refusing his glass,

Classical Dictionary (1788)

BEAST. TO DRINK LIKE A BEAST i.e. only when thirsty.

observed, that he was like a brute beast, never drinking but when he was thirsty, and then nothing but water. (198)

An Irishman explaining the reason why the alphabet is called the Criss-cross Rowe, said, it was because Christ's cross was prefixed at the beginning and end of it. (195)

... there are a set of men, who attend at the Custom-house, under the denomination of *Damned Souls*, in order, for a certain fee, to swear out any goods whatsoever for the merchants ... [they have taken] a previous oath, by which they bind themselves never to swear to the truth, at the custom-house or excise office. (30)

CHRIST-CROSS ROW. The alphabet in a horn book: called Christ-cross Row, from having, as an Irishman observed, Christ's cross *prefixed* before and *after* the twenty-four letters.[56]

DAMNED SOUL. A clerk in a counting-house, whose sole business it is to clear or swear off merchandize at the custom-house; and who, it is said, guards against the crime of perjury, by taking a previous oath, never to swear truly on those occasions.

A further thirty-three entries are listed twice in the second edition of the *Classical Dictionary*. For example, *to flash the hash* "to vomit', is listed both at *flash* and *hash*. At *garret*, we have:

GARRET, or UPPER STORY. The head. His garret, or upper story, is empty, or unfurnished; i.e. has no brains, he is a fool.

while at *upper story* is the very similar:

UPPER STORY, or GARRET. Figuratively used to signify the head. His upper story or garrets are unfurnished; i.e. he is an empty or foolish fellow.

Some new entries contain only a cross-reference, for instance:

UPRIGHT ... Three-penny upright [sic]; see THREE-PENNY UPRIGHT.
THREE-PENNY UPRIGHT. A retailer of love, who, for the sum mentioned, dispenses her favours standing against a wall.

Thirty-two new entries duplicate material from the first edition. They usually offer little new information, but do make what is already in the dictionary more easily locatable. In each of these two examples, the first entry cited is more or less as found in the first edition, but with the addition of a cross-reference:

BARKER. The shopman of a bow-wow shop, or dealer in second-hand clothes, particularly about Monmouth-street, who walks before his master's door, and

---

[56] i/j and u/v counted as two letters rather than four.

deafens every passenger with his cries of—Clothes, coats, or gowns—what d'ye want gemmen?—what d'ye buy? See BOW-WOW SHOP.

BOW-WOW SHOP. A salesman's shop in Monmouth street; so called because the servant barks, and the master bites. See BARKER.

DRAUGHT, OR BILL, ON THE PUMP AT ALDGATE. A bad or false bill of exchange. See ALDGATE.

ALGATE [sic]. A draught on the pump at Algate; a bad bill of exchange, drawn on persons who have no effects of the drawer.

Another thirty-seven new entries appear to be included on the strength of other similarities with existing entries. For example, the first edition includes the entry *master of the rolls* "a baker", which is joined in the second edition by *master of the mint* "a gardener" and *master of the wardrobe* "one who pawns his clothes to purchase liquor". For other headwords, material is added, expanding on what is already there. Sometimes related terms are included:

1785	1788
HUNKS, a covetous miserable fellow, a miser.	Adds: also the name of a famous bear mentioned by Ben Jonson.
KEMP'S SHOES, would I had Kemp's shoes to throw after you. *Ben Johnson*. Perhaps Kemp was a man remarkable for his good luck or fortune; throwing an old shoe, or shoes, after any one going on an important business, is by the vulgar deemed lucky.	Adds: KEMP'S MORRIS. William Kemp, said to have been the original Dogberry in Much ado about Nothing, danced a morris from London to Norwich in nine days; of which he printed the account, A.D. 1600, intitled, Kemp's Nine Day's Wonder, &c.

Six hundred of the entries in the second edition of the *Classical Dictionary* (12.0 per cent) include illustrative citations. Although the proportion of entries including citations in the second edition is slightly higher than in the first, the increase is not statistically significant. Neither, if we look at entries new to the second edition, is there any significant change in Grose's practice with regard to citations (see Appendix, Tables 1.4 and 1.4.1).

Thirty-nine entries in the second edition include named authorities (0.8 per cent). Again, although there is a slight proportional increase in the entries including references to authorities, it is not statistically significant. However, the new entries contain significantly more authorities than those carried over from the first edition ($p = 0.01$). In keeping with Grose's additions to the list of sources in the preface, the dictionary is becoming more overtly authoritative (see Appendix, Tables 1.4 and 1.4.1). Similarly, although there are not enough new entries including etymologies to make a significant different to the dictionary as a whole (see Appendix, Tables 1.4 and 1.4.1), there are significantly more etymologies in the new entries than can be accounted for by chance ($p = 0.01$).

The semantic coverage of the first and second editions is not significantly different. It is more revealing, however, to look at the additions alone, as a representation of Grose's changing practice (see Appendix, Tables 1.2 and 1.2.1). Fewer additions are made than would be expected to CRIME & DISHONESTY and EMOTION (both $p = 0.05$), but there are significantly more miscellaneous terms ($p = 0.05$). The *Classical Dictionary* is thus demonstrably moving further away from the cant of thieves and beggars, and towards slang and non-standard language in general.

A sub-field of PLEASURE & PASTIMES grows markedly in size. There were only six entries for clubs in the first edition; the second adds a further forty-five ($p = 0.01$). Most of these include information about individual clubs, including their meeting place and date of establishment. For example:

BLUE AND ORANGE. This society, styling themselves Loyal and Friendly, met, 1742, at Kouli Kahn's head, Leicester-fields.
CAT AND BAGPIPEAN SOCIETY. A society which met at their office in the great western road: in their summons, published in the daily papers, it was added, that the kittens might come with the old cats without being scratched.[57]
HICCOBITES. The brethren of this most ancient and joyous order, held their general court, Dec. 5, 1750, at the Sun tavern Fish-street hill.
KIT-CAT CLUB. A society of gentlemen, eminent for wit and learning, who in the reign of queen Anne and George I. met at a house kept by one Christopher Cat. The portraits of most of the members of this society were painted by Sir Godfrey Kneller, of one size; thence still called the kit-cat size.
SWIZZLE . . . The 17th regiment had a society called the Swizzle Club, at Ticonderoga, A. D. 1760.

These and the other entries for the names of gentlemen's clubs are also found in the third edition of Grose's dictionary, but most were deleted by the editor of the *Lexicon Balatronicum*. It is worth commenting here that they represent a broadening of Grose's focus, in that they cover the slang of fashionable London society, and not of the

---

[57] Given the evasive definition for *bagpipe*, cited above, this is clearly written with a double audience in mind: it is innocent enough on the surface, but sufficiently explicit for those who might be interested in attending.

lower orders. It seems likely that they come from a common source, not yet identified.

Two other groups of entries in the second edition of the *Classical Dictionary* are worthy of note. One lists non-standard pronunciations, including:

BAG OF NAILS . . . The old BAG OF NAILS at Pimlico; originally the BACCHANALS.

DEAD-LOUSE. Vulgar pronunciation of the Dedalus ship of war.

FOX'S PAW. The vulgar pronunciation of the French words faux pâs. He made a confounded fox's paw.

NEGLIGEE. A woman's undressed gown, vulgarly termed a niggledigee.

NINE SHILLINGS. Corruption of *nonchalance*.

SUCCESSFULLY. Used by the vulgar for *successively*: as, Three or four landlords of this house have been ruined successfully by the number of soldiers quartered on them. *Irish*.[58]

Although Grose did not make any attempt to indicate pronunciation for other entries, these examples demonstrate that his conception of non-standard language included mispronunciations and malapropisms. This new interest in pronunciation was very much in keeping with contemporary interest in accent as an indication of social class, and was demonstrated in a number of popular plays, such as Sheridan's *The Rivals* (1775), in which the eponymous Mrs Malaprop first appeared.[59]

A small number of the additions to the second edition take the form of normal dictionary entries, but are actually jokes or riddles, most of which refer to prostitution. In these Grose usually treats the punchline as the headword and the body of the joke as a definition, for example:

ORTHODOXY AND HETERODOXY. Somebody explained these terms by saying, the first was a man who had a doxy of his own, the second a person who made use of the doxy of another man.

PUBLIC LEDGER. A prostitute: because, like that paper, she is open to all parties.

RICHARD SNARY. A dictionary. A country lad, having been reproved for calling persons by their christian names, being sent by his master to borrow a dictionary, thought to shew his breeding by asking for a Richard Snary.

SQUIRREL. A prostitute: because she, like that animal, covers her back with her tail. *Meretrix corpore corpus alit*. Menagiana, ii. 128.

WASP. An infected prostitute, who like a wasp carries a sting in her tail.

There is no evidence that any of these terms were ever used with the sense that Grose gives. What does seem more likely is that Grose's

---

[58] Grose also comments on this usage in *The Olio*, 94.

[59] Blake, *Non-Standard Language*, 82–4, 111.

contemporaries might have asked each other 'Why is a prostitute like a squirrel?' or 'What is the difference between orthodoxy and heterodoxy?'

The proportion of new entries containing usage labels is in line with Grose's practice in the first edition (see Appendix, Tables 1.3–1.3.2.1). They are also distributed in much the same way, although there are significantly more naval and nautical terms in the second edition, and significantly more terms are labelled as 'jocular' (both $p = 0.05$).

However, comparing the second edition and the first edition together may obscure changes in Grose's practice in the production of the second edition. Concentrating on new entries alone provides a better measure of Grose's changing methodology. In comparison with the first edition, significantly fewer new entries are labelled 'cant', while markedly more terms are labelled 'colloquial' ($p = 0.05$). Even more marked is the increase in the use of the labels 'naval/nautical', 'slang', and 'jocular' (all $p = 0.01$). These changes confirm the impression that Grose's interest in general slang and colloquial language was increasing at the expense of cant terms, and demonstrate that he was not actually in a position to document genuine contemporary cant.

There are 189 entries in the second edition that include cross-references (3.8 per cent). This is proportionally slightly lower than in the first edition, both in the second edition as a whole, and among the new entries, but neither change is statistically significant (see Appendix, Tables 1.4 and 1.4.1). A slightly higher proportion of cross-references in the second edition is accurate, but again this is not statistically significant, and it is because mistakes in the first edition have been rectified rather than because the new entries are any more exact. This indicates that Grose corrected incorrect cross-references as he came across them (usually by inserting an entry to fulfil the cross-reference), but did not work his way through the dictionary systematically correcting errors made in the first edition.

In the preface to the second edition, Grose addressed complaints about the indelicacy of his work:

Some words and explanations in the former edition having been pointed out as rather indecent or indelicate, though to be found in Le Roux, and other Glossaries of the like kind, these have been either omitted, softened, or their explanations taken from books long sanctioned with general approbation, and admitted into the seminaries for the education of youth—such as Bailey's, Miege's, or Philip's

Dictionaries; so that it is hoped this work will now be found as little offensive to delicacy as the nature of it would admit.[60]

A few terms were apparently deleted on the grounds of obscenity, notably *bagpipe*, *bud sallogh*, *huffle*, and *larking*, all quoted above. However, only in the case of *bud sallogh* had the definition been sufficiently explicit to cause offence to those who did not already understand it.

The second edition of Grose's dictionary, as we have seen, contains numerous additions to the first. The *OED* cites most of these additions from the third edition, published in 1796. In fact, the *OED* cites Grose (1788) only thirty-five times. It provides antedatings for eighty-seven existing *OED* entries, most by fewer than ten years, but twice by almost two centuries (see *guzzle-guts* and *shag*):

articles "trousers" (1796)

as like one's father as if he was spit out of his mouth [**spit**] "very like his father" (1825: *the very / dead spit of*)

blow-up "a discovery or disturbance" (1809)

book-keeper "one who keeps borrowed books" (1884: "a hoarder of books")

botch "a tailor" (1829: "an unskilful worker"; 1855: "a cobbler")

bottom "the backside" (1794–6)

breeches Bible "an edition of the Bible, published in 1598, in which Adam and Eve are said to make themselves breeches" (1835: referring to the 1560 Geneva Bible)

bug-hunter "an upholsterer" (1796)

bumping "the ceremony of banging someone's bottom against a boundary-marker" (*a*1888: *to bump*)

to bunt "to jostle" (1825: 'to strike, knock, push, butt')

buzzman "a pickpocket" (1832)

to capsize "to fall over through drunkenness" (*Capsize* is first cited from 1788. The first intransitive citation (for reflexive) is from 1805. It is not recorded with this sense.)

to cascade "to vomit" ([1771], 1805)

cat in hell [**cat's foot**] [with reference to a hopeless situation] (1796)

cat's sleep "faked sleep" (1823: *cat's nap*; 1856: *cat-nap*; 1837: *cat-sleep* "a short sleep")

catamaran 'an old scraggy woman' (1833: "a quarrelsome person, esp. a woman")

cobbler's punch "treacle, vinegar, gin, and water" (1865: 'a warm drink of beer or ale with the addition of spirit, sugar, and spice')

contra-dance "country-dance" (1803)

to cut off one's nose [**nose**] "to hurt oneself through spite" (1796)

dip "a candle-seller" (1815: "a candle")

dished up "ruined" (1798 *to dish*)

doodle-sack "a set of bagpipes" (*a*1846)

---

[60] Grose, *Classical Dictionary* (1788), i.

Dutch comfort "little or no comfort" (1796)

fat "empty space on a page" (1796)[61]

fid "a plug of tobacco" (1793)

figure-dancer "a forger who alters numbers on bank-notes" (1796)

flam "a single stroke on a drum" (1796)

fly-by-night "a witch" (1796)

garret "the head" (1796)

to the little gentleman in velvet [**velvet**] "a toast to the mole that caused King William's horse to stumble" (1814)

glass-eyes "someone who wears glasses" (1796)

go [**go-shop**] "a drinking-vessel" (1796)

the go [**go-shop**] "the rage" (1793)

gooseberry-eyed "grey-eyed" (1796)

gooseberry-wig "a large frizzy wig" (1796)

groggified [**grog**] "drunk" (1796)

guzzle-guts "one who drinks a lot" (1959: "a glutton")

to hoax [**hoaxing**] "to banter, to play jokes on" (1796)

hubble-bubble "confused" (1796)

jog-trot "a slow but regular pace" (1796)

kick-up [**kicks**] "a disturbance" (*a*1793)

like a winter's day [**winter's day**] "short and dirty" (1796)

maggot-boiler "a candle-seller" (1796)

Nazarene foretop [a type of wig] (1796)

negro's head "a brown loaf" (1796)

nip [**nyp, or nip**] "a half-pint" (1796)

nosebag "a bag used to feed a horse" (1796)

old gooseberry "mischief; the devil" (1796)

P.P.C. "pour prendre congé: to take leave (written on a card)" (1809–12)

to pad the hoof "to walk" (1824)

paw-paw "naughty; nasty" (1796)

peeping Tom "an inquisitive man" (1796)

persuaders "spurs" (1796)

to piddle "to urinate" (1796)

to piss down someone's back [**pissing**] "to flatter someone" (1967: *to piss in (a person's) pocket* (Austral.), 'to ingratiate oneself with, be on very familiar terms with')

poke "a punch" (1796)

to polish a bone "to eat a meal" (1908: *to polish one's plate / bowl etc.*)

pope's nose "a turkey's rump" (1796)

pug-nosed "with a snub nose" (1834)

as queer as Dick's hatband [**dick**] "odd" (1796: **hatband**)

rider "a sub-contractor" (1796)

rook "a crowbar" (1796)

rump and dozen "beef and claret" (1796)

---

[61] Typesetters, being paid by the page, were particularly pleased to see empty white spaces.

to run to a standstill [**stand-still**] "to ride (a horse) to exhaustion" (1811)
saddle-sick "saddle-sore" (1823)
schism-shop "a dissenters' meeting-house" (1801)
shag "a sexual partner" (1971)
slabbering-bib "a parson or lawyer's band" (1796)
to slip-slop "to use words incorrectly" (a1791)
to sluice one's gob "to drink" (1796)
snicker "a horse suffering from a swelling of the neck" (1796)
snitcher [**snitch**] "an informer" (1827)
to snooze "to sleep" (1789)
squeaker "an organ-pipe" (1796)
swizzle "an alcoholic drink" (1813)
taradiddle "a petty lie" (1796)
upping-block "a block used in mounting a horse" (1796)
vessel "an eighth of a sheet of paper" (1790)
walking the plank "a method of murder used by mutineers to avoid prosecution"
    (1822: *to walk the plank*)
to warm "to beat" (1824)
Welsh comb "the thumb and fingers" (1796)
whereas "a statement introduced by 'whereas'" (1795)
whistling-shop "an illegal spirits shop in prison" (1796)
the wood "the pulpit" (1854)
wrinkle in one's arse "an additional piece of knowledge" (1818: *wrinkle*)
wry-neck day "execution day" (1796)

The works and authors most frequently predated are: the third edition of Grose's dictionary (1796) forty-three times,[62] magazines six times, dialect glossaries five times, and Scott, Marryat and Coleridge twice each.

The Third Edition (1796)

Eric Partridge based his reprint of Grose's dictionary on the third edition:

I had originally planned to reprint the second edition of Grose's Dictionary, but I have good reason to believe that the third edition incorporates many of Grose's addenda and corrigenda, for the second was published three years before his death: and Grose was not the sort of man to rest upon his laurels. . . . The third edition, 1796, may . . . be considered the most important of those which Grose himself revised.[63]

---

[62] The third edition is once erroneously dated to 1793.
[63] Eric Partridge, *A Classical Dictionary of the Vulgar Tongue by Captain Francis Grose* (1931) (London: Routledge & Kegan Paul, 1963), vii.

Grose died in 1791, five years before the publication of the third edition of his dictionary. Partridge argued that, because no additional editor's name was given, we should see this posthumous edition as the best representation of Grose's own work. It has no new preface, and surely, Partridge reasoned, a new editor would not be able to resist taking credit for his work. The new edition was published by Hooper, as were the first two, and may therefore have represented Grose's own papers left with his publisher or passed on to the publisher by his family as Partridge asserted. But why wait five years before publication? Is there any other evidence to support or disprove Partridge's claim?

It may be that the publication of two editions of Grose's dictionary in the 1780s had been enough to saturate the market for large slang dictionaries for some time. Only minor cant lists were published during the intervening period.[64] It is possible, however, that the publication of a third edition of Grose's dictionary was prompted by the appearance in 1795 of both Caulfield's *Blackguardiana* and Potter's *New Dictionary of all the Cant and Flash Language* (see Chapters 2 and 3), both largely derived from Grose.

The editor of the third edition based it on the second edition of the *Classical Dictionary*, including in it entries not found at all in the first. These include the names for clubs listed above, but also:

BABBLE. Confused, unintelligible talk, such as was used at the building the Tower of Bable. [1796: *Babel*]

BLACK FLY. The greatest drawback on the farmer is the black fly, i.e. the parson who takes tythe [1796: *tithe*] of the harvest.

CONTRA DANCE. A dance where the dancers of the different sexes stand opposite each other, instead of side by side as in the minuet, regadoon [1796: *rigadoon*], louvre, &c. and now corruptly called a country dance.

This edition of the dictionary contains 5,097 entries for 4,054 headwords, as opposed to 4,999 entries and 3,975 headwords in the second edition. That is an increase of just 2 per cent in the number of both entries and headwords. However, there are actually just over a hundred new entries, because there are also some deletions.

---

[64] Although several versions of the Carew word-list were published during the 1780s and 1790s, the public surely bought them because they wanted to read about Carew's life rather than for the vocabulary. In any case, the word-list is presented as a glossary of terms used by gypsies, and this, along with the brevity of the list, meant that these volumes were not competition for Grose's dictionary. Equally, although George Parker published successfully on London street-life during the 1780s, his work made no attempt to challenge the thoroughness and authority of Grose's.

As in the second edition, some of these new entries are merely cross-references to existing entries. For example, at **pig**, the second edition has:

Brandy is Latin for pig or goose; an apology for drinking a dram after either

which the third edition presents at **brandy** as:

Brandy is Latin for a goose; a memento to prevent the creature from rising in the stomach by a glass of the good creature.[65]

All three editions have the entry:

FLAT, a bubble, gull, or silly fellow.

but the third adds another, probably from a different source, but without noticing the duplication:

FLATT. A foolish fellow.

For some entries the third edition provides additional explanation:

AFTER-CLAP. A demand after the first given-in has been discharged, a charge for pretended omissions [1796 adds:] in short, any thing disagreeable happening after all consequences of the cause have been thought at an end.

ANTHONY OR TANTONY PIG. The favourite or smallest pig in the litter.—To follow like a tantony pig, i.e. St. Anthony's pig; to follow close at one's heels. St. Anthony the hermit was a swine herd, and is always represented with a swine's bell and a pig. Some derive this saying from a privilege enjoyed by the friars of certain convents in England and France (sons of St. Anthony) whose swine were permitted to feed in the streets. These swine would follow any one having greens or other provisions, till they obtained some of them [1796 adds:] and it was in those days considered an act of charity and religion to feed them.

or additional illustration:

GUTS AND GARBAGE. A very fat man or woman. More guts than brains; a silly fellow [1796 adds:] He has plenty of guts, but no bowels; said of a hard, merciless, unfeeling person.

In others we are provided with new senses:

BOB TAIL. A lewd woman, or one that plays with her tail; also an impotent man, or an eunuch. Tag, rag, and bob-tail; a mob of all sorts of low people. To shift one's bob; to move off, or go away. To bear a bob; to join in chorus with any singers [1796 adds:] Also a term used by the sellers of game, for a partridge.

---

[65] Francis Grose, *A Classical Dictionary of the Vulgar Tongue. The Third Edition, Corrected and Enlarged* (London: Hooper & Co, 1796).

DICKEY. A woman's under petticoat [1796 adds:] It's all Dickey with him;
   i.e. it's all over with him.
SKIP JACKS. Youngsters that ride horses on sale, horse dealers boys [1796 adds:]
   Also a plaything made for children with the breast-bone of a goose.

or a development of an existing sense, making it more general or
more specific:

CROSS-BITE . . . also, to counteract or disappoint. *Cant* [1796 adds:]—This is
   peculiarly used to signify entrapping a man so as to obtain *crim. con.* money, in
   which the wife, real or supposed, conspires with the husband.
CROSS PATCH. A peevish boy or girl [1796 adds:] or rather an unsocial
   ill-tempered man or woman.

For two terms, synonyms are provided, once within the existing
entry, and once separately:

APRIL FOOL. Any one imposed on, or sent on a bootless errand, on the first of
   April; on which day it is the custom among the lower people, children, and
   servants, by dropping empty papers carefully doubled up, sending persons on
   absurd messages, and such like contrivances, to impose on every one they can,
   and then to salute them with the title of April Fool [1796 adds: This is also
   practised in Scotland under the title of Hunting the Gowke.]

MOTHER OF ALL SAINTS. The monosyllable.
[1796 adds:] MOTHER OF ALL SOULS. The same.

and in another the citation is extended, paraphrasing Dogberry in
Much Ado About Nothing (III v 43–4):

OBSTROPULOUS. Vulgar misnomer of *obstreperous*: as, I was going my rounds,
   and found this here gemman very obstropulous [1796 adds:] whereof
   I comprehended him as an auspicous parson.

Although existing entries are not, on the whole, further censored,
some of the new additions remind us that 'Victorian' prudery was
advancing apace:

INEXPRESSIBLES. Breeches.
UNFORTUNATE WOMEN. Prostitutes; so termed by the virtuous and compassionate
   of their own sex.

which is not to say that the compiler of this edition shied away from
including obscene terms in definitions:

SCOTCH WARMING PAN. A wench [1788] . . . also a fart. [1796]

A closer look at some of the other new entries indicates that
they, like the editorial changes made to existing entries, would have

required a thorough knowledge of the contents of the dictionary. For example:

IRISH BEAUTY. A woman with two black eyes [1796]

is apparently related to:

WEDDING . . . You have been at an Irish wedding, where black eyes are given instead of favours; saying to one who has a black eye. [1788]

The new entry for *pot-wabbler:*

POT-WABBLERS. Persons entitled to vote for members of parliament in certain boroughs, from having boiled their pots therein. These boroughs are called pot-wabbling boroughs. [1796]

appears to be a fuller explanation of the entry found under *wobble* in this and earlier editions:

TO WOBBLE. To boil. Pot wobbler; one who boils a pot. [1788]

There are also new entries of types that we have noted before. These include games and practical jokes:

CHOAKING PYE, OR COLD PYE. A punishment inflicted on any person sleeping in company: it consists in wrapping up cotton in a case or tube of paper, setting it on fire, and directing the smoak up the nostrils of the sleeper. See HOWELL'S COTGRAVE.

TRAVELLING PIQUET. A mode of amusing themselves, practised by two persons riding in a carriage, each reckoning towards his game the persons or animals that pass by on the side next them, according to the following estimation:
A parson riding a grey horse, with blue furniture; game.
An old woman under a hedge; ditto.
A cat looking out of a window; 60.
A man, woman, and child, in a buggy; 40.
A man with a woman behind him; 30.
A flock of sheep; 20
A ditto of geese; 10.
A postchaise; 5.
A horseman; 2.
A man or woman walking; 1.

coffee-houses and pubs:

FINISH. The Finish; a small coffee-house, in Covent-Garden market, opposite Russel-street, open very early in the morning, and therefore resorted to by debauchees shut out of every other house; it is also called Carpenter's coffee-house.

THE RELISH. The sign of the Cheshire cheese.

one non-standard pronunciation:

OYES. Corruption of oyez, proclaimed by the crier of all courts of justice.

and one entry that appears to be a joke rather than a headword and definition proper:

NONSENSE. Melting butter in a wig.

To compliment entries carried over from earlier editions, such as:

THINGUMBOB. Mr. Thingumbob; a vulgar address or nomination to any person whose name is unknown, the same as Mr. What-d'ye-call'em . . . [1788]

we have:

HICKENBOTHOM. Mr. Hickenbothom; a ludicrous name for an unknown person, similar to that of Mr. Thingambob. Hickenbothom is a corruption of the German word *icken-baum*, i.e. oak tree.

While entries for abbreviated terms in earlier editions, both ultimately from B. E.'s dictionary:

PHYZ. The face. Rum phyz; an odd face or countenance. [1788]
TRIB. A prison: perhaps from tribulation. [1788]

are joined by:

HYP. The hypochondriac; low spirits. He is hypped; he has got the blue devils, &c.

Only two of the new entries include dates, and these both precede Grose's demise:

AKERMAN'S HOTEL. Newgate. In 1787, a person of that name was the gaolor, or keeper.
PROPHET. The prophet; the Cock at Temple Bar: so called, in 1788, by the bucks of the town, of the inferior order.

A few of the new entries in the third edition of Grose's *Classical Dictionary* indicate that its compiler had probably looked at other cant dictionaries or works using cant, but not with any great thoroughness:

Parker[66]	*Classical Dictionary* (1796)
Farthing. *A fadge.*	FADGE . . . A farthing.
Glims. Eyes.	GLIMMS. Eyes.

---

[66] George Parker, *Life's Painter of Variegated Characters* (London: R. Bassam, 1789), 1789.

Potter[67]

LUSH, drink.	LUSH. Strong beer.
STONE JUG OR PITCHER, Newgate.	STONE JUG. Newgate, or any other prison.

If Potter's dictionary was a source, which seems unlikely, the entries could only have been added after Grose's death.

The third edition contains relatively few new entries, but it is, nevertheless, a thorough revision of existing material. New cross-references to entries carried over from the second edition suggest an editor who knew the dictionary well. The new entries fit in with Grose's established practice with regard to the rate of inclusion of etymologies, cross-references, authorities, citations, and usage labels (see Appendix, Tables 1.3–1.4.1). There are thus no statistically significant changes in lexicographic practice between the second and the third edition. Semantic coverage also remains pretty well unchanged, although new entries in the third edition include significantly more terms for LAW & ORDER than new entries in the second ($p = 0.05$) (see Appendix, Tables 1.2 and 1.2.1).

Because the new entries are relatively small in number and represent a limited quantity of text, it is impossible to produce any authoritative stylistic analysis to identify Grose's hand in them. However, we cannot assign the changes to Grose on negative evidence alone. Other people involved in the production of earlier editions would also have had a close acquaintance with its contents, and since all three editions bear the name of Hooper as their publisher, we can assume some continuity in production. Moreover, the sources of some new entries may postdate Grose's death.

Along with semantic fields, usage labels give an indication of the type of additions being made to the dictionary (see Appendix, Tables 1.3.2 and 1.3.2.1). Although the number of entries including usage labels is not significantly different overall, the proportion of new entries labelled as various types of jargon is markedly higher than we would expect based on additions to the second edition ($p = 0.01$). This is in continuation of the trend noted in the second edition away from cant and towards non-standard language in

---

[67] Humphry Tristram Potter, *A New Dictionary of all the Cant and Flash Languages*, 3rd edn. (London: B. Crosby, 1797). Note that although this dictionary was apparently first published in 1795, all surviving editions postdate the third edition of Grose's dictionary.

general. What we do not find, despite Grose's extensive travels in Scotland and Ireland after the publication of the second edition of his dictionary, and his evident interest in dialectal variation,[68] are any new Scots or Irish terms.

The third edition is a more thorough revision than the second, in that existing entries are altered as well as new entries being added. Entries emerge as more polished:

1788

APOTHECARY. To talk like an apothecary; to talk nonsense: from the assumed gravity and affectation of knowledge generally put on by the gentlemen of that profession, who are commonly but superficial in their learning.

1796

APOTHECARY. To talk like an apothecary; to use hard, or gallipot words; from the assumed gravity and affectation of knowledge generally put on by the gentlemen of that profession, who are commonly as superficial in their learning as they are pedantic in their language.

easier to follow:

1788

HEATHEN PHILOSOPHER. One whose breech may be seen through his pocket hole: this saying arose from the old philosophers, many of whom despised the vanity of dress to such a point, as often to fall into the excess complained of.

1796

HEATHEN PHILOSOPHER. One whose breech may be seen through his pocket-hole: this saying arose from the old philosophers, many of whom despised the vanity of dress to such a point, as often to fall into the opposite extreme.

more precise:

1788

BLACK INDIES. Newcastle in Northumberland, whose rich coal mines prove an Indies to the proprietors.
HODGE PODGE, OR HOTCH POT. A mixture.

1796

BLACK INDIES. Newcastle upon Tyne, whose rich coal-mines prove an Indies to the proprietors.

HODGE PODGE. An irregular mixture of numerous things.

[68] See the rather laboured dialogues between English and Scottish men in *The Olio*, 105–16.

better informed:

1788

BREWES, OR BROWES. Oatmeal boiled in the pot with salt beef.

DUKE HUMPHREY. To dine with Duke Humphrey; to fast. Humphrey, Duke of Gloucester, surnamed the Good, was famous for his voluntary mortifications, particularly frequent fasting.

1796

BREWES, OR BROWES. The fat scum from the pot in which salted beef is boiled.

DUKE HUMPHREY. To dine with Duke Humphrey; to fast. In old St. Paul's church was an aisle called Duke Humphrey's walk (from a tomb vulgarly called his, but in reality belonging to John of Gaunt), and persons who walked there, while others were at dinner, were said to dine with Duke Humphrey.

fuller:

1788

PEG. Old Peg; poor hard Suffolk cheese . . .

1796

PEG. Old Peg; poor hard Suffolk or Yorkshire cheese . . .

or less risqué:

1788

COLD PIG. To give cold pig, is a punishment inflicted on sluggards who lie too long in bed: it consists in pulling off all the bed clothes from them, and exposing them naked to the cold.

1796

COLD PIG. To give cold pig is a punishment inflicted on sluggards who lie too long in bed: it consists in pulling off all the bed clothes from them, and throwing cold water upon them.

The editor also abridges what is not essential:

1788

HELTER SKELTER. In defiance of order: composed of the Cumberland words, *helter*, to halter, or hang; and *skelter*, or *kelter*, order, or condition; i.e. hang order; as we say hang sorrow, &c.

MISCHIEF. A man loaded with mischief, i.e. a woman on one shoulder, and a monkey on t'other.

1796

HELTER SKELTER. To run helter skelter, hand over head, in defiance of order.

MISCHIEF. A man loaded with mischief, i.e. a man with his wife on his back.

and updates entries that require it:

1788	1796
NOKES. A ninny, or fool. John-a-Nokes and Tom-a-Stiles; two honest peaceable gentlemen, repeatedly set together by the ears by lawyers of different denominations: two fictitious names commonly used in law proceedings.	NOKES. A ninny, or fool. John-a-Nokes and Tom-a-Stiles; two honest peaceable gentlemen, repeatedly set together by the ears by lawyers of different denominations: two fictitious names formerly used in law proceedings, but now very seldom, having for several years past been supplanted by two other honest peaceable gentlemen, namely, John Doe and Richard Roe.

This posthumous edition also modernizes a number of spellings that had become rare by the last quarter of the eighteenth century: <camerade> becomes <comerade> (in the entry for **messmate**), <fidler> becomes <fiddler> (**rum squeeze**), <gate> "posture" becomes <gait> (**slouch**), <gigg> becomes <jig> (**goats gigg**), <jugg> becomes <jug> (**grey beard**), <jugler> becomes <juggler> (**juggler's box**), and <lye> becomes <lie> (**fib**). In addition, <pudden>, found only in representations of speech by this period, is corrected to <pudding> (**jack pudding**, **pickle herring**). It is hard to believe that a man as defiant of convention as Grose, at the age of almost sixty, would update his spelling in this way. This, clearly, is the work of a younger editor.

As well as correcting the second edition, the 1796 edition of Grose's dictionary introduced a number of careless errors, most of which appear to be the result of page-setting and proofreading mistakes. For example:

AGOG, ALL-A-GOG. Anxious, eager, impatient; from the Italian *agogare*, to deire [1788: *desire*] eagerly.

CROAKERS [1788: *CROCKERS*]. Forestallers, called also Kidders and Tranters.

CURJEW. The vulgar seaman's pronunciation of the Courageux [1788: *Couragieux*] ship of war.

JACKMEN. Sea [1788: *See*] JARKMEN.

SINGLE PEEPER. A person have [1788: *having*] but one eye.

We would expect Grose to know his own dictionary better than this, but the introduction of errors into existing entries does not demonstrate that the additions are not Grose's. It was certainly someone else who was responsible for proofreading the third edition, because Grose had been dead for several years by the time this edition came to the press, and it is likely that the typesetters would have introduced some errors.

Although existing entries are quite extensively edited, there is no significant change in lexicographic practice. There are no great increases or decreases in the proportion of entries containing etymologies, authorities, citations, or cross-references. This similarity is all the more striking in comparison with later editors' treatment of Grose's dictionary (see Chapters 2 and 3).

However, what we have here, according to Partridge, is a later version of the working copy discussed above. He argues that Hooper, the publisher, took Grose's unfinished notes on the second edition and incorporated them into this, the third. A number of factors argue against this hypothesis. First, in editing the first edition, Grose left existing entries largely unchanged, but added new entries copiously; here we have radical rewriting of existing entries, including the modernization of spelling, but relatively few new ones. Secondly, the carelessness of some of the editorial work on this edition exceeds Grose's own. Thirdly, and less convincingly, some of the new material in the third edition appears to use a source that postdates Grose's death. I believe that Partridge's hypothesis is part of the story: it is clear that Grose did continue to make notes after the publication of the first edition, and there is no reason to assume that he would not have done the same after the publication of the second. However, although some of the new material may be from Grose's notes, other additions were certainly made by his editor, and the revision of existing entries was also done by another hand. Partridge argues that such an editor would wish to record his own name, and perhaps write a new preface, but if this edition were motivated by new publications in the same field, it is entirely possible that a publisher's commercial instincts would override personal vanity. After all, the competition consisted of versions of Grose's dictionary with other people's names on the title page. If Grose's publisher had produced another such it would just have been one among several. What name could be more authoritative than Grose's own? The title page notes that the edition has been corrected and enlarged and that, presumably, was enough to demonstrate its superiority and also its faithfulness to the earlier editions.

What Partridge did not comment on is the death, in 1793, of Samuel Hooper, Grose's publisher. This was followed by several years in which his widow, Mary, apparently published nothing. In 1796 she entered into a partnership with William Wigstead. The third edition of the *Classical Dictionary* was published by this new partnership, presumably prompted by the success of the related publications by Caulfield and Potter (see Chapters 2 and 3). Although this edition may contain some additions collected by Grose, I believe that its editor was Wigstead.[69]

The *OED* cites the third edition of Grose's dictionary seventy-two times.[70] As has been shown, these citations are frequently predateable by reference to earlier editions of the dictionary, especially the second, and by referring to Grose's sources. It is not surprising that an edition that was used so regularly, despite its limited new material, should provide relatively few antedatings of its own. Three of these predate later slang dictionaries: *fawney* "a ring" (Vaux 1812), *guts* "courage" (Farmer 1893), and *to queer* "to spoil; to mess up" (Vaux 1812). One predates a newspaper: *all dicky with* "all over with" (*Morning Post* 1810). The others are *bone-picker* "a footman", which surely presupposes the sense 'one who lives by collecting bones from heaps of refuse, etc.' (1861), *skip-jack* "a children's toy" (1797), and *tizzy* "a sixpence" (1804). In addition, the *OED* cites *round-about* "a burglar's tool" from Grose (1796), though its first appearance was in the *Lexicon Balatronicum*.

Summary

All three editions of Grose's dictionary published under his name covered general slang as well as cant, jargon, and dialect. Grose went to great lengths to appear authoritative and scholarly, listing his sources both in the preface and in the body of the dictionary. To this end, he made his canting sources seem more extensive than they actually were.

In the first edition, Grose chose first those terms labelled as 'cant' in his dictionary sources, then those illustrated by citation and/or dealing with selected semantic areas. He included relatively few cant terms that were not listed in earlier dictionaries. Modern canting

[69] A more detailed version of this argument is to be found in Julie Coleman, 'The third edition of Grose's *Classical Dictionary of the Vulgar Tongue*: bookseller's hack-work or posthumous masterpiece?', in Julie Coleman and Anne McDermott, *Historical Dictionaries and Historical Dictionary Research* (Tübingen: Niemeyer, forthcoming), 71–81.

[70] Seventy-three if we assume that the 1793 citation for *fid of tobacco* is from the 1796 edition.

works, novels, plays, popular literature, and reference works were among Grose's other sources, some of which are credited where appropriate. It is likely, but unverifiable, that he did use spoken as well as written sources. Although his inclusion of terms dealing with bodily functions is more thorough than that of his main sources, Grose remained euphemistic in spelling and defining them. His moralistic tone is most apparent in the presentation of trades and professions, almost as one, as dishonest and grasping.

Although the second edition was largely passed over in the compilation of the *OED* in favour of the third, it does represent a considerable augmentation of the first. Significant changes were made to the layout of individual entries, but not to the ordering of entries. Some of the mistakes made in the first edition were corrected, and new entries allow easier access to material that might not easily be found. The inclusion of markedly more etymologies and named authorities in new entries for this edition makes the work seem all the more definitive. Grose follows his original practice in exaggerating his new antiquarian sources, and in not giving due credit to contemporary rival publications. As well as using new sources, he consulted volumes used in the compilation of the first edition again, recycled material from the *Provincial Glossary*, and duplicated entries from the first edition of the *Classical Dictionary* under new headwords.

Entries new to the second edition represent a broadening of Grose's conception of 'the vulgar tongue'. He includes more general slang and colloquial language, names of clubs, jokes, mispronunciations, and more naval/nautical terms. The reduced proportion of new entries belonging to two groups—those explicitly labelled as 'cant', and those dealing with CRIME & DISHONESTY—demonstrates the movement away from the language of criminals into more general non-standard English.

The third edition may include some material from notes made by Grose before his death, but it was extensively edited by Wigstead. It includes relatively few new entries, but many existing entries were rewritten and updated. The trend away from cant continued, with an increase in jargon in this edition.

Grose appears to have compiled and edited his dictionary alphabetically. This suggests that he made notes from his sources and later arranged them in the order they were to appear in his word-list. His etymologies display little knowledge of languages other than English. Despite his limitations as a lexicographer, Grose is much cited by the

OED, and could have been even more extensively used. This 'good-humoured Antiquary and Philologist'[71] was certainly the most sensitive and perceptive recorder of contemporary slang and colloquial language of his age. He 'dominated the whole character and trend of slang during the first two decades of the nineteenth century'[72] as well as the last three decades of the eighteenth.

[71] *Gentleman's Magazine*, October 1788, 911.
[72] Eric Partridge, *Slang Today and Yesterday* (1933) (London: Routledge & Kegan Paul, 1950), 80.

2 Dictionaries Based on Grose's

Grose's dictionary established his reputation as the foremost authority on cant and slang, both antiquarian and contemporary. It should come as no surprise, then, that later lexicographers built upon his reputation: some by using his name, and others his work.

James Caulfield, *Blackguardiana* (1795)

James Caulfield (1764–1826) was an author and print-seller. He specialized in portraits of characters 'remarkable for their eccentricity, immorality, dishonesty, and so forth'.[1] This skill in infamous portraiture was what Caulfield brought to Grose's dictionary. The full title of this pirated edition is:

Blackguardiana, or, Dictionary of Rogues, Bawds, Pimps, Whores, Pickpockets, Shoplifters, Mail-robbers, Coiners, House-breakers, Murderers, Pirates, Gipsies, Mountebanks, &c. &c. Illustrated with eighteen Portraits of the most remarkable Professors in every Species of Villainy. Interspersed with many curious Anecdotes, Cant Terms, Flash Songs, &c. The Whole Intended to put Society on their guard against Depredators; and was picked up by an Inhabitant of St. James's, who was a Spectator of a grand Scuffle, on a Birth-day Night. Copied for the Inspection of the Curious; and the Original ready to be returned (on describing the Binding, &c.) to the Loser.[2]

Even the publication details are intriguingly faked, listing real and fictional characters notorious as highwaymen, pirates, pickpockets, jail-breakers, and actresses:

Printed for, and sold by John Shepherd, at the Golden Farmer, Bagshot; Sir John Falstaff, at the Boar's-head, Finchley-Common; Sir Henry Morgan, at the Land-Pirates, Hounslow; Charles Maclean, at the Lady Abbess's, Shooter's-Hill; Mary Cut-Purse, at Fairfax's Head, Hedge-Lane; Mary Flanders, at the Naked Boy, Wapping; Mary Carleton, at the German Princess, Mary le Bone; and Betty Ireland, at the Fair Damsel, Dyot-Street, St. Giles's.

As a further inducement to buy, the public is informed that 'Only a few Copies of this Work are printed'.

---

[1] Biographical details and quotation from *DNB* Vol. ix.329–31.
[2] James Caulfield, *Blackguardiana* (London: John Shepherd, 1795).

Comparison between the layout of this and the first edition of Grose's dictionary reveals that this actually is Grose's first edition: Caulfield must have obtained some remaindered copies and decided that he could mark up his cannibalism of Hooper's book enough to make it profitable. Interpolated into the word-list are portraits of immoral individuals and new entries of a far more discursive style than those adopted from Grose. The new entries are not always in their correct alphabetical position. Oddly, the new entry for *Abbess, Lady Abbess*, which falls between *All-a-mort* and *All-nations*, is preceded by the title 'A Classical Dictionary of the Vulgar Tongue', which takes up the first half of the page:[3]

ABBESS, LADY ABBESS, a Bawd, or the Mistress of a Brothel. One of the greatest adepts in this profession in the last century, was Mrs. Creswell. This infamous woman was, from the natural effects of prostitution in her youth, far advanced in the decline, before she arrived to the meridian of her life. Her great experience in her former occupation qualified her for a procuress, and she soon became an adept in all the diabolical arts of seduction; she lived in town in the winter, and sometimes retired into the country, where she provided convenient lodgings for her customers, some of whom were persons of distinction. Though she appeared in her real character in the stews, she could assume a very decent behaviour on proper occasions, and frequently decoyed young unsuspecting girls to London, in hopes of preferment; she kept a very extensive correspondence, and was by her spies and emissaries informed of the rising beauties, in different parts of the kingdom. The trade which she possessed, was, perhaps, carried to a greater height at this period, than at any other. This is plainly hinted at by a man of wit and pleasure, who sometimes dealt with her.

> To an exact perfection have they brought
> The action Love,—the passion's quite forgot

Mother Ross and Mother Bennett (these flourished at this time), to whom the Plain Dealer is dedicated; which is an admirable piece of raillery on women of this description.

Mother Mosely was a bawd of the same period. Betty Beaulieu, a bawd of Scotland Yard, is celebrated by Wood, who says, that Charles Maurice Tellier, Archbishop and Duke of Rheims and Crequi, who came here concerning the marriage of the Dauphin to the lady Mary, visited the house of this mother strumpet. Of these matrons we have no portraits, nor of Mother Needham, Mother Rawlins of Deptford, Mother Douglas, Mother Eastmead, Mother Phillips, and Mother W—r. Mr. Tyson, however, has preserved the likeness of Mother Lagden, of Bournbridge, in Cambridgeshire. [facing page]

---

[3] The original entry for *Abbess, Lady Abbess*, from Grose's dictionary, is found in its correct place two pages earlier, at the beginning of the dictionary, where it is also preceded by the title.

The most famous places in London, for the resort of women who carried on this vocation, formerly was Moorfields, Whetstone Park, Lukener Lane, and Dog and Bitch Yard. But as every thing has its day, and decline, so these seraglio's now are no more in vogue: and are changed to King's Place, Mary le Bone, and St. George's Fields.

Even more obviously an interpolation is the entry for *Banditti*, which falls in the middle of Grose's definition for *Banyan day*.

The illustrations, Caulfield's main purpose in constructing this volume, are of Mrs Creswell, Mrs Lagden, A Captain of Banditti's [sic], Falstaff, John Weston, George Weston, Miss Nancy Parsons, Mary Carleton, Mother Damnable of Kentish Town, and Phillips the merry Andrew. Several bear Caulfield's name, and are dated 1792 and 1793, but the styles of the others vary markedly.

After the dictionary, Caulfield included flash songs from Richard Head's *Canting Academy*, introducing some careless changes:

Head's *Canting Academy*	*Blackguardiana*
When the Darkmans have been wet	When the darkman's have been wet,
Thou the Crackmans down didst beat	Tho' the crackman's down didst beat
For Glymmar whilst a	For glimmer, whilst a
quacking cheat,	quacking-cheat,
Or Tib o'th Buttery was our meat.	Or rib o'th' buttery was our meat.
Red shanks then I could not lack,	Red-shaks then I could lack,
Ruff-peck still hung at my back,	Ruff-peck still hung on my back,
Grannam ever fill'd my sack,	Crannam ever fill'd my sack,
With lap and poplars held I tack.	With lap and poplats held jack.

Although Caulfield has nothing new to add to slang or canting lexicography, he does demonstrate a continuing fascination with the underworld and its language. The *Blackguardiana* is also testament to the commercial viability of such works, and to the limited effort necessary to benefit from it.

The *Lexicon Balatronicum* (1811)

> One of the many reprints of Grose's second edition, put forth under a fresh, and what was then considered more attractive title. It was given out in an advertisement, &c., as a piece of puff, that it was edited by a Dr. H. Clarke, but it contains scarcely a line more than Grose.[4]

---

[4] Hotten, *Dictionary*, 157.

Twenty years after Grose's death, the 'buffoons' dictionary' or 'chatterers' dictionary' appeared. The title page further describes it as:

A dictionary of Buckish Slang, University Wit, and Pickpocket Eloquence. Compiled originally by Captain Grose. And now considerably altered and enlarged, with the modern changes and improvements, by a member of the Whip Club. Assisted by Hell-Fire Dick, and James Gorden, Esqrs. of Cambridge; and William Soames, Esq. of the Hon. Society of Newman's Hotel.

As the subtitle also suggests, although the work continues to include cant terms, it emphasizes more than ever its coverage of general slang. Two later slang lexicographers differ in their assessments of this edition. Hotten, quoted above, considered it no better than the second edition. John Bee wrote:

To this impression Dr. H. Clarke added 'University Wit' to the 'Pickpocket Eloquence' of a professor in that line, who had been suborned for the purpose, and cannot be named, further than the initial P. comes to: 'Buckish Slang,' and various scraps by several assistants, completed the editorial *pains* of this flashy work; and the publisher dished-up a title conformably thereto, to grace or to sell his books. 'Hell-fire Dick's' name, with some others, bore a prominent feature on the first leaf; Dick Owen, or Vowen, or Vaughan, had, however, nought what-ever to do with 'the writing part,' not being in the habit of penmanship; and he was, moreover, previously dead and buried. The other *names* on the title were fictitious, or not allowable,—it was, in fact, a printer's job; nevertheless, the book contained all that other books of the same profession contained, and much new and interesting matter, and may be pronounced the best edition of Grose, and the farthest-gone thing of the kind ever produced, or probably that ever will be produced.[5]

The preface emphasizes the usefulness of the dictionary to fashionable young men:

The merit of Captain Grose's Dictionary of the Vulgar Tongue has been long and universally acknowledged. But its circulation was confined almost exclusively to the lower orders of society: he was not aware, at the time of its compilation, that our young men of fashion would at no very distant period be as distinguished for the vulgarity of their jargon as the inhabitants of Newgate; and he therefore conceived it superfluous to incorporate with his work the few examples of fashion-able slang that might occur to his observation.[6]

[5] John Bee, *Slang. A Dictionary of the Turf, the Ring, the Chase, the Pit, of Bon Ton, and the Varieties of Life* (London: T. Hughes, 1823), viii–ix.
[6] *Lexicon Balatronicum. A Dictionary of Buckish Slang, University Wit, and Pickpocket Eloquence* (London: Printed for C. Chapel, Pall-Mall, 1811), Preface, v.

After a lengthy discussion of the advantages of being able to discuss unsuitable topics without one's father or the ladies understanding, the preface concludes:

> When the number and accuracy of our additions are compared with the price of the volume, we have no doubt that its editors will meet with the encouragement that is due to learning, modesty, and virtue.[7]

The *Lexicon Balatronicum* contains 5,381 entries for 4,307 headwords, as opposed to 5,097 entries and 4,054 headwords in the third edition. This is an increase of 5.6 per cent in the number of entries and of 6.2 per cent in the number of headwords. It takes most of its word-list from the third edition of Grose's *Classical Dictionary*, including entries only found in that edition:

MOTHER OF ALL SOULS. The same [as *mother of all saints*]. [*Lexicon* adds:] . . . *Irish*.
PIECE. A wench. A damned good or bad piece; a girl who is more or less active and skilful in the amorous congress [*Lexicon* adds:] . . . Hence the (*Cambridge*) toast, May we never have a *piece* (peace) that will injure the constitution . . .

The text of the *Lexicon* is in many instances more efficient than that of the earlier edition. It deletes very few entries, but abridges many, sometimes by merely cutting out a word, phrase, or clause:

Classical Dictionary (1796)	*Lexicon Balatronicum*
HURDY GURDY A kind of fiddle, made perhaps out of a gourd: at present it is confounded with the humstrum. See HUMSTRUM.	HURDY GURDY. A kind of fiddle, originally made perhaps out of a gourd. See HUMSTRUM.
SCUM. The riff-raff, tag-rag, and bobtail, or lowest order of the people.	SCUM. The riff-raff, tag-rag, and bobtail, or lowest order of people.
TEIZE. To nap the teize; to receive a private whipping. *Cant*.[8]	TEIZE . . . To nap the teize; to receive a whipping. *Cant*.

and sometimes by more radical abridgement:

Classical Dictionary (1796)	*Lexicon Balatronicum*
ACADEMY . . . Campbell's Academy; the same [a hulk], from a gentleman of that name, who had the contract for finding and victualling the hulks or lighters.	ACADEMY . . . Campbell's Academy; the same, from a gentleman of that name, who had the contract for victualling the hulks or lighters.

[7] *Lexicon Balatronicum*, Preface, viii.
[8] Not, as it might sound, a sexual perversion, but one of the two judicial alternatives in sentencing a criminal to be whipped: public or private. By the mid-eighteenth century, private whippings were more common.

FLOGGING CULLY. A debilitated
lecher (commonly an old one),
whose torpid powers require
stimulating by flagellation.

FLOGGING CULLY. A debilitated
lecher, commonly an old one.

At the same time, however, the editor increases the length of other
entries. Usually it is because he has a citation to add:

BOG HOUSE. The necessary house. [*Lexicon* adds:] . . . To go to bog; to go to stool.
GAMBS. Thin, ill-shaped legs; a corruption of the French word *jambs* [*Lexicon*
  adds:] . . . Farcy gambs; sore or swelled legs.
MALKIN, OR MAULKIN . . . a figure set up in a garden to scare the birds . . .
  [*Lexicon* adds:] . . . The cove's so scaly, he'd spice a malkin of his jazey: the
  fellow is so mean, that he would rob a scare-crow of his old wig.
PANNY. A house. To do a panny; to rob a house. See the Sessions Papers. Probably,
  panny originally meant the butler's pantry, where the knives and forks, spoons,
  &c. are usually kept . . . [*Lexicon* adds:] The pigs frisked my panney, and nailed
  my screws; the officers searched my house, and seized my picklock keys . . .

Some citations are rather lengthier than mere lexical illustration
requires:

BEAK. A justice of peace, or magistrate. [*Lexicon* adds:] . . . Also a judge or
  chairman who presides in court. I clapp'd my peepers full of tears, and so the
  old beak set me free; I began to weep, and the judge setme [sic] free.
BLOWER OR BLOWEN. A mistress or whore of a gentleman of the scamp. [*Lexicon*
  adds:] . . . The blowen kidded the swell into a snoozing ken, and shook him of
  his dummee and thimble; the girl inveigled the gentleman into a brothel and
  robbed him of his pocket book and watch.[9]
COLLEGE . . . King's College; the King's Bench prison. [*Lexicon* adds:] . . . He has
  been educated at the steel, and took his last degree at college; he has received
  his education at the house of correction, and was hanged at Newgate.
CROWN OFFICE. The head. [*Lexicon* adds:] . . . I fired into her keel upwards; my
  eyes and limbs Jack, the crown office was full; I s—k—d [sic] a woman with her
  a—e upwards, she was so drunk, that her head lay on the ground.

He includes anecdotes and additional information to bring entries
to life:

BOH. Said to be the name of a Danish general, who so terrified his opponent Foh,
  that he caused him to bewray himself. Whence, when we smell a stink, it is
  customary to exclaim, Foh! i.e. I smell general Foh. He cannot say Boh to
  a goose; i.e. he is a cowardly or sheepish fellow. [*Lexicon* adds:] . . . There is
  a story related of the celebrated Ben Jonson, who always dressed very plain; that
  being introduced to the presence of a nobleman, the peer, struck by his homely

---

[9] The headword is reduced to **blowen**.

appearance and awkward manner, exclaimed, as if in doubt, 'you Ben Johnson! why you look as if you could not say Boh to a goose!' 'Boh!' replied the wit.

FELLOW COMMONER. An empty bottle: so called at the university of Cambridge, where fellow commoners are not in general considered as over-full of learning. At Oxford an empty bottle is called a gentleman commoner for the same reason. [*Lexicon* adds:] . . . They pay at Cambridge 250l. a year for the privilege of wearing a gold or silver tassel to their caps. The younger branches of the nobility have the privilege of wearing a hat, and from thence are denominated HAT FELLOW COMMONERS.

and sources to provide an air of authority:

CARVEL'S RING. The private parts of a woman. Hans Carvel, a jealous old doctor, being in bed with his wife, dreamed that the Devil gave him a ring, which, so long as he had it on his finger, would prevent his being made a cuckold: waking, he found he had got his finger the Lord knows where. [*Lexicon* adds:] . . . See Rabelais, and Prior's versification of the story.

In one entry a joke is added:

QUIM. The private parts of a woman: perhaps from the Spanish *quemar*, to burn [*Lexicon* adds:] . . . (*Cambridge*) *A piece's furbelow.*[10]

A new entry for *Jew* is added, which stands alongside one carried over from the third edition:

Classical Dictionary (1796)	*Lexicon Balatronicum*
JEW. An over-reaching dealer, or hard, sharp fellow; an extortioner; the brokers behind St. Clement's church in the Strand were formerly called Jews by their brethren the tailors.	JEW. A tradesman who has no faith, i.e. will not give credit.

apparently under the influence of:

CHRISTIAN. A tradesman who has faith, i.e. will give credit.

Occasionally the editor adds a new cross-reference to an existing entry:

DROP. The new drop; a contrivance for executing felons at Newgate, by means of a platform, which drops from under them: this is also called the last drop. See LEAP.[11] [*Lexicon* adds:] . . . See MORNING DROP.

GUTTING A QUART POT. Taking the lining out of it; i.e. drinking it off. Gutting an oyster; eating it. Gutting a house; clearing it of its furniture. [*Lexicon* adds:] . . . See POULTERER.

---

[10] As well as providing an obscene pun, *furbelow* means 'A piece of stuff pleated and puckered on a gown or petticoat; a flounce; the pleated border of a petticoat or gown' (*OED*).

[11] The editor of the *Lexicon Balatronicum* corrects this to LEAF.

HANK . . . A Smithfield hank: an ox rendered furious by over-driving and barbarous treatment. [*Lexicon* adds:] . . . See BULL HANK.

Additions that modify the sense of an entry are rare:

CLOUT . . . It also means a handkerchief. *Cant.* [*Lexicon* adds:] . . . Any pocket handkerchief except a silk one.

PLANT. The place in the house of the fence, where stolen goods are secreted. [*Lexicon* adds:] . . . Any place where stolen goods are concealed.

Typographical and grammatical errors in the third edition are corrected and updated by amendment:

ARK RUFFIANS. Rogues who, in conjunction with water-men, robbed, and sometimes murdered, on the water, by picking a quarrel with the passengers in a boat, boarding it, plundering, stripping, and throwing them overboard, &c. A species of badgers [*Lexicon: badger*]. *Cant.*

TOTTY-HEADED. Giddy, hair-brained. [*Lexicon: hare-brained*]

while factual errors are usually corrected by addition:

BERMUDAS. A cant name for certain places in London, privileged against arrests, like the Mint in Southwark, *Ben. Jonson.* [*Lexicon* adds:] . . . These privileges are abolished.

BUNDLING. A man and woman sleeping in the same bed, he with his small clothes on, and she with her petticoats on; an expedient practised in America on a scarcity of beds, where, on such an occasion, husbands and parents frequently permitted travellers to bundle with their wives and daughters. [*Lexicon* adds:] . . . This custom is now abolished. See Duke of Rochefoucalt's Travels in America.

The editor of the *Lexicon* also introduces some mistakes into text taken from the third edition. For example:

APE LEADER. An old maid: their punishment after death, for neglecting to increase [*Lexicon: neglecting increase*] and multiply, will be, it is said, leading apes in hell.

CHUB. He is a young chub, or a mere chub; i.e. a foolish fellow, easily imposed on: an allusion [*Lexicon: illusion*] to a fish of that name, easily taken.

TO FULK [*Lexicon: FUNK*]. To use an unfair motion of the hand in plumping at taw. *Schoolboy's term.*

GINNY. An instrument to lift up a grate [*Lexicon: great*], in order to steal what is in the window. *Cant.*

OLD ROGER [*Lexicon: POGER*]. The Devil.

RUSTY GUTS. A blunt surly fellow: a jocular misnomer of *rusticus* [*Lexicon: resticus*].

SNAFFLER. A highwayman. Snaffler of prancers [*Lexicon: prances*]; a horse-stealer.

George Parker's *Life's Painter* (1789), possibly already used by the compiler of the third edition of Grose's dictionary, appears to be the source for some new entries in the *Lexicon*. For instance:

Parker (1789)   *Lexicon Balatronicum*

Flash of lightning. A glass of gin.   LIGHTNING. Gin. A flash of
                                                lightening; a glass of gin.[12]

Breeches. *Kickseys*.   KICKSEYS. Breeches.

Screen. A bank note.   SCREEN. A bank note . . . [13]

Humphry Tristram Potter's *New Dictionary of all the Cant and Flash Languages* derived most of his word-list from earlier editions of Grose's dictionary (see Chapter 3). In his turn, the editor of the *Lexicon* looked to Potter for additions to his word-list, for example:

Potter (1797)   *Lexicon Balatronicum*

——CONOBLIN [RIG], cutting the   KONOBLIN RIG. Stealing large pieces
    string of large coals hanging at the   of coal from coal sheds.
    doors of coal-sheds, &c.

MOUTH, a foolish easy fellow.   MOUTH. A silly fellow. A dupe . . .

PULL, having the advantage over   PULL . . . To have a pull is to have an
    another.   advantage; generally where a
                                                person has some superiority at
                                                a game of chance or skill.

STEPHEN, money.   STEPHEN. Money. Stephen's at home;
                                                i.e. has money.

THIMBLE, OR, TICK, a watch.   THIMBLE. A watch. The swell flashes
                                                a rum thimble; the gentleman
                                                sports a fine watch.

In 1803 'A Pembrochian' produced a dictionary called *Gradus ad Cantabrigiam* (see Chapter 9). Some of its word-list is derived from earlier editions of Grose's *Classical Dictionary*. It contains much of the university slang that is new to the *Lexicon*, but if it is the source it was not used verbatim. For example:

Gradus (1803)   *Lexicon Balatronicum*

POLLOI, οι πολλοι "the many".   ΟΙ ΠΟΛΛΟΙ. (*Cambridge.*) The many;
    Those who take their degree   the multitude; who take degrees
    without any honour. . . .   without being entitled for an honor.
                                                All that is *required*, are three books

---

[12] The third edition already had the entry 'LIGHTNING. Gin'.
[13] Potter also lists this in his dictionary, where it is spelt *skreen*.

of Euclid, and as far as Quadratic
Equations in Algebra. See
PLUCKED.

Despite the overlap in content, it is probable that *Gradus* was not
a direct source for the *Lexicon*, which sometimes disagrees with its
definitions:

Gradus (1803)

APOSTLES; the xii last on the list of
Bachelors of Arts: a degree lower
than the οι πολλοι. "Scape goats
of literature, who have, at length,
scrambled through the pales, and
discipline, of the Senate House,
without being *plucked*, and
miraculously obtained the
title of A.B."

Lexicon Balatronicum

APOSTLES. (*Cambridge.*) Men who are
plucked, refused their degree.

or adds material to it:

Gradus (1803)

NESCIO. "To *sport* a NESCIO;"—to
shake the head, a signal that there is
nothing in it. Strange and
paradoxical as it may seem—to
sport a NESCIO is very common
with those who would, nevertheless,
be thought very KNOWING.

Lexicon Balatronicum

NESCIO. He sports a Nescio; he
pretends not to understand any
thing. After the senate house
examination for degrees, the
students proceed to the schools,
to be questioned by the proctor.
According to custom immemorial
the answers *must* be *Nescio*. The
following is a translated
specimen:
Ques. What is your name?—*Ans*. I
do not know.
Ques. What is the name of this
university?—*Ans*. I do not know.
Ques. Who was your father?—*Ans*. I
do not know.
This last is probably the only true
answer of the three!

A playwright known only as 'T. B.' published a play called *The Pettyfogger
Dramatized* in 1797 (see Chapter 7). The glossary that accompanies it

may be a further source for a few terms in the *Lexicon*, including:

Pettyfogger Dramatized	*Lexicon Balatronicum*
TO BUM. To Arrest.	TO BUM. To arrest a debtor. The gill bummed the swell for a thimble; the tradesman arrested the gentleman for a watch.
SCALY. Mean.	SCALY. Mean. Sordid. How scaly the cove is; how mean the fellow is.

The *Lexicon* is not unusual in repeating information found in existing entries. In this and the first three editions of Grose's dictionary we have:

DEVIL'S BOOKS, cards.

to which a new entry is added in the *Lexicon*:

BOOKS. Cards to play with. To plant the books; to place the cards in the pack in an unfair manner.

The *Lexicon* excerpts new entries from those found as early as the first edition of Grose's dictionary:

Classical Dictionary (1785)	*Lexicon Balatronicum*
BETTY MARTIN, that's my eye, betty martin, an answer to any one that attempts to impose or humbug.	EYE. It's all my eye and Betty Martin. It's all nonsense, all mere stuff.
HAWK, ware hawk, the word to look sharp, a bye word when a bailiff passes . . .	WARE HAWK. An exclamation used by thieves to inform their confederates that some police officers are at hand.
WIPER DRAWER . . . he drew a broad, narrow, cam, or speckt wiper, he picked a pocket of a broad, narrow, cambrick, or coloured handkerchief.	TO DRAW. To take any thing from a pocket. To draw a swell of a clout. To pick a gentleman's pocket of a handerchief . . .

The compiler of the *Lexicon* clearly did not know the contents of the dictionary as well as he should have, because some new entries duplicate existing headwords:

Entries carried over from the 3rd edition	New entries
GYP. A college runner or errand-boy at Cambridge, called at Oxford a scout. See SCOUT.	GIP. From γυπζ, a wulf. A servant at college.
NUTS. It was nuts for them; i.e. it was very agreeable to them.	NUTS. Fond; pleased. She's nuts upon her cull; she's pleased with her cully . . .
TO STRUM. To have carnal knowledge of a woman . . .	STRUM . . . (*Cambridge*) To do a piece. Fœminam subagitare. *Cant*.

There are many new entries in the *Lexicon* that cannot be traced to a specific source. These take some of the forms that we are familiar with from earlier editions of the *Classical Dictionary*. They include names for clubs and fashionable places of resort:

FOUSIL. The name of a public house, where the Eccentrics assemble in May's Buildings, St. Martin's Lane.

FREE AND EASY JOHNS. A society which met at the Hole in the Wall, Fleet-street, to tipple porter, and sing bawdry.

ODD FELLOWS. A convivial society; the introduction to the most noble grand, arrayed in royal robes, is well worth seeing at the price of becoming a member.

jocular names for various professions:

AMBASSADOR OF MOROCCO. A Shoemaker. (See Mrs. Clarke's Examination.)

KNIGHT OF THE WHIP. A coachman.

PARSON'S JOURNEYMAN. A curate.

SHERIFF'S JOURNEYMAN. The hangman.

TORMENTER OF SHEEP SKIN. A drummer.

and one instance of a joke or riddle inserted as a dictionary entry:

FRUITFUL VINE. A woman's private parts, i.e. that has *flowers* every month, and bears fruit in nine months.

Noteworthy in number are new terms to describe skill, alertness, and knowingness, all essential qualities for a law-breaker:

CLEAN. Expert; clever. Amongst the knuckling coves he is reckoned very clean; he is considered very expert as a pickpocket.

FLASH. Knowing. Understanding another's meaning. The swell was flash, so I could not draw his fogle. The gentleman saw what I was about, and therefore I could not pick his pocket of his silk handkerchief . . .

MAN OF THE WORLD. A knowing man.[14]

OFFICE. To give the office; to give information, or make signs to the officers to take a thief.

Although transportation had been revived before the production of the second edition of Grose's dictionary, it is not until the *Lexicon* that we see the practice reflected in the word-list to any extent:

BAY FEVER. A term of ridicule applied to convicts, who sham illness, to avoid being sent to Botany Bay.

BELLOWSER. Transportation for life: i.e. as long.

[14] Because of the inadequacies of the alphabetization of the *Lexicon*, this entry appears twice.

FINE. A man imprisoned for any offence. A fine of eighty-four months; a transportation for seven years.

LAG FEVER. A term of ridicule applied to men who being under sentence of transportation, pretend illness, to avoid being sent from gaol to the hulks.

There are also various new terms for police and policing:

PIG. A police officer. A China street pig; a Bow-street officer. Floor the pig and bolt; knock down the officer and run away.

LIKENESS. A phrase used by thieves when the officers or turnkeys are examining their countenance. As the traps are taking our likeness; the officers are attentively observing us.

as well as citations testifying to improvements in crime detection and prevention:

COLLEGE COVE. The College cove has numbered him, and if he is knocked down he'll be twisted; the turnkey of Newgate has told the judge how many times the prisoner has been tried before, and therefore if he is found guilty, he certainly will be hanged. It is said to be the custom of the Old Bailey for one of the turnkeys of Newgate to give information to the judge how many times an old offender has been tried, by holding up as many fingers as the number of times the prisoner has been arraigned at that bar.

GAME. Any mode of robbing. The toby is now a queer game; to rob on the highway is now a bad mode of acting. This observation is frequently made by thieves; the roads being now so well guarded by the horse patrole; and gentlemen travel with little cash in their pockets.

Improvements in the detection of criminals were beginning to reduce the need for informers. Offering pardons and even shares of the reward to criminals who informed against their confederates had, however, proved particularly productive in effecting convictions during the seventeenth and eighteenth centuries:[15]

BLOOD MONEY. The reward given by the legislature on the conviction of highwaymen, burglars, &c.

NOSE. A man who informs or turns king's evidence.

TO NOSE. To give evidence. To inform. His pall nosed and he was twisted for a crack; his confederate turned king's evidence, and he was hanged for burglary.

One other feature worth noting, given later developments in the slang dictionary tradition, is that there are a few boxing terms among the new additions to the *Lexicon*:

GLUTTON. A term used by bruisers to signify a man who will bear a great deal of beating.

---

[15] McMullan, *Canting Crew*, 89.

MILLING COVE. A boxer. How the milling cove served the cull out; how the boxer
  beat the fellow.
MUZZLER. A violent blow on the mouth. The milling cove tipped the cull
  a muzzler; the boxer gave the fellow a blow on the mouth.
TOPPER. A violent blow on the head.

Because duties on the manufacture and sale of gin were higher than
those on other alcoholic drinks during the early eighteenth century,
cagey synonyms for gin had become a useful way of avoiding tax.
The *Lexicon* records several, including:

DRAIN. Gin: so called from the diuretic qualities imputed to that liquor.
FROG'S WINE. Gin.
JACKEY. Gin.
LADY DACRE'S WINE. Gin.
WHITE RIBBIN. Gin.

However, by the time the *Lexicon* was published, gin-shops were
subject to exactly the same licensing laws as alehouses,[16] and it
is likely that these terms were being used for humour rather than
concealment.

  These additions, along with some deletions made in the compilation of this edition, are not sufficient to make a significant difference
between the subject matter of the third edition and the *Lexicon* as
a whole. However, the new entries are significantly different in subject matter from new additions to the third edition (see Appendix,
Tables 1.2.1 and 2.1), which highlight the diverse approaches of
these two editors. New entries in the *Lexicon* are proportionally more
likely to belong to the fields of CRIME & DISHONESTY, ARTEFACTS,
WORK, AND SPEECH (all $p = 0.01$) than new entries in the third edition, and significantly less likely to belong to the fields of BODY &
HEALTH, CLOTHES, FOOD & DRINK (all $p = 0.01$), GEOGRAPHY &
TRAVEL, and PLEASURE & PASTIMES (both $p = 0.05$). There are also
significantly fewer miscellaneous terms than we would expect ($p = 0.01$). Taken together, this suggests a move away from general slang,
back towards cant and jargon.

  The additions to the *Lexicon* alter the nature of the dictionary in a
number of other ways. They contain significantly more illustrative
citations and named authorities than the existing entries (both

---

[16] Norman Longmate, *The Waterdrinkers. A History of Temperance* (London: Hamish Hamilton, 1968),
10–11. The only people who might have had to pretend that they were not drinking gin at this time
were prisoners, to whom the sale of any alcoholic drink was now prohibited (R. S. E. Hinde, *The British
Penal System 1773–1950* (London: Gerald Duckworth & Co. Ltd., 1951), 16).

$p = 0.01$; see Appendix, Tables 1.4 and 2.3). So many of these new citations are similar in form that it seems likely they were created for the purpose. One group all contain exclamations beginning with 'How . . .':

BLOWER. A Pipe. How the swell funks his blower and lushes red tape; what a smoke the gentleman makes with his pipe, and drinks brandy.

COG. A tooth. A queer cog; a rotten tooth. How the cull flashes his queer cogs; how the fool shews his rotten teeth.

HUNG BEEF. A dried bull's pizzle. How the dubber served the cull with hung beef; how the turnkey beat the fellow with a bull's pizzle.

IVORIES. Teeth. How the swell flashed his ivories; how the gentleman shewed his teeth.

SLOP. Tea. How the blowens lush the slop. How the wenches drink tea!

while in another group the verb *to nap* is used:

MORNING DROP. The gallows. He napped the king's pardon and escaped the morning drop; he was pardoned, and was not hanged.

SCALDER. A clap. The cull has napped a scalder; the fellow has got a clap.

A SCOLD'S CURE. A coffin. The blowen has napped the scold's cure; the bitch is in her coffin.

STOOP. The pillory. The cull was served for macing and napp'd the stoop; he was convicted of swindling, and put in the pillory.

Items of clothing and facial features are invariably *flashed*:

BELCHER. A red silk handkerchief, intermixed with yellow and a little black. The kiddey flashes his belcher; the young fellow wears a silk handkerchief round his neck.

HANDLE . . . The cove flashes a rare handle to his physog; the fellow has a large nose.

and *kiddies* people the citations that were once the domain of *coves* and *culls*:

CRACKSMAN. A house-breaker. The kiddy is a clever cracksman; the young fellow is a very expert house-breaker.

TO DROP DOWN. To be dispirited. This expression is used by thieves to signify that their companion did not die game, as the kiddy dropped down when he went to be twisted; the young fellow was very low spirited when he walked out to be hanged.

TO STRAP. To work. The kiddy would not strap, so he went on the scamp; the lad would not work, and therefore robbed on the highway.

WELL-HUNG. The blowen was nutts upon the kiddey because he is well-hung; the girl is pleased with the youth because his genitals are large.

while their victims are almost all *swells*:

BURNER. A clap. The blowen tipped the swell a burner; the girl gave the
gentleman a clap.[17]
CADGE. To beg. Cadge the swells; beg of the gentlemen.
PIT. A watch fob. He drew a rare thimble from the swell's pit. He took a
handsome watch from the gentleman's fob.
SPICE. To rob. Spice the swell; rob the gentleman.
SWELL. A gentleman. A well dressed man. The flashman bounced the swell of all
his blunt; the girl's bully frightened the gentleman out of all his money.

Terms of approval are a regularly changing feature of slang
language, and the editor of the *Lexicon* adds several:

PRIME. Bang up. Quite the thing. Excellent. Well done. She's a prime piece; she is
very skilful in the venereal act. Prime post. She's a prime article.
RIGHT. All right! A favourite expression among thieves, to signify that all is as
they wish, or proper for their purpose. All right, hand down the jemmy; every
thing is in proper order, give me the crow.
IN TWIG. Handsome; stilish. The cove is togged in twig; the fellow is dressed in
the fashion.

The proportion of entries including cross-references is not significantly different, neither is the level of accuracy of cross-references.
Although rather fewer of the new entries in the *Lexicon* are provided
with usage labels and etymologies than in the third edition, the
differences are not statistically significant (see Appendix, Tables 1.4
and 2.3; 1.3.2 and 2.2; 2.2.1). The *Lexicon* does, however, contain
significantly more terms labelled as 'slang' and 'university' than the
third edition (both $p = 0.05$).

Various new entries contain what were, and in some cases still are,
obscene and profane terms:

ARTICLE . . . She's a prime article (*Whip slang*), she's a devilish good piece, a hell of
a goer.
BALLOCKS . . . His brains are in his ballocks, a cant saying to designate a fool.
BUGGER. A blackguard, a rascal, a term of reproach. Mill the bloody bugger;
beat the damned rascal.
OATHS. The favourite oaths of the thieves of the present day are, 'God strike me
blind!' 'I wish my bloody eyes may drop out if it is not true!' 'So help me God!'
'Bloody end to me!'

---

[17] By some biological quirk, these dictionaries never see a man infecting his female partner.

although other terms continued to be censored:

COOLER. The backside. Kiss my cooler. Kiss my a-es [sic]. It is principally used to
signify a woman's posteriors.
INSIDE AND OUTSIDE. The inside of a **** and the outside of a gaol.

The editor of the *Lexicon* also censored one headword that had been
presented in full in earlier editions:

P—K. The virile member

The *OED* cites the *Lexicon* forty times. Four of these can be predated
by reference to earlier editions of Grose's dictionary, as noted
above. Since the publication of the first edition, twenty-six years had
passed, not a considerable period in itself, but much longer than
most slang terms could be expected to last.

Forty-six further *OED* first citations can be antedated by reference
to the *Lexicon*:

all right [**right**] "ok, fine" (1837)
blue ribbon "gin" (1823: **ribbon**)
blue ruin "gin" (c. 1817: **ruin**)
to bridge "to win a bet by losing a game"[18]
brown George "a type of wig" (1840)
to buff "to swear to" (1812)
buffer "a hired perjuror" (1874)
to cadge "to beg" (1812)
chaw-bacon "a country bumpkin" (1822)
cheese it! "stop it" (1812)
chip: brother chip "a man of the same profession" ([1658] 1815: '*fig.* Something
forming a portion of, or derived from, a larger or more important thing, of
which it retains the characteristic qualities. Usually applied to persons')
crack "a burglary" (1812)
crib "a house" (1812)
cross "dishonest" (1812)
to dance upon nothing "to be hanged" (1837: *to dance in air*, 1839: *to dance upon nothing*)
darkee "a covered lantern" (1812: **darky**)
to diddle out of "to cheat" (1829)
drain "gin" (1836–9)
fakement "a forgery" (1812)
flimsy "a banknote" (1824)
to gaff "to gamble by tossing coins" (1812)
gibbe "a jibbing horse" (1843: **jib**)

---

[18] cf. **1812** J. H. Vaux *Flash Dict.* ('*To bridge a person*, or to throw him over the bridge, is . . . to deceive
him by betraying the confidence he has reposed in you.') (*OED*).

kid "a little dapper man" (1812: "an expert young thief")
lag "a transported convict" (1812)
milling-cove "a boxer" (1812: *milling* ppl a)
nous-box "the head" (1823)
to nut "to curry favour with" (1812)
onion "a seal" (1812)
to patter "to talk" (1812: *to patter flash* "to speak flash")
pimple "the head" (1818)
plummy "very good" (1812)
regulars "one's share of the booty" (1812)
roost-lay "stealing poultry" (1823)
shindy "a dance" (1821)
shove in the mouth "a drink" (1821)
to sing "to call out" (1813: *to sing out*)
smut "a grate" (1812)
to spice "to rob" (1812)
to strap "to work" (1823)
tail "a prostitute" (1846)
varment "stylish" (1823)
to weed "to take part of (the booty)" (1812)
to well "to take part of (the booty)" (1812)
well-breeched [**breeched**] "well off" (1821)
wife "a fetter" (1813: *fig.*)
winder "a sentence of transportation for life" (1812)

Thirty-five of the first citations in these entries are from later slang dictionaries, four from magazines and periodicals. Dickens provides two of the remaining first citations: for *all right* "fine", and *drain* "gin".

The Bang-up Dictionary (1812)

Only a year after the publication of the *Lexicon Balatronicum, The Bang-up Dictionary* appeared.[19] This was merely the *Lexicon* repackaged to appeal to the current fascination with coach-drivers and their *bang-up* vocabulary. The preface, lifted from the *Lexicon* along with the rest of the text, gives due credit to Grose for his work in canting lexicography, but implies that the *Bang-up Dictionary* is superior, and makes many additions, particularly in fashionable slang, none of which is true. Renaming the dictionary and boasting that it included 'a copious and correct glossary of the language of the whips' may have been sufficient to promote further sales. It is fitting

---

[19] *Bang-up Dictionary, or, The Lounger and Sportsman's Vade Mecum* (London: M. Jones, 1812).

that a shamelessly pirated publication like this should advise its readers to behave as they liked, but to avoid being caught.

George Matsell's *Vocabulum* (1859)

By this period, New York was growing even more rapidly than London. Like London, it had extensive slums in which criminals could take refuge and even assert a certain degree of control. Unlike London, it was still in the process of establishing a professional police force. All policing jobs were fixed-term political appointments, so each change of city government led to changes in police personnel. Naturally those in position supported the party that appointed them, so police presence at elections and behaviour between elections could hardly have been less partisan. Although salaries were generous by London standards, some officers chose to pursue rewards rather than criminals. Out of a reluctance to surrender the responsibility for policing to a trained, salaried, and uniformed profession, New Yorkers settled for an amateur, inefficient, corrupt, and entirely politicized force.

George Matsell was a bookseller and a Democrat. He was appointed the first Chief of Municipal Police in New York in 1845, and remained in the position even after it was abolished in 1857. Its abolition was brought about by the creation of the State-run Metropolitan Police department, as a Republican attempt to wrest control of the city from the Democrats. For a time, the two forces both patrolled the streets, each obstructing the other, but eventually the Municipals conceded defeat. Matsell, 'a walking mass of moral and physical putrefaction', somehow acquired sufficient wealth during his time in office to acquire an extensive country estate. Despite his vociferous opponents, Matsell was to serve as police superintendent and president of the Police Commission in the 1870s. The most successful publishing venture of this 'Beastly Bloated Booby' was the *National Police Gazette*, a tabloid newspaper, covering legal and illegal sporting events, giving lurid accounts of crime and accidents, and including advertisements for risqué publications.[20] It was aimed solidly at a working-class male readership.

[20] The historical and biographical information in this section is from James F. Richardson, *The New York Police. Colonial Times to 1901* (New York: Oxford University Press, 1970) and Wilbur R. Miller, *Cops and Bobbies. Police Authority in New York and London, 1830–1870* (Chicago/London: University of Chicago Press, 1977). The assessments of Matsell are both from Mike Walsh, a journalist and political opponent, and are quoted from Miller, *Cops and Bobbies*, 151–2 and Richardson, *New York Police*, 56.

In 1859 George Matsell published his *Vocabulum*, subtitled the *Rogue's Lexicon*. He explains in the preface that it was never his intention to become a lexicographer, but that:

Occupying the position of a Special Justice, and Chief of the Police of the great Metropolis of New York, where thieves and others of a like character from all parts of the world congregate, and realizing the necessity of possessing a positive knowledge of every thing connected with the class of individuals with whom it was my duty to deal, I was naturally led to study their peculiar language, believing that it would enable me to converse with them more at ease, and thus acquire a knowledge of their character, besides obtaining from them information that would assist me in the position I occupied, and consequently be of great service to the public. To accomplish this task was no mean undertaking, as I found that it required years of diligent labor to hunt up the various authorities, and these when found proved only partially available, as much of the language in present use was unwritten, and could only be obtained by personal study among first-class thieves who had been taught it in their youth. The difficulties surrounding it, did not deter me from following out my resolution, and by closely pursuing it, I had opened up to me a fountain of knowledge that I could not have obtained if I had not possessed a clear understanding of this peculiar dialect. Experience has since demonstrated to me that any man engaged in police business can not excel without understanding the rogues' language, in the study of which they will find this Lexicon of invaluable service.[21]

This, Matsell claims, is a practical dictionary: it is intended as an aid in the detection and prevention of crime.

However, Matsell also argues that many terms from rogues' language were being adopted into standard speech, and that the appeal of his dictionary was, therefore, all the wider. He traces thieves' language to the language of European Gypsies, and remarks that although there are national variations, New York rogues speak in essentially the same language as rogues the world over. However:

Among policemen, not only in this city but in the different parts of the United States, the cant language of thieves is attempted to be used; but there being no standard they are unable to do so understandingly, and each one gives to the words the corrupted sense in which he received it; thus speaking as it were, a miserable '*patois*,' to the exclusion of the true 'Parisian French.' This departure from the true meaning of the words used is mischievous in its tendency, as it is calculated to mislead and bewilder, so that the rogues might still converse in the presence of an officer, and he be ignorant of what they said. This I have endeavoured to correct, and although I may not claim infallibility in these matters, yet I believe that I have arrived at as high a degree of perfection as is now attainable.[22]

---

[21] George Matsell, *Vocabulum, or, the Rogue's Lexicon. Compiled from the most authentic sources* (New York: George W. Matsell & Co., 1859), 6–7.   [22] Matsell, *Vocabulum*, 8–9.

Matsell's dictionary contains 2,293 entries for 2,158 headwords. It is followed by a 'Scene in a London Flash Panny', which consists largely of flash dialogue. There is a list of numbers from one to ten, a cant text with its translation, and an intercepted coded letter:

RAED MOT: Ecnis ouy evah neeb ot eht tiw, semit evah neeb llud. Mij dna em evah enod gnihton fo yna tnuocca . . .[23]

Then come four shorter glossaries containing the jargon specific to gamblers, billiard-players, brokers, and pugilists. These short glossaries together contain 206 entries for 203 headwords, and sometimes overlap with the main list. Between the third and the last glossary is inserted a cant song, 'A hundred stretches hence'. The volume closes with an 'Advertisement' in which a reformed thief notifies the public, in cant, that he has set himself up as a tailor. This is derived from Ducange Anglicus (see Chapter 7).

Of the 2,499 entries in Matsell's dictionary, just over two-thirds had been listed in earlier dictionaries (see Appendix, Table 2.4). Matsell's main source is the *Lexicon*, whose lengthy entries he sometimes abbreviates beyond recognition:

Lexicon Balatronicum	Matsell
EMPEROR. Drunk as an emperor, i.e. ten times as drunk as a lord.	EMPEROR. A drunken man.
HASH. To flash the hash; to vomit. Cant.	HASH. To vomit.
MOSES. To stand Moses: a man is said to stand Moses when he has another man's bastard child fathered upon him, and he is obliged by the parish to maintain it.	MOSES. A man that fathers another man's child for a consideration.
ROSE. Under the rose; privately or secretly. The rose was, it is said, sacred to Harpocrates, the God of silence, and therefore frequently placed in the ceilings of rooms destined for the receiving of guests; implying, that whatever was transacted there, should not be made public.	ROSE. A secret.

---

[23] Matsell, *Vocabulum*, 106.

For phrases, Grose's practice, carried over into the *Lexicon*, was to alphabetize under a key-term from the phrase, and then place the phrase after the headword, followed by a definition, as seen above. Matsell generally retained the headword, but omitted the phrase, which may have been the only context in which the headword actually bore the sense given. He usually rewrote the definition (see *rose*), but sometimes did not (see *hash*).

Showing an even greater lack of understanding are those entries derived from terms mentioned in the *Lexicon* as etymologies and explanations:

Lexicon Balatronicum	Matsell
DUN. An importunate creditor. Dunny, in the provincial dialect of several counties, signifies *deaf*; to dun, then, perhaps may mean to deafen with importunate demands: some derive it from the word *donnez*, which signifies give . . .	DONNEZ. To give. DUNNEY. Deaf; to dun.
RASCAL . . . Some derive it from *rascaglione*, an Italian word signifying a man without testicles, or an eunuch.	RASCAGLION. A eunuch.
SKY FARMERS. Cheats who pretend they were farmers in the isle of Sky, or some other remote place, and were ruined by a flood, hurricane, or some such public calamity: or else called sky farmers from their farms being *in nubibus*, 'in the clouds.'	NUBIBUS. In the clouds. 'Blow a nubibus,' make a smoke.

An early commentator on Matsell's dictionary noted some of these parallels, and took them as examples of Americans' tendency to reshape English, rather than demonstrations of Matsell's editorial shortcomings:

In Matsell we find some strange additions to the actual signification of words, *e.g.* "*Tace*. A candle." The following appears in Grose: "*Tace*. Silence, hold your tongue. *Tace* is Latin for a candle; a jocular admonition to be silent on any subject." Ed. 1788. Now this jocular admonition the American rogue thinks proper to take as an actual definition; hence *tace*, a candle.[24]

---

[24] William Cumming Wilde, 'Notes on Thief Talk', *Journal of American Folk-Lore*, 1890, iii.303–10, 305.

There is no doubt, however, that Matsell's source is the *Lexicon* rather than the changing English of American villains. Another early critic wrote:

We must confess that many of Matsell's words appear to us exceedingly fishy, and that the differences between those he gives and those contained in English glossaries may, as it seems to us, be mere careless errors of his own.[25]

Matsell may also have included some terms from Vaux's glossary. For example:

Vaux	Matsell
PUT UP, to suggest to another, the means of committing a depredation, or effecting any other business, is termed, *putting* him *up to it*.	PUT UP. Information given to thieves by persons in the employ of parties to be robbed, such as servants, clerks, porters, etc., whereby the thief is facilitated in his operations.
SCREWSMAN, a thief who goes *out* a *screwing*.	SCREWSMAN. A burglar who works with keys, picks, dubs, bettys, etc., etc.

Since these are so few in number, it may be that Vaux and Matsell recorded them independently.

The inclusion of entries containing Potter's characteristic inversion (see Chapter 3) indicates that Matsell used a dictionary or dictionaries belonging to that group:

BEAKQUERE. A sharp, strict magistrate who is attentive to his duty.
JET AUTUM. A parson.

The dictionaries derived from Potter's share the same core word-list, which also overlaps with the *Lexicon* because of their common source in Grose's *Classical Dictionary*. However, Matsell's reproduction of variant readings and later additions indicates that he certainly used the *Flash Dictionary*:

Flash Dictionary (1821)	Matsell
Danan—stairs.	DANAN. Stairs.
Sherried—ran away.	SHERRID. Run away.
Smiller—a bumper.	SMILER. A bumper.

It is possible that he also used either Kent's dictionary (or the *Sinks of London*), because he includes a number of entries only previously

[25] W. W. N., 'Cant and Thieves' Jargon', *Journal of American Folk-Lore*, 1890, iii.314.

found in these dictionaries, but the dissimilarities argue against a direct dependence:

Kent (1835) [also found in *Sinks* (1848)]	Matsell
Chaff—irritating, or ironical language . . .	CHAFF. Humbug.
Collar—to grab, snatch	COLLAR. To seize or take.
Mazzard—the head	MAZZARD. The face.
Tape—gin	TAPE. Liquor.

Matsell frequently Americanized the entries he took from his sources, usually by changing place-names and currencies, for example:

Lexicon Balatronicum	Matsell
BEAN. A guinea . . .	BEANS. Five-dollar gold-pieces.
SCULL. A head of a house, or master of a college, at the universities.	SKULL. The head of the house; the President of the United States; the Governor; the head man.
SLAT. Half a Crown. *Cant.*	SLAT. A half-dollar.
TRESWINS. Three pence.	THRESWINS. Three cents or pence.

The same processes of naturalization occur in entries derived from the word-lists in the *Vulgar Tongue* (see Chapter 7):

The Vulgar Tongue (1857)	Matsell
Case . . . also a bad crown piece.	CASE. A Dollar.
FROG AND TOE, London. We will go to *frog and toe*. Thieves coming up to London with plunder. *Th.*	FROG AND TOE. The city of New-York. 'Coves, let us frog and toe,' coves, let us go to New-York.
STAIT, *n.* London. *Th.*	STAIT. City of New-York.

Matsell failed to appreciate that some of the entries from Ducange Anglicus are rhyming slang, and thus sometimes carelessly obscured the relationship between headword and definition by losing the rhyme:

The Vulgar Tongue (1857)	Matsell
BILLY-BUTTON, *n.* Mutton. *Th.*	BILLY BUTTER. Mutton.
BOB MY PAL, Gal. *Th.*	BOB MY PAL. My girl.
CHARLEY PRESCOT, *n.* Waistcoat. *Th.*	CHARLEY PRESCOT. A Vest.

There are significantly fewer terms from *The Vulgar Tongue* and the *Lexicon* in the addenda than in the main list (both $p = 0.01$; see Appendix, Table 2.4). Significantly more terms in the additional lists do not have the authority of having appeared in any source ($p = 0.01$), which suggests that their inclusion in the addenda is an expression of Matsell's reduced confidence in his own independent observations. There are significantly fewer terms illustrated by citation in Matsell's additional glossaries than in his main list ($p = 0.01$), but considerably more cross-references in the addenda than can be explained by chance ($p = 0.01$; see Appendix, Table 2.4.2).

Thirty-one of the 206 entries in the additional lists are also in the main dictionary (15.0 per cent). Significantly more of these are in a number of Matsell's sources than would be expected by chance ($p = 0.01$), which indicates that he did not cross-check the main and supplementary lists as he was going through his various sources, and did not weed out entries that he had accidentally copied twice.

The overlap between sources makes it difficult to determine how Matsell used each one, but it does appear that he was influenced by meaning. Although it is by no means certain that the *Lexicon* was the direct source, 1,409 of the entries in his main list (61.4 per cent) could be from that dictionary, and thirty-two entries in the addenda (15.5 per cent). Except where specified below, I will talk about the main list and addenda together. Taking these lists together, well over half (57.7 per cent) of Matsell's entries are (or could be) from the *Lexicon*.

Assuming that the *Lexicon* was the main source, Matsell adopted considerably more terms for CRIME & DISHONESTY, LAW & ORDER, BODY & HEALTH, and ARTEFACTS (all $p = 0.01$) and MONEY ($p = 0.05$) than we would expect in a random sample. He selected fewer terms for SEX ($p = 0.01$) and FOOD & DRINK, PLEASURE & PASTIMES, SPEECH, FOOLS & VICTIMS, and LOOKS (all $p = 0.05$) than can be accounted for by chance. By selecting terms according to meaning from the *Lexicon*, Matsell shaped his sources into what appears to be a more focused glossary of criminal language and interests. Terms for BODY & HEALTH are most likely to be duplicated in the main list and the addenda ($p = 0.01$). They largely occur in the list of pugilists' slang, and include *boko* "nose", *bread-basket* "stomach", *claret* "blood", *conk* "nose", *dukes* "fists", *forks* "the fingers; the hands", *gob* "the mouth", *ivories* "the teeth", *knowledge-box* "the head", *listeners* "the ears", *ogles* "the eyes", *pins* "the legs", and *smeller* "the nose".

Although Matsell did not include any usage labels in his dictionary, having implicitly labelled all terms in the main list as cant and all those in the addenda as belonging to the slang of specific sports, he does make use of the labels in the *Lexicon* (see Appendix, Tables 2.2 and 2.2.1). From it, he selects significantly more terms labelled as cant than can be explained by chance, and significantly fewer naval/nautical and university terms. Even more of the *Lexicon*'s labelled terms are found in the addenda, particularly those belonging to various types of slang and jargon (all $p = 0.01$).

Other considerations also influenced Matsell's use of the *Lexicon* (see Appendix, Table 2.3). Considerably fewer entries contain etymologies, citations, authorities, or cross-references (all $p = 0.01$). Matsell's entries are, therefore, more concise than their main source, although we have seen the consequences of some of his editorial decisions in the nonsensical definitions presented above. At the same time, however, Matsell took the liberty of providing illustrative citations that are clearly fabricated for the purpose. They are characterized by excessive use of cant, by Ducange Anglicus's 'Bill' (see Chapter 7), and sometimes, bizarrely, by painfully stereotypical cockney pronunciation:

ANODYNE. Death; to anodyne, to kill. 'Ahr say, Bill, vy don't yer hopen that
    jug and draw the cole?' 'Vy, my cove, aren't you avare as how a bloke snoses
    hin it?' 'Vell, vot hof it, aren't yer habel to put him to hanodyne?'
DUSTMAN. Dead man. 'Poor Bill is a dustman; he was a bene cove,' poor
    Bill is dead; he was a good man.
GLAZE. Break the glass. 'I say, Bill, you mill the glaze, and I'll touch the swag and
    mizzle,' I say, Bill, you break the glass, and I will steal the goods and run away.

Almost a third of Matsell's entries (29.7 per cent) are not from the sources identified here. Some of these are compounds and derivatives based on terms that are in his sources, such as *addle-cove* "a fool", *autum-cove* "a married man", *high-liver* "an attic-dweller", *kirkbuzzer* "a church pickpocket", *lavender cove* "a pawnbroker", *moll-buzzer* "one who picks women's pockets", and *peter-biter* "a luggage-stealer". The reoccurrence of *cove* and *buzzer*, even in such a small selection, suggests that these may be the product of a not very imaginative mind.

Matsell's new entries are even more focused in subject matter than those he carried over from his sources (see Appendix, Table 2.4.1.1). They belong overwhelmingly to the area of PLEASURE & PASTIMES, FOOLS & VICTIMS, and WAR & VIOLENCE (all $p = 0.01$). The semantic areas to which Matsell adds considerably fewer terms than might be expected include CRIME & DISHONESTY and LAW & ORDER (both $p = 0.01$), rather undermining the emphasis that Matsell placed on the benefit of his experience as a police chief.

A few of Matsell's new entries are very lengthy and detailed. They suggest personal acquaintance with their subject matter. For example:

CONFIDENCE MAN. A fellow that by means of extraordinary powers of persuasion gains the confidence of his victims to the extent of drawing upon their treasury, almost to an unlimited extent. To every knave born into the world it has been said there is a due proportion of fools. Of all the rogue tribe, the Confidence man is, perhaps, the most liberally supplied with subjects; for every man has his soft spot, and nine times out of ten the soft spot is softened by an idiotic desire to overreach the man that is about to overreach us. This is just the spot on which the Confidence man works. He knows his subject is only a knave wrongside out, and accordingly he offers him a pretended gold watch at the price of a brass one; he calls at the front door with presents from no where, as none could be expected; he writes letters in the most generous spirit, announcing large legacies to persons who have no kin on the face of the earth who cares a copper for them. The Confidence man is perfectly aware that he has to deal with a man who expects a result without having worked for it, who gapes, and stands ready to grasp at magnificent returns. The consequence is, that the victim—the confiding man—is always *done*. The one plays a sure game; his sagacity has taught him that the great study of the mass of mankind is to get something and give nothing; but as this is bad doctrine, he wakes up out of his 'brown study,' and finds himself, in lieu of his fine expectations, in possession of a turnip for a watch, a cigar-box in place of a casket. The Confidence man always carries the trump card; and whoever wishes to be victimized can secure his object by making a flat of himself in a small way, while attempting to victimize somebody else.

Reference to the *OED* and to dictionaries of American English and American slang[26] suggests that many of Matsell's additions were indeed current Americanisms. These include *bummer* "a sponger", *chips* "money", *dip* "a pickpocket", *go-away* "a train", *OK* "all right", *to smile* "to have a drink", *sucker* "one who is easily cheated", and *to vamoose* "to run away".

Other terms are marked as Scottish or dialectal in the *OED*. Unaware of their restricted use in Britain, Matsell may have

[26] J. E. Lighter (ed.), *Random House Historical Dictionary of American Slang* (New York: Random House, 1994, 1997); Hyman E. Goldin, Frank O'Leary, and Morris Lipsius, *Dictionary of American Underworld Lingo* (New York: Citadel Press, 1962); William A. Craigie and James R. Hulbert, *A Dictionary of American English on Historical Principles* (London: Oxford University Press, 1938–44).

considered them peculiar to America. These include *anointed* "beaten", *bonnet* "a hat", *copped* "taken, arrested", *to kittle* "to tickle", *land-yard* "a graveyard", *to leg it* "to run away", *pouch* "a pocket", *prim* "an attractive woman", *wame* "the stomach", and *wesand* "the throat".

The *OED* cites Matsell's dictionary sixty-seven times in all, sometimes on the authority of Farmer and Henley. The main list predates a further twenty-nine existing first citations:

Albert "a (watch-)chain" (1861)
artist "a skilled criminal" (1890)
bull "a train" (*a*1889)
chump "the head" (1864: n¹ 7b)
dancing "sneaking upstairs to perform a burglary" (1864: *dancer* "a thief who steals
   from upper floors")
dukes "the hands; the fists" (1874)
flue-scraper "a chimney-sweep" (listed at *flue* n² 6, but no citation given)
to hare it "to return" (1893: "to double back")
hot "dangerous (of a place)" (1925: "stolen (of property); wanted by the police")
kip "a bed" (1879: n³ 2)
leather "a pocket-book" (1883)
lobsneak "one who steals from tills" (1868: **lob** n⁴ *lobsneaking* "stealing from tills")
nish "be quiet" (1903: *nix*)
palling in "associating with" (1879: *to pal in*)
planter "one who hides stolen property" (1890)
played out "exhausted, expended" (1872)
ponce "a pimp" ([1861] 1872)
pongelo "alcoholic liquor" (1864)
prospecting "looking for something to steal" (1867: *to prospect* "to look out for")
put away "locked up" (1872: "to lock up")
scrapper "a pugilist" (1874)
soap "money" (1860)
sport "a gambler" (1861: n¹ 8)
sugar "money" (1862)
tanglefoot "cheap liquor" (1860)
tanglefooted "drunk" (1888: "stumbling")
trick "property stolen in a single theft" (1865: "a robbery")
verge "a watch" (1871)

The lists in Matsell's addenda predate seventeen additional first citations:

barney "a fixed fight" (1865)
burst "A term chiefly used at pin-pool, when a player has exceeded the number
   which is placed as the common limit to the game, and must, therefore, either
   retire from the game, or take a privilege of another life" (1939: **to bust** v² f

"to lose by exceeding a set limit"; 1928: ***bust*** n³ c "a person who exceeds a set limit")

to carom "(of a billiard ball) to rebound" (1860)

to cash "to exchange gambling chips for money" (1888: v² 2a *to cash in*)

corinthian canvas "a boxing enthusiast" (1910: *canvas* 'a covering over the floor of a boxing or wrestling ring')

gaff "a ring worn by a cheating card-dealer" (n¹ 4 cites Farmer, but gives no date)

jollying "abusing an opponent to distract him" (1873: *to jolly* "to ridicule")

lay-out "a piece of cloth on which bets are laid in faro" (1889)

parlieu "the act of leaving a winning stake on the table in order to increase it further" (1904: *parlay*; cf 1710: *paroli*)

piker "a gambler who places only small bets" ([1872] 1889)

rib-bender "a severe blow to the ribs" (1861)

ruby "blood" (1860)

shoe-string "a small stake" ([1882] 1904)

stuck "having lost all one's money" (1865)

tell-box "a box used by cheating card-dealers" (1894)

velvet "winnings" (1901)

wash "a fictitious sale of securities by a broker" (1891)

Herbert Asbury's *Gangs of New York* (1927)

Herbert Asbury was a journalist and popular historian. Rejecting the Methodism of his upbringing, he wrote about the underworld of many American cities. He was sceptical about reformers' attempts to control the morals of the population at large, and although he based his books on sensational newspaper accounts, he adopted an 'uninvolved, non-judgemental attitude' to his lurid subjects.[27]

Asbury included very little cant in the text of the *Gangs of New York*, but he did provide a glossary, entitled 'slang of the early gangsters'. He noted that it was derived from Matsell's dictionary, and wrote:

It is interesting to note that of the words and phrases which are still in use, the meaning of many has entirely changed. Others, however, retain their ancient meanings, and have been appropriated by the modern wise-cracker[28]

---

[27] Biographical information is from *American National Biography*, ed. by John C. Garraty and Mark C. Carnes (Oxford/New York: Oxford University Press, 1999), i.660–1, and *Dictionary of American Biography*, ed. by Allen Johnson, et al. (New York: Charles Scribner's Sons, 1927–) (*DAB*), Suppl. 7.19–20. The quotation is from *DAB*, 20.

[28] Herbert Asbury, *The Gangs of New York. An Informal History of the Underworld* (1927) (New York: Garden City Publishing, 1928), 375.

Following the glossary is an example of its terms in use:

Tim Sullivan buzzed a bloke and a shakester of a reader. His jomer stalled. Johnny Miller, who was to have his regulars, called out 'copbung,' for as you see, a fly-cop was marking. Jack speeled to the crib, where he found Johnny Doyle had been pulling down sawney for grub. He cracked a casa last night, and fenced the swag. He told Jack as how Bill had flimped a yack, and pinched a swell of a spark fawney, and had sent the yack to church, and had got half a century and a finniff for the fawney.[29]

The glossary itself contains 245 entries for 242 headwords, representing 9.8 per cent of Matsell's entries and 10.2 per cent of his headwords. Asbury preserved none of Matsell's cross-references or named authorities, and only one of his etymologies:

O.K. All right. 'Oll kerect.'

all of which is in line with a random selection from Matsell, who retained very few such features in his dictionary in any case. Asbury has considerably fewer citations than can be accounted for by chance ($p = 0.01$), however. Those that remain, little changed, include:

Matsell	Asbury
BLEAK Handsome; 'The Moll is bleak,' the girl is handsome.	*Bleak.* Handsome. 'The moll is bleak'; the girl is handsome.
JOSEPH'S COAT Guarded against temptation. 'I say, my bene blowen, can't you kiddy the bloke?' 'No, Dick, it's of no use trying, he wears a Joseph coat.' I say, my good girl, can't you seduce the man? No, Dick, it's no use trying, he is guarded against temptation.	*Joseph's coat.* Guarded against temptation. 'I say, my bene blowen, can't you kiddy the bloke?' 'It's no use trying, he wears a Joseph coat.' I say, my good girl, can't you seduce the fellow? It's no use trying, he is guarded against temptation.
RABBIT A rowdy. 'Dead rabbit,' a very athletic rowdy fellow.	*Rabbit.* A rowdy. 'Dead Rabbit,' a very athletic, rowdy fellow.

The semantic coverage of Asbury's glossary is entirely in line with a random selection from Matsell's, except that he has considerably more SEX terms than can be accounted for by chance ($p = 0.01$; see Appendix, Table 2.4.1).

---

[29] Asbury, *Gangs of New York*, 379. The original version of this text is quoted below (221).

Cant on Film: Martin Scorsese's *Gangs of New York* (2002)

Martin Scorsese's film, *Gangs of New York*, tells a fictional story set against the historical background provided by Asbury's book. It focuses on the life of Amsterdam Vallon (Leonardo DiCaprio), who returns to the notorious Five Points slum as an adult to avenge the death of his father at the hands of rival mobster, Bill 'the Butcher' Cutting (Daniel Day Lewis). Along the way, Amsterdam falls in love with Jenny Everdeane (Cameran Diaz).

Unfortunately for the scriptwriters, they turned to Matsell's dictionary, presumably through Asbury's acknowledgement, for their authentic period vocabulary. Terms derived from Matsell's dictionary are scattered throughout the film, but a few scenes use slang terms particularly densely. In one, Jenny disguises herself as a housemaid and walks into a wealthy house, secure in the invisibility that her clothes confer. While we watch Jenny, Vallon's voice-over provides us with a little background colour:

> For every lay we had a different name. An angler put a hook on the end of a stick to drop behind store windows and doors. An autem-diver picked your pocket in church. A badger gets a fellow into bed with a girl, then robs his pockets while they're on the go. Jenny was a bludget—a girl pickpocket—and a turtledove. A turtledove goes uptown dressed like a housemaid, picks out a fine house, and goes right through the back door. Robs you blind. It takes a lot of sand to be a turtledove.

Naturally, this account of lays ("criminal schemes") includes several slang terms used by criminals. Except for *lay* itself, each of these is explained in context, because authentic terminology cannot be allowed to stand in the way of comprehension. The two-disc DVD set includes a 'Five Points Vocabulary'.[30] It includes forty entries for forty terms, which represents under 2 per cent of Matsell's dictionary, whether entries or headwords are counted.

The vocabulary acts as a glossary to terms included in the film, and includes most of the slang terms used in the voice-over quoted above:

Matsell's *Vocabulum*	Five Points Vocabulary
ANGLER small thieves who place a hook on the end of a stick, and therewith steal from store-windows, doors, etc. It also applies to fencemen; putters up, etc.	ANGLERS: small thieves who place a hook on the end of a stick, with which they steal from store windows, doors, etc.

---

[30] Martin Scorsese, *Gangs of New York* (Los Angeles: Miramax, 2003).

AUTEM DIVERS pickpockets who practise in churches.

AUTUM-DIVERS: pickpockets who practice in churches.

BLUDGET A female thief who decoys her victims into alley-ways, or other dark places, for the purpose of robbing them.

BLUDGET: a female thief who decoys her victims into dark alleys to rob them.

LAY A particular kind of rascality, trade, or profession; on the look out; watching for something to steal. Sometimes the same as gait. 'What's the cove's lay?' 'Why, you see, he is on the ken's crack'—house-breaking.'

[does not list *lay*]

[does not list *sand*]

SAND: nerve, guts.

Both Matsell and the *Five Points Vocabulary* define *turtle-doves* only as 'a pair of gloves'. *Sand* is listed in the *OED* with the sense 'firmness of purpose; pluck, stamina' between 1867 and 1954, and is labelled 'chiefly US'.

It is not statistically significant that Scorsese preserves none of Matsell's cross-reference, etymologies, or authorities. While it is not statistically significant that he retains one citation, it is probable that:

RABBIT: a rowdy (dead-rabbit: a very athletic rowdy fellow).

remains largely because one of the gangs featured in the film was known as the dead rabbits.

While there are no statistically significant differences between the semantic areas listed in the lists (Appendix, Table 2.4.1), Scorsese's glossary does include a disproportionate number of terms for women who are not prostitutes. The 'Five Points Vocabulary' contains two of Matsell's eighteen ($p = 0.01$), which may represent deliberate political correctness.

Having traced the genealogy of Matsell's dictionary, it comes as no surprise that some of the vocabulary used in the film is rather dubious as a representation of mid-nineteenth-century American cant. For example, *autem-diver* 'a pickpocket operating in church' has an unbroken dictionary-life dating back to the *New Canting Dictionary* of 1725. *Angler* 'a thief using a hooked stick' can trace its dictionary-heritage back to Dekker in 1608, and beyond that to Harman in 1567.

At least one scene in the film might have looked rather different if some of its $100 million budget had been spent on dictionary research. A dance, organized by missionaries, is referred to as a *ballum-rancum*. The *Five Points Vocabulary* defines this term as:

BALLUM-RANCUM: a ball where all the dancers are thieves and prostitutes.

which can be traced to Matsell's identical entry. However, Matsell's entry is ultimately derived from one found in Grose's dictionary in 1785:

BALLUM RANCUM. A hop or dance, where the women are all prostitutes, a dance at a brothel.

In the second edition, as noted above, Grose added:

N.B. The company dance in their birthday suits

Summary

The dictionaries covered in this chapter range from the entirely pirated to the partially original. While the *Lexicon Balatronicum* is by far the most interesting, the others demonstrate the imaginative flexibility with which the same list could be remarketed in line with current fads.

The *Lexicon* increases the size of the word-list by over 300 new headwords and almost 400 new entries. These additions are largely slang terms, particularly university slang. The compiler of the *Lexicon* edited existing entries to make them more concise, correct, modern, and informative. He added citations and authorities to make his work all the more authoritative. However, repetition within the new citations suggests that they were fabricated for the purpose of illustration rather than providing independent evidence of terms in use. His addition of cross-references to existing entries suggests a good knowledge of the contents of the dictionary, but the duplication of existing entries undermines this, as does careless proofreading. *OED* use of the *Lexicon* is rather haphazard. The citations that could usefully be employed outnumber those that actually were, 10 per cent of which can be predated by reference to earlier editions of Grose's dictionary.

Matsell's dictionary is largely derivative. He used his sources extremely carelessly and often without understanding. Among his additions, however, he made a significant contribution towards charting early American slang, and demonstrated that he had a good ear for small shifts in meaning. Asbury's selection from Matsell's dictionary produces a glossary that is concise and much more sensational. Scorsese was unfortunate in his choice of the *Vocabulum* as a source of authentic period language.

3 Humphry Tristram Potter

Although the dictionaries in this section are all ultimately derived from Grose's, they are linked by a common intermediary.

Humphry Tristram Potter's *New Dictionary of all the Cant and Flash Languages* (1795)

The *New Dictionary of all the Cant and Flash Languages* was first published in 1795, but no copies of the first edition are extant.[1] B. Crosby published the first dated edition in 1797. I have seen two copies of an undated edition, published by W. Mackintosh, and sold by J. Downes. One is in Cambridge University Library, dated *c*.1796, and the other in the British Library, dated *c*.1797. J. Downes republished the dictionary in 1800. There are, then, three extant editions. Some authorities date the dictionary to *a*1790, because 1790 is the year in which Potter allegedly died.

Humphry Tristram Potter is not listed in the *Dictionary of National Biography*, but the dictionary gives some information about his life. He was born, it tells, at Clay in Worcestershire, in 1747, attended the Blue Coat School in Stourbridge, and was apprenticed to an ironmonger in Wolverhampton. He became clerk to an attorney in Wolverhampton, and in 1773 became an attorney himself. He was a prominent Methodist and preacher, but was declared bankrupt in 1776, and evidently moved to London. There he was imprisoned under martial law in the Gordon riots of 1780, and sent to Newgate in 1782 for running a gambling den. To avoid paying his debts, he lived within the rules of the King's Bench prison. In 1788 he was imprisoned for libel, and in 1790 he died in a public house.[2]

This account of Potter's life follows the familiar pattern of the rogue biography suspiciously closely, in that he began life in a respectable family, had a good education, and was apprenticed. The heights of social acceptability that Potter reaches before his fall are unusual, but it

---

[1] R. C. Alston, *A Bibliography of the English Language from the Invention of Printing to the Year 1800. A Corrected Reprint of Volumes I–X.* (Ilkley: Janus Press, 1974), ix.67.

[2] Potter, *New Dictionary* (1797), 5–15.

is normal that sin, once begun, leads to ever-greater depths of depravity. The implication is that Potter collected his word-list by personal contact with cant speakers. The dedicatory epistle, apparently written by Potter himself, is addressed to William Addington, Justice of the Peace, and discusses the problem of increasing crime:

In house and street robbery, every week seems to give birth to some new mode of seizing the property of the honest and peaceable subject. The depredator's talent at novelty, almost keeps pace, with the exertions of a police, able, active and vigilant.

The danger to which the public is exposed from thieves of every description, is perhaps greatly increased by the circumstance of their associating together, and forming by the *Language* as well as their crimes a distinct community. By this means their depredatory schemes, are the result of general knowledge of the prevailing rules of practice. Security and danger are pointed out from perilous and past atchievements [sic]; and those who may want experience for a difficult undertaking, are supplied with instructions from the more veteran and hackneyed offenders.

Improvements are thus introduced to simplify their system of plunder, and thus the ignorant and vicious are trained up and educated. They have their terms of Art—their various modes of attack—execution and retreat—their success and miscarriage, all recorded in a language of their own invention, and of which every [sic] few, but themselves, have the least knowledge.

The chief object the Editor had in view in compiling the following Dictionary was by exposing the Cant Terms of their language, FACILITATE THE DETECTION OF THEIR CRIMES. He cannot but indulge the hope that this work, which has occupied much of his time and attention, will be found to be tolerably accurate; and therefore the public will be greatly assisted in the discovery and apprehension of offenders.

Thieves at present, secure that their jargon is unintelligible to others, converse with ease and familiarity in the streets, on plans of plunder and deprdeation [sic]; but when the meaning of those mysterious terms is generally disseminated, the honest subject will be better able to detect and frustrate their designs.[3]

The biographical account is followed by an address to the reader written by an unnamed editor:

As to the work itself, it appears to be the most perfect of the kind; the various scenes of life into which his turn for dissipation led him, especially towards the latter part of it, when his pot companions were of every rank; having furnished him with opportunities that few have met with, of picking up the Cant and Flash terms, and made him an adept in that species of language. Nor is there room to doubt, but that the motives for his intended publication of them, were really such as he alledged to the late worthy magistrate, to whom he has dedicated his dictionary.[4]

[3] Potter, *New Dictionary* (1797), iii–iv.   [4] Potter, *New Dictionary* (1797), 15.

The subtitle further explains that the word-list was:

Carefully arranged and selected from the most approved Authors, and from the Manuscripts of Jonathan Wild, Baxter, and Others.[5]

Despite all assertions and insinuations to the contrary, Potter had three main sources: the *New Canting Dictionary*, Grose's *Classical Dictionary*, and Parker's *Life's Painter* (see Appendix, Table 3.1). In addition, sixteen terms are from the *Discoveries of John Poulter, alias Baxter*, mentioned in the subtitle. Poulter's work certainly seems to be a genuine list of contemporary cant, as used in 1753, but there is no evidence that these terms were still current a generation later.[6]

A further four entries must be from an edition of the life of Bampfylde-Moore Carew, because they contain distinctive variants only found in that source. For example, Potter lists *hum-box* "a pulpit", *to melt* "to spend money", and *togemans* "a gown or cloak" which are found in both the *New Canting Dictionary* and in Grose's *Classical Dictionary*. He also lists the variant forms *hunt-box*, *to meet*, and *tagemans*, found in some versions of the word-list appended to editions of Carew's life, which is itself derived from the *New Canting Dictionary*. Instead of following the *New Canting Dictionary* and Grose in defining *iron-doublet* as 'a prison', Potter follows the erroneous Carew definition 'a parson'. We can further narrow Potter's source down to the five editions of Carew's life that include all of these variant readings and predate the publication of this dictionary. These were issued between 1786 and 1793.[7]

These sources account, in total, for 1,001 entries of Potter's 1,234 (81.1 per cent). The second edition of Grose's dictionary is undoubtedly Potter's main source. Entries that could only be derived from this edition include:

Classical Dictionary (1788)	Potter
FLOGGER. A horsewhip. *Cant.*	FLOGGER, a whip.
READER. A pocket book. *Cant.*	READER, a pocket book.
UPPER BENJAMIN. A great coat. *Cant.*	UPPER BEN, a great coat.

---

[5] Potter does arrange his entries carefully. Unlike either of his main sources, he treats *u* and *v* as separate letters. However, his alphabetical sequence runs *t, v, u, w*.

[6] John Poulter, *The Discoveries of John Poulter*, 5th edition (Sherbourne: R. Goadby, 1753). The terms that Potter takes from it are *queer beak* "a bad or severe justice", *to chaunt* "to sing; to advertise", *crapping-cull* "a hangman", *gaff* "a fair", *to gagg* "to beg", *gloak* "a man", *grabbed* "arrested", *lagged* "transported", *lift* "a shoplifter; shoplifting", *old nob* (a game played by con-men), *noll* "a wig", *oliver* "the moon", *to pinch* "to steal money under pretence of getting change", *quod-cull* "a jail-keeper", *stoop* "pillory", and *swag* "goods".   [7] See Coleman, *Cant and Slang Dictionaries*, i.ch.5.

Although the *New Canting Dictionary* (1725) derived most of its entries from B. E.'s *New Dictionary of the Terms Ancient and Modern of the Canting Crew* (*c*.1698), the inclusion of entries not found in B. E.'s word-list indicates that Potter used the later dictionary as his source. For example:

New Canting Dictionary	Potter
ANTICKS; such as dress themselves up with Ribbons, mismatch'd Colours, Feathers, *&c.* Zanies, Mountebanks, or Merry-Andrews. Also a Species of *Abram-men*; which See.	ANTICKS, morris dancers; a species of abram men, called merry-andrews.
BEEF, to alarm, as *To cry Beef upon us*; they have discover'd us, and are in Pursuit of us.	BEEF, to alarm, to discover, to pursue.
WAPPING, the Act of Coition.	WAPPING, the act of coition.

Some entries, although included in Grose's dictionary, are closer to the *New Canting Dictionary* entries:

New Canting Dictionary	*Classical Dictionary* (1788)	Potter
BEAU-TRAPS; the *Fortieth Order* of Villains, Genteel-dress'd Sharpers, who lie in wait to insnare and draw in young Heirs, raw Country 'Squires, and ignorant Fops.	BEAU TRAP. A loose stone in a pavement, under which water lodges, and on being trod upon, squirts it up, to the great damage of white stockings; also a sharper neatly dressed, lying in wait for raw country squires, or ignorant fops.	BEAU TRAPS, genteel dressed sharpers, fortune hunters.
BELCH, any sort of Malt-Liquor so called.	BELCH. All sorts of beer; that liquor being apt to cause eructation.	BELCH, malt liquor.

while others are closer to Grose's entries:

New Canting Dictionary	*Classical Dictionary* (1788)	Potter
BENE-BOWSE, strong Liquor or very good Drink.	BENE BOWSE. Good beer, or other strong liquor. *Cant.*	—[BENE] BOWSE, good beer, or other strong liquor.

BENFEAKERS,	BENE FEAKERS.	—[BENE] FEAKERS,
Counterfeiters of Notes, Receipts, &c.	Counterfeiters of bills. *Cant.*	counterfeiters of bills.

Potter's use of his sources was not passive. He frequently rewrote definitions, usually to abbreviate them:

Classical Dictionary (1788)	Potter
ADAM TILER. A pickpocket's associate, who receives the stolen goods, and runs off with them. *Cant.*	—[ADAM] TILER, a receiver of stolen goods, a pick-pocket, a fence.
PEG TRANTUM'S. Gone to Peg Trantum's; dead.	PEG TANTRUMS [sic], dead.

He rewrote some entries so radically that it is not at first apparent that they are from Grose's dictionary:

Classical Dictionary (1788)	Potter
TO BUG . . . Bailiffs who take money to postpone or refrain the serving of a writ are said to bug the writ.	BUG, to spoil.
GEE. It won't gee; it won't hit or do, it does not suit or fit.	GEE, suitable.

From the text and word-list of Parker's *Life's Painter*, Potter has, for example:

Parker's *Life's Painter*	Potter
Cant of dobbin. A roll of ribbon.	DOBBIN, ribbon.
	DOBBIN, CANT OF, roll of ribbon.
Crown. *A bull.*	BULL'S EYE and BULL, a crown piece.
Darkey. Night.	DARKEY, night.

He also included a number of the entries in which Parker reverses the order of headword and definition, as shown below (Chapter 7). For example, Potter, like Parker, defines *body* as 'trunk', *lips* as 'lispers', and *purse* as 'a sack', instead of the other way round.

Of the entries that Potter does not derive directly from Grose, the *New Canting Dictionary*, Parker, Carew, or Poulter, there are about sixty that appear to be coined from the material included in these sources. The coinages follow a number of patterns. For example, nouns and adjectives listed in earlier dictionaries are compounded

with a word meaning 'man', and listed as separate headwords.
A dash or series of dashes represents a repeated headword:

New Canting Dictionary	Potter
BLUBBERING, much Crying.	—[BLUBBERING] CULL a crying thief.
BOARDING *school*, in a Canting Sense, is *Bridewell*, or *New-Prison*, or any Work-house or House of Correction, for Vagrants, Beggars and Villains of all Denominations.	—[BOARDING-SCHOOL] GLOAKS, felons in newgate, new prison, clerkenwell bridewell, &c.
DIDDLE, the *Cant Word* for *Geneva*, a Liquor very much drank by the lowest Rank of People.	—[DIDDLE] COVE, the keeper of a gin shop.

Classical Dictionary (1788)	
CROWD. A fiddle: probably from *crooth*, the Welsh name for that instrument.	CROWDSMAN, a fidler.

Another common pattern is that new headwords are made by qualifying existing ones with *queer* or *rum*. Some of these are listed under
the adjective and some under the following noun:

New Canting Dictionary	Potter
BUB, drink . . .	—[BUBB] QUEER, bad liquor.
CLY . . . Also a Pocket, as, *Filed a Cly*, Pick'd a Pocket.	------ [RUM] CLYE, a full pocket.
LAP . . . also strong Drink of any Sort.	—[LAP] QUEER, bad liquor.
	—[LAP] RUM, good liquor.
PEEPERS, Eyes.	—[RUM] PEEPERS . . . or bright eyes.
PROG, Meat . . .	----- [PROGG] QUEER, bad victuals.

Classical Dictionary (1788)	
FEEDER. A spoon. To nab the feeder; to steal a spoon.	------- [RUM] FEADERS, large silver spoons.

The third pattern by which Potter boosted his word-list is the inclusion
of present and past participles and agent nouns as separate headwords,
based on verbs and nouns derived from his sources. The verbs and
nouns are sometimes also included in their own right. For example:

New Canting Dictionary	Potter
KID, a Child.	KIDD, a child.
	KIDDED, a woman with child.
NIM, to steal, or whip off or away any thing . . .	NIM, to steal, to pilfer.
	NIMMER, a thief of the lowest order.

Classical Dictionary (1788)

To Chouse. To cheat or trick: he choused me out of it . . .	Chouse, to cheat.
	Choused, cheated.
To Rap. To take a false oath . . .	Rap, to swear, to give evidence, to take a false oath.
	Rapper, a perjurer.

Potter rarely provides usage labels. His title serves to label all of his entries as 'cant' or 'flash', so it may be that further labelling seemed unnecessary. However, he does make use of the labels that Grose provides, and demonstrates a marked preference for terms labelled as 'cant' ($p = 0.01$). About three-quarters of the terms that Potter selected from Grose are also in the *New Canting Dictionary*. He was much more inclined to adopt terms not labelled 'cant' in Grose if they were in both dictionaries ($p = 0.01$).

If meaning were a further factor influencing Potter's choice, we would expect the semantic coverage of Grose's 'cant' terms and of Potter's selection from them to be significantly different, which they are not. However, in selecting terms that are not labelled as 'cant', Potter was influenced by meaning. There are significantly fewer terms for ARTEFACTS, EMOTION & TEMPERAMENT, and LOOKS than we would expect, and considerably more for CRIME & DISHONESTY and MONEY (all $p = 0.01$). The rise in terms for LAW & ORDER is also significant ($p = 0.05$; see Appendix, Tables 1.2 and 3.2). Taken together, Potter's preference for terms labelled 'cant' in Grose, and for the semantic fields listed above, results in a dictionary that is much more focused on criminals and their language than its main source.

Potter has 157 entries that cannot be traced to a specific source. Some are for new headwords and others add a new sense to an existing headword. These entries are Potter's positive contribution to canting lexicography, and it is among these that we find entries predating *OED* first citations. The *OED* cites Potter's dictionary thirty-six times, dating the first edition to 1790 or *a*1790, and the second to 1795. It often provides the earliest citation for terms it illustrates, and predates a further sixteen existing *OED* first citations (seventeen, if the dubious *dud* is included):

to bluff "to pretend to greater strength or power than one really possesses" (1854)
bobbery "a disturbance" (1816)

to cadge "to beg" (1812)
cadger "a beggar" (1851)
cracksman "a burglar" (1812)
dud cheats "ragged and poor" (1903: *dud* "counterfeit")
jigger "an illicit still" (1824)
lagger "a sailor" (1812)
to ring "to swap" (1812: v^2 13)
rum bow "rope stolen from the royal dockyard" (1846: *rumbo*)
skewer "a sword" (1838: "a weapon")
slanged "in fetters" (1812)
staller (listed twice) "a pickpocket's accomplice" (1812)
stephen "money" (1812: *steven* n^5)
to tease "to flog" (1812)
to wall "to chalk up a reckoning" (1848: v^2)
wallflowers "secondhand clothes exposed for sale" (1804)

Potter also made a negative contribution to canting lexicography. He adopted an unusual method for dealing with headwords repeating terms included in the preceding headword, as we have seen above. For example, after *bene* 'good' come *bene bowse* 'good beer, or other strong liquor', *bene cove* 'a good fellow', *bene darkmans* 'good night', etc. Instead of repeating *bene* in each entry, Potter substitutes a long hyphen, or sometimes a series of dashes, as shown in Figure 3.1.

In the entry—**of gybes**, the hyphen stands not for *bene*, as before, but for *benefeakers*. This is just one of the ambiguities that can arise from this practice. Another occurs where the repeated term, replaced by the long hyphen, should actually follow rather than precede the word that is spelt out. See, for example, the sequence **beak,**—**rum**, and—**queer** in Figure 3.1. Here Potter is clearly listing normal adjectival uses of *queer* and *rum*, and indeed he could be accused of excessive thoroughness in this regard. These headwords are *beak, rum beak*, and *queer beak*. However, he leaves open the possibility of interpreting them as *beak, beak-rum*, and *beak-queer*. As we shall see, later lexicographers did fall into this trap.

It may be this same urge towards concision that led Potter to delete most of the etymologies, citations (both $p = 0.01$), and references to authorities ($p = 0.05$) that he found in Grose's dictionary. Although the proportion of entries including cross-references is lower than we would expect, the fall is not statistically significant (see Appendix, Tables 1.4 and 3.3).

12

B.

BAB

BABES IN THE WOOD, Rogues in the stocks or pillory.
BACK'D, dead.
BACK-GAMMON PLAYER, a sodomite.
BACK-DOOR GENTLEMAN, the same.
BACON, he has saved his bacon, he has escaped.
BACON FACED, full faced.
BADGE, one burned in the hand.
—— COVES, parish pensioners.
BADGER, to confound, perplex or teaze.
BADGERS, forestallers and murderers.
BAGGAGE, a slut, a common whore.
BALLUM RANCUM, a hop or dance where the women are all prostitutes.
BALSAM, money.
BAM, a lie.
BANDOG, a bum bailiff.
BANTLING, a young child,
BARK, an Irishman.
BARKER, a salesman servant, a prowler to pick up countrymen in the street.
BARKING IRONS, pistols.
BARNACLE, a good job.
BASKET-MAKING, copulation.
BASTE, to beat.
BATTER'D BULLY, an old gloak, well mill'd and bruis'd, a huffing fellow.

13

BAU

BAUBEE, a halfpenny.
BEAU TRAPS, genteel dressed sharpers, fortune hunters.
BAWD, a female procuress.
BAWDY BASKET, the twenty third rank of canters, who carry pins, tape, ballads and obscene books to sell, but live mostly by stealing.
BAWDY HOUSE BOTTLE, a very small one, short measure.
BEAK, a justice of peace, or magistrate.
—— RUM, a justice that will do any thing for money.
—— QUEER, one that is a justice, particularly strict to his duty.
BEAR LEADER, a travelling tutor.
BEARD SPLITTER, a man much given to wenches.
BECK OR HARMAN, a beadle.
BEEF, to alarm, to discover, to pursue.
BEGGARS BULLETS, stones.
BELCH, malt liquor.
BELLY CHEAT, an apron, the pad.
—— TIMBER, food of all sorts.
BEN OR SAM, a silly fellow, a novice, a tool.
BENE, good.
—— BOWSE, good beer, or other strong liquor.
—— COVE, a good fellow.
—— DARKMANS, good night.
—— FEAKERS, counterfeiters of bills.
—— OF GYBES, counterfeiters of passes.
BENESHIPLY, worshipfully.
BETT, a wager.

Figure 3.1. Humphry Tristram Potter's *New Dictionary of all the Cant and Flash Languages* (c.1800), 12–13 [BL 12984.bbb.4]

George Andrewes's *Dictionary of the Slang and Cant Languages* (1809)

George Andrewes's *Stranger's Guide* outlined the activities by which thieves, conmen, and prostitutes could ease trusting fools of their money.[8] The types described, like the money-dropper and the duffer (a seller of supposedly contraband goods), are all familiar from earlier canting works. Its mixture of social comment and precautionary advice was clearly sufficiently profitable, even though little in the work was new, to persuade Andrewes to publish further work in this field. The following year he produced his *Dictionary of the Slang and Cant Languages*.

The 'Advertisement' to the dictionary explains Andrewes's purpose:

One great misfortune to which the Public are liable, is, that Thieves have a *Language* of their own; by which means they associate together in the streets, without fear of being over-heard or understood.

The principal end I had in view in publishing this DICTIONARY, was, to expose the Cant Terms of their Language, in order to the more easy detection of their crimes; and I flatter myself, by the perusal of this Work, the Public will become acquainted with their mysterious Phrases; and better able to frustrate their designs.[9]

What Andrewes does not do, however, is give any indication of the means by which he collected his word-list. This is probably because all he had done was rework Potter's dictionary. Most of Andrewes's word-list ultimately goes back to Grose's dictionary, and thus, sometimes, to Grose's much older sources. We can only be sure that Potter was Andrewes's source by his inclusion of some of Potter's additions:

All sett, desperate fellows, ready for any kind of mischief.
Frumper—a sturdy blade.
Lifter—a robber of shops.
Squail—a dram.

as well as his mistakes:

Classical Dictionary (1788)	Potter	Andrewes
GALLIGASKINS. Breeches.	GALIGASKIN, breeches.	*Galigaskin*—breeches.
TO MILL . . . To mill doll; to beat hemp in Bridewell. *Cant.*	MILLDOLL, to beat hemp in bridewell.	*Milldoll*—beating hemp in Bridewell.
WATTLES. Ears. *Cant.*	WHATTLES, ears.	*Whattles*—ears.

[8] George Andrewes, *The Stranger's Guide or Frauds of London Detected* (London/Glasgow: J. Bailey/Messrs. Lumsden, 1808).
[9] George Andrewes, *Dictionary of the Slang and Cant Languages Ancient and Modern* (London: G. Smeeton, 1809), Advertisement.

Andrewes sometimes retains Potter's hyphens and dashes for *queer* or *rum*:

Potter	Andrewes
------ [RUM] BOOZE, wine or any other liquor.	—[*rum*] *boose*—wine, or any liquor.
------ [QUEER] COVE, a rogue.	—[*queer*] *cove*—a rogue; villain.
—[RUM] PRANCER, a good horse.	—[*rum*] *prancer* -- good fine horse.

but usually reinstates the repeated headword. We have seen that Potter's practice sets up a number of interpretative traps, and Andrewes often falls into them:

Potter	Andrewes
DARBIES, irons used in prisons.	*Darbies*—fetters.
—FAIR, removing day at Newgate.	*Darbies Fair*—the day when people are removed to Newgate for trial.
JET, a lawyer.	*Jet*—a lawyer.
—AUTEM, a parson.	*Jet Autum*—a parson.
SCAMP, a highwayman.	*Scamp*—highwayman of the 2d order of thieves.
—FOOT, a street robber—a footpad— a spicer.	*Scamp-foot*—a street robber, a foot pad, spicer.

Potter's intended headwords, based on his sources, were actually *darby fair*, *autem-jet*, and *foot-scamp*.

Andrewes's definitions are frequently slightly shorter than Potter's:

Potter	Andrewes
ACADEMY, a bawdy house, a brothel.	*Academy*, a brothel.[10]
SKINNERS, kidnappers, or sett of abandoned fellows who steal children, or intrap unwary men to inlist for soldiers.	*Skinners*—villains who steal children; kidnappers who entrap uwary [sic] men to inlist for soldiers.
TEARS OF THE TANKARD, drops of good liquor.	*Tears of the tankard*—drops of liquor.

and sometimes more ambiguous:

Potter	Andrewes
DUNNAKIN, a necessary.	*Dunnakin*—necessary.

[10] On the first page, up to the entry for *autem divers*, Andrewes uses commas to separate headwords and definitions. From *autem gogglers* onwards, he uses an em dash, as shown.

Andrewes only rarely added to Potter's entries:

Potter	Andrewes
GROANER and SIGHER, wretches hired by methodists and others to attend their meetings for the purposes of fraud.	*Groaners*—a sort of wretches who are employed by methodists and others, to attend their meetings, for the purpose of sighing, and looking demure, in order to give a colour to the sermon of the fellow who preaches; in the mean time pick the pockets of the good-disposed persons who may be in the same pew with them. Likewise attend charity-sermons, and rob the congregation of their watches on their coming out of church; exchange their bad hats for good ones; steal prayer-books; &c. &c,—*See Sighers.*
HOISTER, a shoplifter.	*Hoister*—shop-lifter—fellows who go into shops, and under the pretence of buying goods, generally conceal some small article under the sleeve of their coat—mostly frequenting jeweller's shops.

These additions are usually in descriptions of types of rogue, and thus reflect the interest demonstrated in Andrewes's *Stranger's Guide*, which itself provides a lengthy digression, doubling as an advertisement, in the entry for *swindlers*. Rarer than such additions is the inclusion of new citations for Potter's existing entries:

Potter	Andrewes
PIKE, to run away.	*Pike*—to run away—'He *piked* it off to sea.'

Andrewes occasionally updated his definitions:

Potter	Andrewes
—[BODY] SNATCHERS, thief takers and bum bailiffs.	*Body-snatchers*—bailiff [sic], Police officers.

redefined them the better to reflect contemporary usage:

Potter	Andrewes
CHUM, a chamberfellow, at the university & in prison.	*Chum* . . good fellow, companion.[11] *Chum* . . school fellow, partner, fellow prisoner.

edited them to improve their precision or intelligibility:

Potter	Andrewes
NOBB, a head, the party wears a good head.	*Nobb*—a head; the fellow carries a high head; a man of money, of respectability.
RATTLING COVE, a coachman.	*Rattling cove*—hackney coach man.

or replaced defining words likely to cause offence:

Potter	Andrewes
—[AUTEM] MORT OR MOTT, a woman of the same sect, a beggar, a whore.	*Autem Mort or Moll*—a woman of the same sect, a beggar, a prostitute.
BAGGAGE, a slut, a common whore.	*Baggage*—a slut, a common prostitute.
BORDELLO, a bawdy house.	*Bordello*—a house of ill fame.
DOXIES AND DRABS, whores, strumpets.	*Doxies*—girls of the town.
FROW, a whore (see mott).	*Frow*—prostitute.

He also introduced errors into a few entries:

Potter	Andrewes
BECK OR HARMAN, a beadle.	*Beck or Hasman*—a beable.
CHIVE, a knife.	*Clive*—a knife.
PRATTS, buttocks . . .	*Pratt*—buttocks.

and, oddly, alphabetized only to the first letter where Potter had alphabetized more or less fully. Moreover, the headwords **the dewbeaters** and **the bower** are both found under 'T'.

Andrewes follows Potter in creating a few new headwords by qualifying existing ones with *rum* or *queer*. These new entries include:

——[*queer*] *amen curler*—drunken parish clerk.
——[*queer*] *buffer*—a cur.
Queer cat-lap—bad tea.
——[*queer*] *Nantz*—bad brandy.

[11] There are seven entries, all under 'C', in which the headword and definition are divided by <. .>. A few entries under *rum* have <. . . .>.

Andrewes also lists thirty-nine new entries for thirty-eight headwords as addenda. These come from a version of the Bampfylde-Moore Carew word-list, probably one published in 1793, and include:

Carew[12]	Andrewes
coblecolter a turnkey [for *turkey*]	*Coble colter*—a turnkey.
cussin[for *cuffin*]a man	*Cussin*—a man.
husbylour[for *husky lour*]a job, a guinea	*Husbylour*—a guinea.

Following the addenda are a 'sketch of the manner of electing a king of the beggars' (which is done using black and white balls), the canting verse 'Cast your cares and nabs away', 'The Sixty Orders of Offenders', and an advertisement for the *Stranger's Guide*.

Andrewes's dictionary contains slightly fewer entries than Potter's: 1,163 entries (94.2 per cent) for 1,126 headwords (96.5 per cent). The semantic make-up of the two dictionaries is very different, however (see Appendix, Table 3.2); there are considerably more terms for LOOKS than we would expect. Indeed, Andrewes almost doubled the size of the field by his additions ($p = 0.01$). There are also considerably fewer terms for SEX than in Potter's dictionary ($p = 0.01$). Moreover, different types of SEX term have different selection rates. Andrewes allowed a far higher proportion of PROSTITUTION terms to stand in his selection of terms from Potter, suitably bowdlerized, as shown above. General SEX terms, however, were largely deleted ($p = 0.05$).

Andrewes tended to delete Potter's cross-references ($p = 0.01$). These deletions, like many of the others that Andrewes made, were presumably for the sake of greater conciseness. An increase from one to two etymologies is also statistically significant ($p = 0.05$), as is the increase from none to two cited authorities ($p = 0.01$; see Appendix, Table 3.3).

The Flash Dictionary (1821)

The anonymous *Flash Dictionary* is a pamphlet printed on pages of only $7^1/_2$ by $12^1/_2$ centimetres, in tiny print. Its publisher was George Smeeton, who published Andrewes's dictionary, historical accounts of the lives of eminent people (largely royalty), anti-Catholic tracts, medical books (particularly on vaccination), and an encyclopaedia of

[12] *The Life and Adventures of Bampfylde-Moore Carew* (London: J. Buckland, C. Bathurst, and T. Davies, 1793).

America and the West Indies, among many other works. The *Flash Dictionary*, however, clearly appeals to the same audience as his sensational accounts of crime and entertaining tours among the low-life of London. Examples include the luridly titled *Account of the dreadful murder of the unfortunate Mary Minting, on Saturday, February 14, 1818, at Union-Street, Mary-le-bone: with the particulars of the suicide of W. Haitch, her murderer: Also, the trial of David Evans, for the wilful murder of his wife. Unfolding another melancholy instance of the horrid effects of drunkeness!* (1818) and *An Account of a most shocking murder committed by Charlotte Lawson on her mistress, by beating her brains out with a brick-bat, and afterwards cutting her to pieces* (1830s). Smeeton's *Life and Death in London, or, The Kaleidoscope of Villainy* (1817) and *Doings in London* (1828) belong to the same tradition as Egan's *Life in London*, but attained nothing like the same popularity.

The *Flash Dictionary* begins with an 'Advertisement' not dissimilar in its opening, to Andrewes's (see above):

One misfortune to which the Public are liable, is, that Thieves have a *Language* of their own; by which means, they associate together in the street, without fear of being over-heard or understood.

One object in publishing this Flash Dictionary, was, to expose the Cant Terms of their Language, in order to the more easy detection of their crimes; and it is presumed, by the perusal of this work, the Public will become acquainted with their mysterious phrases, and better able to frustrate their designs.

By reference to this *Linguist*, the various fashionable Slang Phrases used by Boxiana, the Newspapers, &c. in describing the Boxing Matches, will be readily understood.[13]

followed by a rather uninspiring verse:

> Thro' every age some *master slang* assails,
> And *modern flash* the one that now prevails.
> Each man, each tongue, and pen some *slang* has got,
> In short—name one that *flash* and *cant* has not.
> It glares abroad!—'tis found in every nook,
> And now it stares you in this little book.

The dictionary itself is fifty-nine pages long, and includes 1,210 entries for 1,184 headwords, alphabetized to the first letter reliably, and slightly less reliably to the second. The word-list is largely taken from Andrewes's *Dictionary of the Cant and Slang Languages*, with

---

[13] *The Flash Dictionary* (London: G. Smeeton, 1821), Advertisement. Smeeton also published Egan's *Boxiana* (see Chapter 5 for Egan's works).

apparent additional reference to Potter's *New Dictionary of all the Cant and Flash Languages*:

Potter	Andrewes	*Flash*
BAWD, a female procuress.	*Bawd*—a female procuress, keeper of a bagnio.	Bawd—female procuress, keeper of a bagnio.
BLACK LEGS, a gambler or sharper on the turf or in the cock pit.	*Blacklegs*—sharpers; fellows who lay wages [sic], and after losing them, cannot pay them; a gambler on the turf, billiard-table, or cock-pit.	Black legs—sharpers; fellows who lay wages, and after losing them, cannot pay them; a gambler on the turf, billiard-table, or cock-pit.
BREAD BASKET, the stomach.	[omits]	Bread basket—the stomach.
BROWN BESS, a solder's firelock.	[omits]	Brown Bess—a solder's fire-lock.

Most entries are adopted verbatim, but a few undergo minor editing and correction:

Potter	*Flash*
—[AUTEM] CACKLER, dissenters of every denomination.	Autem cacklers—dissenters of all sects.

Andrewes	
Burn the Ken—vagabonds residing in an ale-house, and leaving it without paying their reckoning.	Burning the ken—vagabonds residing in an ale-house, and leaving it without paying their reckoning.
Catch-pole—bailiff, a fellow of the lowest order, who goes about to distressed people under various pretences.	Catch-pole—bailiff, a fellow of the lowest order, who goes about to distress [sic] people under various pretences.

The compiler of this edition occasionally retained Potter's hyphens to indicate repetition of the headword (see Figure 3.1), especially at *queer* and *rum*, but usually followed Andrewes in replacing the missing terms.

There are a few new entries, for example:

To blab—to chatter, to tell secrets.
Black-boy—a lawyer.
Buttering up—praising, or flattering.

Chuffy—jolly, merry.
To Clink—to snatch.

There is no single obvious source for these and other new terms, although some appear to be related to the second edition of Grose's dictionary:

Classical Dictionary (1788)	*Flash*
DEAD MEN, a cant word among journeymen bakers, for loaves falsely charged to their master's customers . . .	Dead men—bakers; so called from the loaves falsely charged to their master's customers.
FIN, an arm; a one finned fellow, a man who has lost an arm, (*sea phrase*).	Fin—arm.
KNOWLEDGE BOX, the head.	Knowledge box—the head.
PERSUADERS, Spurs.	Persuaders—spurs.

Andrewes's dictionary is, however, the main source for this word-list, and there are no statistically significant differences between the semantic coverage of the two (see Appendix, Table 3.2).

The *OED* does not cite this dictionary at all, but it predates four existing *OED* first citations: *chaffing* "bantering" (1827), *to box* "to overturn (a watchman) in a box" (1851), *farmer* "an alderman" (1848), and *up to slum* "knowing" (1857–9).

George Kent's *Modern Flash Dictionary* (1835)

This pamphlet-dictionary, sometimes referred to by the name of its publisher, Duncombe, is based on the *Flash Dictionary* of 1821, and alphabetized much more reliably to the second letter. The British Library holds one edition, and the Newberry Library in Chicago holds two. Neither of the copies in Chicago has a date on the title page, but one is identical in content with the British Library copy, dated 1835, and is probably from the same year. The other is clearly derived from it, and must therefore have been published later.

We can put together a picture of the target audience by considering the publications advertised in this pamphlet. They are *Billy Black's Cabinet of Conundrums* 'Calculated to afford Wit for a Week, Fun for a Fortnight, Mirth for a Month, and Entertainment for ever',[14] *The*

[14] George Kent, *Modern Flash Dictionary; by George Kent, Historian to the Prize Ring* (London: J. Duncombe, 1835), inside front cover.

Out-and-Outer 'A Right up-on-End Collection of Flash and Amatory Songs',[15] *The Frisky Songster* and *The Singular Life, Amatory Adventures, and Intrigues of John Wilmot, Earl of Rochester*. Taken together with the description of Kent as 'Historian to the Prize Ring' on the title page, we can assume an audience of young men, interested in sport, sex, and drinking. This cheap volume is likely to have been within the reach of working men.

The earliest edition of the dictionary contains 1,639 entries for 1,610 headwords, as opposed to 1,210 entries for 1,184 headwords in the *Flash Dictionary*. Kent also used Egan's dictionary, and sixty-two entries appear to be derived from *Life in London* or one of its dramatic or glossarial off-shoots (see Appendix, Table 3.1.1).

The *Flash Dictionary* of 1821 has a number of characteristic reinterpretations and misreadings, whose reproduction in Kent's list confirms that it is the source, rather than Andrewes or Potter's dictionaries, which obviously share much of its content:

Andrewes	*Flash Dictionary*	Kent
Fambles—gloves.	Fumbles—gloves.	Fumbles—gloves
——[*rum*] *gutlers*— canary wine.	——[rum] gutters— Cape wine.	Rum gutters—cape wine
Trandlers—pease.	Twandlers—pease.	Twandlers—pease

Kent sometimes edited terms taken from the *Flash Dictionary*, often by compression:

Flash Dictionary	Kent
Hempen furniture—money received as rewards for convicting felons by thief-takers and others; commonly called blood money.	Hempen furniture—money rewards for convicting felons by thief takers and others; commonly called blood money
Jock-gagger—a sort of fellows who live on the prostitution of their wives, &c.	Jock gagger—fellows who live on the prostitution of their wives, &c.
Kid-lay—villains who defraud young apprentices and errand boys of their parcels and goods.	Kid lays—villains who defraud boys of their parcels and goods
Lully-prigger—the lowest and meanest order of thieves, who go about decoying little children to some bye corner, and then robbing them of their clothes.	Lully priggers—the lowes [sic] order of thieves, who decoy children to some bye place and rob them of their clothes

---

[15] Kent, *Modern Flash Dictionary*, back cover.

Sometimes he rewrote entries, usually altering small details in grammar, syntax, or spelling, but occasionally producing entirely different definitions:

Flash Dictionary	Kent
Garnish—money demanded of people on their entrance into prisons.	Garnish—money demanded of people entering into prison
Ken-flash [for *flash ken*]—a house appropriated for the reception of thieves and disorderly fellows of the meanest order.	Ken, flash—a house where thieves and vagrants resort
Niggers—fellows who clip the gold coin and file them.	Niggers—fellows who clip and file the gold coin
Philistines—bailiff [sic] and their crew.	Philistines—bailiffs and their crew

Although the general tendency is towards compression, Kent sometimes added synonyms and expanded unclear definitions:

Flash Dictionary	Kent
Bing—to go away.	Bing—to cut, go away
Hobbled on the leg—a transported felon sent on board the hulks.	Hobbled on the leg—a transported felon ironed on the leg, and sent on board the hulks
Luggs—ears.	Lugs, or listeners—the ears

One expansion that Kent makes almost consistently is the insertion of articles into nominal definitions that omit them:

Flash Dictionary	Kent
Bender—shilling.	Bender—a shilling
Glim Jack—link boy.	Glim Jack—a link boy
The lil—pocket book.[16]	Lil—a pocket book
Rattling gloak—simple, easy fellow.	Rattling gloak—a simple easy fellow

As with the *Flash Dictionary*, Kent's use of Egan's dictionary usually involves compression:

Egan (1823)	Kent
ALDERMAN. A roasted turkey garnished with sausages; the latter are supposed to represent the gold chain worn by those magistrates.	Alderman in chains—turkey and sausages

---

[16] This is listed under 'T'. Kent moves it to 'L'.

BULL. A blunder; from one Obadiah   Bull—a blunder
Bull, a blundering lawyer of
London, who lived in the reign of
Henry VII.: by a bull, is now always
meant a blunder made by an
Irishman . . .

JEHU. To drive Jehu-like; to drive   Jehu—a coachman
furiously; from a king of Israel of
that name, who was a famous
charioteer, and mentioned as such
in the Bible.

although there are some additions that update entries with contemporary words and phrases. Others make definitions more specific or more contemporary:

Egan (1823)	Kent
CHAUNT. A song.	Chant—a flash song
NOB-THATCHER. A peruke-maker.	Nob thatcher—a hat maker

Kent often introduced cant and flash terms into his definitions, sometimes using only non-standard terms for definition:

Egan (1823)	Kent
FLY. Knowing. Acquainted with another's meaning or proceeding. The rattling cove is fly; the coachman knows what we are about . . .	Fly—up, acquainted with
FUDGE. Nonsense.	Fudge—gammon
RIFF RAFF. Low vulgar persons, mob, tag-rag and bob-tail.	Riff raff—black beetles, the lower order of people

Citations and etymologies are sometimes deleted, but definitions are made more precise:

Egan (1823)	Kent
COOPED UP. Imprisoned, confined like a fowl in a coop.	Cooped—in durance vile, to lock up in a gaol
HERRING POND. The sea. To cross the herring pond at the king's expense; to be transported.	Cross the herring pond—transported to Botany-bay
SKY PARLOUR. The garret, or upper story.	Sky parlour—a garret, or first floor next the sky

There is no evidence that meaning influenced Kent in his selection of terms from Egan or the *Flash Dictionary*. Neither, in his selection from the *Flash Dictionary*, are there significant differences in the number of entries containing citations, references to authorities, etymologies, or cross-references. This means that Kent's selection from the *Flash Dictionary* is either completely random, or is influenced by some factor that cannot be quantified in this way, like currency. In using Egan, however, Kent selects against entries containing etymologies and citations (both $p = 0.05$).

It is difficult to trace words from *Life in London* to a specific source with any certainty. Various plays and songs were inspired by Egan's account of fashionable town life, and several publications arising from it included glossaries. In Kent's list the following are examples of those whose contents are exactly as in a glossary published in 1822 (see Chapter 5):

Arm props—crutches
Core—the heart
Mazzard—the head
Operators—pickpockets
Right and fly—complete
Tip—money

Others are not verbatim, but are clearly related:

Tom and Jerry (1822)	Kent
Cover me decently, a great coat.	Cover me decent—a top tog, a great coat
Fig out, to fit out.	Fig out—to dress
Moisten your chaffer, to drink.	Moisten your chaffer—drink
Seven pence, a cant phrase among the bunches of *turn-ups* for seven years transportation.	Seven-pence, to stand—to suffer seven years transportation
The time of day, quite right.	Time o' day—quite right, the thing

Kent also lists some terms that seem to be from Egan's work, but are not in this glossary, which suggests that a related version that is no longer extant may have been his direct source. It is also possible that he extracted these terms directly from *Life in London*.

It is clear that Kent was not influenced, like some of his predecessors, by considerations of decency. He is happy to include terms with sexual and defecatory meaning, and does not tend to edit them to exclude potentially offensive terms. Terms like *prostitute*, *whore*, and *slut* are largely carried over uncensored from his sources. Equally, if his sources use euphemisms, like *house of ill fame*, *low-life woman*, *girl of the town*, Kent reproduces those. Once he draws attention to a euphemism, seeing in it an opportunity for double entendre:

Dunnaken—if it be *necessary* to explain the word-privy

The *OED* did not make use of Kent's dictionary at all. It predates thirty-five existing *OED* first citations, mostly by fewer than fifteen years. The most significant antedating is by fifty-eight years, for *swinger*, in the sense 'a lame leg':

bogey "the devil" (1836–40)
bonnetter "a blow on the hat" (1837: *to bonnet* "to pull someone's hat down over their eyes")
booked "arrested" (1841: *to book*)
buster "a loaf of bread" (1839: sense unknown)
chaff "banter" (1840)
cheese-cutters "bandy legs" (1848)
chickster "a prostitute" (1839: *shickster*)
chimmy "a chemise" (1837: *shimmy*)
chummy "a chimneysweep" ([1834: "a chimneysweep's boy"] 1860: "a chimneysweep")
coal-scuttle "a type of bonnet" (1839: *coal-scuttle bonnet*)
communicator "a bell" (*c*.1865: "a device for communicating")
crammer "a lie" (1862)
crikey [an exclamation of astonishment] (1838)
to damp your mugs "to have a drink" (1862: *damp* refl.)
to draw it mild "to refrain from exaggeration" (1837: *draw* v 40b)
fiddler "a sixpence" (1846)
to goose "to hiss like a goose" (1838)
joe "a fellow" (1846)
kibosh: to put the kibosh on "to finish off" (1836)
knacker "a worn-out horse" (1864)
leg of mutton sleeves "sleeves shaped like a leg of mutton" (1840)
no go "an impasse" (1870)
pig's whisper "a quiet word" (1883)
to poke fun "to mock" (1840)
potato: to drop (something) like a potato "to stop at once" (1846: *like a hot potato*)
to pull out "to work hard" (1866: *pull* v 29e)
rivets "money" (1846: n[1] 1e)
to take a sight [to make a gesture of contempt] (1836: n[1] 7c)
spike-hotel "a debtors' prison" (1866: *spike* n[2] 4 "a workhouse")
squeezer "the hangman's noose" (1836)
swankey "weak beer" (1841)
swinger: two legs and a swinger "one leg sound and the other lame" (1893: *swinger*[3] 2b)
tater-trap "the mouth" (1846)

that's the ticket "that's the very thing" (1838: n[1] 9)
tuck "food" (1857)

The Sinks of London (1848)

In 1848, Kent's publisher, Duncombe, reissued the dictionary in a new guise 'embellished with humorous illustrations by George Cruikshank'.[17] This was a marked departure from his normal publication of penny pamphlets accompanying contemporary drama, which all have subtitles ranging from the straightforward 'a farce in one act', 'a domestic drama in two acts', 'a comic drama in three acts', to the self-parodying 'an historical, pantomimical, melo-dramatical, balletical, burlesque burletta in one act'. Although 'The Sinks of London' appears on the title page, every page of the volume is headed 'The Dens of London'.[18] The text begins as a documentary-style account of common lodging houses and beggars, but soon becomes more descriptive and narrative, following characters around and reporting on their experiences, in chapters entitled 'A Quiet Scene', 'A Little Literary Conversation', and 'The Close of the Night'. The author insists that the public's knowledge of beggars is based on fiction rather than fact, and that his work reverses this trend.

The word-list is headed 'Flash Dictionary', and is preceded by an illustration of a rather well-dressed man with a top hat and quizzing stick (see Figure 3.2). This rather undermines the implication made by the rest of the volume, that this is a list of beggars' cant. In fact, it is entirely derived from Kent's word-list, including 1,629 of his 1,639 entries (99.4 per cent) and 1,606 of his 1,610 headwords (99.8 per cent). There are no statistically significant differences between the semantic coverage of *The Sinks of London* and Kent's dictionary. In some respects the dictionary is more thoughtful than Kent's, in that it changes archaic and incorrect spellings:

Kent	*Sinks of London*
Dozing cribb—a sleeping room	Dozing crib, a sleeping room
Grand twig—in prime stile	Grand twig, in prime style
Sling tale and galena—fowl and pickle pork	Sling tale and galena, fowl and pickled pork

---

[17] *Sinks of London laid open: A Pocket Companion for the Uninitiated* (London: J. Duncombe, 1848), title page.
[18] It appears to be the same work as *A Peep into the Holy Land*, published by Duncombe without the dictionary in *c.*1800.

Figure 3.2. Detail from the *Sinks of London Laid Open* (*c*.1890), 95 [Bodleian G.A. Lond. 8°300]

Some of the corrections are mistaken, however:

Kent	*Sinks of London*
Ligating a candle—sneaking out of a public house without paying the reckoning	Lighting a candle, sneaking out of a public house without paying the reckoning
Squeezer—the drop at Newgate	Squeezer, a drop at Newgate

Kent's *ligating a candle* was found in Potter's dictionary over fifty years earlier and there is no reason to think that the spelling is erroneous. By changing *squeezer* "the drop at Newgate" to "a drop at Newgate", the compiler of this dictionary alters the sense from "gallows" to "a hanging" or even "a drink", and demonstrates that he does not always understand his source.

The compiler also rewrites definitions that earlier editors have rendered nonsensical or incorrect. *Captain Hackum* began life as a character in Thomas Shadwell's play, *Squire of Alsatia* (1688). B. E. included the term in his dictionary, defined as "a Fighting, Blustring Bully", and a century later, in Potter's dictionary, it was still listed:

——[CAPTAIN] HACKUM, an impudent blustering fellow, a coward. [Potter]
Captain Hacham—a blustering fellow, a coward. [Andrewes, *Flash Dictionary*]
Captain Flasham—a blustering fellow, a coward [Kent]
Captain Flashman, a blustering fellow, a coward [*Sinks of London*]

The development of *peterees* is indicative of a series of compilers making the best sense they can of what lies before them:

PETEREES, persons who make it their business to steal trunks and boxes from coaches, chaises, and other carriages. [Potter]
Petereess—persons who make it their business to steal boxes from the back of coaches, chaises, or other carriages. [Andrewes]
Peteress—persons who make it their business to steal boxes from the back of coaches, chaises, or other carriages. [*Flash Dictionary*]
Peteress—persons who make it their business to steal boxes from the backs of coaches, chaises, and other carriages [Kent]
Peteresses, persons who make it their business to steal boxes from the backs of coaches, chaises, and other carriages [*Sinks of London*]

The compiler of the *Flash Dictionary*, faced with Andrewes's mis-set <petereess>, deleted an <e> instead of the erroneous <s>. Having made his headword feminine rather than plural, he failed to bring the definition in line. Kent accepted this imbalance, but the compiler of the *Sinks of London* later repluralized the headword to match the definition.

Where Kent inserted commas to indicate that headwords, often those ultimately derived from Potter's dictionary, are to be read in reverse (see Figure 3.1), they are sometimes omitted in this list:

Kent	*Sinks of London*
Gag, high [for *high gag*]—on the whisper, nosing, telling secrets	Gag high, on the whisper, nosing, telling secrets
Kid, with [for *with kid*]—pregnant	Kid with, pregnant

In other headwords, bizarrely, he inserts commas where they are not needed:

Kent	*Sinks of London*
Pockets to let—empty pockets, no money	Pockets, to let, empty pockets, no money
Prate roast—a loquacious fellow	Prate, roast, a loquacious fellow

Some entries become more accurate or more precise:

Kent	*Sinks of London*
Poney—money	Poney, money, £50[19]
Queer plungers—fellows who pretend to be drowned	Queer plungers, fellows who pretended to be drowned[20]

but this dictionary was not well typeset or proofread, and not all changes were for the better:

Kent	*Sinks of London*
Bever—an afternoon's luncheon	Bever, an afternoon's luncneon
Fork it out—to produce any thing by the hand	Forh it out, to produce anything by the hand
Hempen widow—a woman whose husband has been hanged	Hempen widow, a woman husband has been hang'd
Nab the bib—to cry and wipe the eyes	Nob the bib, to cry and wipe the eyes
Siester—a nap after dinner, a short sleep	Sigster, a nap, after dinner, a short sleep

These headwords are alphabetized according to Kent's spelling.

The Bodleian library has a copy of *Sinks of London*, dated in the catalogue to *c*.1890 (see Figure 3.2). I could find no differences between this and the 1848 edition.

Duncombe's New and Improved Flash Dictionary of the Cant Words (*c*.1850)

The Newberry Library Chicago holds this undated edition, listed in the catalogue as having appeared *c*.1820. It cannot, however, have been published before 1835, because it is based on Kent's dictionary.

---

[19] £25 (*OED*).

[20] The Royal Humane Society was established in 1774 to encourage the resuscitation of the apparently drowned. Unscrupulous heroes were thus motivated to throw their accomplices into the Thames for the life-saver's reward. By this period, however, medals had replaced cash payments (http://www.royalhumane.org/history/history.htm).

My reasons for assigning it a rather later date than this are discussed below.

The address 'To the Learned Reader' is self-consciously pompous and inelegant:

In this age, cultivated as it is, in art and science from the Pharo Table to the Scratch Court, and from the Fancy *Noblisse* to the Dover-street ken student; in this improved and evidently improving state of Polished Society, when elegant Literature is sought, pursued, and studied with unremitting avidity, and while the *March of Intellect* is proceeding with such rapid and gigantic strides towards the completion of its laudably energetic desire under the *impetus* of sapient emulation, that, erudition must ultimately and speedily arrive at its utmost summit, acme and apex of perfectitude, it cannot but be submitted that (at the present period of mental thirst) it becomes, and is a desideratum of the last importance for completing the finish of society, that the *Literary World* be furnished with DICKSINEARY dil RUMBO GREEKCUM, or DICTIONARY of the MODERN FLASH-PHRASES, TERMS and WORDS (*whids,*) alphabetically arranged, for the advantage and convenience of the Flash-lingo student.

Having *whidded* thus much in prefatory illustration of our purpose, and the important utility of the plan we herein adopt, it is now only incumbent to add that, our Flash Lexicon, compiled from the best authorities, will be found to contain some hundreds of *whids* never heretofore published.

With this assurance we proceed *sans* let or hindrance to the Lexicographical developement [sic] of the Lingo alluded to.[21]

The dictionary contains 1,251 entries for 1,199 headwords, as opposed to 1,639 entries for 1,610 headwords in the 1,835 edition of Kent's dictionary. Thus this volume is about three-quarters of the size of Kent's. It is not merely a selection of the terms included in the earlier dictionary, however. It uses at least one other glossary, and over 40 per cent of its entries, as promised in the preface, are altogether new to the slang dictionary tradition. More than half of Duncombe's entries are from earlier cant and slang lists, but he uses his sources critically. For example, although 31.4 per cent of Duncombe's entries are from Kent's dictionary (see Appendix, Table 3.1.2), this represents fewer than a quarter of the entries that could have been adopted from Kent.

Numbers and percentages alone do not demonstrate how Duncombe uses his sources, however. Entries from Kent's dictionary include some that are adopted verbatim:

Angling-cove—a receiver of stolen goods
Lap, queer—bad liquor

---

[21] *Duncombe's New and Improved Flash Dictionary of the Cant Words, Queer Sayings, and Crack Terms, now in use in the Politer Circles, and the most accomplished Flash Cribb Society* (London: Edward Duncombe, *c.*1850), iii–iv.

Scamp foot—a street robber
Stifle a squeaker—to murder a child
Yack and onions—watch and seals

and others that are edited, often to shorten them:

Kent	Duncombe
Beak, queer,—a magistrate that is particularly strict to his duty	Beak, queer—a conscientious magistrate
Gaffing—tossing with the pie-man	Gaffing—tossing with pie-men, &c.
Kiddiess—a slap up well-dressed girl	Kidlesses [sic]—flashy prostitutes
Mauns, tip us your—give me your hand	Mauns—to tip us your mauns; shake hands, or give me your hand

Duncombe also used an edition of the Carew glossary published in 1812. He updated spellings in these definitions, and sometimes expanded upon or condensed them:

Carew (1812)[22]	Duncombe
Autumn [for *autem, autum*] church	Autumn—a church
Bambee [for *baubee, bawbee*] halfpenny	Bambee—a halfpenny
Bing to go, . . . Bing we to Rumvilek [for *rumville, romeville*], shall we go to London?	Bing we abs Rumvilk—shall we go to London
Families [for *fambles*] Rings	Fammilies [sic]—rings
Hazel golds [for *hazel-geld*] to beat any one with a hazel stick, or plant	Hazel golds—to beat with a hazel stick
Henfright [for *hen-(pecked) frigate*] those commanders and officers who are absolutely swayed by their wives [not included, but see *bing*]	Henfrights—men governed by their wives
	Rum-vileck—London
Trundles [for *trundlers*] Pease	Trundles—peas

Some entries represent an amalgamation of Duncombe's two sources:

Carew (1812b)	Kent[23]	Duncombe
[omits this, but spells all *autem-* entries <autumn>]	Autem quaver's tub, a quaker's meeting house	Autumn quaver's butt—quaker's meeting house
Barnacles a good job, or a snack easily got; also the irons worn in gaols by felons	Barnacles, spectacles	Barnacles—spectacles; the irons worn by felons; a share of stolen goods easily got

---

[22] *The Surprising Adventures of Bampfylde Moore Carew* (Tiverton: W. Salter, 1812).
[23] Note that although Kent usually has an em dash between headword and definition, there are occasional commas, as shown here.

Facer a bumper without lip room	Facer—a blow on the face; a bumper	Facer—a bumper with hip-room [sic]; also a blow on the face

The only statistically significant changes are that Duncombe adopted more terms for LAW & ORDER from Kent than can be explained by chance ($p = 0.01$), and more for DOMESTIC LIFE than we would expect in a random selection from Carew ($p = 0.05$). He also chose from this list a significantly higher proportion of terms including citations than we would expect in a random selection ($p = 0.01$).

More interesting than Duncombe's use of his sources, however, are his new entries. These include a number linked by the prefix *abb-*, which all refer to punishment of various kinds:

Abb-clouts—prison dress
Abb-discipline—whipping in court-yard, either publicly or privately
Abb-gammonry—a condemned sermon
Abb-tanger—the passing bell at execution
Abb-whack—gaol allowance

Also noteworthy are the slang names for places in London:

Burrowdamp Museum—Newgate
Cobblers' Hall—Hick's-hall Session House
Conjuror's Abbey—Guildhall
Cowboy Castle—the Mansion-house
Culpgill college—Giltspur-street compter
Tower of Babel—the Mansion-house

Unique in the cant and slang dictionary tradition is Duncombe's inclusion of prepositions and conjunctions, one of which also serves as a prefix.

Abs—to, from, gone, at, out
Abs-lushery—at a drinking house
Abs-nunks—gone to the pawn-shop
Abs-smash-rig—out passing bad notes, &c.
Bene abs gybes—counterfeiters or forgers of passes
Ca—used as a Preposition, in
Cab—from, through. They snitched me cab the glaze; they eyed me from or through the window
Cas—as because
Clamn—(used as a Preposition) without, or by

Dabe—to give. (Cant Preposition). Dabe him the double; give him the slip; she
   dabed da cove da double; she gave the fellow the slip
Dil—(Preposition) of; out of, to

Duncombe's provision of grammatical labelling, although not always
accurate, is also novel in the cant and slang dictionary tradition. One
further entry is provided with grammatical labelling:

Krich—(used as the adjective) good

Also unique, at this period, is Duncombe's provision of a system of
counting, described on the title-page as 'the Cracksman's new mode
of counting':

Twibecs—two; one of the ordinarily numbers [sic] in the flash language:—
videlicit—1 Yunibec 2 Twibecs 3 Tribecs 4 Katrambecs 5 Knimtrambecs
6 Hexambecs 7 Septzambecs 8 Octzambecs 9 Nouxambecs 10 Dyams 11
Dy-zunibec 12 Dy-twibecs 13 Dy-tribecs 14 Dy-katrambecs 15 Dy-knintrambecs
16 Dy-hexambecs 17 Dy-septzambecs 18 Dy-octzambecs 19 Dy-nouzambecs 20
Twyams 21 Twy-zunibec 22 Twy-twibecs 23 Twy-tribecs 24 Twy-katrambecs
30 Tryams 31 Try-yunibec 32 Try-twibecs, &c. 40 Katryams 41 Katry-yunibec 50
Knintryams 51 Knintry-yunibec 60 Hexyums 70 Septzyams 80 Octzyams
90 Nouzyams 100 Dyam-dyams 101 Dy-dyam zunibec 102 Dy-dyams twibec 200
Twyams-dyams 201 Twy-dyams zunibec 300 Tryams-dyams 301 Trydyam yunibec
400 Katryams-dyams 401 Katry-dyams yunibec 500 Knintryams-dyams, &c.

These numerals are derived from a mixture of English (*yun*, *twi*),
French (*katra-*, *noux-*), and Latin and Greek (*tri-*, *hex-*, *oct-*, *sept-*).
There is no other evidence of their use.
   In some cases Duncombe's terms had appeared in a less slangy
form in earlier dictionaries. Where these terms were included in
Duncombe's sources, the changes could be his own:

Carew	Duncombe
Cup hot drunk [for *cup-shot*]	Cupsweat—drunk
Kent	
Gin spinner—proprietor of a gin shop	Diddle-spinner—landlord of a gin-shop
Patter slang—to talk flash	Repatter—to repeat: repeat again
Quod—Prison	Quodlings—felons
South sea mountain—gin	South-sea sherry—Geneva
Coriander seed—money	Succory-seed—money

but in other cases, it is possible that he was merely illustrating the natural semantic and morphological developments of slang:

Earlier forms	Duncombe
SPOONY . . . it is usual to call a very prating shallow fellow, a rank spoon [Egan]	Ladle—a numskull, silly fellow
MOON CURSER, a link boy, (cant) link boys are said to curse the moon, because it renders their assistance unnecessary: these gentry frequently under cover of lighting passengers over kennels, or through dark passages, assist in robbing them. [Grose (1785)]	Moon-queerer—a linkboy
RIB, a wife, an allusion to our common mother Eve, made out of Adam's rib. [Grose (1785)]	Ribbery-plague—a termagant wife

The *OED* does not cite this dictionary, and most of the new terms it lists are not included in the *OED* at all. Without a publication date, it is difficult to say that it predates any existing citations. Although it is later than Kent's dictionary (1835), there is no way of dating it any more certainly than that. My feeling is that it postdates the *Sinks of London* (1848), because it is the better list of the two, and it seems unlikely that Duncombe would publish the defective list in preference to it if this were already in existence. Assuming publication in *c.*1850, it antedates five existing *OED* entries:

faddish "whimsical" (1855)
flag "an apron" (1851: n^4 3)
flipper "a whip" (1861: *to flip* 'to strike smartly and lightly (with a whip or the like)')
hush-soap "hush-money" (1860: *soap* 1e 'money; now esp. that used in bribery')
jack at the stiff "a friend in need" (1919: *stiff* A 2g "unlucky"; 1899: *stiff* B 4a "a penniless person")

In addition, *angury-chant* "the death psalm" and *angury clack* "prayers said at an execution", appear to predate the 1880 citation for *right of angary* 'the right of a belligerent to use and destroy, if necessary, the property of neutrals'. The *OED* does not cite *belly-ache* "a querelous complaint" until 1930, or the verb *to bellyache* until 1888, but Duncombe has:

Belly-ache Belfry—a lawyer's mouth. He opened his belly-ache belfry, he began to state the charge, &c.

The *OED*'s first citation for *to bounce* with reference to a cheque that fails to clear is from 1927, but Duncombe has:

Bounce rag—a forged check

The first *OED* citation for *sugar* "money" is from 1862. Duncombe has:

Brown sugar—counsel fees

For *cave*, an interjection meaning "look out; beware", the *OED*'s first citation is from 1868. Duncombe has:

Cavey—to know, to understand, to be acquainted with; I'm cavey to the smezzle; I know or am in the secret

Summary

Potter's dictionary has a dishonest bibliography and a dubious biography. Over 80 per cent of its word-list is derived from earlier slang dictionaries, some up to fifty years old. From these, he selected terms labelled as 'cant' and those dealing with crime and punishment. Terms listed in both *The New Canting Dictionary* and the second edition of Grose's dictionary also had a good chance of selection. Potter deleted citations, authorities, and etymologies found in his sources. He thus produced a more concise dictionary. However, some of his efficiencies led to ambiguities that left a characteristic signature on all later dictionaries derived from his. Although some of his additions appear to be fabricated from the raw material found in his sources, Potter does have some new entries that seem to represent contemporary cant, or at least slang.

Andrewes's dictionary is largely derived from Potter's. It reproduces his mistakes, and introduces a few of its own. However, addenda from the Carew list ensure that Andrewes does produce a distinctive dictionary. He replaces offensive terms by euphemisms, and deletes most of the sex terms that do not relate to prostitution. He tends to abbreviate Potter's definitions, especially by deleting cross-references, but occasionally adds new material.

The tiny *Flash Dictionary* is largely derived from Andrewes's and Potter's. It edits the material that it takes from them, and appears to have reference to other sources including Grose's dictionary. Its new entries, few as they are, predate a handful of *OED* first citations, which suggests that, where he did add entries, the compiler was representing contemporary cant and slang usage.

The compiler of the *Modern Flash Dictionary* used several sources, including the *Flash Dictionary*, Egan's edition of Grose, and possibly a version of the *Tom and Jerry* glossary. His definitions are normally briefer than those of his sources. Just over a fifth of his entries cannot be traced to an earlier dictionary, and among those are a reasonable number that predate *OED* first citations, indicating that Kent was probably representing contemporary speech as well as his written sources. He seems unusually unaffected by the obscenity of his word-list.

The Sinks of London contains no new terms. The compiler of this glossary adopted his entire word-list from Kent's. A small proportion of entries are omitted, probably by chance. He updated the spellings of his source and tried to make sense of the corrupt text before him, not always successfully. The list adds nothing other than its errors to the cant and slang dictionary tradition.

Unlike most of the other dictionaries in this group, *Duncombe's New and Improved Flash Dictionary* did make significant additions to the material from its sources. Although it is only three-quarters of the size of Kent's dictionary, over two-fifths of its entries were entirely new. Unfortunately for the compiler, he was using two rather corrupt sources, and he thus reproduced errors introduced by earlier lexicographers and printers. The additional terms include prepositions and conjunctions as well as numerals, and the dictionary appears to show how terms listed in earlier dictionaries had developed through continued slang use.

The Potter-group dictionaries have little to offer, on the whole. They are characterized by careless copying rather than original lexicography. Most add a few new entries to those they take from their sources. They testify to the continuing existence of a market for slang and cant dictionaries among those who could not afford Grose's more extensive (and more expensive) work.

4 James Hardy Vaux

Transportation to America ended with the War of Independence. Despite questions raised about the efficacy of transportation as both punishment and deterrent, by this time the alternatives seemed worse. The hulks, instituted in 1776, were intended as a temporary solution. These ships, moored on the Thames and used as prisons for those sentenced to hard labour, were first brought into disrepute by an inquiry of 1778. By the end of the following year, more than 500 hardened criminals had escaped. Rioting on the hulks was commonplace, mortality rates were unacceptably high, and hard labour proved to be more expensive and less productive than anticipated. Despite these problems, the system was extended to the rest of the country, and continued in use for over a century. Australia provided a possibility for the resumption of transportation, which no longer seemed so bad now that the alternatives had been explored. The first convicts arrived in Botany Bay in 1788, and at least 160,000 English and Irish convicts were sent to Australia before transportation eventually stopped in 1852.

More English cant terms are found in Australian than American English, presumably because convicts made up a larger proportion of the immigrant population, which was also less racially mixed than the population of America. Terms listed in British cant and slang dictionaries and now used mainly in Australia include *bolter* "a fugitive", *cove* "a man", *dunny* (and variants) "a toilet", *to plant* "to conceal", *prad* "a horse", *to shake* "to steal; to rob", *Sheila* "a girl", *shicer* "a worthless person", *to snavel* "to steal; to snatch", *to speel* "to make off", *spieler* "a gambler", and *trap* "a police officer" (*OED*). The techniques of rhyming slang, used for humour as much as concealment, were also adopted, and a separate body of Australian rhyming slang developed.[1]

The Memoirs of James Hardy Vaux (1819)

Among the thousands of convicts transported to Australia was one who wrote an autobiography.

It has been thought that the Public would benefit in more ways than one, by the publication of a work, in which the philosopher may read the workings of an

---

[1] Julian Franklin, *A Dictionary of Rhyming Slang* (London: Routledge & Kegan Paul, 1961), 16–21.

unprincipled conscience, the legislator to be let into the operations of the law upon the criminal's mind, and the citizen derive a key to the frauds by which he is so easily and constantly beset; and it is not often that thieves are possessed of sufficient truth, memory, vanity, and literature, to tell the story of their own lives.[2]

The 'Advertisement' cautions the reader against believing too much in Vaux's honesty:

As for the truth of the following tale—nobody can vouch for it . . . The reader must, therefore, believe as much or as little as he pleases of the following story. Of him who confesses himself a liar, the voice must necessarily be listened to with distrust.[3]

According to this work, which follows many of the conventions of criminal autobiography, James Hardy Vaux was born in East Clandon in 1782, the son of a butler. His parents and grandparents spoilt him, and after his apprenticeship to a linen-draper he took to gambling in the cockpits. He scraped a living as a hack-writer for a time, then fell in love with a prostitute and turned to robbery and fraud. Eventually he was transported, but his appointment as storekeeper's clerk allowed him to continue exercising his talent for fraud. Despite this, the remainder of his sentence was remitted when he returned to England with the Governor of his penal colony. He resolved to live a good life, but fell in with former acquaintances and was fortunate to have his subsequent execution commuted first to hard labour on the hulks and then to transportation. A further resolution to lead an honest life failed, and the autobiography closes with yet another declaration of good intentions.[4] At the end of the *Memoirs* is a letter, dedicated to Thomas Skottowe, a Justice of the Peace in New South Wales:

With the utmost deference and respect, I beg leave to submit to your perusal the following sheets. The idea of such a composition first originated in the suggestion of a friend; and however the theme may be condemned as exceptionable by narrow minds, I feel confident you possess too much liberality of sentiment to reject its writer as utterly depraved, because he has acquired an extensive knowledge on a subject so obviously disgraceful. True it is, that in the course of a chequered and eventful life, I have intermixed with the most dissolute and unprincipled characters, and that a natural quickness of conception, and most retentive memory, have rendered me familiar with their language and system of operations.

---

[2] James Hardy Vaux, *Memoirs of James Hardy Vaux. Written by Himself*. . . (London: W. Clowes, 1819), xi.

[3] Vaux, *Memoirs*, xi, xii–xiii.

[4] Published accounts of Vaux's life are heavily dependent on the *Memoirs*. However, there is independent evidence of his existence, which confirms some of the details of the autobiography, including his repeated transportation to Australia.

Permit me, Sir, to assure you most seriously, that I view with remorse the retrospect of my hitherto misspent life, and that my future exertions shall be solely directed to acquire the estimable good opinion of the virtuous part of the community.

I trust the Vocabulary will afford you some amusement from its novelty; and that from the correctness of its definitions, you may occasionally find it useful in your magisterial capacity.

I cannot omit this opportunity of expressing my gratitude for the very humane and equitable treatment I have experienced, in common with every other person in this settlement,* under your temperate and judicious government.

*The author (a prisoner under sentence of transportation for life) having, by an alleged act of impropriety, incurred the Governor's displeasure, was at this period banished to Newcastle, a place of punishment for offenders: these sheets were there compiled during his solitary hours of cessation from hard labour; and the Commandment was accordingly presented by the Author with the first copy of his production.[5]

The dedicatory letter is dated 1812, which is the date that the *OED* adopts for Vaux's glossary. Its role in the cant and slang dictionary tradition began upon its publication in 1819, however, which is the date that I have used here. I also believe it to be closer to the date of composition. The Newcastle penal settlement was 'a place of secondary punishment', where life was even harder than elsewhere in the colony.[6] I find it hard to believe that a convict would have had the leisure and facilities to write an autobiography and compile a lengthy glossary under these harsh and punitive conditions. No matter what the circumstances of its compilation, it was 'probably the first dictionary compiled in Australia [and] gives a valuable glossary of London slang'.[7]

The word-list contains 332 entries for 303 headwords. Eighty-eight entries (26.5 per cent) are for words also found in the *Lexicon Balatronicum*, and forty (12.0 per cent) for words also found in Potter's dictionary (see Chapters 2 and 3). Twenty-eight of these entries are in both, so the two dictionaries combined overlap with 100 of Vaux's entries (30.1 per cent). As we have already seen, lexicographers are not always scrupulously honest where their commercial interests and integrity collide, so it is necessary to account for this overlap and to subject Vaux's account of the compilation of his glossary to critical scrutiny.

[5] Vaux, *Memoirs*, 151–2.
[6] Robert Hughes, *The Fatal Shore. A History of the Transportation of Convicts to Australia, 1787–1868* (London: Collins Harvill, 1987), 437.
[7] *Australian Dictionary of Biography*, ed. A. G. L. Shaw and C. M. H. Clark (London & New York: Cambridge University Press/Melbourne: Melbourne University Press, 1967), 552.

Let us begin with entries that support the idea that Vaux may have used Potter's dictionary and the *Lexicon* in the compilation of his own:

Potter (1797)	Vaux
CLY, a pocket.	CLY, a pocket.
NIX, OR NIX MY DOLL, nothing.	NIX, OR NIX MY DOLL, nothing.
RATTLER, a coach.	RATTLER, a coach.

Lexicon Balatronicum	
DARKEE. A dark lanthorn used by housebreakers . . .	DARKY, a dark lanthorn.
FAMMS, OR FAMBLES. Hands; (cant) famble cheats, rings or gloves.	FAM, the hand.
SPANGLE. A seven shilling piece.	SPANGLE, a seven-shilling piece.
SPREAD. Butter.	SPREAD, butter.
STICKS. Household furniture.	STICKS, household furniture.

None of this provides compelling evidence of any direct debt to either dictionary. Such brief definitions could easily have been reached independently. More interesting are entries engaging with cant terms and senses that Vaux marks as obsolete and which, therefore, he could only have known through written sources:

Potter (1797)	Vaux
BARKING IRONS, pistols.	BARKING-IRONS, pistols; an obsolete term.

Lexicon Balatronicum	
FILE, FILE CLOY OR BUNGNIPPER. A pick pocket . . .	FILE . . . *File*, in the old version of cant, signified a pickpocket, but the term is now obsolete.
STAG. To turn *stag*; to impeach one's confederates: from a herd of deer, who are said to turn their horns against any of their number who is hunted.	STAG, to *turn stag* was formerly synonymous with *turning nose*, or *snitching*, but the phrase is now exploded.

It is much more common, however, that entries in Vaux's dictionary bear little resemblance to those in Potter's or the *Lexicon*, despite their co-occurrence:

Potter (1797)	Vaux
RUSH, a number of persons rushing into a house together to rob it.	RUSH, *the rush*, is nearly synonymous with *the ramp*; but the latter often applies to snatching at a single article, as a silk cloak, for instance,

from a milliner's shop-door; whereas *a rush* may signify a forcible entry by several men into a detached dwelling-house for the purpose of robbing its owners of their money, *&c.* A sudden and violent effort to get into any place, or *vice versâ* to effect your exit, as from a place of confinement, *&c.,* is called *rushing them,* or *giving it to 'em upon the rush.*

Lexicon Balatronicum

AWAKE. Acquainted with, knowing the business. Stow the books, the culls are awake; hide the cards, the fellows know what we intended to do.

AWAKE, an expression used on many occasions; as a thief will say to his accomplice, on perceiving the person they are about to rob is aware of their intention, and upon his guard, *stow it,* the *cove's awake.* To be awake to any scheme, deception, or design, means, generally, to see through or comprehend it.

DUMMEE . . . A dummee hunter. A pick-pocket, who lurks about to steal pocket books out of gentlemen's pockets.

DUMMY-HUNTERS, thieves who confine themselves to the practice of stealing gentlemen's pocket-books, and think, or profess to think, it paltry to touch a *clout,* or other insignificant article; this class of depredators traverse the principal streets of London, during the busy hours, and sometimes meet with valuable prizes.

Even if Vaux did use earlier dictionaries as his sources, he clearly had much to add to them, presumably from his own experience.

Vaux included none of the etymologies or cited authorities found in Potter's dictionary or the *Lexicon.* In fact, only one authority is named in the whole of Vaux's dictionary, but it is an anecdotal, rather than a bibliographical reference:

LIFE, by this term is meant the various cheats and deceptions practised by the designing part of mankind; a person well versed in this kind of knowledge, is said to be one that knows *life;* in other words, that knows the world. This is what Goldsmith defines to be a knowledge of human nature on the wrong side.

Thus we have no concrete evidence that Vaux did use any earlier dictionaries in the compilation of his own. If Vaux had listed the shared terms independently, we would expect there to be no statistically significant differences between previously recorded and unrecorded terms. However, entries for previously unrecorded terms include significantly more cross-references, but fewer citations (both $p = 0.01$) than we can account for by chance (see Appendix, Table 4.3),[8] and deal disproportionately with GEOGRAPHY & TRAVEL ($p = 0.01$; see Appendix, Table 4.1).

It is possible to explain these differences. Given what we know of Vaux's life, we would expect him to be well-versed in travel terms. The increased rate of cross-reference among the previously unrecorded terms might indicate that Vaux appreciated that some of the terms he recorded would be less widely known than others. General slang terms, as recorded in Potter's dictionary and the *Lexicon*, would have been known to many, while cant terms would have been less familiar. Thus Vaux expended greater energy on explaining the shades of meaning of canting terms.

Given that there is no strong evidence to disprove it, we can accept Vaux's claim that his dictionary is a genuine and original record of contemporary cant and slang. The overlap with Potter's dictionary and the *Lexicon* identifies the terms among their contents that were still valid by the time Vaux compiled his glossary.

In comparison with the *Lexicon* and with Potter's dictionary, Vaux provides many more terms with citations (both $p = 0.01$). Thus his dictionary is considerably more lively than concise. This is not the only function that his citations serve, however. They indicate finer shades of meaning than the definition always can, for example *to bug* appears to be restricted to reference to money, while *dues* is used with reference to punishment:

BUG, or BUG OVER. To give, deliver, or hand over; as, *He bug'd me a quid*, he gave me a guinea; *bug over the rag*, hand over the money.

DUES. This word is often introduced by the lovers of *flash* on many occasions, but merely *out of fancy*, and can only be understood from the context of their discourse; like many other cant terms, it is not easily explained on paper: for example, speaking of a man likely to go to jail, one will say, there will be *quodding dues concerned*, of a man likely to be executed; there will be *topping dues*, if any thing is alluded to that will require a fee or bribe, there must be *tipping dues*, or *palming dues* concerned, *&c.*

---

[8] Vaux notes (149 n.) that cant terms in his citations are italicized, and that readers can look them up elsewhere in the glossary if necessary. Most entries contain these implicit cross-references, which I have not counted.

Citations can also make an apparently general term seem more specifically criminal:

BUSTLE, any object effected very suddenly, or in a hurry, is said to be *done upon the bustle*. To *give it to* a man *upon the bustle*, is to obtain any point, as borrowing money, *&c.*, by some sudden story or pretence, and affecting great haste, so that he is taken by surprise, and becomes duped before he has time to consider of the matter.

CAZ, cheese; *As good as caz*, is a phrase signifying that any projected fraud or robbery may be easily and certainly accomplished; any person who is the object of such attempt, and is known to be an easy dupe, is declared to be *as good as caz*, meaning that success is certain.

MOVE, any action or operation in life; the secret spring by which any project is conducted, as, There is *move* in that business which you are not *down to*. To be *flash to every move upon the board*, is to have a general knowledge of the world, and all its numerous deceptions.

Citations also indicate grammatical and syntactical information. *Jogue* and *stretch*, for example, are both unchanged in the plural, *ridge* can be either adjective or noun, while *kick* is used only in the construction specified:

JOGUE, a shilling; *five jogue* is five shillings, and so on, to any other number.

KICK, a sixpence, when speaking of compound sums only, as, *three and a kick*, is three and sixpence, *&c.*

RIDGE, gold, whether in coin or any other shape, as a *ridge-montra*, a gold watch; a *cly*-full of *ridge*, a pocket full of gold.

STRETCH. Five or ten *stretch*, signifies five or ten yards, *&c.*; so in dealing for any article, as linen, *&c.*, I will give you *three hog* a *stretch*, means, I'll give three shillings a yard. *See* HOG.

Occasionally citations are used to explore the shades of meaning between apparently synonymous terms:

SUIT, in general synonymous with *game*; as, what *suit* did you *give it to 'em upon?* in what manner did you rob them, or upon what pretence, *&c.*, did you defraud them? One species of imposition is said to be *a prime suit*, another *a queer suit*: a man describing the pretext he used to obtain money from another, would say, *I draw'd him of a quid upon the suit of* so and so, naming the ground of his application. *See* DRAW. A person having engaged with another on very advantageous terms to serve or work for him, will declare that he is *upon a good suit*. To use great submission and respect in asking any favour of another, is called *giving it to him upon the humble suit*.

An unusual feature of Vaux's citations is that they are often attributed to a category of people (e.g. 'the knucks') or to an individual representing such a category (e.g. 'a thief', 'a rogue', 'a family man'):

SHAKE, to steal, or rob . . . A thief, whose *pall* has been into any place for the purpose of robbery, will say on his coming out, Well, it is all right, have you *shook*? meaning, did you succeed in getting any thing? . . .

SPICE, *the spice* is the *game* of footpad robbery; describing an exploit of this nature; a rogue will say, I *spiced* a *swell of* so much, naming the booty obtained . . .

SPOKE TO, alluding to any person or place that has been already robbed, they say, that place, or person, has been *spoke to* before. A *family man* on discovering that he has been robbed, will exclaim, I have been *spoke to*; and perhaps will add, *for* such a thing, naming what he has lost . . .

UNSLOUR, to unlock, unfasten, or unbutton. *See* SLOUR. Speaking of a person whose coat is buttoned, so as to obstruct the access to his pockets, the *knucks* will say to each other, *the cove* is *slour'd up*, we must *unslour him* to get at his *kickseys*.

Unattributed citations are also common:

SNOOZE . . . a *snooze* sometimes means a lodging; as, Where can I get a *snooze* for this *darky* instead of saying a bed.

SPEAK, committing any robbery, is called *making a speak*; and if it has been productive, you are said to have *made a rum speak*.

STING, to rob or defraud a person or place is called *stinging* them, as, that *cove* is too *fly*; he has been *stung* before; meaning that man is upon his guard; he has already been trick'd.

TOOLS, implements for house-breaking, picklocks, pistols, &c., are indiscriminately called *the tools*. A thief, convicted on the police act, of having illegal instruments or weapons about him, is said to be *fined for the tools*.

The extensive use of the second person pronoun is also characteristic of Vaux's dictionary (see the entries for *rush* and *stretch* cited above). This not only emphasizes Vaux's familiar knowledge of the language he is recording, it also implicates the reader in some of the activities described.

Another striking feature of Vaux's dictionary is his extensive use of cross-references (see Appendix, Table 4.3). He uses them, often reciprocally, to show semantic relationships between terms, whether synonymy, near-synonymy, or antonymy:

CROSS-CRIB, a house inhabited, or kept by *family people*. *See* SQUARE CRIB.

SQUARE-CRIB, a respectable house, of good repute, whose inmates, their mode of life and connexions, are all perfectly *on the square*. *See* CROSS-CRIB.

KNUCKLE, to pick pockets, but chiefly applied to the more refined branch of that art, namely, extracting notes, loose cash, &c., from the waistcoat or breeches pocket, whereas *buzzing* is used in a more general sense. *See* BUZ.

BUZ, to *buz* a person is to pick his pocket. *The buz* is the *game* of picking pockets in general.

In other cases, phrases are entered under each of their constituent words and cross-referenced back to a single headword instead of repeating the definition unnecessarily:

CUE, *See* Letter Q.
Q, *See* LETTER Q.
LETTER Q, the *mace*, or *billiard-slum*, is sometimes called *going upon the Q*, or *the letter Q*, alluding to an instrument used in playing billiards.

WEAR THE BANDS, *See* BANDS.
BANDS. *To wear the bands*, is to be hungry, or short of food for any length of time; a phrase chiefly used on board the hulks, or in jails.

WALKING-DISTILLER. *See* CARRY THE KEG.
CARRY THE KEG, a man who is easily vexed or put out of humour by any joke passed upon him, and cannot conceal his chagrin, is said to *carry the keg*, or is compared to a *walking distiller*.

Occasionally the reader who follows cross-references will be sent on a tour around the dictionary. For example:

CONCERNED. In using many cant words, the lovers of *flash*, by way of variation, adopt this term, for an illustration of which, *see* BOLT-IN-TUN, ALDERMAN LUSHINGTON, MR. PARMER, *&c.*
ALDERMAN LUSHINGTON. *See* LUSH.
LUSH, to drink; speaking of a person who is drunk, they say, *Alderman Lushington is concerned*, or, he has been *voting for the Alderman*.

Some definitions make little sense without the information contained in the cross-referenced entry:

BILLIARD SLUM. The *mace* is sometimes called *giving it to 'em on the billiard slum*. *See* MACE.
MACE, to *mace* a shopkeeper, or *give* it to him *upon the mace*, is to obtain goods on credit, which you never mean to pay for; to run up a score with the same intention, or to spunge upon your acquaintance, by continually begging or borrowing from them, is termed *maceing*, or *striking the mace*.

while others seem to be included merely to provide another example of the headword in use:

STASH. To *stash* any practice, habit, or proceeding, signifies to put an end to, relinquish, or quash the same; thus, a thief determined to leave off his vicious courses will declare that he means to *stash* (or *stow*) *prigging*. A man in custody for felony, will endeavour, by offering money, or other means, to induce his prosecutor's forbearance, and compromise the matter, so as to obtain his liberation; this is called *stashing the business*. To *stash* drinking, card-playing, or any other employment you may be engaged in, for the time present, signifies to *stow* it, *knife* it, *cheese* it, or *cut* it, which are all synonymous, that is, to desist or leave off. See WANTED.

STINK. When any robbery of moment has been committed, which causes much alarm, or of which much is said in the daily papers, the *family people* will say, there is a great *stink* about it. See WANTED.

WANTED, when any of the *traps* or runners have a private information against a *family person*, and are using means to apprehend the party, they say, such a one is *wanted*; and it becomes the latter, on receiving such intimation to keep *out of the way*, until the *stink* is over, or until he or she can find means to *stash the business* through the medium of *Mr. Palmer*, or by some other means.

In one case, a cross-reference is for additional contextual flavour rather than linguistic information:

YARN, *yarning* or *spinning a yarn*, is a favourite amusement among *flash-people*; signifying to relate their various adventures, exploits, and escapes to each other. This is most common and gratifying, among persons in confinement or exile, to enliven a dull hour, and probably excite a secret hope of one day enjoying a repetition of their former pleasures. *See* BONED . . .

BONED, taken in custody; apprehended; Tell us how you was *boned*, signifies, tell us the story of your apprehension; a common request among fellow-prisoners in a jail, &c., which is readily complied with in general; and the various circumstances therein related afford present amusement, and also useful hints for regulating their future operations, so as to avoid the like misfortune.

This extensive and careful use of cross-references indicates that Vaux knew the material in his dictionary extremely well. It also demonstrates that a great deal of conscientious effort went into constructing and checking the word-list. Unlike some of the earlier rogues who appended glossaries to their autobiographies, Vaux is no accidental lexicographer dashing off a haphazard selection of entries from earlier sources.

The *OED* makes good use of Vaux's dictionary and memoirs, citing them 428 times. The dictionary is often given credit for terms also found in the *Lexicon*. It provides the only citation for fifty-seven entries, and the first citation for another 133 entries. This confirms that Vaux was listing genuine examples of contemporary slang and cant.

Notwithstanding the *OED*'s full use of Vaux's dictionary, a further fourteen entries predate existing first citations. The most striking of these is the first citation for *tool*, which Vaux antedates by over a century:

black diamonds "coal" (1849)
bloody jemmy "a sheep's head" (1836: *jemmy*)
to draw "to extract information from" (1857)
good for "able to pay (a stated amount)" (1865)
grunter "a policeman" (1823)
lushington [referring to drink] (1823)
to nob "to live without labour" (1851: "to collect (money)")
stall "a pretext for a crime" (1851)
string "a trick" (1851)
tool "a weapon" (1938)
trick "a robbery" (1865)
upper tog "an overcoat" (1830 *tog* n^1 2b)
wanted "sought by the police" (1903)
to work "to deal with; to hawk" [12 j] (1839)

Canting Literature: W. Harrison Ainsworth's *Rookwood* (1834)

Harrison Ainsworth's *Rookwood* is the tale of a fortune reclaimed and lost again by Luke Rookwood, the abandoned son of a deservedly cursed family. This plot is intertwined with the story of Dick Turpin, climaxing in his legendary ride to York. Luke's Gypsy friends and their associates are the main users of cant terms in the novel. In this extract, the Gypsies admire Dick Turpin. The explanatory footnotes are Ainsworth's own:

'I believe ye' returned the Ruffler; stroking his chin,—'one may see that he's no half swell, by the care with which he cultivates the best gifts of nature, his whiskers. He's a rank nib.[†]

'Togged out to the ruffian, no doubt,' said the Palliard, who was incomparably the shabbiest rascal in the corps. 'Though a needy mizzler myself, I likes to see a cove vot's vel dressed. Jist twig his swell kickseys and pipes;[*] if they ain't the thing, I'm done. . . .'[9]

[†] A real gentleman.
[*] Breeches and boots.

Ainsworth cites both Vaux (IV,1) and Grose (III,5), and appears to have used both dictionaries in the construction of his novel. In this

[9] W. Harrison Ainsworth, *Rookwood: A Romance in Three Volumes* (London: Richard Bentley, 1834), Bk III, ch.5, 319–20.

extract, *half-swell* (under **nib**), *needy mizzler*, *nib*, and *to tog* are in Vaux's word-list, and thence in Egan's; *to the ruffian* and *pipes* only in Vaux's; *palliard*, *ruffler*, and *to twig* are in all editions of Grose's dictionary, but not in Vaux's; *kickseys* is in the *Lexicon*, Vaux, and Egan. *Cove* is in all of these lists. Ainsworth must have used Vaux's list and either the *Lexicon* or Egan's edition of Grose. There is no way to determine which of these editions he used, but since Ainsworth cited Grose by name, Egan's edition is the more likely source. Because Egan did not always label terms as obsolete, Ainsworth mingled sixteenth-century cant, originally from Harman, with nineteenth-century London flash in his surprisingly popular depiction of the eighteenth-century rural underworld.

Averil Fink's selection from Vaux (1962)

In a paper entitled 'James Hardy Vaux, Convict and Fatalist', Averil Fink gave an account of Vaux's life, concluding that if he had not come from a broken home, he might not have turned to crime.[10] She includes a brief glossary of 'some flash language', but provided no explanation of her selection process.

The glossary contains forty-five entries for forty headwords, each representing 5.6 per cent of Vaux's total. In its selection of terms including citations, etymologies, cross-references, and usage labels, and in its coverage of subject matter, it is entirely in keeping with a random selection from Vaux's glossary (see Appendix, Tables 4.1–4.3).

Fink tends to select only the definition from lengthy entries. For instance, from Vaux's entry for *to bounce*:

BOUNCE, to bully, threaten, talk loud, or affect great consequence; to *bounce* a person out of any thing, is to use threatening or high words, in order to intimidate him, and attain the object you are intent upon; or to obtain goods of a tradesman, by assuming the appearance of great respectability and importance, so as to remove any suspicion he might at first entertain. A thief, detected in the commission of a robbery, has been known by this sort of finesse, aided by a genteel appearance and polite manners, to persuade his accusers of his innocence, and not only to get off with a good grace, but induce them to apologize for their supposed mistake, and the affront put upon him. This masterful stroke of effrontery is called *giving it to 'em upon the bounce*.

[10] In *The Royal Australian Historical Society Journal and Proceedings*, December 1962, 48.321–43.

Fink extracts only:

bounce—to bully, threaten, talk loud or affect great consequence.

In a few entries Fink makes other minor changes, usually to make the definition more concise. For example:

Vaux	Fink
BLUE-PIGEON FLYING, the practice of stealing lead from houses, churches, or other buildings, very prevalent in London and its vicinity.	*blue-pigeon flying*—the practice of stealing lead from buildings, very prevalent in and around London.
CAT AND KITTEN RIG, the petty game of stealing pewter quart and pint pots from public-houses.	*cat and kitten rig*—stealing quart and pint pots from public houses
GAMS, the legs, to have queer gams, is to be bandy-legged, or otherwise deformed.	*gams*—the legs; to have 'queer gams' is to be bandy.

Canting Literature: Bernard Cornwall's *Gallows Thief* (2001)

Cornwall, best known for his Sharpe novels and their television adaptations, also wrote this tale of an honourable and naive ex-soldier, called Sandman, who turns private detective out of a desperate need for cash. He is set the task of investigating the murder of a countess, and discovers corruption at all levels of early nineteenth-century London society. The novel is full of authentic incidental detail, and Cornwall notes his debt to Vaux's glossary for the cant found throughout the text:[11]

Flash was the slang name for London's criminal life and the label attached to its language. No one stole a purse, they filed a bit or boned the cole or clicked the ready bag. Prison was a sheep walk or the quod, Newgate was the King's Head Inn and its turnkeys were gaggers. A good man was flash scamp and his victim a mum scull. (78)

Cornwall's use of cant is interesting in two main respects. First, he uses a variety of techniques for ensuring that the unfamiliar vocabulary is not off-putting to his readers. Sometimes one character, usually Sandman, will ask another for explanation:

'Are you carrying a stick, sir?'
'A stick?'
'A pistol, sir . . .' (50)

---

[11] Bernard Cornwall, *Gallows Thief* (London: HarperCollins, 2002), 405.

Sometimes there is no explicit request for a translation:

'What are you napping your bib for? Sally demanded, and Meg, uncomprehending, just stared at her. 'Why are you bleeding crying?' Sally translated. (322)

There are also a few cases where the translation is provided by the narrator, and not through dialogue, indicating that Sandman is beginning to understand for himself:

'There are some coves to see you in the back slum, Captain,' he said, meaning that there were some men waiting for Sandman in the back parlour. (197)

Occasionally the context alone is enough:

'How do you know what kind of a soldier I was, Sergeant?'
'I know exactly what sort of swoddy you was,' Berrigan said. (151)

Several terms are revealed to Sandman's friend, Lord Alexander, who is happy to buy drinks in exchange for disreputable vocabulary. For example:

The Reverend Lord had taken notes, delighted to discover that the lower rank of cly-faker was the clouter, a child who snitched handkerchiefs, while the lords of the buzzing trade were the thimble-coves who stole watches. (208)

The second interesting feature of Cornwall's use of cant is that he does so creatively. An example of this is *fake away*, which Vaux defines:

FAKE AWAY, THERE'S NO DOWN, an intimation from a thief to his *pall*, during the commission of a robbery, or other act, meaning, go on with your operations, there is no sign of any alarm or detection.

but which Cornwall invariably uses as an obscene request to leave. For example:

'Now, on your trotters and fake away off!' (33–4)

Cornwall also creates new compounds from the vocabulary found in Vaux's glossary. For instance, Vaux lists *crap* "the gallows", and *prig* "a thief":

'And what will you do, Mister Hood,' he asked, 'when they catch you?'
'. . . When I'm caught?' Hood asked. 'I'll come to you for help, Captain. Sally says you're a crap prig.'
'A gallows thief.' Sandman had learnt enough flash to be able to translate the phrase. (195)

Cornwall's choice of *Gallows Thief* as his title, rather than *Crap Prig*, is entirely understandable.

Summary

Despite Vaux's doubtful reliability as an author, his glossary appears to be a genuine record of the language used by English felons at the beginning of the nineteenth century. He gives us no indication of how he collected the word-list, leaving us to surmise that he used his own experiences of crime and its consequences to document contemporary cant. This lively and informative word-list demonstrates the transportation of English slang and cant across the world and confirms the continued currency of many terms found in the *Lexicon* and Potter's dictionary. Fink used it reasonably impartially to illustrate her article on Vaux's life, and Cornwall used it creatively to bring to life his fictional account of the seedier and shadier side of life in London. Ainsworth's use of cant was considerably less convincing.

5 Pierce Egan

Flash Literature: Pierce Egan's *Life in London* (1821)

Neither the date nor the place of Pierce Egan's birth is certain. It is known that he was apprenticed to a printer in London in 1786, and later worked as a compositor, proofreader, and probably also a hack-writer. He travelled around the country to report on sporting events, and by 1812 was well-known as a sporting writer. He began publishing the boxing journal *Boxiana* in 1818, and continued to issue it until 1824, thus establishing his authority as 'the most popular and successful of all the sporting journalists in an age when noblemen and dustmen alike shared a passion for sport':[1]

> having seen that Londoners read with avidity his accounts of country sports and pastimes, he conceived the idea of a similar description of the amusements pursued by sporting men in town. Accordingly he announced the publication of 'Life in London' in shilling numbers, monthly, and secured the aid of George Cruikshank and his brother, Isaac Robert Cruikshank, to draw and engrave the illustrations in aquatint to be coloured by hand.[2]

Life in London describes Jerry Hawthorn's introduction to the excesses of the capital by his cousin Corinthian Tom, a fashionable man about town, helped by Tom's friend, Bob Logic, and mistress, Kate (see Figure 5.1). Although there were no complaints about its immorality from those who adored the work, Egan produced a conclusion to the adventures of Tom and Jerry in 1828, which saw:

> Tom breaking his neck while hunting, his mistress Kate dying of drink, Logic succumbing to his excesses, and Jerry settling down to a quiet life in the country.[3]

Life in London is a leisurely and digressive work, that claims a place in the tradition of Sterne, Smollett, Fielding, Goldsmith, and Sheridan, but whose literary merits do not deserve such company. The Cruikshanks both claimed credit for initiating the work, and it is

---

[1] Pierce Egan, *Boxiana; or, Sketches of Antient and Modern Pugilism* (London: G. Smeeton, 1818–1824). J. C. Reid, *Bucks and Bruisers. Pierce Egan and Regency England* (London: Routledge & Kegan Paul, 1971) and *DNB*, xxvii.142–4, are my sources for biographical information about Egan. The quotation is from Reid, *Bucks and Bruisers*, 1.   [2] *DNB*, xvii.142.   [3] Ousby, *Cambridge Guide*, 557.

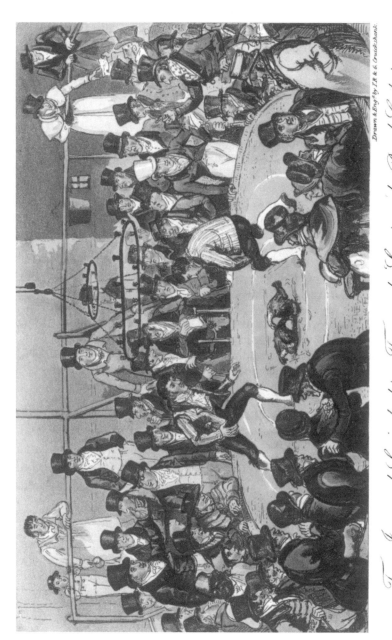

Figure 5.1. A Cock-fight (George Cruikshank), from Pierce Egan's *Life in London* (1821), 318 [BL C.59.f.23]

certainly true that the text is largely structured around the engravings. The narrative is episodic and the characters undeveloped. For example, while he was writing Book II, Egan was obviously busy with something else, because in chapter four there is a fourteen page account of the furnishings and art work of Carlton Palace, worthy of a guidebook. Egan claimed that his pocketbook, containing notes for chapter five, was stolen after a night of debauchery with Bob Logic:

In consequence of BOB LOGIC's *Daffy*, only one sheet of Letter Press accompanies the Plates of No. 5; but to make up for this unavoidable deficiency, THREE SHEETS of Letter Press will be given in No.6.[4]

Despite its many flaws, *Life in London* was such a success that each issue was produced in greater numbers than the last, and the colourists had trouble keeping up with the rate of publication. Imitated and pirated versions of both the text and the illustrations soon appeared, along with tea-trays, snuff-boxes, and handkerchiefs. At least four dramatic versions were produced in 1821 alone, one written by Egan himself. A contemporary theatre-goer commented that it was:

beyond every thing vulgar I eversaw . . . the people were hollowing & talking to each other from the pit to the gallery, & fighting & throwing oranges at each other . . . it is impossible to describe the sort of enthusiasm with which [the play] was received by the people who seemed to enjoy a representation of scenes, in which, from their appearance, one might infer they frequently shared.[5]

One of the work's most popular features was its inclusion of contemporary metropolitan slang terms, which caught on throughout the country at all levels of society. Egan was presented at court and allowed to dedicate the work to George IV when it was reissued in book form:

. . . I am further emboldened by the numerous opportunities which your Majesty has had of witnessing LIFE IN LONDON, as well in the humblest of dwellings as in the most splendid of palaces . . . Pardon me, most gracious SIRE, in remarking, that the exalted Personage whom we all look up to has been, without adulation, enabled, by such opportunities, to have, as it were, the PULSE of the people in his hands, to feel how it beats, and to prescribe accordingly. That your MAJESTY'S people may never be insensible to your MAJESTY'S care and exertion for their

---

[4] Pierce Egan, *Life in London; or, the day and Night Scenes of Jerry Hawthorn, Esq. and his Elegant Friend Corinthian Tom, Accompanied by Bob Logic, The Oxonian, in their Rambles and Sprees through the Metropolis* (London: Sherwood, Neely, and Jones, 1821), 279.

[5] From Harriet Arbuthnot's journals, quoted by Marc Baer, *Theatre and Disorder in Late Georgian England* (Oxford: Clarendon, 1992), 51.

welfare; that the heart of the KING may be always directed towards the happiness of his subjects, and his ears open to a "bit of good truth," Is the most sincere and honest wish of YOUR MAJESTY'S Very humble, loyal, and obedient subject.[6]

From 1824 Egan also published a weekly newspaper called *Pierce Egan's Life in London and Sporting Guide*. He died in 1849, the admiration once bestowed upon him having withered to the mild and amused curiosity generally awarded to the faded has-been. By 1888 Charles Hindley could write:

But although LIFE IN LONDON, or, TOM and JERRY did make our grandfathers so very—*very!* merry in the first quarter of the Nineteenth Century, we are constrained to admit; that it is a terrible dull and tedious work to read through in the present day . . .[7]

Glossaries to *Tom and Jerry* (1822, *c.*1823)

So successful was Egan's *Life in London* that several dramatic versions appeared soon after its publication. A version of one of these plays was published in Dublin in 1822, and included a glossary consisting of 317 entries for 311 headwords. The glossary is alphabetized more or less fully, with only a few lapses. It is partially derived from Egan's footnotes, often somewhat abbreviated. For example:

Life in London footnotes	1822 glossary[8]
[dead-beat] '*Dead beat!*' or '*beat to a stand still!*' Common phrases in the Sporting World, when a man or a horse is so completely exhausted from over-exertion, or the constitution breaking down, as to give up the object in view, not being able to pursue it any further. (96)	*Dead beat*, same as 'beat to a stand still.' q.v.
[the grin] A low *slang* term made use of in opposition to the *stylish* phrase of QUIZ. It is considered rather an	*Grin*, a low slang term, made use of in opposition to the *stylish* phrase of *quiz*.

---

[6] Egan, *Life in London*, Dedication, v–viii.
[7] Charles Hindley, *The True History of Tom and Jerry* (London: Reeves and Turner, 1888), ii–iii. I will discuss Hindley's glossary in volume III of this series.
[8] *Tom and Jerry; or Life in London. A Musical Extravaganza in Three Acts. To Which is affixed, the most Copious Vocabulary of Flash and Cant yet published. Founded on Pierce Egan's popular work of "Life in London"* (Dublin: The Bookseller, 1822).

unpleasant circumstance to persons entering a splendid ball-room who are not accustomed to it. As all times it should be executed in a graceful manner. (299)

[his uncle] *Cant-term for a Pawnbroker*: this class now prefer the term *Silversmith*!

Who lives where hang those golden balls,
Where Dick's poor mother often calls,
And leaves her *dickey*, gown, and shawls?
MY UNCLE.
Who, when you're *short* of the *short* stuff,
Nose starving for an ounce of snuff,
Will '*raise the wind*,' without a *puff*?
MY UNCLE. (65)[9]

Uncle, a pawnbroker.

A second *Tom and Jerry* glossary, containing eighty-eight entries for eighty-seven headwords, was published in *c.*1823, in an undated pamphlet consisting of a single sheet of paper, folded to make twelve leaves.[10] Two copies survive in the Bodleian library, one of which is uncut. Its entries are largely also found in the 1822 Dublin glossary. The following are not found among Egan's footnotes:

1822 glossary	c.1823 glossary
Gay tyke boys, dog fanciers.	Gay Tyke Boys, Dog Fanciers
Holy Land, St Giles's.	Holy Land, St. Giles's
Natty, very neat.	Natty, Very Neat
Sufferer, a tailor . . .	Sufferer, a Tailor

The Bodleian catalogue dates this glossary to 1810, but not only is that before *Life in London* was written, but also before the 1822 glossary from which it is clearly derived. The following entries demonstrate that this is the later of the two glossaries, because entries in the 1822 glossary are often closer to Egan's footnotes,

[9] Robert Bruce of the Bodleain Music Library and Max Tyler of the British Music Hall Society were kind enough to help me to locate the earliest published version of this song, which is in *The Universal Songster, or, Museum of Mirth*, Vol. II (London: John Fairburn, 1826), 224 [private correspondence].
[10] *Songs, Duets, Choruses, &c. in Tom and Jerry. As Sung at the Newcastle Theatre for Several Successive Nights, With Unbounded Applause. With a Glossary of all the Cant and Flash Phrases* (Newcastle: J. Marshall, *c.* 1823).

with changes and errors in the *c.*1823 glossary not reproduced in 1822:

Life in London footnotes	1822 glossary	*c.*1823 glossary
[back-slums] Low, unfrequented parts of the town. (274)	*Back slums*, beggars' place of resort; low unfrequented parts of the town.	Black Slums, Beggars' retreat or place of resort
[duce] Two-pence. (180, 228)	*Duce*, two-pence.	Deuce, Two-pence
[morleys] Hands. (207)	*Morleys*, fists.	Mawleys, Fists
[out-and-outer] A phrase in the sporting world for *goodness*; a sort of climacteric—the *ne plus ultra*. (43)	*Out and outer*, a real good one; a sort of climacteric—the *ne plus ultra*.	Out and Outer, A real good one

Seven entries (2.2 per cent) in the 1822 glossary contain citations, not all of which illustrate the use of the headword. They include:

A Benefit. Persons assembling by invitation at any one's house, are said to be 'taking a benefit' at the house of that person.
Dandies, '*a tribe of fops*, got between sleep and wake.'
Die proud, an expression among abandoned women of the town when any of them lose their flashman, as, 'Well, how did Bob die?'

Three entries (0.9 per cent) in the 1822 list include cross-references. In addition to *dead beat*, cited above, they are:

Diddler, see *Neat Article*.
Sponger, one who makes it a rule to call in on his acquaintances during meal time, in order to be invited to take share.—see 'Neat Article'

These both refer the reader to:

Neat Article, a good time-*ist* in calling, upon very slight acquaintance, at the juncture of meal time, when good manners, though often painful in this case, compels the housekeeper to invite him to partake of the meal.

None of the entries in the 1822 glossary includes etymologies. The *c.*1823 glossary has no citations, authorities, cross-references, or etymologies.

Although some of the entries in these glossaries are derived from Egan's footnotes, the semantic coverage is very different (see Appendix,

Table 5.1). There are a disproportionate number of additional terms for EMOTION & TEMPERAMENT and CRIME & DISHONESTY ($p = 0.05$) in the 1822 glossary. Fields that are supplemented less than can be accounted for by chance are LAW & ORDER, PLEASURE & PASTIMES, and FOOD & DRINK ($p = 0.01$). The semantic coverage of the *c.*1823 glossary is entirely in line with a random selection from the 1822 glossary list.

Egan's edition of Grose's *Classical Dictionary of the Vulgar Tongue* (1823)

Following the phenomenal success of *Life in London*, Egan became something of an authority on fashionable slang. It was perhaps inevitable that he would capitalize on this by producing a slang dictionary:

> *Grose's Classical Dictionary of the Vulgar Tongue* became one of Egan's most popular publications. Its greater fullness, comprehensiveness and liveliness won it wider acceptance than any of the other many slang and cant glossaries circulating at the time. It was reprinted again and again until late in Victorian times, and because a popular source-book . . . for such novelists as Ainsworth, Bulwer Lytton and Disraeli seeking for some authentic phrases with which to pepper their novels of low life or with which to define a criminal character.[11]

The most extensive slang dictionary then available was Grose's, and what could be better for sales than to combine two such well-known names on a single title page? If further inducement were needed to buy, Egan provides it in the form of a quotation from his own work:

> A kind of *cant* phraseology is current from one end of the Metropolis to the other, and you will scarcely be able to move a single step, my dear JERRY, without consulting a *Slang* Dictionary, or having some friend at your elbow to explain the strange expressions which, at every turn, will assail your ear.
>
> *Corinthian Tom*—LIFE IN LONDON[12]

Egan's motivations are familiarly commendable:

> every exertion has been made to collect and arrange, under their proper heads, all the new phrases which have occurred since the last edition. To improve, not to

---

[11] Reid, *Bucks and Bruisers*, 102. Reid overestimates the originality of Egan's dictionary at a sixth of the total (99).   [12] Egan, *Grose's Classical Dictionary*, title page.

degrade mankind; to remove *ignorance*, and put the UNWARY on their guard; to arouse the *sleepy*, and to keep them AWAKE; to render those persons who are a *little UP*, more FLY: and to cause every one to be *down* to those tricks, manœuvres, and impositions practised in life, which daily cross the paths of both young and old, has been the sole aim of the Editor; and if he has succeeded in only one instance in doing good, he feels perfectly satisfied that his time has not been misapplied.[13]

Egan reprints Grose's prefaces to the first and second editions, and uses his arguments as justification for producing another edition of the work, which he calls the third. He does not acknowledge the *Lexicon*, although that was his source.

Naturally he emphasizes that slang and cant are always changing. Despite the need for innovation to evade the understanding of law-enforcers, Egan notes similarities between the language of the Elizabethan and Victorian underworlds:

> But, notwithstanding the Protean nature of the *Flash* or *Cant* language, the greater part of its vocabulary has remained unchanged for centuries, and many of the words used by the Canting Beggars in Beaumont and Fletcher, and the Gipsies in Ben Jonson's Masque, are still to be heard among the *Gnostics* of Dyot-street and Tothill-fields. To *prig* is still to steal; to *fib*, to beat; *lour*, money; *duds*, clothes; *prancers*, horses; *bouzing-ken*, an alehouse; *cove*, a fellow; a *sow's baby*, a pig, &c. &c.[14]

While this comment demonstrates that Egan had consulted earlier literary authorities, several of the terms cited, including *boozing-ken*, *lour*, *prancer*, and *sow's baby*, were by this time obsolete other than in cant dictionaries and in works derived from them, demonstrating Egan's limited knowledge of contemporary cant. The preface is followed by a lively biographical sketch of Francis Grose, which provides some of the anecdotes given in Chapter 1.

Egan's dictionary contains 5,714 entries for 4,549 headwords. Eighty-seven per cent of these are from the *Lexicon* (see Appendix, Table 5.2). Terms including *ambassador of morocco, apostles, article,* and *awake*, to take only those from the letter 'A', confirm that this, and not an earlier edition, was Egan's source. There is no evidence that he looked at earlier editions of Grose's dictionary.[15] The *Lexicon* was not Egan's only dictionary source, however. He also used Vaux's *Memoirs* (1819), *The Life of David Haggart*, the *Flash Dictionary*, and

---

[13] Egan, *Grose's Classical Dictionary*, xxviii.   [14] Egan, *Grose's Classical Dictionary*, xxi.
[15] Reid, *Bucks and Bruisers*, 99, writes that Egan compared the *Lexicon* with the 1796 edition, but I have found no evidence to support this.

Burrowes's *Life in St George's Fields*, all published in 1821 (see Chapters 3, 4, and 7).

Since Egan's dictionary is presented as an edition of Grose's, it is no surprise that most of the word-list is derived from that source, if only indirectly. Egan's editorial intervention is largely orthographical. He modernizes spelling, particularly of *shew, stiled, taylor*, and *Welch*, and tends to respell *Shakespeare* as <Shakspeare> and *seize* as <sieze>. Agent nouns ending in <-or> are often respelt with <-er>. Egan tends to insert commas after clause-qualifying adverbs and around sub-clauses. He also inserts commas between listed adjectives, sometimes even between the last adjective and the noun it qualifies:

APPLE-PYE [Egan: *PIE*] BED. A bed made apple-pye [Egan: *pie*] fashion, like what is called a turnover apple-pye [Egan: *pie*], where the sheets are so doubled as to prevent any one from getting at his length between them: a common trick played by frolicsome country lasses on their sweethearts, male relations, or visitors [Egan: *visiters*].

DUNGHILL. A coward: a cockpit phrase, all but game cocks [Egan: *gamecocks*] being styled [Egan: *stiled*] dunghills. To die dunghill; to repent, or shew [Egan: *show*] any signs of contrition at the gallows. Moving dunghill; a dirty, filthy man or woman. Dung, an abbreviation of dunghill, also [Egan: *also,*] means a journeyman taylor [Egan: *tailor*] who submits to the law for regulating journeymen taylors' [Egan: *tailors'*] wages, therefore deemed by the flints [Egan: *deemed, by the flints,*] a coward. See FLINTS.

HOITY-TOITY. A hoity-toity wench; a giddy, thoughtless, romping [Egan: *romping,*] girl.

ROMP. A forward wanton girl, a tomrig. Grey, in his notes to Shakespeare [Egan: *Shakspeare*], derives it from arompo, an animal found in South Guinea, that is [Egan: *Guinea; that is,*] a man eater. See HOYDEN.

SWEET. Easy to be imposed on, or taken in; also [Egan: *in: also,*] expert, dexterous clever. Sweet's your hand; said of one dexterous at stealing.

Egan also italicizes cited terms and *see*, used to introduce cross-references. He modernizes French spellings, and inserts accents, though not always correctly:

P.P.C. An inscription on the visiting cards of our modern fine gentleman, signifying that they have called *pour prendre conge* [Egan: *congé*], i.e. 'to take leave.' This has of late been ridiculed by cards inscribed D.I.O. i.e. 'Damme, I'm off.'

RESCOUNTERS [Egan: *RECOUNTERS*]. The time of settlement between the bulls and bears of Exchange-alley [Egan: *Stock-Exchange*], when the losers must pay their differences, or become lame ducks, and waddle out of the Alley.

SALMON-GUNDY. Apples, onions, veal or chicken, and pickled herrings, minced fine, and eaten with oil and vinegar; [Egan: *vinegar*:] some derive the name of this mess from the French words *selon mon goust* [Egan: *goût*], because the proportions of the different ingredients are regulated by the palate of the maker . . .

SOUSE [Egan: *SOU*]. Not a souse [Egan: *sou*]; not a penny. *French.*

Egan makes relatively few lexical changes, but he regularly replaces *Exchange Alley* with *Stock Exchange* (**rescounters**). Only once does he comment on what he finds in his source:

EVIL. A halter. *Cant.* Also a wife [*Lexicon*] . . . an admirable synonyme. [Egan]

The entries drawn from Vaux's *Memoirs* are generally edited to the same extent as those from the *Lexicon*: on an orthographical level only. Because Vaux's list is more modern, there are even fewer changes to make. With a confidence that he does not show in editing the *Lexicon*, however, Egan sometimes rewrites entries from Vaux:

Vaux	Egan
BRADS, halfpence; also, money in general.	BRADS. Money; but generally meant for halfpence. *Cant.*
COVER, to stand in such a situation as to obscure your *Pall*, who is committing a robbery, from the view of by-standers or persons passing, is called *covering* him. Any body whose dress or stature renders him particularly eligible for this purpose, is said to be *a good cover.*	COVER . . . Among the *family people*, it is to stand in such a situation as to obscure your *pal*, who is committing a robbery, from the view of the by-standers or persons passing, it is called *covering him*. Any person belonging to the gang, whose dress or stature renders him particularly eligible for this purpose, is termed a *good coverer.*
DRAKED, ducked; a discipline sometimes inflicted on pickpockets at fairs, races, &c.	DRAKED. A thief forced into a pond by a mob, as a summary mode of punishment, is termed being *draked*, or *ducked*. *Cant.*
FAMILY, thieves, sharpers and all others who get their living *upon the cross*, are comprehended under the title of '*The Family*'.	FAMILY. Thieves, and others who live upon *the cross*, are denominated '*the family*'.

In these entries, Egan follows Vaux in using italics both for usage labels and as implicit cross-references.

Egan sometimes includes extra material:

Vaux	Egan
BASTILE, generally called, for shortness, *the Steel*; a cant name for the House of Correction, Cold-Bath-Fields, London.	BASTILE. A flash term for the House of Correction, in Cold Bath Fields: so termed when under the management of Governor Aris. For shortness termed the *Steel*.
SCURF'D, taken in custody.	SCURFED. Laid hold of; taken up: an allusion to the head. It is a cant phrase to say such a one is *scurfed*: i.e. he has been pulled.

and excludes what he feels to be unnecessary:

Vaux	Egan
JOGUE, a shilling; *five jogue* is five shillings, and so on, to any other number.	JOGUE. A shilling. *Cant.*
LAG SHIP, a transport chartered by Government for the conveyance of convicts to New South Wales; also, a hulk, or floating prison, in which, to the disgrace of humanity, many hundreds of these unhappy persons are confined, and suffer every complication of human misery.	LAG SHIP. A vessel chartered by government for the conveyance of convicts to *Botany Bay*.

He updates a few entries:

Vaux	Egan
WEIGH FORTY, term used by the police, who are as well versed in *flash* as the thieves themselves. It is often customary with the *traps*, to wink at depredations of a petty nature, and for which no reward would attach, and to let a thief *reign* unmolested till he commits a capital crime. They then *grab* him, and, on conviction, share (in many cases) a reward of 40*l.*, or upwards; therefore these gentry will say, Let him alone at present, we don't *want* him till he *weighs his weight*, meaning, of course, forty pounds.	WEIGH FORTY. A term formerly used by the police, who are as well versed in *flash* as the thieves themselves and of whom it is said, did often wink at depredations of a petty nature, for which no reward would attach, and to let a thief *reign* unmolested till he commits a capital crime; they then *grab* him, and, on conviction, share (in many cases) a reward of £40, or upwards; therefore these gentry will say, Let him alone at present, we don't *want* him till he *weighs his weight*, meaning, of course, forty pounds.

Occasionally, in redefining them, Egan changes the meanings of terms he takes from Vaux:

Vaux	Egan
GUN . . . To *gun* any thing, is to look at or examine it.	GUN. To *gun*, among flash people, is to be noticed. Do not you see we are *gunned*? an expression used by thieves when they think they are being watched.

Although all of Vaux's entries could be understood to be cant:

Vaux	Egan
CROAK, to die.	CROAK. To die. *Cant.*
MANCHESTER, the tongue.	MANCHESTER. The tongue. *Cant.*
WRINKLE, to lie, or utter a falsehood.	WRINKLE. To utter a falsehood. *Cant.*

Egan does not consistently label them as such. He introduces other usage labels with little apparent justification:

Vaux	Egan
ANDREW MILLER'S LUGGER, a king's ship or vessel.	ANDREW MILLER'S LUGGER. A king's ship or vessel. *Sea cant.*
CABIN, a house.	CABIN. A house. *Irish term.*

Entries derived from the *Life of David Haggart* and from Burrowes's *Life in St George's Fields* (see Chapter 7) are generally quite short, and Egan's editorial interventions are minor. He often inserts usage labels into entries from the *Life of David Haggart*, frequently labelling these terms as cant, Scottish or nautical. Haggart was certainly a Scottish thief, but the nautical labels are more difficult to justify:

Life of David Haggart	Egan
Cuddie, *a jack-ass.*	CUDDIE. A Jack-ass. *Sea cant.*
Deeker, *a thief kept in pay by a constable.*	DEEKER. A thief kept in pay by a trap. *Scotch cant.*
Dot, *a ribbon.*	DOT. A ribbon. *Sea cant.*
Geach, *a thief.*	GEACH. A thief. *Cant.*
Jaun, *to discover.*	JAUN. To discover. *Scotch cant.*
Nippers, *handcuffs,*	NIPPERS. Handcuffs. *Cant.*

Egan also supplies usage labels for entries from Burrowes, which he generally treats as cant, with the odd 'sea term' thrown in for seasoning:

Burrowes	Egan
Ball of fire, *glass of brandy*	BALL OF FIRE. A glass of brandy. *Cant.*
Hop, *a dance*	HOP. A dance. *Sea term.*
Listener, *the ear*	LISTENER. The ear. *Cant.*
Tough yarn, *a long story*	TOUGH YARN. A long story. *Cant.*

A few entries from Burrowes appear in an expanded form in Egan's dictionary:

Burrowes	Egan
Blue moon, *a long time*	BLUE MOON. In allusion to a long time before such a circumstance happens. 'O yes, in a blue moon.'
Cat's meat, *the lungs*	CAT'S MEAT. A slang phrase for the lungs: applied when any person is touched with a consumption; i.e. his *Cat's meat* is bad.
Ear-wigging, *whispering*	EAR-WIGGING. A snake in the grass; a fellow fond of telling tales about those persons he may be employed with. A whisperer.

Egan often labels terms selected from the *Flash Dictionary* (see Chapter 3) as 'cant':

Flash Dictionary	Egan
Bowman—a thief.	BOWMAN. A thief. *Cant.*
Cogue—a glass of gin.	COGUE. A glass of gin. *Cant.*
Null-gropers—people who sweep the streets, in search of old irons, nails, &c.	NULL-GROPERS. Persons who sweep the streets, in search of old iron, nails, &c. *Cant.*
Shoving the moon—moving goods by moonlight, to prevent them being seized by the landlord.	SHOVING THE MOON. Moving goods by moonlight to prevent their being siezed [sic] by the landlord. *Cant.*
Stark naked---gin.	STARK NAKED. Gin. *Cant.*

and makes a few other small changes:

Flash Dictionary	Egan
Abbott's priory—the King's Bench prison.	ABBOT'S PRIORY. The King's Bench Prison; this bit of *flash* generally

Cadger—beggar, mean sort of thief, of the lowest order.

CADGER. A beggar. One of the lowest of the low. *Cant.*

changes when the Lord Chief Justice of the above court retires from his situation

Drawing a cork—giving a person a bloody nose.

DRAWING THE CORK. To give a man a bloody nose: i.e. I have drawn his cork. *Pugilistic cant.*

Ignoramus—a novice, a stupid fellow.

IGNORAMUS. A stupid fellow.

Mufflers—sparring gloves.

MUFFLERS. Boxing-gloves, used in sparring.

He inevitably introduces a few errors in spelling:

Lexicon

Egan

PUNCH. A liquor called by foreigners Contradiction, from its being composed of spirits to make it strong, water to make it weak, lemon juice to make it sour, and sugar to make it sweet . . .

PUNCH. A liquor called by foreigners, contradiction, from its being composed of spirits to make it strong, water to make it weak, lemon-juice to make it sour, and sugar to make it sweat . . .

Burrowes
Scuddick, *a halfpenny*

SCURRICK. A halfpenny. *Cant.*

sense:

Vaux

Egan

GRAY, a half-penny, or other coin, having two heads or two tails, and fabricated for the use of gamblers, who, by such a deception, frequently win large sums.

GRAY. A copper coin, having two heads and two tails, to answer the purposes of gamblers, who, by such deceptions, frequently win large sums.

and division between headword and definition:

Haggart

Egan

Sweeten a grawler, *satisfy a beggar.*

SWEETEN. A grawler. To give money to a beggar. *Cant.*

In a few cases, Egan combined material from more than one of the dictionaries he had consulted:

Source

Egan

BLACK SPY. The Devil. [*Lexicon*]
Black Spy—an informer [*Flash Dictionary*]

BLACK SPY. The Devil; a smith; an informer. *Cant.*

JUMPERS. Persons who rob houses by getting in at the windows. Also a set of Methodists established in South Wales. [*Lexicon*]

Jumper, *a tenpenny-piece*. [Haggart]

MUFF. The private parts of a woman. To the well wearing of your muff, mort; to the happy consummation of your marriage, girl; a health. [*Lexicon*]

MUFF, an epithet synonymous with *mouth* [Vaux]

JUMPERS. Persons who rob houses by getting in at the windows: also, a set of Methodists established in South Wales: also, a ten-penny piece. *Scotch cant.*

MUFF. The monosyllable. To the well wearing of your muff, mort; to the happy consummation of your marriage, girl; a health: also, a fool.

Dictionaries were not Egan's only sources, however. He noted in his preface that:

> To the cultivation, in our times, of the science of Pugilism, the *Flash* Language is indebted for a considerable addition to its treasures.[16]

and made extensive use of two eulogistic poetic works on pugilism: *Tom Crib's Memorial* and *Jack Randall's Diary*.[17] Sometimes these provide illustrative citations for entries taken from Egan's dictionary sources (here all are from the *Lexicon*):

DEW BEATERS. Feet. *Cant.* [Egan adds:] . . . 'Long may you stand on your *dew-beaters* well.' *Vide Randall's Scrap Book.*

FUNK . . . I was in a cursed funk . . . [Egan adds:] . . .
'Up he rose in a *funk*, lapp'd a toothful of brandy,
And to it again,' &c.
Vide Crib's Memorial

WHITE FEATHER. He has a white feather; he is a coward: an allusion to a game cock, where [Egan: *which*] having a white feather is a proof he is not of the true game breed. [Egan adds:] . . . Speaking of *Randall*, the author of *Randall's Diary* says,
'He never yet has shown in fight
The snow-*white feather's damning shade*.'
Recounting a meeting at *Belcher's*, the author of *Crib's Memorial* says they were
'All high-bred heroes of the *ring*,
Whose very *gammon* would delight one,
Who, nurs'd beneath *the Fancy's* wing,
Show all her *feathers* but the *white one*.'

[16] Egan, *Grose's Classical Dictionary*, xxii.
[17] *Tom Crib's Memorial to Congress . . . by one of the fancy* (London: Longman et al., 1819); *Jack Randall's Diary of Proceedings at the House of Call for Genius*, ed. Mr Breakwindow (London: W. Simpkin and R. Marshall, 1820). The pieces contained in *Tom Crib's Memorial*, written by Thomas Moore, are political satires written in the form and style of pugilistic works (Blake, *Non-Standard Language*, 129–30).

while others form the basis of new entries:

QUILT. To thrash. *Cant.*
'Up with your hat in the Surrey air
And turn to and *quilt* the Nonpareil.'
Lines to Martin, the Baker, in Randall's Scrap Book

SCUTTLE . . . To scuttle a nob; to break a head.
'See the *Captain* and *Caleb* are chuckling around him,
As he offered to *scuttle a nob* o'er again.'
Lines on Randall's Fight with Turner, vide Randall's Diary.

The *Lexicon* contains 5,381 entries for 4,239 headwords. Egan adopts 4,972 entries for 3,888 headwords: about 92 per cent of each. The semantic coverage of the terms that Egan selects from his main source is in line with a random selection, except that there are significantly fewer miscellaneous terms than we would expect ($p = 0.01$; see Appendix, Tables 2.1 and 5.2.1).

Neither, apparently, was Egan particularly influenced by the usage labels he found in the *Lexicon*. Their distribution is also largely as we would expect in a random selection. There is a slight increase in the proportion of obsolete terms, but this is because Egan marks as obsolete several entries carried over from the *Lexicon*. For example:

CAPTAIN PODD. A celebrated master of a puppet show, in Ben Jonson's
  time, whose name became a common one to signify any of that fraternity.
  Obsolete.
LARRY DUGAN'S EYE WATER. Blacking: Larry Dugan was a famous shoe black
  at Dublin. *Obsolete.*
SORROW SHALL BE HIS SOPS . . . Sorrow go by me; a common expletive used by
  the Presbyterians in Ireland. *Obsolete.*
WHITHER-GO-YE. A wife, wives being sometimes apt to question their husbands
  whither they are going. *Obsolete.*

Apart from the addition of 'obsolete', and a few small orthographical changes, these entries are exactly as in the *Lexicon*.

There are significantly fewer terms labelled 'Irish' than we might expect in a random selection from the *Lexicon* ($p = 0.05$). Of the forty-two Irish terms in the *Lexicon*, Egan adopts only thirty-seven. He may have been influenced by his own knowledge of contemporary Irish speech, as used by his parents, to reject terms that were no longer in use. Alternatively, he may have found the inclusion of stage-Irish offensive, and chosen to omit them for nationalistic reasons. The terms he rejects are indistinguishable from the rest in their offensiveness and currency, but all five are among the first thirteen terms labelled as 'Irish' in the *Lexicon*. It seems, then, that Egan began with the intention of deleting terms marked as 'Irish', but did not maintain this practice.

Egan provides fewer than a fifth of his entries with usage labels (see Appendix, Table 5.2.2). Most of the labelled entries are marked as 'cant'. Egan's overall distribution of usage labels is markedly unlike that of his main source in only three respects. There are significantly more terms labelled as 'university cant', 'Scottish', and 'obsolete' in Egan's dictionary than in the *Lexicon* ($p = 0.01$). The 'Scottish' terms, as noted above, are from the *Life of David Haggart*, and the 'obsolete' entries are largely relabelled terms from the *Lexicon*.

Terms marked 'university cant' are largely from Egan's own *Life in London*. They generally appear in the laboured puns of Bob Logic, the rather less than diligent Oxford scholar whose income does not match his lifestyle:

Life in London

In the *Kingdom of Sans Souci* he proved himself a *brilliant* of the first water; and from the figure he had cut in the *Province of Bacchus* and the *Dynasty of Venus*, LOGIC had been pronounced a hero. On the *Plains of Betteris* he had shown himself a general of no mean stamp: and his knowledge of *Navigation* was so good, that he had been enabled to steer clear of the shoals and rocks of *Dun Territory* and the *River Tick*.[18]

Egan's dictionary

UNITED KINGDOMS OF SANS SOUCI AND SANS SIX SOUS. Riddances of cares, and, ultimately, of sixpences. *Oxf. Univ. cant.*

PROVINCE OF BACCHUS. Inebriety. *Oxf. Univ. cant.*

DYNASTY OF VENUS. Indiscriminate love and misguided affection. *Oxf. Univ. cant.*

PLAINS OF BETTERIS. The diversion of billiards. *Oxf. Univ. cant.*

DUN TERRITORY. Circle of creditory to be had. *Oxf. Univ. cant.*

RIVER TICK. Standing debts, which only discharge themselves at the expiration of three years by leaving the Lake of Credit, and meandering through the haunts of 100 creditors. *Oxf. Univ. cant.*

---

[18] Egan, *Life in London*, 73.

I have found no evidence that anyone other than Bob Logic used these terms, and there is no reason to believe that Egan was a particularly knowledgeable authority on university slang.[19] Nevertheless, because of these additions, this work functions both as a slang dictionary and as a glossary to *Life in London* and its dramatic offshoots.

In Vaux's dictionary there are 800 entries for 715 headwords. Egan selects from these 385 entries (48 per cent) for 328 headwords (46 per cent). Their semantic coverage is in line with random selection.

Egan's introduction of illustrative citations from Randall and *Crib's Memorial* means that his dictionary contains significantly more citations and authorities than the *Lexicon* (both $p = 0.01$). There is no statistically significant difference between the proportions of entries containing cross-references in the two dictionaries, but Egan does have significantly fewer entries containing etymologies ($p = 0.01$; see Appendix, Tables 2.3 and 5.2.3). It is not that he deleted etymologies or avoided selecting terms from his sources that contain them: the proportion of entries including etymologies adopted from the *Lexicon* is in keeping with random selection. The falling proportion is because Egan generally did not provide etymologies for terms he gathered from other sources.

In his preface, Egan noted that:

In the present edition, for myself, I have strongly to re-echo the sentiments of for-mer editors, namely, that I have neglected no opportunity of excluding indelicate phrases, which might have been adopted by my predecessors, nor of *softening* down others, where propriety pointed out such a course as not only necessary, but, perhaps essential to render palatable this CLASSICAL DICTIONARY OF THE VULGAR TONGUE.[20]

His bowdlerization was generally of sexual terms, particularly those relating to venereal disease, and to the genitals. He less often censored terms dealing with prostitution. While never actually obscuring the sense of his definitions, he adopted two techniques for rendering them less indelicate. The first of these is the omission of offensive terms, or their replacement by a variety of euphemisms and obscure slang terms. In the case of euphemisms, offence to the reader is avoided. In the case of slang terms, readers who have

---

[19] Reid, *Bucks and Bruisers*, 55, comments that Egan, who was 'always conscious of his own scanty education', 'put a great deal of himself' into Logic, playing him on stage on several occasions.
[20] Egan, *Grose's Classical Dictionary*, xix–xx.

looked up defining terms elsewhere in the dictionary and been offended have only themselves to blame:

Lexicon Balatronicum	Egan
ACADEMY, OR PUSHING SCHOOL. A brothel . . .	ACADEMY, OR PUSHING SCHOOL. A cyprian lodge . . .
BURNT. Poxed or clapped. He was sent out a sacrifice, and came home a burnt offering; a saying of seamen who have caught the venereal disease abroad . . .	BURNT. Poxed or clapped. He was sent out a sacrifice, and came home a burnt offering; a saying of seamen who have been 'in for the plate' abroad . . .
CLAP. A venereal taint . . .	CLAP. A delicate taint . . .
COMMODITY. A woman's commodity; the private parts of a modest woman, and the public parts of a prostitute.	COMMODITY. A woman's commodity, the monosyllable of a modest woman, and the public parts of a prostitute.
COVENT GARDEN AGUE. The venereal disease . . .	COVENT GARDEN AGUE. The ladybird disease . . .
HAIR SPLITTER. A man's yard.	HAIR SPLITTER. A thing *with* use *without* ornament.
VENUS'S CURSE. The venereal disease.	VENUS'S CURSE. The enviable disease.
WHORE PIPE. The penis.	WHORE PIPE. The sugar-stick.

Egan's second technique for avoiding offence is the obliteration of letters in tabooed terms. This is far more extensive than in any earlier version of Grose's dictionary, but is inconsistently performed:

Lexicon Balatronicum	Egan
To FRISK. . . . Blast his eyes! frisk him	FRISK. . . . B—t his eyes! frisk him . . .
To KEEP. To inhabit. Lord, where do you keep? . . .	KEEP. To inhabit. L—d, where do you keep? . . .
To NAP . . . Also to catch the venereal disease . . .	NAP. . . . also, to catch the **** disease . . .
SILENCE . . . Silence in the court, the cat is pissing; a gird upon any one requiring silence unnecessarily.	SILENCE . . . Silence in the court, the cat is p—ing; a gird upon any one requiring silence unnecessarily.
WIND MILL. The fundament. She has no fortune but her mills; i.e. she has nothing but her **** and a*se.	WIND-MILL. The fundament. She has no fortune but her mills: i.e. she has nothing but her **** and ****.

Egan's other works feature much more often in the *OED* than does his dictionary, which is cited fifty-nine times, sometimes under his own name, and sometimes Grose's. Nine of these citations can be predated by reference to Egan's sources. Egan provides several first citations, including *collywobbles* 'indigestion', *to cross* 'to cheat', *fogle-hunter* 'a pickpocket', *short* 'an undiluted shot of spirits', *the stiff* 'a document', *stiff 'un* 'a corpse', and *top-sawyer* 'a skilled craftsman'. For a few entries, Egan's is the only citation, including *stale-drunk* 'hung-over' and *stump* 'money'. The dictionary antedates a further twenty-six existing *OED* first citations, mostly in the first half of the alphabet. As we come closer to the date of the composition of the *OED*, we should expect to see fewer terms that predate its earliest citations, and we should expect the antedatings to be shorter. It is, therefore, no surprise that two-fifths of these predate the *OED* by fewer than ten years. The most significant is ninety-nine years earlier than the first citation, however (*putty*):

balderdash "lewd conversation" (1849)
board of green cloth "a billiard table" (1871: **green cloth**)
boozed "drunk" (1850)
bugaboo "a debt-collector" (1827)
to chaff "to banter" (1827)
chancery 'Getting your head "in chancery," among pugilists, is when your nob is completely at the mercy of your opponent; or, in other words, you cannot protect it' (1832)
to cover "to put down one's bet; to match an opponent's wager" (1857)
to cut one's stick "to be off" (1825)
domino-box "the mouth" (1828: *dominoes* "the teeth")
eye-water "gin" (1869)
figure "an amount (of money)" (1842)
finger-smith "a thief" (1884)
flipper "the hand" (1832)
four bells at night "ten o'clock" (1836: *bell* n¹ 3b 'The bell which is struck on ship-board, every half hour . . . a period of half-an-hour thus indicated')
jawing-tackle "the jaws" (1859)
old chap [an affectionate term of address] (*OED* lists an example of this usage from 1892 under *old*, but citations from as early as 1865 are scattered elsewhere throughout the dictionary)
pewter "silver" (1829: "a tankard or 'cup' given as a prize; prize-money, money")
putty cove or *covess* 'A man or woman upon whom no dependence can be placed; i.e. they are as liable [sic] as putty, which can be bent any way' (1924: with reference to malleable people)
to quilt "to beat" (1836)
rat "a worker who accepts wages below the market-rate; a strike-breaker" (1836)
to scuttle "to break (a head)" (1834)

stinker "a black eye" (1917: 'something repugnant because of its difficulty or unendurable nature')

stumped "destitute" (1828: *to stump* v¹ 11 "to render penniless")

to swipe "to drink" (1829)

to tramp "to wander as a beggar" (1846)

in the wind "drunk" (1835)

Canting Literature: Charles Dickens's *Oliver Twist* (1837)

Some of the most famous villains of literature people Dickens's *Oliver Twist*. First published in 1837, the tale of a poor orphan boy who eventually finds his wealthy family was a immediate success. Much of the force of the novel lies in the criminal characters: Fagin, Sikes, and the Artful Dodger. They and their colleagues (and some of the police officers) use cant, much of which was clearly widely-known by the time Dickens was writing. Nevertheless, these are 'introduced so carefully that the genteel reader need never be at a loss for their meaning',[21] and include *beak* "magistrate", *caster* "hat", *flat* "a fool", *ken* "house", *prig* "thief", and *trap* "police-officer". Other terms and phrases had been popularized through their use in Egan's hugely successful *Life in London*, which was undoubtedly one of Dickens's influences.[22] These include *cleaned out* "ruined", *downy* "knowing", *make one's lucky* "make one's escape", *staunch* "reliable, faithful", and *that's the time of day* "that's perfect". In his preface, Dickens wrote:

> I had read of thieves by the scores . . . But I had never met (except in HOGARTH) with the miserable reality. It appeared to me that to draw a knot of such associates in crime as really did exist . . . would be a service to society. And therefore I did it as I best could.[23]

It would be odd if Dickens had not read *Life in London*, or seen one of the dramatic adaptations, since they took the capital by storm during the first few years that he and his family lived there, but it seems that his debt to Egan was greater than this. Egan listed most of the canting terms found in *Oliver Twist* in his edition of Grose's dictionary,

---

[21] Keith Hollingsworth, *The Newgate Novel 1830–1847. Bulwer, Ainsworth, Dickens, & Thackeray* (Detroit: Wayne State University Press, 1963), 121.

[22] See Reid, *Bucks and Bruisers*, 214–18.

[23] Charles Dickens, *Oliver Twist*, ed. Peter Fairclough (1966) (Harmondsworth: Penguin, 1983), 33–4. The 1838 edition does not include this preface.

deriving some from Grose and some from Vaux. In this extract, Sikes and Fagin plan a robbery at Chertsey:

Egan	Oliver Twist[24]
PUT UP AFFAIR. A preconcerted plan or scheme to rob a house, at the suggestion of the porter, or servants belonging to it; they, possessing a knowledge of the premises, are the most competent to advise the best and safest mode to carry it into effect; pointing out all the places where the plate and other valuable articles are deposited, &c. Instances of this kind are too frequent in London. The *putter-up*, as he is called, comes in for a share of the booty, although he may take no active part in the robbery.	'. . . it can't be a put-up job, as we expected. . . . I tell you that Toby Crackit has been hanging about the place for a fortnight, and he can't get one of the servants into a line.'
LINE. To get a man into a line, i.e. to divert his attention by a ridiculous or absurd story. To humbug.	'Do you mean to tell me, Bill,' said the Jew: softening as the other grew heated: 'that neither of the two men in the house can be got over?'
IN IT. To let another partake of any benefit or acquisition you have acquired by robbery or otherwise, is called *putting* him *in it:* a *family-man* who is accidentally witness to a robbery, &c., effected by one or more others, will say to the latter, Mind, I'm *in it*; which is generally acceded to, being the established custom; but there seems more of courtesy than right in this practice.	'Yes, I do mean to tell you so,' replied Sikes. 'The old lady has had 'em these twenty years; and if you were to give 'em five hundred pound, they wouldn't be in it.' (i.317: ch. 19)

Canting Literature: George Borrow's *Lavengro* (1851)

Better known for his use of Romany, Borrow also depicted some cant speakers in his novels. *Lavengro* is 'a series of brilliantly conceived episodes concerning the adventures of an almost penniless young man who, leaving London in 1825, wanders about England for a year or more, consorting with tinker, innkeepers, Non-conformist

---

[24] Charles Dickens, *Oliver Twist; or, The Parish Boy's Progress* by "Boz" (London: Richard Bentley, 1838), i.317 (ch. 19).

ministers, eccentric old gentlemen, chaste young women, and gypsies.'[25] In his travels, Lavengro encounters several speakers of cant, including an apple-seller on London Bridge. She takes his interest in the Thames as an indication of suicidal intent, and approaches to dissuade him, assuming that he is a thief fallen on bad luck:

'. . . we never calls them thieves here, but prigs and fakers: to tell you the truth, dear, seeing you spring at that railing put me in mind of my own dear son, who is now at Bot'ny . . .'[26]

He sees that she is reading *Moll Flanders*, and asks to buy it. She refuses to sell it to him, but asks instead for a *tanner* for *baccy*:

'What's a tanner?' said I.
'. . . a tanner is sixpence; and, as you were talking just now about crowns, it will be as well to tell you that those of our trade never calls them crowns, but bulls; but I am talking nonsense, just as if you did not know all that already, as well as myself; you are only shamming . . . If you have any clies to sell at any time, I'll buy them of you; all safe with me; I never 'peach, and scorns a trap . . .'[27]

He returns on several occasions, reads her book, and exchanges it, on her request, for a Bible. Being of a philological bent, he asks her for more of the canting language, and is rewarded with *pannam* 'bread'. This, and the inclusion of another ancient canting term, *harmanbeck*, uttered by a boxing promoter in chapter 24, indicates that Borrow's source had a wide chronological range. The only dictionary I could find listing all of them was Egan's.

Summary

Egan capitalized on his fame as a sporting writer and as the author of *Life in London* in producing his edition of Grose's dictionary, which was 'designed less . . . to "improve" Grose than to advertise Egan's *Life in London* (1821) and his *Boxiana*.'[28] He used several slang dictionaries in addition to the *Lexicon*, and fewer than 4 per cent of his entries were entirely new to the slang dictionary tradition. He edited entries from the *Lexicon* only superficially, but displayed more

[25] Ousby, *Cambridge Guide*.
[26] George Borrow, *Lavengro; The Scholar—The Gypsy—The Priest* (London: John Murray, 1851), ii.29: ch. 3 (ch. 31).   [27] Borrow, *Lavengro*, ii.32–3: ch. 3.   [28] Partridge, *Slang*, 80.

confidence in his treatment of terms from Vaux's *Memoirs* and minor slang dictionaries. He also realphabetized the word-list.

In selecting terms from the *Lexicon*, Egan tended to omit marginal terms and concentrate on its core semantic coverage. He selected against terms labelled as 'Irish', but included more labelled 'Scottish', 'obsolete', and 'university cant'. The university cant was derived from Egan's own *Life in London*. He also used poetic works dealing with pugilism to provide illustrative citations for the word-list. He tended to clean up definitions relating to sex, sexually transmitted diseases, and sexual organs.

Egan derived most of his word-list from earlier dictionaries, and the *OED* made fairly extensive use of his work. However, it predates enough *OED* first citations to suggest that the additional terms, excluding the dubious university slang, do represent contemporary non-standard usage.

Egan's work had an important influence on several later novelists, not least in demonstrating how popular slang literature could be. Dickens and Borrow may both have used Egan's dictionary, though his debt to Grose and Vaux and the slang craze created by *Life in London* make that difficult to prove beyond doubt. Dickens and Borrow, like many of the other contemporary novelists discussed in this volume, came to be seen as useful sources for cant and slang, and Hotten, Partridge, and the *OED* all looked to them for evidence of continued usage.

6 John Bee

John Badcock published 'a variety of works on pugilism and the turf' using the names John Bee and John Hind, between 1816 and 1830.[1] I refer to him here as 'John Bee', because that is the name under which his slang dictionary appeared. Nothing is known of his personal life, and his professional career can only be guessed at from his publications. These include *The Fancy, or True Sportsman's Guide*, in monthly parts from 1821, and the *Annals of Sporting and Fancy Gazette*, in thirteen volumes between 1822 and 1828. He produced several volumes on farriery, and editions of Samuel Foote's plays and of the life of Bampfylde-Moore Carew, as well as books on natural history, anatomy, travel, history, politics, theology, and criminal trials. He also published several translations from French and German.

Bee's dictionary[2] shares its publication date with Egan's slang dictionary, although Egan's appeared in December 1822. Although Bee, like Egan, made extensive use of Grose's dictionary, he used it for reference rather than as the basis of his own. Bee's preface, dated May 1823, clearly shows his exasperation at Egan's publication, which involved considerably less work. He was concerned to ensure that no reader could consider him indebted to Egan's work, and noted that his own was in press when Egan's appeared:

> Wholly unlike any of its precursors, the present laborious Dictionary claims for its characteristics a good portion of originality . . . no *modern compiler* will please to have the arrogance to consider himself *consulted* . . .[3]

After lamenting, at length, the inadequacies of each cant and slang dictionary following Grose's, Bee goes in for the kill:

> A reprint,* of Grose's old edition appeared last year, with copious extracts from this last-mentioned edition,† and the introduction of several inventions of the editor's own manufacture.‡ These latter were necessarily impertinent; besides, a man who makes cramp words and invents arbitrary names in one place for the purpose of giving explanations in a fresh book, does but increase the evil by creating error and uncertainty.[4]

---

[1] *DNB*, ii.381–2.   [2] Republished as *Sportsman's Slang* in 1825.   [3] Bee, *Slang*, iii, xiv.
[4] Bee, *Slang*, ix.

* This reprint was undertaken in great haste, upon the printer thereof learning that materials for the present dictionary were in train, (April 28, 1822;) and it appeared in December, a time too short for the research necessary to such a work. How it failed a comparison will show.

† Like every other work of the same nature, Clarke's edition of 1811 [the *Lexicon*] contained a few misprints or errors of the press. These have been copied, with *Simian* servility, into the publication of last year; thus is error propagated. In ten minutes, ten such blundering mishaps of the copyist caught our eye; take for example, 1st "To BLOT THE SKRIP AND JAR IT," Edition of 1811; the *k* in Jark is *dropped out*, leaving a *white* space:—the careful editor of 1822 has left it out also! 2d. "CARVELS RING," in the edition of 1811, Hans Carvel, is misprinted *Ham* at one place—so the *new edition* of last year.

‡ Mr Egan, we have shewn (with small exertion of critical acumen) is wholly incapable of undertaking a work requiring grammatical accuracy—to say no more *here*.

Bee argues that Egan's previous work, including the sporting periodicals that far outsold his own, did not equip him with any particular qualification for the task of producing a dictionary of slang:

Fitness for an undertaking of this nature is not *always* to be found in the aptitude or similarity of an author's previous pursuits. Some pounce upon and perform (a novelty) a miracle at once, by a single effort as it were: this is *genius*; but genius is poetical, and belongs not to a critical glossary or explication, particularly of sporting terms. Hard work, years of drudgery, and *labour upon labour*, is his lot who undertakes the composition of a *dictionary*; and, notwithstanding his utmost care, he subsequently reviseth his pages with a plush for such as seem too positively penned.[5]

The animosity towards Egan is unmistakeable, and requires some explanation. Each of Egan's most popular works was preceded by a similar but less successful work by Bee: *Boxiana* by Bee's *Lives of the Boxers*, *Life in London* by Bee's *Letters from London*. Although Bee was not an innovator in either field, it is easy to see how it might have seemed to him that Egan was not only stealing his ideas, but also making a much better living out of them. The bitterest irony is that Bee was then reduced to cashing in on Egan's success: both *Real Life in London* and the fourth volume of *Boxiana* (1824) have been attributed to him.[6]

The preface is not merely a rant against Egan, however. Bee writes scornfully about all other cant and slang lexicographers, excepting only Grose. This serves to demonstrate the breadth of his reading as well as the superiority of his own work. In apologizing for his general failure to cite his sources, Bee presents the excuse that there are just too many of them:

And, truly some of our authorities would be *none*, as Dogberry might say, not being drawn from *books*, or other *written* documents; but being *dictæ*, aptly *drawn* from the

[5] Bee, *Slang*, xii.
[6] *Real Life in London; or, the Rambles and Adventures of Bob Tallyho, Esq. and his cousin, The Hon. Tom Dashall, through the Metropolis; exhibiting a living picture of fashionable characters, manners, and amusements in high and low life. By an Amateur* (London: Jones & Co., 1821). See also Reid, *Bucks and Bruisers*, 17, 51, 74, 104.

mouths of *downie coves*, phrases over-heard in the market-place, or slang picked up in the coffee-panny, around *the ring*, and at other verbal sources equally authentic, where *the people* do not make parade of their *deep reading* or facile penmanship, the quoting of names would redound little to our—purpose. What satisfaction could be derived from the knowledge that such and such phrases fell in the super-finest style from the potatoe-traps of Harry Lemoine, or Harry Dimsdale, of General or Joe Norton? What though we cited to reappear Bill Soames, or Mister G. Pound, or, indeed, to say no more, of Mr. William Perry [note omitted], each, in his distinct degree, a *professor*? In another walk of *life's varieties*, would our readers balance the preference to be given, in this respect, to those *par nobiles*, Bill Gibbons, Jack Scroggins, or Jack Carter? or those other great *orators*, Jack Atcherlee, Harlequin Billy, or Jack Goodlad?[7]

Framing the preface is the image of the Castle of Lexicography. Slang dictionaries belong, because of their base nature, at the bottom of its structure, but the fortifications at the base of a castle are by no means the least important of its defences. Perhaps in response to Johnson's famous description of the lexicographer:

whom mankind have considered, not as the pupil, but the slave of science, the pionier [sic] of literature, doomed only to remove rubbish and clear obstacles from the paths of Learning and Genius . . .[8]

Bee describes the construction of his own dictionary:

Having well cleared away the rubbish, the elevation proceeds without interruption.[9]

Bee's dictionary contains two lists: the main dictionary, and an 'Addenda of Obsolete and Far-fetched Words and Phrases'. They were clearly compiled together: there are references to the Addenda from within the main list, and terms from the *Lexicon* are found in both. The Addenda is not, like Andrewes's, merely a list of terms that turned up too late for inclusion in the main dictionary. The dictionary proper has 2,237 entries for 1,469 headwords. There are 145 entries for 129 headwords in the Addenda. Bee's main source was the *Lexicon*, but he clearly used several dictionaries, and half of his terms are not found in any earlier cant or slang list (see Appendix, Table 6.1).

<hr/>

[7] Bee, *Slang*, x–xi. Harry Dimsdale was the last Mayor of Garratt (see 29); Bill Soames and Jack Scroggins were boxers. William Perry wrote the *London Guide* (see Chapter 7). It is likely that all the individuals mentioned were familiar names in sporting circles.
[8] Johnson, *Dictionary*, 'Preface'.   [9] Bee, *Slang*, xi.

It is far more difficult to identify Bee's sources for individual entries with any certainty than it is for any of the other slang and cant dictionaries I have looked at. Bee clearly consulted various dictionaries in writing his own entries, rather than merely editing an existing word-list. He often expanded upon what he found in his sources:

Lexicon Balatronicum	Bee
JOBBERNOLE. The head.	*Jobbernoul*—the head, and a thick one too. '—At Troy—' 'Axylus then, an honest soul, Got a great knock o'th' *jobbernoul*.
MAX. Gin.	*Max*—gin, originally of the best sort, abbreviated from *Maxime*; but now, any kind of 'the juniper' is *Max*, Old Tom, the Creature, Eye-water, or Jackey; all meaning 'Blue-ruin.'

or rewrote entries completely:

Lexicon Balatronicum	Bee
DEVILISH. Very: an epithet which in the English vulgar language is made to agree with every quality or thing; as, devilish bad, devilish good; devilish sick, devilish well; devilish sweet, devilish sour; devilish hot, devilish cold, &c. &c.	*Devil . . . Devilish* is used as a superlative by many men, who are *devilish foolish* when they say, they are either devilish queer or devilish cold, devilish glad or devilish sad—*the devil* being neither of these.
SANDWICH. Ham, dried tongue, or some other salted meat, cut thin and put between two slices of bread and butter: said to be a favourite morsel with the Earl of Sandwich	*Sandwich* (a)—an apology for treating the stomach—cold meat between bread and butter.
BRAY. A vicar of Bray; one who frequently changes his principles, always siding with the strongest party: an allusion to a vicar of Bray, in Berkshire, commemorated in a well-known ballad for the pliability of his conscience.	*Vicar of Bray*—one who acts now with this party now that. Bray lies near Putney, and one of its *incumbents* (*circa* 1680) changed to opinions most diametrical, repeatedly.

Occasionally Bee engaged with Grose's definitions without including the material alluded to:

Lexicon Balatronicum	Bee
COCKNEY. A nick name given to the citizens of London, or persons born within the sound of Bow bell, derived from the following story: A citizen of London being in the country, and hearing a horse neigh, exclaimed, Lord! how that horse laughs! A by-stander telling him that noise was called *neighing*, the next morning, when the cock crowed, the citizen, to shew he had not forgot what was told him, cried out, Do you hear how the *cock neighs?* . . .	*Cockney*—See 'Cock.' *Quere*, 'Is he a *cock?*' 'nay'–is the answer, i.e. not a game one. The tale about the cock crowing and the horse neighing, is not worthy of credit—not pointed or semblable. . . .

Bee treated entries from his other sources in much the same way. Despite his insistence that he did not use Egan's list, Bee includes a number of the same terms and tends to be particularly disparaging in their definitions:

Egan	Bee
DEADY. One of the multitudinous epithets applied to gin; used by the poets of the *Holy Land* in many instances, as 'Grows your hand more firm and steady, In handing out the cheering *Deady?*' *Epistle to Randall, vide Randall's Diary.* 'Taught by thee, we've quaff'd the *Deady's* stream At Belcher's or at Randall's seat of strife.' *Lines to Caleb Baldwin, Ibid.* Speaking of pleasure, the bard says, 'I've sought her face on *Moulsey's* ground, Her aërial form in *Deady's gin.*' *Vide Randall's Scrap Book.*	*'Deady's*, a drop of'—Gin,—so called after the rectifier's name in reality, without slangery. *Deady* is dead, now; and this word must be transferred to our addenda in the next edition.

EYE-WATER. Gin. *Cant.*

> *Eye-water*—Brandy—mistakenly used
> of *gin* also—'Wet the other eye,'
> take another glass; probably the
> word should be *whet*, from *to whet*, to
> sharpen, or brighten up the eyes—
> which drams effect awhile . . .

He missed no opportunity to criticize Egan's earlier works:

> *Boxiana*—pron. *Box-hanny* on the frontiers of Cockaigne, and *Box-eye-knee* by the
> *canaille* of Bristol, Birmingham, &c. The word is compounded of the verb to
> *box*—as above; and *ana*, trivial remains, scraps, or forgotten trifles, left by
> learned men. '*Boxiana*, or sketches of pugilism,' is the title of three vols. on
> those subjects, the first of which is alone entitled to our regards here; it was
> compiled in 1811, and 12, by *old* John Smeeton, (the sixpenny *Mæcenas* of our
> earliest flights,) upon the basis of Bill Oxberry's *Pancratia*; the second and third
> by Egan. This publication is the only work of so much bulk in the market; it
> contains numerous details and many good portraits. Whoever possesses either
> of those works, and would correct its errors, fill up its omissions, and see every
> fight at a glance, should add thereto, a compressed tract, entitled '*Fancy
> Chronology*; a history of 700 battles; by John Bee, Esq.' the fancy writer, and
> present quill-man. See *Pancratia*. [Addenda]
> '*Historian* of the prize-ring'—all *fudge*; no such *thing*; *He* of whom it was said
> being incapable of *history*, as we have shewn in 'this *here* book.' Spoken
> ironically by the Blackwood. [Addenda]

or to praise his own:

> *Flabbergasted*—staggered, whether physically or mentally. His colleagues were
> *flabbergasted* when they heard of Castlereagh's *sudden* death: as the Slang-
> whangers and Jargonic writers will be when they consult this work. In
> ring-affairs, a man may be *flabbergasted* by a flush hit between the eyes,
> whether with the gloves or without them.
> *Flat*—one who pays money when he can avoid it, is reckoned *a flat* by most
> people; if he gets done out of any, we also consider him *a flat*, and
> recommend him to take vinegar that is *sharp*, to whet up his wits. He may
> avoid much evil by studying these pages.
> *Life* . . . Few people generalise their ideas so far as to visit *every variety* of life.
> The writer of these sheets has seen ALL except being presented at court, and
> feeling the delights of a prison . . .
> *Novice*—one not initiated into the affairs of town; a new or untried boxer, is a
> novice; all inexperienced persons are *novices*, until they peruse this Volume.

Egan is not Bee's only predecessor to emerge bruised (see Figure 6.1).
The entry for *to box*, shown in Figure 6.1, is also a good example of

BAS—BOX

Bas-bleu—literally, blue stockings; the obsolete name given to a *club* or assembly of *dames sçavantes* (circa 1778) Bath and London. Mesds. Moore, Carter, Montagu, led the way; Mesds. Hurst, Warrens, Mashams, closed the vagary: name obnoxious to the survivors. Their aversions were manifold: 1st. The ascendancy of males. 2nd. *Crim-con.* 3rd. Man-milliners and all male shopkeepers. 4th. Subjection in the marriage-state. 5th. The dance, theatricals, and opera. 6th. All scandal not of their own making; *ergo*, parson Bate, soldier Topham, counsellor Boremy, Jack Bell—his sister, and the Della-Cruscans.

Bazaar—a market-place in the eastern countries; imported here, 1815, and applied by a host of speculators to certain uninhabitable houses, fitted up with myriads of yard-long shops for little dealers, like nests of Dutch pill-boxes—*parvorum succubit magno.* The tumour absorbed in three years.

Bean—a guinea, but this coin being abrogated, so must *bean* be as its surname.

Belch—malt-liquor, beer, ale.

Bilboa—a sword. *Bilboes*—the stocks, or irons—naval. Derived from *Bilbao*, a Spanish port, whence, in the 16th century, issued immense privateers, the piratical crews whereof confined their prisoners thus, in pairs, treys, &c.

Blank—baffled—no proceeds.

Box, to—is 'derived from the noun, *a box*; six pieces of wood fastened together; or *a snuff-box*—Johnson knows not which. Indeed, how should he? Nor does he amend the matter by telling us, that "boxing is fighting with the fist," whereas nothing can be less true, neither one fist or two fists would constitute *fighting*, unless they belonged to different persons, as in the case of two one-armed men. See *Lick, Fighting*. In support of his definition, the doctor adduceth for *authorities*, L'Estrange and Grew, one of whom says, 'the ass stood quietly by, whilst they *boxed* each other a-weary;—the other, *still better*, tells that 'the leopard *boxes* with his paws like a cat.' These extracts *boxes* the doctor's derivation *a-weary*; for a man is only *boxed* when put in prison, and then 'tis the incarcerator who *boxes* him. Unfortunately, for most inquiries respecting the oddities of our language, when old Johnson is but adverted to, all persons are struck dumb,—flabbergasted, put down and done for; notwithstanding the old

BOX   201

boy might happen not to know an atomy of the subject he was expounding—as in the present case. For example: this Johnson (Sam) a lexicographer by trade, having to fight Tom Osborne who lived at the sign of *the folio*, behind Belcher's back-door, instead of turning out fairly, Sam took up a thundering large vol. and floored Tom in a pig's whisker, so that he could not come again. In fine, the name of Johnson has been the *bug-a-boo* to frighten cowards with for half a century. If the verb ' to Box, is to be retained at all—and really we feel no hopes of erasing it, by reason of the great preponderance of fools to be found in the world,—why then, in the names of Harry Stephens, old Ainsworth, and Stemmata Salmon, let us carry *hoc verbum* to its extreme cases. Then will *Boxology* mean the knowledge of boxing and boxers, as taught in these pages; *Boxosophy*—the philosophy of boxing, as exhibited monthly in.'The Annals of Sporting'; *Boximania* —is the passion or desire to behold manful exertions at fisty-cuffs; but more finely exalted by another denomination, viz. 'THE FANCY';—to satisfy which *passion* we publish monthly details of such occurrences, with scrupulous regard to truth, and the exactitude of *the Gazette*. *Box* (v.)—to fight with the fists, but without science. As *pugilism* is the highest species of man-fight, so is *boxing* the lowest. Several intermediate degrees of fighting capabilities are described in the foregoing pages, of which *milling* and *hammering* are most distinctly marked; the latter including those who *slash* away as if they were mowing, and *wallop* their antagonists about the carcase or *maw* (whence ' maw-wallop, and the term ' great wallop-ing chap,' for a big country booby); the preceding terms comprise those who rush in, roley-poley-fashion, alike uncertain of what is to become of themselves or their blows.   Refer back to both terms.   A ' boxing-bout, and 'boxing-match,' is said properly of boy-fights, or the contests of boobies, ploughmen, and navigators.

Boxiana—pron. *Box-hanny* on the frontiers of Cockaigne, and *Box-eye-knee* by the *canaille* of Bristol, Birmingham, &c. The word is compounded of the verb *to box*—as above; and *ana*, trivial remains, scraps, or forgotten trifles, left by learned men. " *Boxiana*, or sketches of the pugilism," is the title of three vols. on those subjects, the first of which is alone entitled to our regards here; it was compiled in 1811,

Figure 6.1 John Bee's *Slang* (1823), 200–1 [BL 626 h 38]

Bee's predilection for gossipy anecdotes, of which there are well over 100, including:

Go along Bob—Bob Bussicks was a notorious sheep-drover in St. John-street, and the word of command 'when flock follows flock in quick succession moving,' was naturally enough extended to all who might engage in the same occupation. 'Come along Bob,' had the same origin. Bob died of old age some thirty years ago, but his tom[b]-stone (if his mortality had such a *thing*,) would not contain the foregoing surname, which was applied to the shape of his legs, that were of this form ( ) or some thicker part of his body; derived from the compound *bi* and *sex* or *section*, or bi-section which his lower members described in walking, or else the double (bi) sex which Robert was supposed to enjoy. Either Hybrid or Hermaphroditical, Bob's choler could not be excited by all the girls in Cow-cross.

Jemmy (bloody)—a sheep's head; so called from a great dealer in these delicious *morceaux*, Jemmy Lincomb, who lived near Scotland-yard, and who, from his occupation, would necessarily be bedaubed with blood. His customers mostly addressed him with 'B—Jemmy, bring us a b—y head, and lend us von o' your b—shlivers,—mine's at my uncle's' *Jemmy*. 'Now, gemmen, there you are, in a pig's vhisper, if you vants it viping, vy there's the bitch ye know.' And the legend adds, that a she-dog's shaggy back served for knife-cloth to his dainty guests. We never *saw it done*, though there was the canine means of cleanliness.

Other entries are encyclopaedic, especially those dealing with sporting matters:

A. M.—Ancaster Mile, at Newmarket, is 1778 yards long . . .

King's plate—King's hundred. 'His majesty's plate.'—A hundred pounds were given by Charles II. to be run for at Newmarket, the best of three four-mile heats, B. C. carrying twelve stone. He afterwards extended the bonus to several other courses, and the number now amounts to twenty-three in Great Britain, and sixteen in Ireland. The stewards give a certificate of the race, and the master of the horse pays by an order on the treasury: there *the tellers* take their toll off, and the balance is then about ninety-five pounds. Heats are disused, horses of all ages now run for 'the king's hundred,' and weights as low as 8st. 4lb. are carried; at Edinburgh less.

'Skool! a skool!'—the cry all along the southern coast when the herrings appear first for the season. We had it from the Bergen fishermen; in English 'tis *shoal*. Herrings swim with their heads turned S. S. W. and drift *tail-in*, or sideways, to those inlets which *stand* differently.

while others contain moral and social commentaries rather than definitions:

Marriage Act—of 1822; the laughing-stock of all sound moralists, the harbinger of unlegal attachments, and the quarterly annoyance of the religiously

disposed, when it was read instead of a sermon. On one such occasion, a pious
Devonian addressed his dumpling-head congregation thus:
'I shall preach no sermon this morning, as you will see:
But shall read what will tire both you and me.'

Worthy—commonly applied to magistrates of police, when they 'act with a
vigour beyond the law.' The scrap-news reporters use it once a week at least, lest
they attract censure and lose their bread; 'tis usually *set down* with a grin—'worthy
of the police,' is *police worthiness (vaut-rien.)* When Home Sumner committed *poor*
Joyce for not telling his name, he too was a *worthy* magiste—rate [sic]. Like-wise
Sir William C. 'I shall send you to Bridewell for a month, said the *worthy*
alderman, where you will have bread and water sufficient to keep soul and body
together, and light enough to let you know there's a god in heaven.' Sublime and
true; therefore not *worthy*.

Bee also takes on the role of guardian of English usage, though his
own prose is often far from clear:

Jargonic-writers—those who adopt a style of their own, which is either not
grammatical, affected, or vulgarly phraseological: 'tis a good North-American
term, (naturalized here) for what we of the *old world* call 'slang-whangery.' A
'Western Luminary,' has this *fine passage*—'Our river Exe, winding her
serpentine course down her beautiful vallies, *was so dilated* by the rains, as,
every here and there, to *extend her fin over her banks*. Sea-gulls mingling with her
swans, were seen floating, &c.' Another says—'A *Phillip* is about to be given to
the book-selling trade, by the publication of a *Methodical Cyclopædia*.'—Vide
Globe, Nov. 18. N.B. This *advertisement*, so luminously drawn up, is meant to be
a pun upon *fillip*, which 'the Trade' did not experience, as none perceived the
intended *wit*: said publisher also printed his own work in some (so called)
Evangelical prints—styling it the 'Methodistical Cyclopedia.' Blackwood
revels in Jargonie, at times—like a drunken schoolmaster, who knows better,
but has lost self-control. But above all persons who ever held a pen in the
service of the public, none surpassed the *sporting editor* of the Weekly
Dispatch;[10] from numerous instances take the latest date, Dec. 15, 1822,
page 8, col. 2. '*Had* Shelton *have* been a younger man, it *might have been* a
different thing.' [To be sure!] '*Had* Hudson *have proved* the conqueror: it was
said *to have been* the intention of his friends *to have backed* him against Gas.' Gas,
however, was *dead!* and the sportful writer knew it—'but,' (says he) 'he was as
dead as a house to their endeavours.' . . .

He shows a particular interest in pronunciation, especially in 'h'
dropping and insertion, which were, by this time, recognized indica-
tors of social class:

Argument.—He attains the best of any tavern *argument*, who has the best pair of
lungs; whence we are inclined to fall in with that pronunciation of the word

[10] None other than Pierce Egan.

which calls it 'Hard gumment.' The next best to him, is he who can *offer* to lay very heavy sums that are quite *un*coverable.

Horse's night-cap—a halter, in which many die, as many more will, unless they *alter* their conduct.

as was 'r' insertion:

Mawley, mawlies—the hands; from *to mawl*, to beat. Pronounced by some thorough-bred cockneys *'Maw'r les,'* and written by some fancy *jargonic-writers*—*'morleys.'* We have 'the *right mawley* of Jem Wines met Warton's *left mawley*, and smash'd it.'

and the replacement of /v/ with /w/, a pronunciation characteristic of contemporary literary representations of cockney dialects:

Veighty-von—a fat landlady, who has a good run of custom, is a weighty one in both senses of the word.

'Way of life' (the)—a state of prostitution. To the question 'What are you, young woman?' a prisoner replies, 'I am in the *vay of life*, your vorship.'

Irish and provincial pronunciations were also staples of popular literature:

Bog-trotter—an Irishman just arrived; pronounced *'bahg-throtter'* by his countrymen of the Long Town. Also *bog-lander*, for ever.

Bull . . . To *bullock*—to bully, hector, or maltreat others. Pron. *boloc*, in Lancashire, where 'tis practised among the Vulgar . . .

Dirty-butter—a handsome lass with a thousand or two, is no *dirty butter*. Adopted out of the Irish; and by them pron. *'Dirirty buttra.'*

Fly—is a corruption of *Fla* (for *flash*), and is but one further step towards that complete abasement in language which is always sought after, and is sometimes partially attained. Already we have it *floi*, from the mouth of the new Yorkshire bruiser. To be *fly* to every thing that is said, any man, however uppish, must pretend to a great deal more *nous* than any one every did or will possess.

as were malapropisms and 'unlettered pronunciations':

Fit—meant to be the preterite of *to fight*. 'Ben's ould father *fit* him last night.' And see *Misfit*.

Massacree—unlettered pronunciation for massacre.

Obstacle (the)—it stands in St. George's Fields, and commemorates the 'No. 45' men, and is written 'obelisk.' Old Calvert, when he began the *rot-gut* trade, grinded his malt by *horse-power*, and being in the habit of riding out one of these rotatory animals, when 'the pair of 'em' arrived at this monument to liberty, 'My horse,' said the brewer, 'vent round and round the obstacle till he vas tired, and me too'.

Bee is also unusual among slang lexicographers in providing gram-matical labelling for a small proportion of the terms he includes. Sometimes this is implied by the inclusion of an article after nouns (see *obstacle* and *sandwich*, above). For verbs, the labelling tends to be explicit:

> *Chise* . . . *Chise-it*—is also a verb inactive, and means 'give over,' whether that be
> *the talk*, or some *action*, as robbery. *Chise* is a knife, sometimes called a *chiser*, from
> *chisel*, a carpenter's sharp instrument: all mean *to cut*, to divide or separate; to
> cut the string, thread, or concatenation of a discourse, and to cut or sever the
> design from the execution thereof, is to *chise* it . . .
> *Spout*—to make a speech. 'To *spout Billy*,' (v.) to recite passages out of
> Shakespeare, in a pompous mouthing manner. Many there are, who go about
> from club to club, and from Free and Easy to midnight, 'spouting Billy,' to
> gaping mechanics, ground-rent bricklayers, and lucky-escape shop-clerks . . .
> '*To Tip*'—to give; a noun as well as verb. '*To tip*,' is to pay . . .
> *Tout*—(v.) to watch. *Touting*—is eying the women generally, or spoiling an amour,
> platonically. 'Tis extended to 'stagging,' also.

For all his criticism of earlier lexicographers, Bee's dictionary is flawed in one other basic respect: its alphabetization is frequently imperfect. *Yam*, for example, occurs in the sequence *yarn, yam, yapp, Yarmouth*; *Cock and Hen* is between *cap* and *cabbage-leaf.*

There are no significant differences in the distribution of terms from Bee's sources between the main listing and the Addenda. In other words, despite his scornful references to Egan, Bee does not show any greater tendency to include terms from his dictionary, or any other, in the list of 'Obsolete and Far-fetched Words and Phrases'. He was, however, particularly reluctant to discard terms for which he had evidence of origin or use, so there are significantly more entries with authorities cited, and significantly more with etymologies in the Addenda than the main list (both $p = 0.01$) (see Appendix, Table 6.3).

In terms of subject matter, the only significant difference is that there are fewer terms for CRIME & DISHONESTY in the Addenda than in the main list ($p = 0.05$). Bee's dictionary represents a move away from the concentration on CRIME & DISHONESTY that we have seen in earlier slang dictionaries, and lives up to its claim to be a diction-ary of sporting life (see Appendix, Table 6.2). Comparison with the *Lexicon* demonstrates that Bee was influenced by subject matter in his selection of terms from it. He chose significantly more terms for FOOD & DRINK than we would expect in a random selection ($p = 0.01$), and significantly fewer for LAW & ORDER ($p = 0.05$).

Bee's dictionary contains considerably more citations, authorities, cross-references, and etymologies than the *Lexicon* (all $p = 0.01$). Although he selected in favour of entries including authorities in the *Lexicon* ($p = 0.01$), Bee was not otherwise influenced by the lexicographic features of his source. This demonstrates how extensive his additions were: all of the new information is culled from outside his main dictionary sources.

Bee was clearly influenced, in part, by semantic considerations in selecting terms from his main source. He also preferred entries citing authorities. Having culled these from the *Lexicon*, he added citations, authorities, etymologies, and cross-references of his own, as well as the social, moral, phonetic, grammatical, encyclopaedic, and usage-related comments that we have seen above. Bee's dictionary is evidently the product of a great deal of independent thought and research. We can probably accept on face value his division into common and unusual terms represented by the main list and the addenda. We might also assume that his selection from his sources was motivated, above all, by a desire to produce an up-to-date list of contemporary slang. This is confirmed by comparison with the *OED*.

The *OED* cites the two lists in Bee's dictionary 141 times. Thirty-seven of these citations provide an early usage.[11] However, despite the *OED*'s extensive use of this dictionary, its 1,400 new entries predate a further seventy-three existing *OED* first citations, by up to seventy years (see *jumble shop*):

beery "drunk" (1848)
blow-out "a feast" (1824)
bogy "a ghost; a spirit" (1836–40: "the devil")
bugaboo "a silly, imposing, talkative man" (1897: "loud or empty talk; nonsense")
casual "a casual lodger" (*a*1852: "a casual worker or visitor, etc.")
casualty "an animal driven or baited to death" (1844: "Used of an individual killed, wounded, or injured")
cheek ". . . but when any one becomes a greedy guts and sups up all, he 'takes it all to his own cheek.' " (1851: *to one's own cheek* "for one's private use")
to cut out "to separate a cockerel from a brood in order to take a measure of their skill in fighting" (1862: *to cut out* "to detach an animal from the herd")
dandy [a type of ship] (1858)
deadly-lively "combining dullness and liveliness" (1838)

---

[11] These include *allowance* "a reduction in the weight carried by a race-horse", *bob* [a bowdlerized form of *God*], *Greek* "an Irishman", *possibles* "money", *ripe* "drunk", *slap-up* "(of a meal) excellent", *snigger* "an ill-suppressed laugh", *snotter* "a handkerchief", *snuffy* "drunk", *sukey* "a tea-kettle", and *wallop* "a heavy blow".

derby [used in the combination *Derby-weights* with reference to the race-course]
   (1838: *Derby day*)
do "an imposture" (1835: n[1] 3)
dose "a thrashing" (1847: "an unpleasant experience")
down on one's luck "temporarily hard-up" (1849: *luck* n 3a)
draw "a game that neither party wins" ([1825] 1856)
to draw "to elicit information from (someone)" (1857: *draw* v 53)
to draw "to pull a badger from its hole" (1834: *draw* v 36)
Eccentrics [the name of a club] (1832: "someone with strange whims")
evergreen [used figuratively with reference to people] (1878)
fence "a receiving house for stolen goods" (1847)
to fence "(of a horse) to leap over a fence" (1884)
fencer "a horse that leaps over fences" (1852)
(bunch of) fives "the fist" (1825: *five* a & n 3b)
flat "a (level) race-course" (1836: n[3] 1c)
to flog "to beat; to excel" (*a*1841)
to be floored "to be baffled or confounded" (1830: *to floor* 'to confound, non plus')
gin-twist "a drink made with gin" (1826)
ye gods and little fishes [an oath] (1871)
gorge "a feast" (1854: n[3])
grubby "dirty" (*a*1845)
guy "a person of grotesque appearance" (1836)
habit-shirt [a type of undergarment] (1834)
infant "an exceptionally large person" (1832)
jumble-shop "a shop where miscellaneous goods are sold" (1893)
juniper "gin" (1857)
kite-flying "raising money" (1834)
Mr Know-me-all "one who pretends to great knowledge" (*know-all* 1881: a; 1895: n)
leader "the leading article (in a newspaper)" (1837)
to nipper "to arrest" (1832: v[1] 2)
off: they're off [said at the start of a horse race] (1833)
out-fighting "fighting at arms' length" (1848)
to pigeon "to send (news) by carrier pigeon" (1870)
to pitch (it) into "to attack (someone)" (1829)
to place "to state the position in which (a horse) finished a race" (1826: 5d)
plated butter "lard coated with butter" (1846: *plated* "having an outer surface . . . of
   finer material than the body")
pleb "a member of the lower orders" (1865)
produce "progeny" (1845)
pussy-cat "a pert coxcomical little lass, with a round face, and nose curled up"
   (1859: 'applied to a person . . . ; now esp. one who is attractive, amiable, or
   submissive')
queer-looking "having an odd appearance" (1825)
referee "one who decides disputed points (in sport)" (1840)
to ride to hounds "to hunt with dogs" (1848: *hound*)

ring "an association" (1869: n^1 11a)

roll "a rolling gait" (1836–7: n^2 1c)

to rush "to make a sudden attack" (1863: v^2 5b)

to get the sack "to be dismissed" (1825: *sack* n^1 4)

shindy "a riot" (1829)

slashing "vicious (of a fighter)" (1827: 'that slashes')

snake-headed "long-faced" (1856)

soft is your horn "you have made a mistake" (1837: *soft-horn* "a fool")

spittoon "a receptacle for spittle" (1840)

stinted "(of a mare) pregnant" (1847)

to take in "to accept stocks as security on a loan" (1893: *take* 84q)

to take it out of (someone) "to exhaust" (1847: *take* 88d)

tapped on the shoulder "arrested" (1859: *tap* v^2 1c)

thick-head "a stupid person" ([1785] 1824)

thing-like "like a material or impersonal thing" (*c.*1854)

that sort of thing phr (1848: n^2 10 a)

turnip "a large watch" (1840)

up: all up "completely finished" (1825: *all* adv^2 12e)

uppercrust "(socially) superior" (1836)

used-up "worn out by hard work" (1848)

to walk over "to treat with contempt" (1851: v^1 5p)

to yap "to speak snappishly" (1864)

Summary

In all of his previous publications, John Bee had been overshadowed by Egan. It was Egan's pugilistic periodical that took the sporting world by storm, and Egan who was allowed to dedicate his work to George IV. As if that were not enough, Egan had the temerity to issue a slang dictionary before Bee had a chance to finish his. Bee's desire to demonstrate his greater knowingness and erudition is apparent throughout his dictionary. In his preface, Bee carefully established his position in the slang dictionary tradition, and mercilessly dismissed contemporary competitors as well as many of his predecessors.

Bee followed Grose in demonstrating an interest in non-standard pronunciation and, unusually, he provided some headwords with grammatical labelling. Not content with merely defining his word-list, Bee produced a self-laudatory work that provides anecdotal and encyclopaedic information, moral and social commentary, and guidance on usage. This wider scope is also indicated by his move away from crime and punishment and towards alcohol and other social and sporting pleasures. The significance of the dictionary as a representation of contemporary slang and colloquial language is demonstrated by its extensive use in the *OED* and by the additional antedatings it provides.

Opinionated and rambling as it sometimes is, the *Dictionary of the Turf* offers a comprehensive and authoritative guide to contemporary sporting slang. Bee's knowledge of the cant and slang dictionary tradition is such that he could confidently claim to be building on the best work available: Grose's dictionary. Like Grose, he made sure that his readers were aware of his extensive written sources; unlike Grose, he used them critically. Both attempted, through extensive use of citations and authorities, and particularly in Bee's case, etymologies, to present scholarly and authoritative reference works. Both also emphasized their use of slang-speaking informants, but Bee commented on non-standard pronunciation much more than Grose had.

Hotten dismissed Bee's dictionary as a 'wretched performance . . . with forced and low wit' and Partridge remarked that 'as an editor [Bee] is inferior to even Pierce Egan'.[12] I disagree with both. This is, in many ways, better than the either the *Lexicon* or Egan's dictionary. Its coverage is more limited both chronologically and in terms of register, which demonstrates that Bee had a clearer and more focused purpose. He also avoided the *Lexicon*'s characteristic carelessness. Egan's dictionary was largely derivative, and added little to the record of slang. Bee was an accurate and observant recorder of contemporary slang, especially sport slang. There is no denying his pompous and rancorous tendencies, but many slang lexicographers are unforgiving critics and unrelenting self-publicists. Unfortunately for Bee, even the production of a far better dictionary than Egan's was not enough to allow him to escape from his rival's shadow. Egan was to be, at least for a time, the Fancy's favourite; Bee a mere also-ran.

---

[12] Hotten, *Dictionary*, 150; Partridge, *Slang*, 84.

7 Minor British Cant and Slang Lists

Although the dictionaries discussed so far are the most significant in terms of size and influence, the late eighteenth and nineteenth centuries also saw the production of numerous minor cant and slang word-lists. These were not issued as dictionaries in their own right; indeed, some were not published at all. Instead, they made up part of larger works, being provided as appendixes or glossaries to them. These word-lists were attached to song-sheets, plays, autobiographies, guidebooks for the visitor to London and for the working policeman, and usage guides. A few appeared in articles in periodical publications. One is a handwritten list in a notebook.

Perhaps the public were dissatisfied with the antiquarian bent of the Grose tradition. It may be that observers of contemporary slang felt that those works did not serve them well. It is possible that they were unaware of earlier publications in this field: some of the lexicographers certainly were. These shorter lists were aimed at a public that could not afford the more extensive volumes produced by the likes of Grose, Egan, and Bee. Independent of the main slang dictionary tradition, these lists make a significant contribution to the record of non-standard English in this period.

George Parker's *Life's Painter* (1789)

George Parker (1732–1800) tried his hand at the navy, the army, running a public house, working as a strolling player, and lecturing on elocution:

His wit, humour, and knowledge of the world, rendered him at one time an indispensable appendage to convivial gatherings of a kind; but in his later days he was so entirely neglected as to be obliged to sell gingerbread-nuts at fairs and race-meetings for a subsistence. He died in Coventry poorhouse in April 1800.[1]

---

[1] The quotation and other biographical information are from *DNB* xliii.235–6.

Despite his many failures, Parker did find some success in publishing. His *View of Society and Manners in High and Low Life*, published in 1781, had included cant words within the text, and Grose had used it as one of his sources. *Life's Painter*, a collection of anecdotes padded out with quotations and overlaid with moralistic comment, has not been universally fêted. With reference to the glossary, which explains terms included in the text, Bee wrote:

In this volume, the vocabulary was extended to the utmost pitch of the author's means, and this might be confined to a mile round Covent Garden.[2]

Part of the description of a ballad singer in the neighbourhood of St Giles's will serve as an example of the content of this part of the volume:

Ballad Singer. Come, my lucky masters, here's a choice collection of songs, that have been sung at Drury-lane, *Common Garden*, Sadler's Wells, the *Uproar-House*, *Fox-Hall*, and other places, out of the most *famoustest roratorios.*—Bless your eyes and limbs, lay out a *mag* with poor *chirruping Joe.*—I don't come here every *darkey*—but come, I'll *lip ye a chaunt*—as *rum* a one as you ever heard—it's intitled and called *The Masqueraders*; or, *The World as it wags.*

> Song
>
> Ye flats, sharps, and rum ones, who make up this pother;
> Who gape and stare, just like stuck pigs at each other,
> As mirrors, wherein, at full length do appear,
> Your follies reflected so apish and *queer.*
>
> Tol de rol, &c. . . .
>
> Attend, while I *sings*, how, in ev'ry station,
> Masquerading is practised throughout ev'ry nation:
> Some mask for mere pleasure, but many we know,
> To lick in the *rhino*, false faces will *show.*
>
> Tol de rol, &c. . . .
>
> Twig methodists phizzes, with mark sanctimonious,
> Their rigs prove to judge that their phiz is erroneous.
> Twig lank-jaws, the miser, that skin-flint old elf,
> From his long meagre phiz, who'd think he'd the pelf?
>
> Tol de rol, &c. . . .

What, no *copper clinking* among you, my hearties? No one to give me hansel? What, have you got *red-hot heaters* in your *gropers*, that you're afraid to thrust your daddles in them? It won't do I say, to stand here for *nicks*—all hearers and no

[2] Bee, *Slang*, vii.

buyers—what, will none of you drop your loose *kelter? Crap* me but I must *shove my trunk,* and *hop the twig*—I see as how there's nothing to be got in this here place.
HIS BLOWEN, *a* FEMALE BALLAD-SINGER, *now joins him.*
Female ballad Singer. Don't mizzle yet.
Male ballad Singer. The kelter tumbles in but *queerly*—however we'll give 'em one
more chaunt . . .[3]

The glossary is presented as a separate chapter. Some entries are extremely lengthy, and their prolixity is excused as follows:

The explanation of the *Cant, Flash* and *Slang* terms, takes in the minutest trifle that relates to the chicanery of frauds, and gives the reader at one view, a perfect knowledge of the artifices, combinations, modes and habits of those invaders of our property, our safety and our lives, who have a language quite unintelligible to any but themselves, and an established code of laws productive of their common safety at the same time, and live in splendor, without the exertion of industry, labour or care.[4]

Before the glossary begins, Parker lists some of the terms he is to explain in it. This would have been useful for locating terms in the glossary, which is not alphabetical, if all of them were included in the preliminary list. As it is, the only possible purpose is padding, and the two extra pages represent no additional effort for Parker or value for the reader.

Some of the cant terms in the glossary occur in the order they appear in the text. Compare the following run of entries with the ballad singer's patter following his song, for example:

Copper clinking. A knowing phrase, such as, what, have you got no halfpence
about you? Nor, I don't hear any *copper clinking.*
Gropers. Pockets.
Daddles. Hands.
Nicks. How they have brought a German word into *cant* I know not, but nicks
means *nothing* in the cant language.
Kelter. Money.
Crap. Hanged.
Shove my trunk. To go away. *Shove my trunk. Trunk* is the *body.*
Hop the twig. Is pretty near the same as Shove the Trunk. It means to depart suddenly.
Blowen. A woman. A *Rum* Blowen. A pretty woman.

In other parts of the glossary the arrangement appears to be semantic, for example:

Calp. Hat.
Wig. *Jasey.*

---

[3] Parker, *Life's Painter*, 124–6.   [4] Parker, *Life's Painter*, 136–7.

Hair. *Strummel.*
Neckcloth. *Squeeze-clout.*
Shirt. *Lally.* To wash your own shirt, that is *dabble your lally.*

This selection also illustrates the list's tendency to shift between presenting the cant term as headword and giving the standard English term first, with the cant term italicized in either case. There are a number of trends: longer entries tend to have a cant headword and where synonyms only are given, the headword is often standard English. This has the advantage, in places, of allowing the presentation of more than one cant term with the same meaning, for example:

Eyes. Peepers or ogles.
Guinea. Ned, quid, or ridge.
Sixpence. A bender, crook, or cripple.

Sometimes, instead of providing a synonym, Parker defines his headword:

Flats. Men who are easily taken in, imposed on, or in their language, *to be had, or spoke to.*
Sharps. Men of a contrary nature. This term is applied to sharpers in general, who are continually looking out for flats, in order to do them upon the *broads,* that is *cards,* or in short, any thing else, from pitch and hustle in Moorfields to the Pharo table at St. James's.

The definition is occasionally introduced by 'meaning' or 'is':

Cherruping Joe. Meaning a good ballad singer.
Mizzle. Is sneaking away, or running away. When they make their escape from a constable, I tipt him the *rum mizzle.*
Rum one. Meaning a good one.

In a few cases the grammar of the headword and definition do not match, for example:

Dubber mum'd. To keep your mouth shut, or be obliged to hold your tongue.
Drop the glanthem. Parting with money.

The glossary also contains some terms more than once, including:

Gammon. Gammon and Patter is the language of cant, spoke among themselves; when one of them speaks well, another says he gammons well, or he has got a great deal of *rum patter.*

Gammon and Patter. Jaw talk, &c. A fellow that speaks well, they say he gammons well, or he has a great deal of rum patter.

Ken. Is a house.

Tick. Is your watch.

Ken. A house.

Tick. A watch.

Some entries tend towards the anecdotal. For example:

Hot. A mixed kind of liquor, of beer and gin, with egg, sugar and nutmeg, drank mostly in night-houses, but when drank in a morning, it is called *flannel*. This was a favourite liquor of the celebrated Ned Shuter's: I remember spending an evening with him, in company with that darling of his age, doctor Goldsmith; staying rather late, as we were seeing the doctor to his chambers in the Temple where he then lived, Shuter prevailed on him to step into one of these houses, just to see a little *fun*, as he called it, at the same time, assuring the doctor, that no harm might be apprehended, as he was well acquainted with the *cove* and *covess*, *Slavey* and *Moll Slavey*, that is, the landlord and landlady, man and maid servant; upon the strength of this, we beat our rounds till we arrived at the door of the house; in the middle of the door was a wicket, through which the landlord looked, and the moment he saw Shuter, without any questions the door flew open as by enchantment; we entered, the doctor slipt down on the first seat he saw empty, Shuter ordered a quart of *gin hot*; we had no sooner tasted it but a voice saluted Shuter thus, 'I say, master Shuter, when is your benefit? Come tip us a *chaunt*, and hand us over a ticket, and here's a bobstick.' Shuter took this man by the hand, and begged to introduce him to the doctor, which he did in the following manner: 'Sit down by my friend; there, doctor, is a gentleman as well as myself, whose family has made some noise in the world; his father, I knew, a drummer in the third regiment of guards, and his mother sold oysters at Billingsgate; he's likewise *high borned* and *deep learned*; for he was borned in a garret and bred in a night-cellar.' As I sat near, the doctor whispered me, to know whether I knew this gentleman Mr. Shuter had introduced; I replied, I had not that honour, when, immediately, a fellow came into the box, and in a kind of an under voice asked the person Mr. Shuter had introduced, 'How many there were crap'd a Wednesday?' The other replied, 'three.' 'Was there ere a *cock* among them?' resumed the other, (meaning a fellow who died game.) 'No, but an old *pal* of your's, which I did a particular piece of service to as he was going his journey; I took the liberty of troubling him with a *line*, which he had no sooner got about his neck, than I put my thumb under the bur of his left ear, and at the same time, as I descended from the cart, I gave him such a gallows snatch of the *dew-beaters*, that he was dead near twenty minutes by the sheriff's watch before the other two. I don't recollect that I have *crap'd* a man better for this twelvemonth.' The doctor beckoned to Shuter, and in the same breath cried out, 'For Heaven's sake who is this man you have introduced to me?' 'Who is he?' says Shuter; 'why he's squire Tollis, don't you know him?' 'No, indeed,' replied the doctor: 'Why,' answered Shuter, 'the world vulgarly call him the *hang-man*, but here he is stiled the *crap-merchant*.' The doctor rose from his seat in great perturbation of mind and exclaimed, 'Good God! and have I been sitting in company all this while with a hang-man?' The doctor requested I would see him out of the house, which I did, highly pleased with the conversation of two men, whose feelings of Nature as widely differed as those of the recording angel in Heaven's high chancery (as mentioned in Sterne's story of Le Fevre) to the opposite one of the midnight ruffian, who murdered the ever to be lamented Linton*. [note: Mr. Linton, a musician, who was robbed and most inhumanly murdered in St. Martin's-lane.]

and they emphasize that whatever Parker's skills may have been as an observer of the language, he was not a disciplined lexicographer.

There is some variation in order between the three editions of the list that I have examined, but nothing significant. Errors, repetitions, and inconsistencies are not corrected. The 1800 edition adds a few terms, including:

Ballooning. When a balloon is to be liberated it occasions a great concourse of people, and the pick-pockets can work better then, and with more ease and safety than at any other public amusement.

Cligh. A purse.

Squeeze clout and nap his rum twang. This is a boast of what a person can do at the time of the ascending of a balloon. She says she has robbed one man twice the same day, and if she should see him to-morrow she verily believes, that at the time of the balloon being liberated, he will stand his Squeeze Clout being unbuckled, that is, his stock, and nap his Rum Twang, which is his silver stock-buckle.

but also omits some, with no apparent pattern, except that a sequence of several entries is often deleted together (*whip, horse,* and *pistols* occur together, as shown below). Deleted entries include:

Fire Priggers. No beast of prey is so noxious to society, or so destitute of feeling as these wretches. The tyger who leaps on the unguarded passenger will fly from the fire, and the traveller shall be protected by it, while these wretches who attend fires, and rob the sufferers under pretence of coming to give assistance, and assuming the style and manner of neighbours and acquaintances, take every advantage of distress and confusion; a recent instance of the late fires which have happened at the Opera-House, &c. is a convincing proof how far these pests of society have carried their unhallowed depredations. People who like the late sufferers, should endeavour to collect themselves as well as the dreadful situations at such alarming times will admit. And though they have been imposed upon by the Fire Priggers, yet by advertising the articles, and setting forth that you have a recollection of the persons to whom you delivered the effects, there may be some chance of your getting them back, especially if they should have been given to neighbours or housekeepers, as those persons will be afraid to hold them after such advertisements appearing in the public papers, hand-bills, &c.

Whip. *Flogger.*

Horse. *Prad.*

Pistols. *Barking-irons.*

Gob-stick. A silver table spoon.

The 1789 editions have 158 entries for 154 headwords, and the 1800 edition has 118 entries for 114 headwords (counting repeated terms twice). Despite the deletions and additions in the 1800 edition, none of the differences in the overall semantic make-up of the word-lists is statistically significant (see Appendix, Table 7.1). Parker's list focuses on the fields of CRIME & DISHONESTY and on terms for objects that are moveable and therefore stealable, such as MONEY and CLOTHES. Terms for parts of the body, which would be essential in any code used to give instructions between thieves, are also common. These fields, together with LAW & ORDER, account for about two-thirds of the entire content of Parker's list.

Parker gives only one etymology: for *nicks*, as shown above. Although his list is a glossary to the text, Parker provides twenty-two of his headwords with further illustrative citations. Eighteen of these are in the first half of the list ($p = 0.05$).

The *OED* lists *Life's Painter* fifty-five times, and it often provides the earliest citation for the term it illustrates. It predates fifteen existing *OED* first citations by up to eighty-one years (see *rum snoozer*):

bender "a sixpence" (1836)

bull "a crown" (1812: n[1] 7)

to chaunt "to advertise" (1816: *chant* 'to sell (a horse) fraudulently')

chirruping "that sings" (1826: "that chirrups")

the drop [a method of cheating] (1812)

to fix "to hand over to the authorities" (1836: 14c)

glim "an eye" (1820)

to hobble "to transport" (1812: "to arrest"; 1831: "to tie the legs (of an animal) together to prevent straying")

kelter "money" (1807)

mizzle "the slip" (1912)

prad "a horse" (1798)

scrag "the neck" ([1756] 1829)

skylarker "one who breaks into a house through sky-lights" (compare, 1839: 'one who skylarks')

rum snoozer "a sound sleeper" (1878: *snoozer* "one who snoozes")

village bustler "a kleptomaniac" (1795: *village butler*)

Parker's dictionary has no obvious single source, although some of the terms listed are familiar from earlier cant dictionaries. The chaotic arrangement and unsatisfactory definitional style of his list also suggest that he compiled the list independently. The glossary functions as an explanation of terms included in the text, but the additional anecdotes render it entertaining in its own right. The erratic order and manner in which terms are listed make it unlikely that the dictionary could have been intended for any function other then entertainment. Parker's list is, however, a valuable independent source of information about canting terms and dishonest practices during the 1780s, and was consequently used by many later cant and slang lexicographers.

T. B.'s *The Pettyfogger Dramatized* (1797)

This short glossary was appended to a self-published play. The play itself, dealing with the problems of debt and the corruption of lawyers, has little merit. It is dedicated to Lloyd, Lord Kenyon, who is praised for his knowledge and integrity, and encouraged to use these qualities to prevent 'the depredations unprincipled attornies are committing.'[5] The identity of the author is unknown. The list contains just seventy-eight entries, and confirms the currency of twenty-nine terms in Grose's dictionary, including *bit* "money; property", *flat* "a fool; a victim", and *seedy* "poor".

Entries in the glossary tend to take the grammatical form in which they appear in the play. For example:

The Pettyfogger Dramatized	The *Pettyfogger* glossary
I thought he'd have struck me: Dam'me, I wish he had! I'd have *crown-officed* him. (II i)	CROWN-OFFICED HIM. The most litigious and expensive way of proceeding against a person for an Assault.
. . . come, my *little Goliah*—there's only two of these *good looking pictures* betwixt you and the Pillory, hand 'em over (I iii)	GOOD LOOKING PICTURES. Alluding to his Majesty's Profile on a Guinea.
That fellow Sly always *kicks* me, in spite of my soul (I iii)	KICKS-ME. Obtains his Ends of me.
Dam'me, where am I to get the pieces? (I iii)	PIECES. Guineas.
Bring any with you who has the *quids*; you know I keep open house of Sundays. (I i)	QUIDS. Cash.
Damn the fellow, he sticks to one as fast as old mortar! (I iii)	STICKS TO ONE. Will not be refused.

[5] T. B., *The Pettyfogger Dramatized; in Two Acts* (London: the Author, 1797), vi.

The list, like the play it glosses, is largely concerned with debt and with the exploitation of debtors by their creditors and by lawyers (see Appendix, Table 7.2):

CAPTION FEE. The Bailliffs Fee for the Arrest.
OUTNUMBER AND OUTVALUE THEM. Four Parts in five, in Number and Value of the Creditors proving under a Commission must sign the Consent to the Certificate.
SHY COCK. A Debtor who a long time eludes the Officer.
WARRANT OF ATTORNEY. The Confession of a Debt, subjecting the Party to an Execution against his Person and Effects, by which he is imprisoned without Bail.

Many entries include encyclopaedic and anecdotal information. For example:

DR. DUMAINAUDUC. A Professor of Animal Magnetism (lately deceased), much encouraged about eight year ago by H.R.H. the D--- of G----r; and persons of distinction.
JONES AND IDSWELLS. Three notorious Jew Rogues. Jones was convicted of robbing a Banker's Clerk, and confining him in a house in Hatton-Garden; the night before his intended execution, he hung himself in the cell, and was buried in Hatton-Garden. --- *Idswells*, two young men were his nephews; the one was shot in endeavouring to escape from his keeper, who imprudently conducted him out of jail in the night under a pretence of seeing a sick aunt. The other was hung. They were both charged with forging Stamps for Seamens Wills and Powers.

The *OED* does not cite this glossary at all. It predates one existing *OED* first citation but see also 196, above:

to be had "to be taken in" (1805 *to have* 15c "to deceive").

'The Diary of a Celebrated Police Officer' (1799)

In 1799 the *Morning Herald* published an extract from a diary, allegedly written by a police officer. It was reproduced in 1810 in the *Rambler's Magazine* of New York, under the title 'From an English Magazine. Diary of a celebrated Police Officer'.[6]

This comic diary is interlarded with cant and slang phrases and jocular malapropisms, and runs from Monday to Sunday of a single week. It presents its writer as idle, drunken, corrupt, ignorant, incompetent, and motivated only by the hope of financial reward.

---

[6] 'The Diary of a Celebrated Police Officer', *Rambler's Magazine*, New York, 1810, ii.65–8. I have been unable to gain access to the original.

He mixes both with the capital's low life and with the highest ranks, including royalty, thus implicating the whole of society in his corruption. Criminals operate without fear of prosecution, even braving execution by returning from transportation. The victims of crime have to be coerced into appearing against them. Nobility, royalty, and the diarist himself, consider the malefactors' language and behaviour to be sources of amusement rather than alarm. The lower orders have no respect for their superiors, and even turn executions into entertainment by writing canting songs. In its first publication, this piece was a satirical comment on contemporary life; republished in America its purpose is to criticize English society and institutions.

The alphabetical glossary that accompanies this diary contains only nineteen entries, largely for terms included in it. Its focuses are CRIME & DISHONESTY, LAW & ORDER, and FOOD & DRINK, mostly drink (see Appendix, Table 7.3):

'Diary'

... *Tuesday.* Did not get up till noon, having drank rather too freely of *black strap* the night before ...
Memorandum. If any thing done by *scamps-men* on the Fulham road, send the *traps* to *pull up* Bounce and Blunderbuss, two *forties* at least, besides what the *prads* will fetch at the repository. ...
Friday. Attended at the office—three boys brought in for *prigging* of *wipes*—no prosecutors appeared— blew up the patrole for not apprehending them, as well as the thieves. At twelve o'clock, went to the lectures at St. James's ... sir John *lipt* us the favorite *chaunt* of poor *Jerry Abershaw's.*
Sunday. Put on my best mourning— went to Chapel Royal—lost my new *caster,* cost twenty five shillings—the king and all the royal family (god bless 'em) laughed ready to split their sides to think how the knowing one was done. ...

Glossary

Black-strap—Red Port.
Traps—Runners.
Grabbed—*Pulled up*—Synonymous for apprehending.
Forties—Rewards.
Prads—Horses.

Wipes—Pocket handkerchiefs.

Lip a chaunt—Sing a song.

Caster—A Hat.

There is no single source for the glossary, so we can take it as independent confirmation of terms listed elsewhere, several of which are found in a variety of other lists. The text itself is so obviously contrived that we should not necessary believe that the previously recorded terms in it were still in use. They may simply have become part of clichéd literary faux-cant. The list antedates only one existing *OED* first citation: *forties*, is cited from Australian slang with the sense "A 'crook', thief, sharper . . . convict" from 1879 onwards.

James English's 'A New Vocabulary of Fashionable Phrases' (1813)

In 1813 the *European Magazine* published a piece on fashionable language by James English, who wrote from Cornwall after a recent trip to London 'a place I have not been in these forty years before'.[7] Asking his cousin about a recently married niece:

I was told, with an air of seeming indifference, 'that she was in *confinement.*' Alarmed at this news, I exclaimed, 'Good G—! what has she done to incur this disgrace?'—'Disgrace!' replied my cousin, 'what disgrace can there be in an *accouchement?*'—Here I was as much at a puzzle as ever, till, upon a further explanation, I was told that my niece was *lying-in*, and that *confinement*, or *accouchement*, was the fashionable word to convey the meaning of my *horrible country phraseology.*

On request, the lady provided a list of fashionable phrases for her country cousin, reprinted in the magazine for the benefit of other travellers. The glossary contains forty-three headwords, with one entry each. The first is unrepresentative, in that it does not consist of headword and definition:

The parts of a lady's person that can be described either physically or in polite conversation	The head—the neck—extremity of the neck—stomach, arms, and sides—and feet—*Cætera desunt.*

Later entries continue this ridicule of fashionable squeamishness about the body and its natural functions:

A Lady's pockets	Ridicules.
Ditto petticoats	Under garments.* [note: Invisibles]
Ditto shift	Chemise.
Man-midwife	Accoucheur.

---

[7] James English, 'A New Vocabulary of Fashionable Phrases', 111–12, *European Magazine* 64 (1813), 111.

| Pregnancy .... | In a family way; or, to speak poetically, in that way in which 'Women wish to be who love their lords.' |

Accoucheur is just one of a number of pretentious names for familiar occupations and locations. For example:

A Barber	Peruqueur.
A Hair-dresser	Frizeur.
A Milk-house	Lactarium.
A Coachmaker's-yard.....................	Harmatopoloterion.

Euphemisms for debt and the debtor's fate are grouped together:

Debts	A temporary embarrassment.
Bankruptcy....................................	A Misfortune.
Flying from creditors	Retirement.
King's Bench Prison	Ellenborough Lodge.
Address to a prisoner in the King's Bench Prison	Charles Rackitt, Esq. K.B.
The Fleet	No. 9 Fleet market.

and the list closes with a selection of terms for sexual misconduct:

Adultery	A delicate attachment.
Female fornication	A Slip.
An adulterer	A Cher Ami.
A cuckold	A Good-natured man.

thus emphasizing that fashionable Londoners were both more libertine and more hypocritical than their country counterparts. As is clear from the closing comment,

'Lud! Lud!' (as the man in the play says) 'what a fashionable age do we live in!'

this list comments as much on fashionable life as fashionable language. Euphemisms often reveal areas of anxiety, so it is interesting that the largest semantic area in this list is that of WORK (24.5 per cent), which represents contact between the leisured classes and the working people who serve them (see Appendix, Table 7.4). CLOTHES (14.3 per cent), BODY & HEALTH (8.2 per cent), SEX (8.2 per cent), and also, to a lesser extent, ANIMALS (6.1 per cent) are all included because of their relationship with changing ideas about sexual morality and physical modesty. This is even reflected in the FOOD terms (4.1 per cent):

A Buttock of beef .... A round of beef.
Lamb's-fry .... Lamb's appurtenances.

Debt, as has already been noted, is another area of anxiety for these new middle classes. It is also worth remarking that this glossary deals with servants, clothes and looks, childbirth, and shopping. It clearly represents the fashionable vocabulary used by women, who are thus held responsible for the hypocrisy of modern life. Like modern lists of politically correct language, this may include terms invented purely to discredit the trend.

The *OED* does not cite this list at all and predates many of the terms listed here by thirty or forty years. This list antedates two existing *OED* first citations: for *peruqueur* "hairdresser" (1823: ***perukier***) and *cob* "a strong little horse" (1818 n[1] 4).

A Crime-fighter's Notebook (*c.*1816)

In the British Library's manuscript collections are two notebooks dating from the period 1812 to 1816. They once belonged to Sir John Silvester, who was Recorder of London from 1803–22:

Widely known as a randy reprobate—'Black Jack' he was called—he demanded sexual favours from any lady who came to beg him for mercy or justice. He was also slapdash in his trying, though not alone in this . . . and prejudice against the prisoner always ruled.[8]

The Recorder was responsible to the aldermen of London for civil and criminal jurisprudence, and the contents of the notebooks certainly indicate an interest in the dubious activities of London's inhabitants. One contains lists of thieves' dens, receivers of stolen goods, and felons returned from transportation. There are also detailed notes about the case of a fence named Benjamin Farmer.[9] The other notebook lists houses of resort and more receivers of stolen goods, but much more interestingly for our purposes, on pages 49r–51v, is 'A List of Cant Words with their Meaning' (see Figure 7.1).[10]

[8] V.A.C. Gatrell, *The Hanging Tree. Execution and the English People 1770–1868* (Oxford: Oxford University Press, 1996), 359.   [9] British Library Additional MS 47466.
[10] British Library Egerton MS 3710.

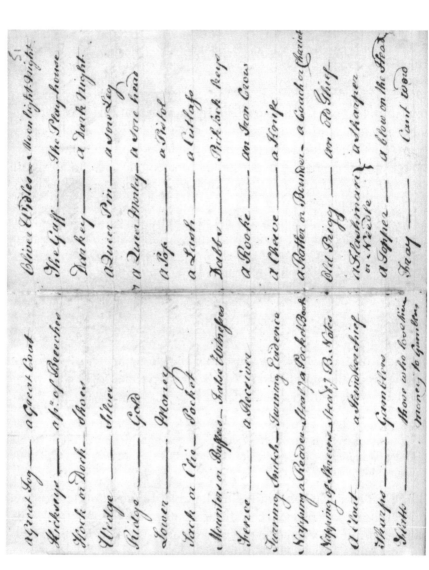

Figure 7.1. A Handwritten Cant List, 50v–51 [BL MS Egerton 3710]

It contains seventy-seven entries for some eighty-nine cant terms. There appears to be some semantic grouping, but it is not carried through consistently, and the list is so focused that terms of similar meaning were likely to fall close to one another by chance alone:

Crapping—Hanging
Teased—Whipping
Standing in the stoop—Pillory
Lagged—Transported
Start—Newgate
Done in the Start—Imprisoned in it
Tumbler—a Cart
Shoving the Tumbler—Whipped at Cart tail
Patter—To try
Pattered—to be tried
Making Whites—Coining Shillings
Making Browns—Coining Halfpence

Note that phrases (*done in the start, shove the tumbler*), follow entries for terms included in them, and that derived forms (*pattered*) follow the root.

Most of these terms had been recorded in cant and slang dictionaries before, but the compiler would have had to have consulted the *Lexicon* and the dictionaries of Potter and Vaux to have gathered them all. This is clearly unlikely, and the unusual spelling of some of the headwords supports the supposition that the list was independently compiled from the spoken word:

usual form	Notebook
fawney	A Fawnee—a Ring
castor	A Cast—a Hat
smish	A Smitch—a Shirt
cly	Sack or Clie—Pocket
screen	Napping of Skreens—Steal[in]g of B[ank] Notes
whiddles or widdles	Oliver widles—Moonlight Night
chive	A Cheive—a Knife

The glossary fulfils our expectation of the semantic range of the cant terms that a crime fighter was likely to come into contact with in the course of his duties (see Appendix, Table 7.5), focusing on CRIME & DISHONESTY and LAW & ORDER. Although this is a very short list, it predates two existing *OED* first citations. These are *bounder* "a coach" (1842) and *burst* "house-breaking" (1857).

William Perry's *London Guide* (1818)

This book, priced at 3*s* 6*d*, was presented as a guide for unwary visitors to London. It warned them against cheats, swindlers, and pickpockets, and aimed:

To supply the place of a *living friend*, and in some cases to perform the necessary part of one, by directing the stranger in the choice of companions, and what characters he should avoid . . .[11]

Two voices speak in this volume. Its editor is identified only as 'a Gentleman, who has made The Police of the Metropolis, an Object of Enquiry Twenty-Two Years'. This gentleman used 'the verbal communications of William Perry, and Others'[12] in the compilation of the work.[13] Perry, who also addresses the reader directly, claims to have acquired his understanding of the activities of London's cheats and frauds by personal experience and acquaintance. He resents the gentleman's interference in his written style:

. . . I am willing to make amends for my past life, by disclosing such secrets as never were made public before, not upon paper; and I thought I would have a few words of my own put down in *genuine* at the beginning, without any of *his* 'making or meddling'.[14]

The body of the volume consists of descriptions of the techniques used by criminals, and advice on how to avoid falling victim to them. For example, to avoid burglary one should burn a light at night, fix an alarm bell to the outside of the house, put a chain on the door, and keep an eye on the neighbours' houses in the hope that they would do the same in return. Now less familiar anti-burglary measures, at least in London, are the warnings to suspect the servants and keep firearms well maintained.[15]

The cant list, containing eight-nine entries, follows immediately after the introduction:

The *terms of art* are explained in the vocabulary; to which the reader may have recourse whenever he is under any difficulty. Among them will be found, also, the English rendering of foreign phrases, which have been retained in the body of the work only because they make part of *the flash* as used by such topping ones as Tom Furby, the young ruffian, Bob Holloway, and such like old ones who knew well how to astonish the natives with scraps of Latin, &c. and who are imitated or

---

[11] William Perry, *The London Guide, and Stranger's Safeguard* (London/Liverpool: J. Bumpus, W. Sharpe/T. Hughes et al, 1818), iv.   [12] Perry, *London Guide*, title page.
[13] Bee, *Slang*, xi *n*. implies that the gentleman in question was the reformed Perry's employer, a brewer.   [14] Perry, *London Guide*, v.
[15] Perry, *London Guide*, 144–62.

copied by great numbers of lads upon every kind of *lay*. Women street walkers of the better sort affect to talk French upon all occasions, as a means of showing their breeding.[16]

The list is arranged in more or less alphabetical order, with occasional lapses. What is unusual in such a short list, is that it contains etymologies, variously giving the language of origin:

C'est toute autre chose, French, quite a different sort of thing.
Felo-de-se, Latin. Self-murderer.
Gusto, Italian, taste, feeling.
Hygeia, Greek for health.
Penchant, French, love, attachment.
Sanctum Sanctorum, Latin, inner or sacred place.

or indicating semantic development:

Stag (to) to look hard at; as stags or deers do on all intruders.
To have *Turnips* (turn-ups) a refusal or denial.

There are also some indications of register and geographical distribution:

Carney, softening talk, common in Ireland.
Let In, at gambling, a betraying.
Massacree, vulgar for massacre, murder.
Vestal, ironical for an incontinent person.

Fewer in number are citations and compounds, cross-references, authorities, and indications of grammatical category and pronunciation:

Cove, a man: thus, Mace Cove, Ding Cove, are 1. a cheating fellow; 2. a robbing fellow.
Ding, to carry off hastily. See Cove.
Galimaufry, odd mixture, revelry; from *Gallimatia* probably: see Amelia, B. 7. ch. 4.
Game, verb, to wink at or encourage theft.
Outre Cela, French, beyond the mark or pitch; *Pron.* 'outray slang.'

There are, however, several entries where the parts of speech in headword and definition do not match, or where different parts of speech are presented under a single headword, for example:

Draw, an entrapping question: to pick a pocket.
Flash, to be knowing to brag. [sic]
Had-Up, to be, police examination.
Mealy-Mouthed, backwardness of speech.
Upon the Town, street walkers, men or women.

[16] Perry, *London Guide*, vii.

There are, additionally, a few errors that appear to have been introduced by the typesetters, such as the omission of a comma in the definition for *flash*, above, and the spellings for *verbum* and *conciliating*:

Sweet, kind, concilating.
Verburn Sat, Latin, means—'a word to the wise is enough.'

and the inclusion of 'slang' in the pronunciation for *outre cela* (above), where it is obviously intended as a usage label. Although this is clearly a list compiled by an amateur and inadequately proofread, it still demonstrates a well-developed sense of what a dictionary ought to contain.

Like the word-list in the British Library's notebook, this one also concentrates on the language of CRIME & DISHONESTY, although EMOTION & TEMPERAMENT also figure fairly largely (see Appendix, Table 7.6).

Forty-nine of Perry's cant terms had not been listed in cant dictionaries before. Of those that had, the *Lexicon* contains thirty-one, Potter's dictionary sixteen, and Andrewes's twelve. Vaux's dictionary, which may have predated this in manuscript form, contains nineteen of its entries. No single source contains all the terms that had been recorded in earlier dictionaries. This, and the fact that over half of Perry's terms are new, suggests that he compiled the list himself, rather than deriving it from an earlier dictionary.

The *OED* cites the *London Guide* four times. It predates another seven existing first citations, for *lag* "transportation" (1821), *to let in* "to betray" (1832: 'to involve in loss or difficulty by fraud, financial failure, etc.'), *nutty* "amatory" (1821), *opaque* "stupid" ([1755] 1850), *plant* "a planned fraud" (1825), *snuffy* "drunk" (1823: a² 3), and *whop* "a blow" (a1825).

John Hamilton Reynolds's *The Fancy: A Selection from the Poetical Remains of the late Peter Corcoran* (1820)

Reynolds (1796–1852) was a poet and lawyer. He was a regular correspondent of Keats's, and was also much influenced by the work of Byron and Wordsworth. He was never able to fulfil his potential in either of the professions competing for his time.[17]

---

[17] *DNB*, xlviii.50–2.

Published anonymously, this volume gives a fictional account of the life of Peter Corcoran, born in Shrewsbury in 1794. As a young man, he became interested in 'the fancy' (i.e. boxing), and as a result was rejected by Kate, the woman he had hoped to marry. The volume contains 'King Tims the First: An American Tragedy', 'The Fields of Tothill: A Fragment', and other short poems, some of which appear at appropriate points in the account of his life. The poems contain a few slang terms, but their densest occurrence is in a letter written to Kate, using an extended boxing metaphor to describe their relationship:

I assure you I am not *fibbing*, when I say, I regret that my last letter proved so severe a *punisher* to you. You have, however, *returned upon* me pretty smartly. You have quite *hit me off* my pugilistic legs,—*doubled* me and my letter up at a *blow*,—and actually *floored* me. And though (as this may serve to show) you have not altogether 'taken the *fight* out of me,' yet you see I come very languidly *up to the scratch*; and this will be in all probability the last *round* in which I shall present myself before you in a *milling* attitude. You are *too much* for me. I am but a *light weight*, and you carry too much *gravity*. . . .[18]

Judging by her response to an earlier letter, we can assume that Kate would not have been impressed:

I glanced my eye over line after line, and page after page, in hopes of meeting with something that was intelligible, and (shall I add?) interesting . . .[19]

The 'almost obligatory'[20] glossary deals largely with VIOLENCE (19.6 per cent), ALCOHOL (17.9 per cent), and PLEASURE & PASTIMES (14.3 per cent) (see Appendix, Table 7.7). There is no indication of how it was collected, but several of its forty-six entries, for forty-four headwords, are not found in the text. Entries are more or less fully alphabetized:

BLUE RUIN.—*Stark-naked*. Gin.
BLUNT.—*Coal*. Money
BROWN.—Porter.—*Heavy Brown*. Stout.—*Heavy Brown with a dash of Blue in it*. Stout mixed with Gin.—Also, a Penny-piece.—*A Georgy*.
BUFF.— *To peel*. To strip.
BOXIANA.—The Lives of the Pugilists in 2 vols.[21]

---

[18] *The Fancy: A Selection from the Poetical Remains Of the late Peter Corcoran* (London: Taylor and Hessey, 1820), xxii.   [19] *The Fancy*, xxi.
[20] Reid, *Bucks and Bruisers*, 89.
[21] One of several tributes to Egan, who was already making his name as a sporting writer.

Four entries, three of which are shown above, include slang synonyms listed before the definition. Other synonyms are sometimes provided after or in place of the definition:

FLOOR.—To knock down. To *grass*.
GIVER.—A *punisher*.
SCRATCH.—The *line* to which the Boxers are brought when they *set to*.

A few entries contain other related terms:

CHATTERING.—A blow that *tells*.
DAMP.—To wet with *heavy brown*, or *stark-naked*.

The *OED* cites the *Fancy* seventeen times: under Corcoran's name three times, and fourteen times under Reynolds's (all from 'M' onwards). It predates three existing first citations: for *damp* "to take a drink" (1862), *raw* "an innocent" (1868), and *short* "undiluted gin" (1823: "undiluted spirit").

The Life of David Haggart (1821)

David Haggart (1801–21), the son of a gamekeeper, was born in Edinburgh. He enlisted as a drummer in the Norfolk militia, but was discharged when the regiment left for England. He was then apprenticed to a millwright, but on his master's bankruptcy he resorted to picking pockets, shoplifting, and burglary. His limited skills as a criminal led to six imprisonments, followed by four escapes. During one of these escapes, he killed a Dumfries turnkey, and when he was next arrested for theft he was recognised and tried as a murderer:

between the trial and his execution he partly wrote, partly dictated, an autobiography, which was published by his agent . . . It is a curious picture of criminal life, the best, and seemingly the most faithful of its kind, and possesses also some linguistic value, as being mainly written in the Scottish thieves' cant, which contains a good many genuine Romany words.[22]

The *Life* accords with contemporary accounts of Haggart's trial, and includes some cant in the text. For example:

I had not been long seated [at the theatre] till I observed a cove and blone, the latter sporting an elegant dross-scout, drag, and chats. In the course of the evening

---

[22] This quotation and all of the biographical information about Haggart are from *DNB* xxiii.438.

I got a seat behind them, and succeeded in undubbing the stretch which slung the scout round her waist, and got clear off with all.[23]

The word-list contains 128 cant terms in 122 entries, including most of the cant in the text. There are no differences between the lists in the two extant editions. It is fully alphabetized, with occasional lapses. Most entries are very short, containing only the cant term and a standard English synonym:

Benjy, *a vest.*
Blink, *light.*
Blone, *a girl.*
Budge, *drink.*
Budge kain, *a public-house.*

Some include cant synonyms, usually reciprocally:

Bit, *money; blunt.*
Dumbie, *a pocket-book; lil.*
Prig, *a pickpocket; snib.*
Tile, *a hat; toper.*

Blunt, *money; bit.*
Lil, *a pocket-book; dumbie.*
Snib, *a pickpocket; prig.*
Toper, *a hat; tile.*

There are a few slightly more expansive definitions:

Coreing, *picking up small articles in shops.*
Gammon, *to take up a person's attention while your neighbour is picking his pocket.*
Mang, *to boast; to talk of.*
Stretcher, *a web; also a string.*

and two entries provide citations:

Down, *alarm; rose the down, gave the alarm.*
Whack, *share;* whack't the smash, *divided the silver.*

The semantic focuses of Haggart's word-list are stealable objects (MONEY, CLOTHES, ARTEFACTS), CRIME & DISHONESTY, and LAW & ORDER. Together these fields make up 55.7 per cent of the dictionary (see Appendix, Table 7.8).

The *Lexicon* contains forty-one of Haggart's slang terms, Vaux's dictionary has forty-six, and Potter's thirty. Despite the considerable overlap between these dictionaries, Haggart would have had to consult all three. It is more likely that none of these was his source, since

[23] David Haggart, *The Life of David Haggart, Alias John Wilson, Alias John Morison, Alias Barney McCoul, Alias John McColgan, Alias Daniel O'Brien, Alias the Switcher.* Written by himself, while under sentence of death (Edinburgh: James Ballantyne & Co., 1821), 28.

sixty-two of his entries are not recorded in any of them. The unusual spellings that Haggart gives even for those terms that are in earlier dictionaries, also suggest that he did not use any of these dictionaries as his source:

Usual form	Haggart's glossary
beak	Beek, *a magistrate.*
ken	Kain, *a house.*
tog	Tuig, *a coat, also clothes.*
quod	Quoad, *a prison.*

The spellings may, moreover, represent Scottish pronunciation. There is no evidence to suggest that this is anything other than an independent cant list compiled by an individual whose life certainly equipped him to produce one. We can, therefore, take this glossary as independent confirmation of the currency of the terms contained within it.

The *OED* cites Haggart's *Life* twenty-three times, and the glossary twice. Nevertheless, the word-list predates four existing *OED* first citations: *bulky* "a policeman" (1827), *squeal* "an informer" (1872: "an act of informing" (US); 1846: "to inform"), *whidding* "talking slang" (1823: v¹), and *yelper* "an animal that yelps" ([1673, 1825] 1847). *Slangs*, defined as "shows", could be a verb or noun. In either case it would be a useful addition to *OED* citations. If a noun, "a show", it would predate the first citation by thirty-eight years (n³ 5a). If a verb, "to show", it is an additional example of a usage supported by only one citation, from *c*.1789.

J. Burrowes's *Life in St. George's Fields* (1821)

This work is clearly an attempt to cash in, at the very reasonable price of 1*s*, on the success of Egan's *Life in London* (see Chapter 5). The other publications advertised in this volume give an indication of the target audience: *Reading Made Easy* (4*d*), *Letter Writer* (1*s*), *Life of the Queen*, *Life in London*, and *Boxiana* (all in 6*d* numbers). It describes the adventures of Flash Dick and Disconsolate William in St George's Fields:

Not at all dismayed at the many attempts which have been made of presenting to the world a living picture of men and manners, under the various titles of '*Life in London*', '*Real Life in London*', '*Original Life in London*', and '*Life in Ireland*'. As we flatter ourselves that every *kiddy* who travels with us will confess, before he is half through his journey, that SURREY is a world of itself, that *St George's Fields* is the Capital where, and only where, *prime fun* is to be found![24]

Dick shows Disconsolate William the prime fun that is to be had in the capital, and he soon loses his claim to the soubriquet. During their wanderings they encounter some Gypsies using thieves' slang:

Thus ended their ramble of pleasure, which Bill confessed had far exceeded his expectation; and, willing that the gentle reader should share the profits of this excursion, he is presented with a SLANG DICTIONARY.[25]

The word-list contains 163 entries for 167 cant terms. They are alphabetical to the first letter only. The definitions are very brief, usually taking the form of a standard English synonym:

All my eye, *a lame story*
Buck, *a kiddy*
Black-strap, *red-port*
Blunt, *money*
Bread-basket, *stomach*
Brads, *cash*
Body-snatcher, *a resurrection man*

Burrowes is markedly euphemistic in defining terms dealing with sexual matters, although several of his entries clearly relate to prostitution:

Blowing, *a fancy girl*
Doxy, *a woman of the town*
Mot, *a lady of easy virtue*
Mutton-walk, *the saloon of a theatre*
Work-bench, a bedstead

Many of the terms that Burrowes includes had been listed in earlier cant and slang dictionaries. The *Lexicon* contains eighty-five, Vaux's dictionary sixty-six, Potter's fifty-three, and Parker's twenty-three. No single dictionary source accounts for all of the previously listed terms, however. Almost a third of Burrowes's entries had not previously been listed in cant and slang dictionaries with the senses that he gives, including:

Carver and gilder, *a match maker*
Daffy, *gin*
Greek, *a gambler*

---

[24] J. Burrowes, *Life in St. George's Fields or, The Rambles and Adventures of Disconsolate William, Esq. (From St. James's,) and his accomplished Surrey Friend, Flash Dick* (London: J. Smith, 1821), 3.
[25] Burrowes, *Life in St. George's Fields*, 24.

Hell, *a gaming house*
Hingy-wipe, *an India handkerchief*
Set-to, a fight
Uproarious, noisy
White-bait, silver

This suggests that Burrowes's dictionary was independently compiled, and that it should, therefore, be taken as confirmation of the continued use of terms that it contains. Unusually, Burrowes's list has more words for BODY & HEALTH than for CRIME & DISHONESTY (see Appendix, Table 7.9).

The *OED* cites Burrowes only once. The word-list antedates eight existing *OED* first citations:

brickish "hearty" (1856)
bunch of fives "the fist" (1825)
ear-wigging "whispering" (1837: **earwig** v)
heavy "porter" (1823: a[1] (n) B3)
miler "a donkey" (1838: "A man or horse specializing in mile-long races")
scuddick "a halfpenny" (1823)
Snoosey "a night constable" (1823: **snoozy**)
yard of clay "a tobacco pipe" ([1828] 1842)

The Vulgarities of Speech Corrected (1826)

This anonymous work is designed to warn against various types of linguistic vulgarity, so its interest is in non-standard language generally. It is dedicated to Maria Edgeworth 'whose works on education have had so much influence on the spirit of the age', and the publisher advertises guides to etiquette and grammar for young ladies 'to be printed uniformly with this volume'.[26] It includes sections on language that is affected, over-learned, provincial, awkward, slovenly, vulgar in subject matter, ungrammatical, and so on. It also talks at some length about the influence of cant and slang on standard English:

It is but very recently that the peculiar secret language of vagabonds, pick-pockets, swindlers, professed boxers, and horse-jockies, has obtained a partial currency among some of the middle, and even of the upper, ranks of society; and in consequence of this, a few of the terms and expressions which are known under the various names of slang, cant, or flash language, have been introduced into common

---

[26] *The Vulgarities of Speech Corrected; with Elegant Expressions for Provincial and Vulgar English, Scots, and Irish* (London: James Bulcock, 1826), i, ii.

discourse . . . it is by no means uncommon to hear the thoughtless imitating the slang of the prize-ring, or the tap-room, under the very mistaken notion, that it is an indication of spirit, wit, and knowledge of life; whereas it is unquestionably low and vulgar. One principal cause of the diffusion of slang may be traced to the extensive circulation of newspaper reports of boxing-matches, drawn up in the peculiar language current at such assemblies. The memoirs of pick-pockets also, such as those of Hardy Vaux; and the Police-office reports, have tended to render slang familiar to the public. . . .[27]

The table of slang vulgarities contains 364 entries for 313 headwords; 255 of the headwords are from the *Lexicon*, and twenty-nine are from Vaux's dictionary. Eighteen are in both. Since the compiler of this list cites these dictionaries in his introduction, there is no reason to assume that he did not use them both. He usually abbreviates the entries he adopts from his source, and always deletes citations:

Lexicon Balatronicum	*Vulgarities*	
	VULGAR	CORRECT
ABIGAIL. A lady's waiting-maid.	*Abigail.*	A waiting-maid.
BAGGAGE . . . Also a familiar epithet for a woman; as, cunning baggage, wanton baggage, &c.	*A Baggage.*	A worthless woman.
Vaux		
TO THE NINES; or, TO THE RUFFIAN. These terms are synonymous, and imply an extreme of any kind, or the superlative degree.	Done *to the Nines.*	Done excellently or correctly.

Phrases are alphabetized according to their keyword, so *baggage* is under 'B', *to be in it* under 'I', and *done to the nines* under 'N'.

Unusually, the compiler gives us some indication of the method of selection from his sources:

In making this table, I have, in most instances, avoided those slang terms and expressions which are more peculiar to profligates, as a secret language for the purposes of concealment . . .[28]

[27] *Vulgarities*, 158, 160–1.   [28] *Vulgarities*, 173–4.

In fact, only two of the terms selected from the *Lexicon* are labelled 'cant' there (*to bilk* "to cheat", and *to melt* "to spend (money)").

The compiler of this list did not make a random selection from among the terms not labelled as 'cant' in the *Lexicon*, however (see Appendix, Table 7.10). The list contains more terms for EMOTION & TEMPERAMENT ($p = 0.01$) than can be accounted for by chance, and fewer for POVERTY ($p = 0.05$) and SEX ($p = 0.01$). The selection from Vaux, small as it is, also contains significantly more terms for EMOTION & TEMPERAMENT than we would expect ($p = 0.01$).

The bowdlerization involved in the production of this list is worth looking at in more detail. Of 329 entries referring to sexual matters in the *Lexicon*, only one makes its way into this list, and it is a term with a suitably puritanical tone: *smutty* "obscene". None of the *Lexicon*'s sixty-two defecatory terms survives, but these are too few in number for their omission to be statistically significant.

The compiler of this list gives only three etymologies, none of which is derived from his sources. They are:

Bam [contracted from] *Bamboozle*. To play a trick, to deceive.
Bitched. [contraction.] Bewitched.
Seedy. [run to seed.] Poor, mean, shabbily dressed.

The second is folk-etymological, but the other two are correct.

Although all headwords in this list are 'vulgar', the compiler provides a few terms with further usage labels:

Morning. [Scots.] A dram before breakfast.
Plucked. [University cant.] Refused a degree.
Potatoe trap. [Irish.] The mouth.
Spliced. [sea term.] Married.
To tip. [this is very vulgar.] To give or lend.

which sometimes apply to the following synonym rather than to the headword:

To budge, [in Scotland] *to mudge.* To move, or to quit.
Duke, [in Scotland] *Laird.* A fellow profligate, or low acquaintance.

The *OED* does not use the *Vulgarities* at all. Despite its dependence on earlier lists, it does include some new entries. These predate three existing *OED* first citations, and make a useful addition to one other entry: *to catch it* "to get a thrashing or scolding" (1835: v 41), *to give it* "to abuse or scold" (the first citation after 1612 is from 1831), *music* "fun" (1859), and *rap* "a criminal accusation" (1903: n[1] 4b "a false oath").

Henry Brandon's 'Dictionary of the Flash or Cant Language' (1839)

Brandon's cant-list appeared as an appendix to W. A. Miles's *Poverty, Mendicity and Crime*, an account of the fieldwork underlying a parliamentary report into conditions in London. Miles noted that:

A few years since, just previous to instituting the new and efficient police, a burletta was presented at the minor theatres, called 'Life in London,' in which were exhibited the orgies, houses of meeting, and all the tricks resorted to by the thief and the beggar generally the *par nobile fratrum*. A knowledge of which until that period was a secret save to a few select—the elect of the young blood about town;—but once made the subject of public notoriety, all London, from the sprig of fashion to the dapper apprentice, became inoculated with the mania peculiar to the natives of this country, and they determined to gratify their curiosity by visiting the scenes in real life they had witnessed the performance of on the stage; while some among them, more daring, could not rest satisfied until they had all acted their feats of prowess by creating a 'row with the Charlies,' agreeable to the fashion of the three celebrated worthies, Messrs. Tom, Jerry, and Logic.

   The disgraceful riots that took place in consequence of this exposure were such as to call loudly for interference by some strong measures on the part of the executive, for the system of police and night watch, as then in operation, was utterly incompetent to maintain that quiet in which a well-regulated city ought to be kept; and it is not to be doubted but to these disgusting disturbances solely the country is indebted for the present police.[29]

The report itself contains much slang and cant in reported speech, and the glossary seems to have been compiled from it. The list contains 258 entries for 256 headwords, and uses three usage markers:

Those words which are marked thus * are peculiar to the Scotch; those marked thus † to the Gipseys; and words marked thus ‡ are only used in Calmet's Buildings, Oxford-street; they are Clockmakers and Watchmakers,—mention of it is made at page 140.[30]

   [29] W. A. Miles, *Poverty, Mendicity and Crime; or, the facts, examinations, &c. upon which the Report was founded, Presented to the House of Lords . . . to which is added a Dictionary of the Flash or Cant Language, Known to Every Thief and Beggar edited by H. Brandon, esq.* (London: Shaw and Sons, 1839), 4.
   [30] Miles, *Poverty*, 161. Page 140 reads: 'Low lodgings are in Calmet-buildings, Oxford-street, inhabited by low Irish, four or five families in a room. Men, women, and children, 4*d.* a night. They are not used as brothels,—considers the people hard-working men. In this court, however, there are two classes, namely, the industrious and the idle, which are distinguished by titles peculiar to this court, and which are often the cause of serious party fights; the parties are the *clock makers*, i.e. the hard-working people, and the *watch makers*, who are the most dissolute persons and young prostitutes.'

Usage markers generally precede the headwords, while usage labels follow after the definition in parentheses:

* *Chattry Feeder*—spoon.
‡ *Clockmakers*—Industrious people living in Calmet's buildings, Oxford-street.
Deaner—a shilling, (country phrase.)
† *Dee*—a pocket book.

In the event, only a handful of terms are labelled (see Appendix, Table 7.11.1). The symbols * and † are also used as footnote markers, and precede the headword whether they are functioning as usage or footnote markers. Footnotes refer the reader to glossaries of terms for money and coloured handkerchiefs at the end of the word-list, which include:

FLASH NAMES FOR THE POCKET HANDKERCHIEFS
Billy—is the general name for silk pocket handkerchiefs of all sorts.
Belcher—close striped pattern.
Blood-red Fancy—all red.
Blue Billy—blue ground, with white spots.
Cream Fancy—any pattern on a white ground.
Green King's-man—any pattern on a green ground.
Randle's-man—green, with white spots.
Water's-man—sky-coloured.
Yellow Fancy—yellow, with white spots.
Yellow-man—all yellow.

and it is only by cross-referring that we can determine which function is intended. These mini-thesauruses are followed by a handful of 'sundry phrases', including:

Tied up prigging—given over thieving.
To go on the shallows—to go half-naked.
Gadding the hoof—going without shoes.
To fly a window—to lift a window.
To go the jump—to steal into a room through the window.
To Speel the drum—to run away with the stolen property.

The phrases are followed by 'specimens of flash'. For example:

I buzzed a bloak and a shakester of a reader and a skin. My jomer stalled. A cross-cove, who had his regulars, called out 'cop bung,' so as a pig was marking, I speeled to the crib, where I found Jim had been pulling down sawney for grub. He cracked a case last night and fenced the swag. He told me as Bill had flimped a yack and pinched a swell of a fawney, he sent the yack to church and got three finnips and a cooter for the fawney.

TRANSLATION.
I picked the pocket of a gentleman and lady of a pocket-book and a purse. My
fancy girl stood near me and screened me from observation. A fellow-thief, who
shared with me my plunder, called out to me to hand over the stolen property, so as
somebody was observing my manœuvres, I ran away to the house, where I found
James had provided something to eat, by stealing some bacon from a shop door.
He committed a burglary last night and had disposed of the property plundered.
He told me that Bill had hustled a person and obtained a watch; he had also
robbed a well-dressed gentleman of a ring. The watch he sent to have the works
taken out and put into another case, (to prevent detection,) and the ring realized
him three five-pound notes and a sovereign.[31]

Although Hotten described the list as 'a very wretched perform-
ance',[32] it is cited by the *OED* twenty times in all. The names of both
Brandon and Miles are included seven times, Brandon appears
alone five times, and the list is attributed to Ducange Anglicus twice.
It is also cited as 'Slang Dict.' once. Miles's text is cited twice more.
The list antedates a further thirteen existing first citations:

bloke "a man" (1851)
buttoner "a con-man's apprentice" (1841)
cadging "begging" (1859)
to church "to remove distinguishing marks from (a watch)" (1868)
couter "a sovereign" (1846)
crow "a lookout" (1851)
to gad the hoof "to go without shoes" (1846)
gonnoff "a thief" (1852: "a pickpocket")
nobbler [a type of con-man] (1876)
padding-crib "a tramps' lodging house" (1851)
soot-bag "a handbag" (1864)
watchmaker "a watch-thief" (1859)
water's man "a blue handkerchief" (1860: *waterman*)

Henry Mayhew's *London Labour* (1851)

Henry Mayhew (1812–87) was the son of a London attorney, and
was himself trained to make a living in the law. He ran away to sea,
and although later articled to his father, chose instead to become a
writer, producing drama, farce, fairy tales, and comedy. He edited
Punch for a while, but became most famous for his contributions to

[31] Miles, *Poverty*, 167. This passage was later to be reworked by Matsell, via Ducange, as an example
of American cant (101).   [32] Hotten, *Dictionary*, 151.

the *Morning Chronicle* under the title 'London Labour and the London Poor'. These were later reissued as a periodical in their own right.[33]

In his chronicle of 'the Condition and Earnings of those that will work, those that cannot work, and those that will not work,' Mayhew records and comments on the language of the London poor and includes a few brief glossaries. In speaking of the costermongers, for example, he writes about their use of back-slang:

The slang language of the costermongers is not very remarkable for originality of construction; it possesses no humour: but they boast that it is known only to them-selves; it is far beyond the Irish, they say, and puzzles the Jews. The *root* of the costermonger tongue, so to speak, is to give the words spelt backward, or rather pronounced rudely backward,—for in my present chapter the language has, I believe, been reduced to orthography for the first time. With this backward pro-nunciation, which is very arbitrary, are mixed words reducible to no rule and seldom referrable to any origin, thus complicating the mystery of this unwritten tongue; while any syllable is added to a proper slang word, at the discretion of the speaker.

Slang is acquired very rapidly, and some costermongers will converse in it by the hour. The women use it sparingly; the girls more than the women; the men more than the girls; and the boys most of all. The most ignorant of all these classes deal most in slang and boast of their cleverness and proficiency in it. In their con-versations among themselves, the following are invariably the forms used in money matters. A rude back-spelling may generally be traced:

Flatch	Halfpenny
Yenep	Penny
Owt-yenep	Twopence
Erth-yenep	Threepence
Rouf-yenep	Fourpence
Ewif-yenep	Fivepence
Exis-yenep	Sixpence
Neves-yenep	Sevenpence
Teaich-yenep	Eightpence
Enine-yenep	Ninepence
Net-yenep	Tenpence
Leven	Elevenpence
Gen	Twelvepence
Yenep-flatch	Three half-pence

and so on through the penny-halfpennies. . . .[34]

Mayhew noted that this form of slang was used mainly to ensure that the costermongers could converse privately within the hearing

---

[33] All biographical information is from *DNB*, xxxvii.153–4.

[34] Henry Mayhew, *London Labour and the London Poor* (London: George Woodfall and Son, 1851), i.23–4.

of their customers and other traders. He wrote that even illiterate boys who became costermongers quickly acquired a command of it:

I saw one lad whose parents had, until five or six months back, resided in the country. The lad himself was fourteen; he told me he had not been "a coster-mongering" more than three months, and prided himself on his mastery over slang. To test his ability, I asked him the coster's word for 'hippopotamus;' he answered, with tolerable readiness, 'musatoppop.' I then asked him for the like rendering of 'equestrian' (one of Astley's bills having caught my eye). He replied, but not quite so readily, 'nirtseque.' The last test to which I subjected him was 'good-naturedly;' and though I induced him to repeat the word twice, I could not, on any of the three renderings, distinguish any precise sound beyond an indistinct gabbling, concluded emphatically with 'doog;'—'good' being a word with which all these traders are familiar. It must be remembered, that the words I demanded were remote from the young costermonger's vocabulary, if not from his understanding.[35]

Mayhew held this form of slang in low regard, commenting that it:

is utterly devoid of any applicability to humour. It gives no new fact, or approach to a fact, for philologists. One superior genius among the costers, who has invented words for them, told me that he had no system for coining his term. He gave to the known word some terminating syllable, or, as he called it, 'a new turn, just,' to use his own words, 'as if he chorussed them, with a tol-de-rol.' The intelligence communicated in this slang is, in a great measure, communicated, as in other slang, as much by the inflection of the voice, the emphasis, the tone, the look, the shrug, the nod, the wink, as by the words spoken.[36]

This is, indeed, the first significant discussion of back-slang, whose use seems to have been as limited as Mayhew notes.[37] However, the *OED* lists a few terms as having entered into more common usage, including some not in Mayhew's list: *pennif*, for *finnip* "five-pound note", *yob* "boy", and possibly *naff*, for *fan* "female genitals".

In total, the word-lists consist of only thirty-nine entries, containing fifty slang terms, arranged by meaning. MONEY is by far the largest field, which is what we would expect in such a specialized form of slang (see Appendix, Table 7.12). There are relatively few terms for food, which is odd, given that that is what the costermongers were selling, but in secret conversations between themselves there would probably be no need to conceal words like *apple* from customers standing by.

---

[35] Mayhew, *London Labour*, i.24.   [36] Mayhew, *London Labour*, i.24.
[37] Eric Partridge, *A Dictionary of Slang and Unconventional English* (1938) 8th edition, ed. by Paul Beale (London: Routledge, 2002), 1376, notices a reference to back-slang from 1839, and there is some evidence that it was still in use among retail butchers in the late twentieth century.

The two food terms that are included are for sub-standard stock and for the costermonger's own dinner (*kennetseeno* "stinking (of fish)", *do the tightner* "go to dinner").

Without detracting in any way from 'his incomparable knowledge of familiar, lowly London speech',[38] Mayhew appears to have had little or no acquaintance with the slang and cant dictionaries that preceded his. Correspondents' queries to *London Labour* about the origin of terms like *beak* "magistrate" and *mot* "woman" are met with speculation that is usually ill-informed. For example:

There are two explanations that may be given as to the meaning of the slang term "beak," but both requiring proof. The one is, that in accordance with the *metaphorical* origin of many of the words in the slang language, the term may have been formed from the beak being the organ of seizing or apprehension with birds, and so have been whimsically applied to the functionary connected with the apprehension of criminals.

The other derivation is referrible to the principle laid down by Dr. Latham, that the 'lower orders' are the conservators of the Saxon part of the English language—a point which all those who have looked even superficially into the construction of their native tongues will readily admit. Assuming then the word *beak* to be of Saxon origin, we find the Anglo-Saxon term *beag* to signify, among other things, a necklace or ornament to hang about the neck, a collar of state; and when we remember that in Saxon times the aldermen were the sole magistrates (*ealdordom* means authority, magistracy), and that part of the aldermen's insignia of office consists of a chain or collar similar to this *beag*, the transition becomes easy from the emblem of the office to the office or officer himself; even as the 'gold-stick-in-waiting' is the title given to the functionary occupying that post; and the policeman is called a 'blue-bottle,' from his blue uniform; and a soldier a 'lobster' from his red coat. Hence a beak would mean simply an alderman or magistrate decorated with a *beag* or gilt collar, as indicative of the magisterial office. As was before stated, however, proof is required; and perhaps some 'constant reader' may be able to cite something tending either to confirm or set aside the above suggestion.[39]

Although the *OED* concedes a possible connection with the *beak* of a bird, it opts for 'etymology unknown'. Although we need not accept Mayhew's analysis uncritically, we can take at face value his claims about how he collected the word-list. As an independently produced fieldwork glossary, it is an invaluable contribution to cant and slang lexicography.

Because this type of slang was so restricted, the *OED* rightly includes little of it. Mayhew thus predates only two existing first

---

[38] Partridge, *Slang*, 94.   [39] Vol III, No. 51, Nov. 29th, 1851.

citations: *esclop/slop* "policeman" (1859: *slop* n⁴) and *neves* "seven" (1901: "seven years' hard labour").

The *Yokel's Preceptor* (*c*.1855)

This anonymous work 'the Greenhorn's Guide thro' little Lunnon' advertises itself at length on the title-page as a volume that will alert the newcomer to London to the tricks that will be used to part him from his money. The word-list is only a small part of a work that, for all its apparent public-spiritedness, is intended mostly for entertainment: exactly the format in which some of the earliest cant and slang glossaries appeared.[40]

The word-list, covering only three pages, is headed 'A Key to the Flash Words made use of in this work.' The compiler notes that:

The slang or flash patter differs much according to the parties by whom it is used. Those who speak it most readily are gypsies, showmen, itinerant dealers, 'travellers,' as they are called, who have so many significations for one thing, it is very difficult to comprehend them.[41]

The list itself contains sixty-eight slang terms in forty-three entries. Two semantic areas, MONEY and CRIME & DISHONESTY, dominate the list, accounting between them for 41.8 per cent of the list's total coverage (see Appendix, Table 7.13). Some semantically related terms are grouped together, with *denaly, blunt,* and *tin* sharing the definition 'Money', and *scarper, hookit, bolt, speal,* and *cut* collectively defined as 'To run away: Make off'. Other related terms are listed contiguously, for example:

Dossing. Sleeping
Doss. To sleep
Dab. A bed

but there is no over-riding organizational principle.

Most entries consist of a slang headword and a standard English synonym as definition, for example:

Bender. A shilling
Cripple. Sixpence

---

[40] Coleman, *Cant and Slang Dictionaries*, i.142–7.
[41] *Yokel's Preceptor: or, More Sprees in London . . . To which is added A Joskin's Vocabulary of the various Slang Words now in constant use . . .* (London: H. Smith, *c*.1855), 31.

Red rag. The tongue
Stiff'un. Dead body

A small number include slang synonyms, for example:

Divers. Fogle hunters, pickpockets
Flummixed. Diddled
Quisby. Queer, bad

A few of the definitions are very broad:

Casey. House, Iron, &c.
A Slum. Any thing you see: A spoon: A knife: A rope: A house, &c

which is probably a good indication of the compiler's determination to capture the variety of meanings with which these terms were used.

The *OED* cites this work only once, accepting the tentative dating to *c.*1855, and the glossary not at all. The word-list antedates four existing *OED* first citations:

busker "a begging street-entertainer" (1857)
donner "a woman" (1873: **dona**)
shicker "a thing or person that cannot be depended upon" (1892: "drunk")
spifflicated "fooled; cheated" (1906: "drunk")

Most of the terms in this list are confirmed from other sources. Those that are not include:

Face makers. Coiners
Nanty. Without, Easy, Be quiet, &c.
Pavé thumper. A whore
Pegging cribs. Bawdy houses
Sups. Supernumeraries

What is interesting about this word-list, given that the words are attributed to gypsies and other itinerants, is their etymologies, as given by the *OED*. In this short list there are terms recently acquired from Dutch and German (*boss* "an overseer", *nix* "nothing", *soskins* "money"), French (*ocre* "money", *pavé* "pavement"), Spanish (*donner* "woman"), Italian (*to scarper* "to run away"), and more to the point, Yiddish (*schofel* "forged money", *shicker* "bad", *shickster* "a prostitute"), Romany (*couter* "a sovereign", *posh* "money"), and various English dialects (*to flummox* "to defraud", *?to speal* "to run away"). The list may well be a genuine representation of the speech of London's ethnically and geographically mixed underclasses.

Archbold's Snowden's Magistrates [sic] *Assistant* (1857, 1859)

Published first by Ralph Leconby Snowden, in 1852, and edited by John Frederick Archbold in 1857, this clumsily titled work contained everything that contemporary law-enforcers needed to know.[42] Its chapter headings demonstrate the increasing professionalization of metropolitan policing during this period: 'Apprehension of Offenders', 'Justice of the Peace and their Jurisdiction', 'Commitment for Indictable Offences', 'Convictions', 'Proceedings for Rates', 'Evidence', 'Duties of Constables in Particular Cases', and 'Proceedings before Justices'.

Archbold claimed to have used earlier dictionaries as well as inside information in the compilation of his glossary:

I shall add the flash or cant language used and known by every thief and itinerant beggar in the kingdom, and collected down to the present period. I had in custody a short time ago an old cadger, who had been in almost all the gaols throughout England, and who furnished me, for a trifling fee, with the same. I have since compared it with my own and with others, and made what alterations I thought proper; that is, in leaving out what was old and not now in use.[43]

This suggests more than one written source, but 149 of the 161 entries are from Brandon's list (92.5 per cent). Their semantic distribution is entirely in keeping with a random selection (see Appendix, Table 7.11). Archbold does, however, select against Brandon's labelled terms ($p = 0.01$). Only three of Brandon's 'Scottish' terms are found in Archbold's list (see Appendix, Table 7.11.1), where they are not marked as Scottish. One, *moll* "a girl", is labelled as an 'old phrase', which is the only usage label in the list.

Two editions, listed in the bibliography, contain the glossary. Its contents in each are identical. The glossary is arranged standard English term first, followed by one or more flash synonyms. Although there is some evidence of organization by meaning, in that the first ten entries are all terms for money, it is by no means sustained:

Sixpence - Downer, also sprat.
Shilling - Deaner, also twelver.
Two shillings and sixpence - - - - - - - - - - - - - - Alderman.
Bad half-crown - Half case.

---

[42] The name of Archbold is still found on the title-pages of guides to the criminal law of Britain and Hong Kong.   [43] *Archbold's Snowden's Magistrates Assistant* (1857), 444.

Five shillings - Bull.
Bad five shillings - - - - - - - - - - - - - - - - - - - Case.
Sovereign - Cooter.
Five-pound notes - - - - - - - - - - - - - - - - - - - Finnips.
Ten-pound notes - - - - - - - - - - - - - - - - - - - Double finnips.
Large notes - Long-tailed finnips.
A house - Crib.
The tread-mill - Everlasting staircase.
Beggar - Cadger.
Begging letter - Fakement.
Gift of clothes - Cant of togs.

A few carelessly edited entries contain grammatical mismatches:

Brandon	Archbold
The Highfly—beggars, with letters, pretending to be broken-down gentlemen, captains, &c.	Begging letters - - - - - - The highfly.
Buttoner—one who entices another to play.	To entice another to play - - - Buttoner.

The *OED* cites Snowden's *Magistrate's Assistant* twelve times in all. All but two of these citations are from an edition I have not been able to trace, from 1846. It antedates no existing first citations.

Ducange Anglicus *The Vulgar Tongue* (1857, 1859)

Published under the pseudonym 'the English Ducange', this list claimed the authority of the seminal dictionary of late (and therefore corrupt) Latin published by Du Cange in 1678.[44] Its publisher, Bernard Quaritch, who specialized in works on language, grammar and translation (especially Indian and Arabic languages), pronunciation, and medieval alphabets, probably compiled it. It is a curious selection of non-standard English in various forms. It includes two glossaries, a flash song, and a tailor's handbill in flash language (see 234). This disparate material can have served no purpose other than entertainment, despite the claims of the preface:

This little volume has been printed with the view of assisting Literary Men, the Officers of the Law, and Philanthropists, in their intercourse with Classes of

[44] John Considine, 'Du Cange: lexicography and the medieval heritage', in Coleman and McDermott (eds.), *Historical Dictionaries*, 1–10.

English Society who use a different Phraseology, only understood by their own fraternity.[45]

The first glossary was, it is claimed, collected in London during 1856 and 1857. It contains 481 entries for 480 headwords, and employs a number of abbreviated usage labels, including 'Pugil' for *pugilistic*, 'Gen' for *general*, 'Th' for *thieves*, and 'L.Life' for *low life*, for example:

ALBONIZED, *adj*. Whitened.	*Pugil*
BAZAAR, *n*. Counter.	*Th*.
CHOAKER, *n*. Cravat or neckcloth.	*Gen*.
KEGMEG, *n*. Tripe. "A *kegmeg* shop."	*L.life*.

All but nineteen entries (4.0 per cent) are provided with usage labels, and three entries contain two usage labels each (see Appendix, Table 7.14.1).

In this edition of the list, 395 entries (82.1 per cent) include grammatical labelling. This is inconsistently performed, in that both 'a' and 'adj' are used for adjectives, and 'n', 's', and 'sub' for nouns, for example:

BOOZY, *adj*. Drunk.	*Gen*.
COPPER, *sub*. Penny. "Give us a *copper*."	*Gen*.
COPPER, *n*. Policeman.	*Th*.
LUSH, *s*. Strong drink.	*Gen*.
TIGHT, *a*. Drunk.	*Gen*.

Neither is the grammatical labelling entirely accurate. In the frequent grammatical mismatches between headword and definition, the label sometimes refers to one, sometimes the other, and sometimes neither, for example:

CHEEK, *n*. Impudent. "Don't you be so *cheeky*."	*Gen*.
CLINCHER, *n*. Incontrovertible. "I gave him a *clincher*."	*Gen*.
OBFUSCATED, *n*. Drunk.	*Gen*.
PEG, *v*. To lower. "Take you down a peg or two."	*Gen*.
PLOWED, *n*. Drunk.	*Gen*.

[45] Ducange Anglicus, *The Vulgar Tongue, comprising Two Glossaries of Slang, Cant, and Flash Words and Phrases used in London at the Present Day* (London: Bernard Quaritch, 1857), Preface.

Over three-quarters of the entries labelled are marked as nouns, thus over-representing the proportion of the word-list made up of nouns and noun phrases. This is partly because a few entries are wrongly labelled as nouns, and partly because nouns are far more likely to be labelled than other grammatical categories (see Appendix, Table 7.14.2).

While verbs are sometimes classed as nouns, past and present participles are frequently lumped together with interjections and prepositional phrases as verbs, regardless of the grammatical category of their definition, for example:

BLACKFRIARS, *v.* Look out.   *Th.*
CHAFFING, *v.* To quiz, or ridicule.   *Gen.*
DARKENED, *v.* Closed.   *Pugil.*
SLUM, *v.* Up to *slum*, knowing.   *Th.*

Phrasal entries, including sentences, clauses, and prepositional phrases, are least often provided with a grammatical label, for example:

CAN'T SEE A HOLE THRO' A
    LADDER. Being nearly drunk.
EBONY OPTICS ALBONIZED.
    Black eyes painted white, an art
    much practised amongst pugilists.
SNUFF. Up to *snuff*. Not easily deceived.   *Gen.*

A noteworthy feature of this list is the inclusion of citations in the form of dialogue and monologue—usually featuring an individual called Bill, although Jack puts in an occasional appearance, for example:

CHINKERS, *n.* Money. 'Got any
    chink, Jack?'   *Th.*
PATTER, *n.* Trial. 'Bill is "to rights"
    at his *patter.*' No chance at his trial,
    is sure to be convicted.   *Th*
ROWDY, *n.* Money. 'Got any *rowdy,*
    Bill?' Also *rhino.*   *Gen.*
SIDE-BOARDS, *n.* Shirt-collar. 'Are
    you in mourning, Bill?' 'No; why?'
    'Because you have got your *side-
    boards* up,' alluding to shops having
    their shutters put up.   *L.life.*
WARM, *n.* A rich person. 'Has he got
    any blunt, Bill?' 'Oh yes, he's *warm.*'   *Th.*

This is the earliest list to include rhyming slang terms, although it does not mark them as such:

BARNET-FAIR, *n.* Hair.	*Th.*
EAST AND SOUTH, *n.* Mouth.	*Th.*
MINCE PIES, *n.* Eyes.	*Th.*
PLATE OF MEAT, *n.* Street.	*Th.*
ROUND ME HOUSES, *n.* Trousers,	
pronounced trouses.	*Th.*

These are generally labelled as thieves' slang, but there are a few exceptions:

BRYAN-O'LYNN, *n.* Gin.	*Gen.*
JACK-DANDY, *n.* Brandy.	*Gen.*
LEAN AND FAT, *n.* Hat used by	
marine store-shop keepers, &c.	

There is no indication, at this stage, that the rhyming slang terms could be abbreviated in any way. It seems to be *barnet fair* that means "hair", and not *barnet* alone.

The second glossary is derived from Brandon's word-list (see above). Differences between the two lists are minor, and largely accidental. The format of Brandon's list, very different from that of the first list in this volume, is preserved. Thus, headwords in the Brandon list are italicized, and usually followed by an em dash, instead of capitalized and followed by a comma.

The Brandon list is much more focused in subject matter than the first *Vulgar Tongue* list. It has significantly fewer terms for the fields of ALCOHOL and WAR & VIOLENCE, and significantly more for ARTEFACTS, CLOTHES, CRIME & DISHONESTY, and MONEY (all $p = 0.01$; see Appendix, Tables 7.11 and 7.14). Also significant is the lower proportion of terms for BODY & HEALTH ($p = 0.05$). This focus on crime and on stealable objects is a characteristic feature of lists of cant rather than general slang.

The *Vulgar Tongue* was reissued in 1859, with the glossaries combined and some additions. There are also some changes in alphabetization. Although the two lists are very different in appearance and content, the second editor combines them as they stand. Words from the first list keep their parts of speech; words from the second list keep the dashes dividing headword and definition.

Terms found in both 1857 lists are listed twice in the 1859 list, for example:

CADGING. Applied to Cabmen
   when they are off the ranks, and
   soliciting a fare.   *Gen.*
Cadging—begging.
CRIB, *n.* House. 'Crack a swell's *crib*,'
   'break into a gentleman's house.'   *Th.*
Crib—a house.
DUMMY, *n.* Pocket-book.   *Th.*
Dummie—a pocket-book.
YAC, *n.* Watch.   *Th.*
Yack—a watch.

In the 1857 edition, the usage labels had been justified to the right at the end of the entry to which they belonged, sometimes occurring alone on a new line. These labels are occasionally lost in the 1859 edition, for example:

1857		1859
COACH-WHEEL, *n.* A crown,		COACH-WHEEL, *n.* A crown,
or five shillings.	*Gen.*	or five shillings.
FLIMP. Putting on the *flimp*.		FLIMP. Putting on the *flimp*.
Garotte robbery.	*Th.*	Garotte robbery.

To the usage labels used in the first list in 1857, the 1859 edition adds 'Sc' for *Scottish*, 'Gp' for *Gypsy*, and 'C.B.' for *Calmet's Buildings*, replacing the symbols used in the second list (see Appendix, Table 7.14.1.2). In the integrated glossary, * is used to indicate terms originally from Brandon's word-list.

The editor of the 1859 edition, not only combines the two lists from the 1857 edition, but also makes some additions, collected, he says, in 1858–9. The † symbol is used to mark these additions. In a few cases the symbol is omitted, falsely indicating that the term was carried over from the earlier edition. A few others are erroneously marked as new.

In compiling his additions to this list, the editor made extensive use of an article in *The Times*, which gives an account of the 'Robbery of the Countess of Ellesmere's Jewels', translating some terms in square brackets, as shown here.[46] The article quotes extensively from the

---

[46] *The Times*, 5th December, 1857, 12.

testimony of William Attwell, and is cited several times in the additions to this word-list:

The Times

Whitty said 'There go Port St. Peters,' which means trunks . . . I asked Whitty which one he was 'going on to?' he said the big one. I replied, 'You can't get it,' and he replied 'May I be lagged [transported], but I'll have it.' I replied, 'If you do you will "tumble" the coachman.' . . . There was a thing in the shape of a butterfly, and I said to Jackson, 'Why, these things are sparks,' meaning diamonds . . . While in the parlour I said, 'Here's a name on the box; what's to be done with that?' and Jackson said, 'Oh, I'll soon put the monicker [name] out of that,' and he took a knife and began scraping the name off . . .

The Vulgar Tongue (1859)

† Port St. Peters, *n.* Trunks. 'There go Port St. Peters.'–*The Ellesmere Jewel Robbery, Times,* Dec. 5, 1857.

† Lag, *v.* To transport. 'May I be lagged (transported).' *The Ellesmere Jewel Robbery, Times,* Dec. 5, 1857.

† Tumble, *v.* To alarm. 'You will tumble the coachman.' *The Ellesmere Jewel Robbery, Times,* Dec. 5. 1857.

† Spark, *n.* Diamond. 'These things are sparks.' *The Ellesmere Diamond Robbery, Times,* Dec. 5, 1857.

† Monicker, *n.* The name. 'I will soon put the monicker out of that.' *The Ellesmere Jewel Robbery, Times,* Dec. 5, 1857.

A few other citations and authorities are included, resulting in some rather more extensive entries among these additions, for example:

† Blackleg, *n.* 'A person who gets his living by frequenting racecourses, and places where games of chance or skill are played, giving as small odds as he can, and getting as much as he can when he bets or plays, but he is not necessarily an habitual cheat.'—*The Chief Baron.* 'A man who habitually cheats at games of cards or otherwise.'—Justice Earle, see the Trial Barnett v. Allen, *Times,* May 31, 1858.

† Nard, *n.* A person who obtains information under seal of confidence, and afterwards breaks faith.—*Times, Police case,* April 2, 1859.

The compiler shows a particular interest in terms for non-standard language:

† Slang. What is Slang? Where do you draw the line? We answer, by Slang we understand, first, technical expressions peculiar to a body of men, forming part of their customs, and a bond of union and fellowship, such as the cant terms of students, political nicknames, and the special phraseologies of particular trades and professions. Secondly, and more generally,—expressions consecrated, as it were, to Momus, from their birth, devoted to comic, or would-be comic literature and conversation, always used with a certain amount of ludicrous intent, and which no person, except from a slip of the tongue or pen, or unfortunate force of habit,

would employ in serious writing or discourse.—*Charles Astor Bristed, in Cambridge Essays*, 1855, p. 66 (See Chapter 9)

The list concludes with some slang phrases, including:

Fence my snibbed lays. Sell my stolen goods.
The only snibs in the gaff. The only prigs in the fair.
Three screaves in a lil which I fork't from a suck. Three bank notes in a pocket
    book which I took from a breast pocket.
A down in the voil. A hue and cry in the town.

The additions are largely in the style of the first list, in that many of them include grammatical labelling. Where they differ is in the inclusion of citations with complete references. However, this does not mean that the 1857 and 1859 lists are the work of different lexicographers. Because these citations date from October 1857 to April 1859, and because they are largely from *The Times*, we can assume that the compiler of the first edition showed a continued interest in cant, and noted down examples from his daily reading.

The two lists that were combined in the 1859 edition of *The Vulgar Tongue* are very different from each other. However, once they are combined, the new entries added to them do not make a significant difference to the overall semantic make-up (see Appendix, Table 7.14).

Following the glossaries in both editions are some samples of flash language, as in Brandon. These are followed by a canting song 'The Leary Man' and a flash tailor's advertisement:

Mr. H. nabs the chance of putting his customers awake, that he has just made his escape from Russia, not forgetting to clap his mawleys upon some of the right sort of Ducks to make single and double-backed Slops for gentlemen in black, when on his return home he was stunned to find one of the top manufacturers of Manchester had cut his lucky, and stopped off to the Swan Stream, leaving behind him a valuable Stock of Moleskins, Cords, Velveteens, Plushes, Swans Downs, &c. and having some ready in his kick—grabbed the chance—stepped home with the swag—and is now safely landed at his crib. He can turn out Toggery of every description very slap up, at the following low prices for
READY GILT—TICK BEING NO GO
. . . A decent allowance made to Seedy Swells, Tea Kettle Purgers, Head Robbers, and Flunkeys out of Collar, N.B. Gentlemen finding their own Broady can be accomodated.[47]

There is a considerable overlap with the content of the word-lists, but the lists do not provide a complete glossary to the texts. The editor of

---

[47] Ducange Anglicus, *The Vulgar Tongue* (1857), 45.

the 1859 edition also included an essay on slang first published in *Household Words*.[48]

The *OED* cites the 1857 edition of *The Vulgar Tongue* thirty-eight times, dating it to 1839 at *gammy* and *squeeze*. It predates a further seventeen existing *OED* first citations:

brief "a (pawnbroker's) ticket" (1860)
cartwheel "a large coin" (1867)
out of collar "out of work" (1862: *collar* n 8a)
cure "a odd person" (1873: **curiosity**)
fast "in a fix" (1863: a 4d)
fiddling "gambling" (1884: "swindling")
gun "a thief" (1858)
joey "fourpence" (1865)
liver-faced "cowardly" (1867)
neddy "a cosh" (1864)
rogue and villain "a shilling" (1859)
to have one's shirt out "to lose one's temper" (1859: *to get (a person's) shirt out*)
souper "a watch" (1859: *super*)
spread "a shawl" (1859)
suit "watch and seals" (1869: *suite* "a set of matching jewellery")
on the tiles "out getting drunk" (1887)
to turn "to rob" (1859: *to turn over* 78j)

In addition, the new terms in the 1859 edition predate four existing *OED* first citations: *chump* "a blockhead" (1883), *leaving-shop* "an unlicensed pawnbroker's" (1865), *to round on* "to inform against" (1882: "to abuse, berate"), and *to swag* "to carry off" (1861).

Summary

The word-lists included in this chapter demonstrate the continued independent documentation of non-standard language in the face of Grose and Egan's otherwise overwhelming influence. Publishers clearly considered that a variety of different readers might be interested in cant and slang lists. They appealed to readers of penny-dreadfuls and periodicals, and to people hoping to achieve a greater understanding of the life and language of the poor, to avoid falling prey to crime, or to avoid using vulgar terms themselves. Their authors include journalists and hack-writers, but also criminals and

[48] 'Slang', *Household Words*, Saturday, September 24th, 1853, 73–8.

officials involved in the detection of crime, both of whom might be expected to have an insight into secret languages used by contemporary villains.

Several of these glossaries cash in on the craze for flash language arising from the phenomenal success of Egan's *Life in London*. Flash language occupied the area between London's wealthy inhabitants and its underworld—particularly in the realms of boxing and prostitution. Well-off young men with nothing better to do could gain excitement and a reputation for worldliness by flirting with the dangers of London's seedier quarters. The less adventurous could explore on paper, and the inclusion of glossaries in so many of these works suggests the perceived importance of understanding the appropriate lingo.

While middle- and upper-class men were busy associating with their social inferiors, the lists included here suggest that their wives and daughters were frantically trying to sever all connection. Those seeking to produce refined language were required to abjure all slang terminology and to avoid direct reference to anything bodily or financial.

8 Some American Cant and Slang Lists

From the end of the sixteenth century until the War of Independence, England transported felons across the Atlantic. This answered the need for a lesser punishment than execution once branding had become little more than a formality. It was also a logical and practical, if brutal, response to Britain's labour surplus and to the desire to populate and thus defend the colonies. Most of the earliest transportees were poor children and vagrants, and it was originally only with the consent of condemned criminals that their execution could be commuted to exile. By the Transportation Act of 1718, however, courts were allowed to impose sentence of transportation directly, and contracts were established to ensure that sentences were carried out. Thus extended to non-capital offenders, transportation quickly became the main method for disposing of criminals, and tens of thousands were shipped off to a new life. On arrival, contractors sold their human cargo into service for seven years, thus covering their costs and making a tidy profit. Many transportees settled and prospered, much to the disgust of those that sent them. Others found means to return to England, where they became 'peculiarly attractive accomplices'[1] because they were already guilty of capital offences and thereby disqualified from turning king's evidence. The crime waves of the 1750s demonstrated that, whatever part these returned convicts were themselves playing, transportation was failing to deter offenders. Moreover, they were no longer welcome in America, and their sale into service had become unprofitable. Even before the War of Independence, the rate of transportation had fallen back to a trickle.

If the cant represented in dictionaries from England is a genuine reflection of the language of contemporary criminals, we would expect these terms to have been exported along with them to America. Some transportees would have taken their cant vocabulary into their new honest lives, while others would have tried to maintain its use as a secret

---

[1] J. M. Beattie, *Crime and the Courts in England 1660–1800* (New Jersey: Princeton University Press, 1986), 540–1.

language to conceal criminal acts and intentions. Some such terms were later imported back into Britain with a decidedly American ring to them, like *moll* "a criminal's female companion", recorded in the sense "a prostitute" in eighteenth-century English cant dictionaries. We would also expect American criminals to have devised new terms, both because of their changed surroundings, and because cant has constantly to mutate if it is to remain an effective means of secret communication.

The earliest American cant dictionaries date from thirty years after transportation to the United States ceased. They range from independently compiled lists of contemporary cant to careless plagiarisms of English dictionaries. Like their English counterparts, American publishers could see the advantages of adapting someone else's work, especially since they did not have to worry about copyright. All of these dictionaries, like Matsell's (see Chapter 2), originate from the heavily populated regions of the east coast.

The Life of Henry Tufts (1807)

Henry Tufts was 'a legendary horse-thief, a capable burglar, a part-time bigamist and full-time philanderer, a convincing conjurer, an aimless vagabond, a good doctor, a pilfering parson, a palmist, a work resistor, a dropout, a soldier, a draft-dodging fugitive, a prisoner, an unknowing agent of genocide, and forever a ne'er-do-well.'[2] The autobiographical *Narrative of the Life, Adventures, Travels and Sufferings of Henry Tufts* was published in 1807. It includes what been described as 'probably the first published glossary of flash lingo in America'.[3] To my knowledge, there are none earlier.

Tufts, or his ghost-writer, explains that he learnt his fellow inmates' secret language while he was incarcerated:

A number of my fellow prisoners were flashmen, (as they termed themselves) an appellation appropriate to such rogues and sharpers, as make exclusive use of the flash lingo. This is partly English and party [sic] an arbitrary gibberish, which, when spoken, presents to such hearers, as are not initiated into its mysteries, a mere unintelligible jargon, but in the flash fraternity is, peculiarly, significant. As I have once made mention of the above language, and learned the use of it while

---

[2] Keating, Neal, 'Henry Tufts, Land Pirate' [http://www.charm.net/~claustro/outlaw/land_pirate/default.htm].

[3] William Jeremiah Burke, *The Literature of Slang* (New York: New York Public Library, 1939), 77.

at the castle, I here subjoin a specimen of sundry fashionable words and phrases of that infernal dialect. It was imported in gross from Europe, and no part of it, to my knowledge, has been hitherto communicated to the public.[4]

The word-list, which occurs in the midst of the autobiographical action, is headed 'Nomenclature of the Flash Language'. It contains only seventy-three entries, with no citations, no etymologies, and only very brief definitions. The entries are not arranged alphabetically, but there does seem to be some semantic grouping in places. For example, near the start of the list, terms for clothing and objects to be carried around the person are listed together:

Mitre	a hat
Long tog	a coat
Jarvel	a jacket
Kickses	breeches
Leg bags	stockings
Crab	a shoe
Quillpipes	boots
Smish	a shirt
Clout	a handkerchief
Trick	a watch
Chiv	a knife
Pops	pistols

Terms relating to imprisonment and punishment are also grouped together:

Jigger	a door
Qua	a jail
Qua keeper	a jail keeper
Drag	a prisoner
Slangs	irons or handcuffs
Nipping jig	a gallows

Longer entries, mostly for phrasal verbs and other phrases, are grouped at the end of the list, for example:

Petre yourself	(a watchword) take care of yourself
You're spotted	you are like to be found out
I'm hammers to ye	I know what you mean
I'm dead up to the cove	I know the man well
A horney's a coming	a sheriff is coming

---

[4] Edmund Pearson (ed.), *The Autobiography of a Criminal. Henry Tufts* (London: Jarrolds, 1931), 291.

Almost half of Tufts' terms (49.5 per cent) are for crime, stealable objects, and punishment (see Appendix, Table 8.1).

After the glossary, Tufts comments:

> From this sample it may appear, that nouns and principal verbs, as being the more important words in a sentence, are generally flashified; while pronouns, auxiliary verbs and abbreviations retain their English uniform; so that the flash tongue is nothing else than a mixture of English, with other words, fabricated designedly for the purposes of deception; it can be useful to rogues and sharpers only. I once acquired such a facility in this dialect, as to converse in it with much the same ease as in plain English, although now I have lost its familiar use. But no more of this futile language; may it return to Europe, where it received its misshapen birth.[5]

These comments betray a peculiar mix of knowledge and ignorance. Tufts knows the vocabulary to be from Europe, but claims not to know that it had been published in any part before.[6]

Twenty-two entries (30.1 per cent) in the list are also in the third edition of Grose's dictionary, published in 1796. Twenty-one entries (28.8 per cent) are found in some form in Potter's *New Dictionary of all the Cant and Flash Languages*. Seventeen entries (23.3 per cent) are similar to those found in Poulter's *Discoveries*, and nine (12.3 per cent) similar to entries found in Parker's *Life's Painter*. None of these dictionaries is a direct source, however, as indicated by differences in spelling and definition:

Earlier dictionary form	Tufts
Darkey. Night. (Parker)	Darky . . . . cloudy
Douss the Glims; *put out the Candles*. (Poulter)	Douse the glin . . . . put out the light
—[SNEAK] EVENING, the same at shutting. (Potter)	Evening sneak . . . . .going into a house by night the doors being open
GLAZE. A window. *Cant*. (Grose 1796)	Glaze . . . . a square of glass

Tufts would have had to work his way through all four of these dictionaries if he had used them as sources. This would be a disproportionate amount of effort for such a short list, so we can accept that he compiled it independently. A further forty-one entries (56.2 per cent)

[5] Pearson, *Henry Tufts*, 294.
[6] Pearson, 294, takes the remark 'imported in gross from Europe', cited above, as a punning reference to Francis Grose, but notes, correctly, that the list is not derived from the *Classical Dictionary*.

are not from any of these possible sources. They include a number of terms for criminals' tools, which all cluster together:

Briar............................... a saw
Wibble .... an auger
Gentleman .... a crow bar
Spiker .... a nail
Flamer .... vitriol

The *OED* cites Tufts's list eight times, dating it to 1807 except under *prad*, where it is dated to 1798. It predates a further three existing *OED* first citations: *dinge* "a dark night" (1846: n² "dinginess"), *slangs* "fetters" (1812), and *water-sneak* "theft from a boat" (1812). In addition *dingy cove* "a Black man" is probably related to *dinge* "a Black person" (1848: n³). *Hookses* "cattle" appears to be related to the dialect term *hook* "the upper part of the thigh-bone of cattle" (1808). *Leg bags* "stockings" predates *bags* "trousers" (1853) by forty-six years.

'The Flash Language' (1848)

The Reverend B. F. Tefft D.D. edited *The Ladies' Repository* 'A Monthly Periodical Devoted to Literature and Religion', published in Cincinnati. In October 1848, in a feature called 'Pencilings from Pittsburg', which appears to be Tefft's account of his own travels, is a section entitled 'The Flash Language'. Tefft explains how he came to know about the secret language of criminals during a series of interviews with a convict in Pennsylvania Penitentiary:

> This language is known to all experienced, or as my informant would say, "well-educated" rogues. It came to this country from England, though many new terms have been added to it here. I have had, for a long time, a great desire to get possession of this dialect; but never, until this opportunity occurred, could obtain more than here and there a word. Toward the end of my stay at the Penitentiary, I ventured to request a vocabulary of this strange tongue. For several days he hesitated, but at length consented, saying, that he ought to give it to me for the benefit of the world.[7]

The burglar provides a manuscript to Tefft: 'a specimen of which I subjoin'.[8] The word-list provided contains 199 entries for 192 headwords. They are arranged alphabetically to the first letter, so

---

[7] 'The Flash Language', in *The Ladies' Repository*, October, 1848, viii.315.
[8] 'The Flash Language', 316.

the entries for B, for example, run: *buffer, buff, buff to, buff for, booze, boozing-ken, blunt, blunted, blunted crib, blunt ken, bolus, beak, blink, briar, brad, blowen, blow, bluff,* and *blirt.* The largest category by far is CRIME & DISHONESTY (23.3 per cent). Added together, the categories of crime, punishment, and stealable objects account for 47.2 per cent of the word-list (see Appendix, Table 8.2).

Several entries contain detailed descriptions of tools used by criminals, some including diagrams:

BRAD, A small saw, to cut fetters or bars in prison.
CALEBS, An instrument to unlock a door with the key in the lock, by inserting it through the key-hole and hooking it over the handle of the key; made thus: [diagram omitted]
LIMMY, OR JIMMY, A tool or set of tools for breaking open houses.

Some criminal methods are also described, including a few terms that are familiar from earlier dictionaries:

COVER, To conceal the operations of a thief while engaged at work, by standing between him and those you wish to screen him from, or to draw attention from him in any way.
CRACK, To enter a house by violence.
KNUCK, To pick pockets.

and others that are not:

STUFF, To sell articles for what they are not, such as galvanized copper watches for gold, &c
STUFF COVER, A man who assists the stuffer, by introducing himself as a stranger to both parties, and praising the article to be sold.
STUFFER, One who stuffs.

Terms that we have seen in earlier dictionaries take on a more American note:

BEAK, A mayor, or magistrate.
SNEAK, One who robs houses and steamboats by means of calebs, outsiders, &c., who never resorts to violence, but does every thing quietly. A professional sneak is considered as the very highest in the profession.

In American cant we would expect not only to see terms that are peculiar to the States, but also some that were dialectal or archaic in Britain, and this list does not disappoint that expectation:

CADY, A man's hat. [*OED:* 'local']
CARDER, A professed gambler. [*OED:* 'obs']

"PEG UP AND MORRICE," Get up and come, or go. [*OED:* 'dial and colloq']
SHERRY, To run quick. [*OED:* 'dial']
SING DUMMY, Say nothing; make no answer. [*OED*, not labelled, but all
    citations are Scottish]

The compiler of this list is rather euphemistic when it comes
to sexual terms, going so far as to adopt a Biblical phrase to avoid
giving offence to his female readership:

BLOWEN, A 'strange woman.'

Mott, or *mort,* usually defined as "a woman" or "a prostitute", takes
a more respectable form here:

MOTT, Any decent female, generally a mother, or sister, or wife.

The list includes only one authority, which might, in this case, also
be taken as an etymology:

OGRE, OGRESS, Liberated convicts who keep a house of resort for thieves. Words not
    generally used. Taken from Eugene Sue's novel entitled, The Mysteries of Paris.

What we do not see in this list is the repetition of errors made in
earlier dictionaries. Indeed, some familiar terms are included with
entirely new definitions, like *boozing-ken,* which is defined in most
earlier dictionaries as "an ale-house":

BOOZING KEN, A coffee-house.

As well as semantic development, we would expect to see morphological extensions, like *tobe,* apparently a back-formation from *toby*
"road, highwayman":

TOBE, To rob; to knock down.

which in turn affects the definition of *tobyman,* defined merely as
"highwayman" in earlier dictionaries:

TOBYMAN, Highwayman; one who robs by knocking down.

Based on *to mang* "to talk", is a previously unrecorded term:

MANGSMAN, A lawyer.

To bluff is defined as "to look big, to bluster" in Potter's dictionary
and in those derived from it. This word-list includes the term, clearly
in the same sense, but independently defined:

BLUFF, To attempt to frighten by talking or showing weapons.

Because there is no obvious dictionary source for this list, and because it contains the sort of material that we would expect in an American cant-list, we can take the compiler's claims at face value. What we cannot possibly know, however, is how good an informant his villain was or what his motivations were. However, where independent confirmation is available, this is a very useful resource.

The *OED* cites the word-list seven times, and it predates a further seven existing *OED* first citations: *dot* "a worthless fellow" (1859: n[1] 7 "a little child or other tiny creature"), *duck* "a simple fellow" (1857: "a fellow"), *gassy* "boastful" (1863), *to haze* "to subject to cruel horse-play" (1850), *lusher* "a drunkard" (1895), *outsiders* "tools for turning a key from the outside" (1875), and *spread* "a newspaper" ([1858] 1877: "printed matter on facing pages").

Edward Judson's *The Mysteries and Miseries of New York* (1848)

Edward Zane Carroll Judson (1823–86) ran away to sea as a boy, and later fought in the Seminole and Civil Wars, incited riots (including one described by Asbury and depicted in the *Gangs of New York* film: see Chapter 2), took part in a fatal duel, and was lynched by an angry mob, but always lived to tell the tale. He married six times, undertook lecturing tours on temperance, and wrote at least one hymn. He published a sensational magazine, *Ned Buntline's Own*, and hundreds of dime novels, some of which were incidental in transforming plain William Cody into the legendary Buffalo Bill.[9]

In the 'Prefatorial' to *Mysteries and Miseries*, Judson explains that although the story is fictional, the scenes depicted are realistic:

Not one scene of vice or horror is given in the following pages which has not been enacted over and over again in this city, nor is there one character which has not its counterpart in our very midst. I have sought out and studied the reality of each person and scene which I portray. Accompanied by several kind and efficient police officers, whom, were it proper, I would gratefully name, I have visited every den of vice which is hereinafter described, and have chosen each character for the work during these visits. Therefore, though this book bears the title of a *novel*, it is written with the ink of truth and deserves the name of a *history* more than that of a *romance*.[10]

[9] Biographical information about Judson is from Albert Johannsen, *The House of Beadle & Adams and its Dime and Nickel Novels: The Story of a Vanished Literature* (University of Oklahoma Press: http://www.niulib.niu.edu/badndp/judson_edward.html, 1999–2003).

[10] Edward Z. C. Judson, *The Mysteries and Miseries of New York: A Story of Real Life, By Ned Buntline* (New York: Burgess & Garrett, 1848), 5.

His aim in publishing this work, he claimed, was to inspire philanthropy, and to guide it toward suitable recipients.

The word-list is at the end of Part One, and is entitled 'A glossary of "flash terms" and "slang language" used in this work.' It contains 113 entries for 112 headwords. Although sixty-one of these (54 per cent) are also listed in the *Lexicon*, there is no evidence that that is Judson's source. Thirty entries (26.5 per cent) are not in any of the earlier dictionaries. These include:

"*Bus.*" Diminutive of omnibus, a common abbreviation.
"*Coppers.*" Officers of the police; also termed "pig," "nabs," &c.
"*Jug.*" The prison.
"*Kicking the bucket.*" To die.
"*Panel-thief.*" A woman who entices a man to her house, and there has him robbed.
"*Salt-water-vegetables*" Oysters and clams.
"*Tramp.*" To walk. To go on the tramp, is to start off on a thieving expedition.
"*Whiff.*" A puff of smoke.

The list is very much focused on terms for CRIME & DISHONESTY (23.5 per cent). No other field is even half the size. Once terms for punishment and stealable objects are included, this proportion rises to 42.6 per cent (see Appendix, Table 8.3).

The *OED* cites this work ten times, sometimes through the medium of Farmer and Henley's dictionary, dating it variously to 1848, *c.*1848, and 1852. It predates three further *OED* first citations: for *buck* "a cheating cab-driver" (1851: n[1] 2c), *gonoph* "a thief" (1852), and *star* "A badge of rank, authority, or military service" (1890).

Summary

This period saw the beginning of the systematic documentation of American English. Webster set out to provide Americans with their own authoritative reference work, so that they need no longer look back to England for linguistic approval.[11] Bartlett restricted himself to terms peculiar to the United States, and thus included much colloquial, dialectal, and slang material ('those perversions of language which the ignorant and uneducated adopt'), but specifically excluded cant.[12] The glossaries discussed in this chapter were

[11] Noah Webster, *An American Dictionary of the English Language* (New York: S. Converse, 1828).
[12] John Russell Bartlett, *Dictionary of Americanisms. A Glossary of Words and Phrases Usually Regarded as Peculiar to the United States* (1848), 3rd edn. (London: John Camden Hotten, 1860), viii. Bartlett provides

independent productions by users or hearers of the terms they include. Unlike Webster and Bartlett, they owe more to spoken than written sources. They are, therefore, useful witnesses to the development of American cant and slang. Partially derivative works, like Matsell's (see Chapter 2), should be treated with much greater caution.

a list of shorter glossaries of Americanisms that preceded his own (xxx). It is striking that many of the terms he excluded from the third edition, as not peculiar to America (iv), are to be found in the slang dictionaries discussed in this volume.

9 College Dictionaries

English slang dictionaries began to include terms restricted to the universities as early as 1785. Grose listed nineteen terms as university slang, usually noting whether they were specific to Oxford or Cambridge. For example:

FELLOW COMMONER, an empty bottle, so called at the university at Cambridge, where fellow commoners are not in general considered as over full of learning; at Oxford an empty bottle is called a gentleman commoner for the same reason.
KEEP, to inhabit; Lord, where do you keep, i.e. where are your rooms, (*accademical phrase*).
SCOUT, a college errand boy at Oxford, called a gyp at Cambridge.

The 1788 edition added two university terms, and the *Lexicon* brought the total up to thirty-five. Egan's edition of Grose's dictionary includes seventy-nine terms marked as university slang, but he cannot be considered a reliable source in this respect, as we have seen. No other dictionaries surveyed for this volume added any new university slang terms, although many list those derived from Grose's dictionary.

In December 1794 and January 1795, correspondents to the *Gentleman's Magazine* discussed the peculiar language of Cambridge University, noting some of the same terms as Grose.[1] The terms noted are a mixture of slang and jargon, ranging from *scholarship* and *fellowship* to *cole* "money", *to sport* "to wear; to carry", and *row* "a disturbance; a fight". The interest in the language of the universities reflected in this correspondence was to produce a number of specialist dictionaries during this period.

Gradus ad Cantabrigiam (1803)

The *Gradus ad Cantabrigiam* is subtitled 'A Dictionary of Terms, Academical and Colloquial, or Cant, which are used at the University of Cambridge', indicating that it contains university jargon as well as slang. The preface, signed 'A Pembrochian', apologises for the

---

[1] 'An Enemy to all Ambiguity', *Gentleman's Magazine*, December 1794, 1084–5. The discussion continued in two letters published in January 1795, 18–20.

dictionary's inadequacies, and promises that a later edition would include more terms.[2] He makes no excuse, however, for its jocular tone:

> . . . in writing to *Cambridge* men, there can be no need of apology for being too much addicted to *joking*. You will perceive, that I have no *puns* to gratify you. This species of wit (*punning*) has been, time immemorial, in request at our most famous University.[3]

He acknowledges his use of various periodical magazines for 'some most exquisite pieces of humorous poetry',[4] and concludes that 'the merit of the Work, if it possessed any, would be that of forming a complete LOUNGING BOOK,'[5] that is, a book used for passing time in idle amusement.

The dictionary has 157 entries for 152 headwords. Unsurprisingly, its main subject is EDUCATION, followed by terms for positions and ranks within the university (see Appendix, Table 9.1). A few terms are provided with additional usage labels (see Appendix, Table 9.1.1), including:

> ABSOLUTION. It is expressly ordered by the statutes, that the Vice-Chancellor shall pronounce *Absolution* at the end of every term.—OBSOLETE! Such is the good order and regularity, may we not *suppose!* that prevails in the University, that there is no occasion to enforce this, with a variety of other statutes respecting discipline?—*Requiescant in pace!*
> TO SCONCE; 'to impose a fine. (*Academical Phrase.*') *Grose's Dict.* This word is, I believe, wholly confined to Oxford.—'A young Fellow of Baliol [sic] College, having, upon some discontent, cut his throat very dangerously, the Master of the College sent his servitor to the buttery-book, to SCONCE (i.e. fine) him 5s. and, says the Doctor, Tell him the next time he cuts his throat, I'll *sconce* him *ten.*' (*Terræ Filius*, No. 39.)

These entries illustrate some of the striking features of this dictionary, which includes many illustrative and anecdotal citations, and many named authorities (see Appendix, Table 9.1.2). There are 253 citations and 243 cited authorities: an average of 1.6 citations and 1.5 authorities for each entry. The entry for *punishment*, which is too long to reproduce here, quotes Milton, Johnson, Aubrey, 'an old poet, Thomas Tusser', the statutes of Trinity College, James the

---

[2] Christopher Stray, *English Slang in the Nineteenth Century* (Bristol: Thoemmes Press, 2002), I.ix–x, implies that its author may be William Paley, son of the moral philosopher of the same name.
[3] *Gradus ad Cantabrigiam, or, a Dictionary of Terms, Academical and Colloquial, or Cant, which are used at the University of Cambridge*, by 'A Pembrochian' (London: Thomas Maiden for W. J. and J. Richardson, 1803), A.3.r   [4] *Gradus* (1803), A.4.v.
[5] *Gradus* (1803), A.4.v.

First, an unnamed school-master, 'the late Reverend and learned Thomas Warton', and 'one of the GENTLE sex'. In addition, it mentions Sir John Fenn, Horace, and the *Iliad*. Moreover, in citing his authorities, the compiler often includes dates, and sometimes line or page references, thus increasing the impression of scholarliness. Dates are also frequently included in the anecdotal and encyclopaedic information:

> BURSAR. *Bowser, Bouser,* or *Bourser,* in a Colledge; a Gal. BOURSE *a purse.*
> *(Minshew.)* So in *Thre Sermons preached at Eton College,* by *Roger Hutchinson,* 1552, printed in 1560. B. L.
> 'Maisters of Colleges do cal their stewardes, and BOWSERS, to an accompt and audit, to know what they have received, and what they have expended.'
> BURSARS, in short, are the *æruscatores magnæ matris.* The sixth statute of Trinity College enjoins, that they, the Bursars, are to receive the college rents, and to put them into the treasury;—from thence, to take out what is for the daily and necessary expence of the college, and to write down the sum, and the day of the month, with his own hand, in an accompt book to be kept for that purpose! 'Nothing like this,' says Sergeant Miller, in his Account of the University of Cambridge, (*Lond.* 1717. *p.* 106.) 'is ever practised.' He adds; that 'another part of their duty is to take care that there be wholesome meat and drink; which,' he says, 'is wholly neglected by them.'

In a further show of learning, the compiler often includes Latin and Greek terms and quotations, and assumes understanding among his educated readership, for example:

> EXCEEDING DAY;—a dinner *extraordinary*; answering to the *cæna adjicialis* of the Romans. Fuller, the ingenious historian, under the words,
> *Cantabrigia petit æquales, aut æqualia,*
> says—'This is either in respect of their *Commons*—all of the same mess have equal shares; or in respect of *Extraordinaries,* they are all ισοσυμβολοι—*club alike.*

Anecdotal and encyclopaedic information is provided in fifty-three entries (33.8 per cent). The entry for *apollo* "a man who wears his long hair loose", for example, tells us that:

> His Royal Highness Prince William of Gloucester was an APOLLO during the whole of his residence at the University of Cambridge!!

Later in the same entry, we are told that hair worn below the ears had once been considered reprehensible, but that hair cut above the ears had, within the memory of the compiler, been considered vulgar. We also learn that a tax upon hair powder had the effect of popularizing short hair, and that Charles II forbade members of Cambridge

University to wear wigs, smoke, and read sermons. Moreover, before short hair became fashionable:

> ... no young man presumed to dine in hall till he had previously received a handsome trimming from the hair-dresser ... Mr. [Thomas] E[rskine] having been disappointed of the attendance of his college barber, was compelled to forego his *commons* in hall!

and consequently wrote a poem in imitation of Gray, of which twenty-six lines are inserted into the dictionary.

Synonyms or related terms are included in forty-one entries (26.1 per cent). For example, the synonym, *greyhounds*, is included in the entry for *clarians* "members of Clare Hall". In the same entry, we are also told that members of other colleges are called *Johnian Hogs* and *Trinity Bulldogs*.

Thirty entries contain thirty-seven etymologies, for example:

> EXEAT, vulg. voc. EXIT. Leave of absence for the vacation.
>
> HARRY SOPH; or, HENRY SOPHISTER; students who have kept all the terms required for a law act, and hence are ranked as Bachelors of Law by courtesy. They wear a plain, black, full-sleeved gown. Many conjectures have been offered respecting the origin of this term, but none which are satisfactory. First: That King Henry the Eighth, on visiting Cambridge, staid all the Sophisters a year, who expected a year of grace should have been given them.' Secondly: Henry the Eighth being commonly conceived of great strength and stature, these *Sophistæ Henriciani* were elder, and bigger than others.' Thirdly: 'In his reign, learning was at a loss, and the University stood at a gaze what would become of her. Hereupon many Students staid themselves two, three, some four years, as who would see how their degrees before they took them would be rewarded and maintained.' ...

Twenty-eight include cross-references to other entries (17.8 per cent). In addition, twenty-two entries contain a total of twenty-nine footnotes. For example:

> COPUS—Of mighty ale, a large quarte.
>
> *Chaucer.*
>
> 'Vast *toasts* on the delicious lake,
>   Like ships at sea, may swim,'
>   Laden with nutmeg—
>   The conjecture is, surely, ridiculous and senseless, that COPUS is contracted from *EPIS*COPUS, a bishop—'a mixture of wine, oranges, and sugar.' *Dr. Johnson's Dictionary.*—A *Copus* of ale is a common fine at the Students' table in Hall, for speaking Latin, or for some similar *impropriety!*"* [note: *Tempora mutantur*. By an old statute, the Students of Trinity College are enjoined to speak no other languages at meals than *Latin*, *Greek*, or HEBREW!!]

These usually provide additional encyclopaedic information, but also contain illustrative citations, glosses on obsolete terms, bibliographic references, cross-references, synonyms, and jokes. In short, they contain nothing that is not elsewhere contained within the entries, and thus serve only to contribute towards the dashed-off mock-learned air of the dictionary.

The *OED* cites this edition of the *Gradus* nineteen times. It antedates fourteen existing first citations:

aegrotat "permission to be absent from lectures or examinations" (1864)
apostles "the lowest passing students in a year" (1829: "a secret society at Cambridge")
commemoration day "a feast day" (a1884)
convention "a university court" (1811)
daylight "the portion of a glass remaining empty once a drink is poured" (1820)
to fag "to study hard" (1826)
lounge "a stroll" (1806)
plucked "rejected; failed" (1827)
to prose "to tire by talking too much" (1825: 'To bring into some specified condition by prosing')
to read "to study" (1823)
retro "an overdue account" (the first citation for any nominal sense of *retro* is from 1974)
Simeonite "a follower of Simeon" (1823)
skylight "the portion of a glass remaining empty once a drink is poured" (1816)
to sport "to force (a door)" (1806)

Gradus ad Cantabrigiam (1824)

In 1824 another edition of the *Gradus* was published. This contains 257 entries for 251 headwords, an increase of about two-thirds in both entries and headwords. Stray comments that:

. . . the best way to express the relationship is to describe the 1824 book as a new work which took over the title of its predecessor. It is fairly clear that some of the entries were taken over from the earlier Gradus, but it is quite possible that the terms common to the two books were simply those current in the 1800s which remained in use two decades later.[6]

In fact, all of the 1803 *Gradus* entries are found in this later edition, largely little altered.

---

[6] Stray, *English Slang*, I.vi. Later on, in contrast, he writes 'The two editions of the *Gradus* share a core of definitions, taken over in 1824 from the 1803 edition.' (I.x).

The compiler of this edition did edit entries from the earlier edition. Fifty-nine entries (23.0 per cent), evenly spread through the alphabet, are modified in some way. In all, the editor adds twenty-four footnotes, twenty citations, eighteen authorities, and six etymologies to existing entries. Synonyms and related terms are added to seven existing entries that did not already contain them, cross-references to three, anecdotal or encyclopaedic information to one, Latin words and phrases to four, and Greek to two. To the entry for *granta* he adds a table showing when the colleges were founded. In some cases the editing is restricted to minor spelling modifications. For example, the 1803 edition has <connoisseur> in the entry for *loungers*, and <errour> in the entry for *a reading ægrotat*, which are changed to <connoisseur> and <error> in the 1824 edition.

Significantly fewer of the new entries, which are also reasonably evenly spread through the alphabet, contain citations, authorities, dates, anecdotal or encyclopaedic information, and synonyms or other related terms (all $p = 0.01$). As a result of these new entries and of changes made to existing entries, the 1824 edition of the *Gradus* has significantly fewer citations and authorities than the first (both $p = 0.01$), and significantly fewer entries containing anecdotal or encyclopaedic information ($p = 0.05$).

Several of the new entries expand and explain abbreviations for different types of degree, for example:

B. D. (Baccalaureus Divinitatis.) A Bachelor in Divinity must be a M.A. of seven
   years standing: his exercise is one act (after the 4th year), two opponencies, a
   clerum, and an English sermon. (See also ten year men.)
D. D. A Doctor in Divinity must be a Bachelor in Divinity of five, or a Master of
   Arts of twelve years standing. The exercises are one act, two opponencies, a
   clerum, and an English sermon. When, however, a M.A. takes his Doctor's
   degree in any of the three faculties, he is said to graduate *per saltum*, though
   properly this phrase belongs only to the degree of D.D.
S. T. B. Sanctæ Theologiæ Baccalaureus, vide B. D.[7]

The entries for *B. D.* and *D. D.* are characteristic of these additions, in that they explain how a candidate qualifies himself for each award. This greater interest in the affairs of the university is reflected in the significant increase in terms dealing with EDUCATION and with FAILURE (both $p = 0.01$). There is also a significant decrease in

---

[7] *Gradus ad Cantabrigiam; or New University Guide to the Academical Customs, and Colloquial or Cant Terms Peculiar to the University of Cambridge. Observing Wherein in Differs from Oxford*, 'A Brace of Cantabs' (London: John Hearne, 1824).

new terms for EMOTION & TEMPERAMENT ($p = 0.01$), but this does not affect the relative size of the field in the 1824 edition as a whole.

The second edition of the *Gradus* includes plates illustrating, variously, the academic costumes of various members of the university, a fight between town and gown, and a student caught with a prostitute by college officials. This last may be intended to illustrate the entry for *proctor*, who ensured that there was 'no chambering and wantonness', but is mainly included to spice up the dictionary.

The 1824 edition of the *Gradus* has an appendix, called 'The Reading and Varmint Method of Proceeding to the Degree of Bachelor of Arts'. This guides the new undergraduate to 'amusements for his leisure moments', 'as he cannot be expected to devote every hour of his undergraduateship to reading'.[8] The guide uses slang terms included in the dictionary, but also many others, to explain how close the student can sail to the wind in avoiding undue academic exertion. It concludes that those who win prizes and attain positions in the university 'are by no means the most gifted men, the men of the most brilliant talent, or the greatest genius. But they are the *steady* men, who owe all their knowledge to hard reading, and desperate perseverance in study.'[9]

The *OED* cites this edition of the *Gradus* five times in all. It antedates three existing first citations:

absit "permission to be absent" (1884)
to degrade "to postpone one's examination(s)" (1829)
tuition "fee paid for tuition" (1828 US)

Benjamin Homer Hall, *A Collection of College Words and Customs* (1851)

Benjamin Homer Hall was 'a lawyer, poet, and New York jurist'. He built the Rice Building, which once bore his name, on First and River Street, New York.[10] Like the *Gradus*, but to a lesser degree, his *Collection of College Words and Customs* contains some college slang among its collection of technical terms and anecdotal entries.

---

[8] *Gradus* (1824), 121.   [9] *Gradus* (1824), 131.
[10] James R. Elkins, *Strangers to Us All. Lawyers and Poetry* [http://www.wvu.edu/~lawfac/jelkins/lp-2001/hall.html].

For that reason, I have not surveyed it in full. Hall includes some college slang terms that appear to have been widely employed:

HAULED UP. In many colleges, one brought up before the Faculty is said to be *hauled up*.

KNUCKS. From KNUCKLES. At some of the Southern colleges, a game at marbles called *Knucks* is a common diversion among the students.[11]

some used at specific American colleges:

BARNEY. At Harvard College, about the year 1810, this word was used to designate a bad recitation. To *barney* was to recite badly.

CURL. In the University of Virginia, to make a perfect recitation; to overwhelm a Professor with student learning.

DOUGH-BALL. At the Anderson Collegiate Institute, Indiana, a name given by the town's people to a student.

FAT. At Princeton College, a letter with money or a draft is thus denominated.

GORM. From *gormandize*. At Hamilton College, to eat voraciously.

LAP-EAR. At Washington College, Penn., students of a religious character are called *lap-ears* or *donkeys*. The opposite class are known by the common name of *bloods*.

SHIP. At Emory College, Ga., one expelled from college is said to be *shipped*.

and others employed at universities in Britain:

POKER. At Oxford, Eng., a cant name for a *bedel*. . . .

RETRO. Latin; literally, *back*. Among the students of the University of Cambridge, Eng., used to designate a *behind*-hand account. . . .

TUFT-HUNTER. A cant term, in the English universities, for a hanger-on to noblemen and persons of quality. So called from the *tuft* in the cap of the latter.—*Halliwell*.

He even translates some German college slang:

OLD HOUSE. A name given in the German universities to a student during his fifth term.

YOUNG BURSCH. In the German universities, a name given to a student during his third term, or *semester*.

The entries for slang terms are not representative of the dictionary as a whole, whose entries often include citations and cited authorities, for example:

EXEAT. Latin; literally, *let him depart*. Leave of absence given to a student in the English universities.—*Webster*.
    The students who wish to go home apply for an "*Exeat*," which is a paper signed by the Tutor, Master, and Dean.—*Alma Mater*, Vol. I. p. 162.

[11] Benjamin Homer Hall, *A Collection of College Words and Customs* (Cambridge, MA: John Bartlett, 1851).

MATRICULATE. Latin, *Matricula*, a roll or register, from *matrix*. To enter or
admit to membership in a body or society, particularly in a college or univer-
sity, by enrolling the name in a register.—*Wotton.*
In July, 1778, he was examined at that university, and *matriculated.*—*Works of R.T. Paine,*
Biography, p. xviii.
In 1787, he *matriculated* at St. John's College, Cambridge.—*Household Words*, Vol. I. p. 210.

TERM. In universities and colleges, the time during which instruction is
regularly given to students, who are obliged by the statutes and laws of the
institution to attend to the recitations, lectures, and other exercises.—*Webster.*

Entries describing college customs, disproportionately those of
Harvard, are sometimes several pages long (e.g. *Class Day, Liberty
Tree, Phi Beta Kappa, Wrestling Match*).

The *OED* cites Hall's dictionary twenty-nine times in all, usually
dating it to 1851, but occasionally to 1856, the revised and enlarged
edition, towards the beginning of the alphabet. I have not surveyed
its contents completely, but none of the terms I have noted here
antedates an existing first citation.

Charles Astor Bristed, *Five Years in an English University* (1852)

Bristed arrived in Cambridge from New York in October 1840, having already studied at Yale. He was an outstanding student, and won
prizes from both universities. He wrote for sporting journals and,
later in life, was 'known in literary circles as a scholar and to his
friends as a hospitable but not indiscriminate host.'[12]

In *Five Years in an English University*, already quoted via Ducange in
Chapter 7, Bristed explained English university life and customs for
the benefit of American readers. Volume I contains a five-page
vocabulary of 'The Cantab Language'. He notes that:

One of the first and most necessary things to be acquired by a resident in a new
country is some knowledge of its language. Even in the few pages we have thus far
gone through, terms have frequently occurred which required explanation; and
without some insight into the Cambridge vocabulary, it would be impossible to
describe Cambridge life intelligibly, or to understand a true description of it.
I therefore subjoin a list of the principal cant terms and phrases in use, translating
them, when possible, into equivalent slang of our own.[13]

[12] *DAB* ii.53–4.
[13] Charles Astor Bristed, *Five Years in an English University* (New York: G. P. Putnam, 1852), 30.

The glossary, which is not arranged alphabetically, contains forty-three entries for forty-one headwords. It begins:

Gownsman.—A student of the University
Snob.—A townsman as opposed to a student, or a blackguard as opposed to a gentleman; a loafer generally.
Cad.— A low fellow, nearly = snob.
Reading.— Studying.
A reading man.— A hard student.

Only two entries include citations:

Like bricks, Like a brick or a bean, Like a house on fire, To the nth. To the n+1th.— Intensives to express the most energetic way of doing anything. These phrases are sometimes in very odd contexts [sic]. You hear men talk of a balloon going up *like bricks*, and rain coming down *like a house on fire.*
No end of.—Another intensive of obvious import. *They had no end of tin*, i.e. a great deal of money. *He is no end of a fool*, i.e. the greatest fool possible.

One entry gives an indication of pronunciation:

A rowing man—(*ow* as in *cow*).— A hard case, a spreër

A few consider the different shades of meaning among equivalent slang and standard English terms, for example:

Brick.—A good fellow; what Americans sometimes call a *clever* fellow.
Fast.—Nearly the French *expansif. A fast* man is not necessarily (like the London fast man) a *rowing* man, though the two attributes are often combined in the same person; he is one who dresses flashily, talks bigs, and spends, or affects to spend, money very freely.
Little-Go.—The University Examination in the second year, properly called the *Previous Examination.*

and two entries refer back to the previous definition:

Pill.—Twaddle, platitude.
Rot.—Ditto.

Proctors.—The Police Officers of the University.
Bull-dogs.—Their Lictors, or servants who attend them when on duty.

Not surprisingly, the largest semantic area is EDUCATION (33.3 per cent). SUCCESS and FAILURE each account for 5.6 per cent of the glossary's semantic coverage, as does SPEECH. The only other significant fields are EMOTION & TEMPERAMENT (14.8 per cent), and RANK and PLEASURES & PASTIMES, each accounting for 7.4 per cent of the whole (see Appendix, Table 9.2).

After the glossary, Bristed includes a number of more widely-known slang words in his discussion:

Add to these some words previously explained, as *gyp, sporting-door, questionist,* &c., and a number of London slang words with which *Punch* has made up familiar, e.g. *lush* and *grub,* for meat and drink; *weed,* for cigar; *tin,* for money; *governor,* for father; *sold,* for exceedingly disappointed or deceived; and a few pure Greek words, of which the most generally used are, νούς (sense) and χύδος (credit, reputation), and you have a tolerable idea of the Cambridge vocabulary—chiefly confined to the Undergraduates (except in the technicals like *proctor, wrangler,* etc.), but understood and acknowledged by the stiffest Dons.[14]

He notes that it is not just the less academic rowing-men who use unintelligible vocabulary, but that the scholarly reading-men are prone to insert Greek terms into conversation and correspondence. 'And this is not altogether affectation; to many of these men the strange words they use have become more familiar and convenient than the corresponding English ones'.[15]

The *OED* cites Bristed's text and glossary forty-eight times in all, often for college slang. It antedates one existing first citation: for *pill* "nonsense" (1935).

Summary

These word-lists involved much more effort than some of the hastily plagiarized throwaway glossaries of flash language discussed in earlier chapters. The *Gradus* is characterized by its mock-scholarship, which excludes all who fail to appreciate the in-jokes and abstruse quotations. Hall's dictionary is more ambitious, and aims to document at least some of the language of universities throughout the world. Bristed's aims are more modest, and he alone focuses on slang, excluding the university jargon found in the other three lists.

There are a number of reasons why dictionaries of college slang should emerge as specialized publications at so early a date. First, this is the language of a well-defined group: like thieves, beggars, or gypsies, whose glossaries predate these by centuries, students can be easily identified. Secondly, the language they use is different enough from normal speech to make it worth cataloguing. Thirdly, there is a reasonable market for these word-lists: each year a new cohort

---

[14] Bristed, *Five Years,* 34.   [15] Bristed, *Five Years,* 35.

of excited freshmen would strive to fit in without exposing their inexperience. What finer gift could an anxious parent or knowing older brother give than a dictionary of university slang? Fourthly, the intended audience is literate and has some disposable income. Fifthly, people outside the target group might also be interested in their vocabulary: parents, ex-students, prospective-students, etc. Finally, the vocabulary is reasonably stable: once produced, a dictionary might sell for several years or even decades with minor changes. Naturally then, the earliest specialized slang lists were lists of student slang. Combining the weight of tradition with the glamour of undermining it, these dictionaries had a captive target market.

10 Conclusions

The dictionaries surveyed in this volume are markedly different in methodology, type, and content from those that preceded them. A comparison between these and the earlier dictionaries reveals some interesting changes in linguistic theory and practice, in attitudes towards non-standard registers, and in publishing. There are continuities, of course, and I will discuss those first.

Amateur glossaries, apparently independently produced by people with first-hand experience of the criminal underworld, like Haggart and Tufts, belong to a tradition of confessional lexicography, including works by Hitchin, Dalton, and Poulter.[1] Several such glossaries are mediated by a respectable member of society, who protects the reader from individuals like Perry and Vaux, if only by the inclusion of an admonitory preface. These can trace their heritage to Head's *English Rogue*. At one further remove from the source of their word-lists are those glossaries produced by an altruistic expedition into the underworld. Like the contributor to the *Ladies Repository*, Head collected terms for the *Canting Academy* during prison visits. Others, like Matsell, claim to have compiled their lists in the course of their official duties, and can trace their ancestry, and even some of their contents, to Harman's *Caveat*. Even Grose and Egan, compiling their lists, at least in part, from the written sources around them, were copying B. E.'s example. Largely derivative lists also have a long history: Potter and Caulfield follow in the dishonourable footsteps of Smith and Hall, cashing in on the popularity of earlier works without any extra exertion than thinking up a new title and a new marketing angle.[2]

What has changed is that cant has become stylish: it has become flash. Where the earlier glossaries presented the secret language of thieves and beggars, many of the later ones list the slick lingo of London's ultra-fashionable world. While still edgy enough to imply

[1] Charles Hitchin, *The Regulator or, a Discovery of the Thieves, Thief-Takers and Locks, alias Receivers of Stolen Goods in and about the City of London* (London: T. Warner, 1718); James Dalton, *A Genuine Narrative of all the Street Robberies Committed since October last, by James Dalton, and his Accomplices* (London: J. Roberts, 1728); Poulter, *Discoveries*.

[2] Alexander Smith, *The Thieves New Canting Dictionary* (London: Sam Briscoe, 1719); John Hall, *Memoirs of the Right Villainous John Hall* (London: H. Hills, 1708).

knowledge of the seedy underworld, the use of flash language did not indicate criminality in the same way as the use of cant. Sixteenth- and seventeenth-century users of cant fumed and raged when their vocabulary was revealed; nineteenth-century users of flash merely basked in the warm glow of increased admiration. Egan is the best example of how profitable a reputation for such knowledge could be.

This period saw an increasing geographical separation between rich and poor. Instead of having a cross-section of society in each parish, London began to develop wealthy districts and slums. As the growing middle classes employed ever more servants, contact between employer and employee was becoming more distant and formal. Conscious of their own ignorance, mid-nineteenth-century readers turned to works like Brandon's and Mayhew's for information about the lives of the less fortunate. At the same time, the concentration of population in large towns, and especially London, created a market for cheap pamphlets, and working-class readers must have enjoyed a particular pleasure in seeing high society invaded and parodied by flash-speaking anti-heroes. Separation between the classes appears to have created a mutual fascination with how the other half lived and talked.

What made flash so dangerous, and therefore so appealing, was that it occupied the area between the classes: between those who were respectable and those who were not. Cant was frightening enough— a language that could be used, within one's hearing, to plot against one's life—but flash threatened to bring the disreputable, immoral, enticing world of gambling, drinking, and prostitution into one's own drawing room. Cant respected class, in that its speakers knew not to use it outside its proper sphere; flash had no such respect. Thus flash language was, for users of any class, an expression of defiance.

One glossary from before 1785 that explored the idea of flash was Moll King's.[3] Although the text and glossary covered only the language of criminals, we are told that it was adopted and used by the fashionable patrons of Moll's coffee house. It is a fascinating document for many reasons, not least because it is unusual among the cant and slang lists in giving a woman a prominent role. This is another difference between the two periods. In the earlier lists, we can assume that female criminals also used canting language; in the

---

[3] *The Life and Character of Moll King, Late Mistress of King's Coffee-house in Covent Garden* (London: W. Price, 1747).

later ones we can see from the introductions and prefaces that
women, or at least ladies, should be protected from exposure to flash
terms at all costs. In other words, although flash transcended class
boundaries, it identified new divisions between the genders. Before
he embarked on his account of life in St Giles's, Parker wrote:

With a fearful foot, I enter on the soil of the following chapter, and I do beseech
my fair readers to shun it, lest, in this primrose path, they meet a snake in the
grass; therefore, ye dear delights of the universe, to man, more precious than honour, wealth, or friendship, stop short, I once more beseech you, lest twining round
your light heels, like the original serpent, a vicious variety may level your delicate
imaginations, and leave them in a state, dangerous, as delightful.

But, if female curiosity will prevail, and still the peeping eye would pervade the
midnight orgies of the moderns, I must first inform them, that the following compositions are intended only for that *part* of the *public*, who has so generously
patronized my undertaking; that species of people, who at the same time that they
can enjoy the flights of fancy on an attic wing, yet, stooping their pinions, feel as
much pleasure in the effusions of what is termed *cant*, *flash*, *low wit* and *humour*,
which substantially are quickened by the same *orb*, as the witty compositions of a
more refined taste.

For them, and them alone, the following traits of low characters are introduced,
and as a dancing star ruled my birth, and on my first onset in life, set me off with
the most eccentric and convivial disposition, I once more conjure the fair reader
will pass over the following pages; for the man who could be capable of instilling
poison into the chaste recesses of a female breast deserves not the name of man,
nor the happiness a virtuous and fond woman can bestow.[4]

This probably served the same function as modern media warnings of
foul language and scenes of explicit sex: to entice audiences to perse-
vere while covering writers, broadcasters, and film-makers against
criticism for causing offence. Indeed, the *Lexicon Balatronicum* suggested
that flash language could actually protect the delicate from vulgarity:

We need not descant on the dangerous impressions that are made on the female
mind, by the remarks that fall incidentally from the lips of the brothers or servants of
a family; and we have before observed that improper topics can with our assistance be
discussed, even before the ladies, without raising a blush on the cheek of modesty.[5]

While affluent young men were dressing as coachmen and adopting
flash language, their sisters and mothers were valiantly attempting to
preserve themselves from all hint of impropriety. Both English's list
and the *Vulgarities of Speech* explore ideas of decency in language, which

[4] Parker, *Life's Painter*, 122–3.   [5] *Lexicon Balatronicum*, Preface, vii.

differ for men and women. A gentleman might enjoy and use, or at least understand, terms that a lady must never acknowledge. Backing away rapidly from crudeness beyond their comprehension, middle-class women created and observed whole new areas of lexical anxiety.

This growing sense of obscenity all around is reflected, in its turn, in the dictionaries' coverage of tabooed terms. Even in these defiantly risqué publications, it became increasingly necessary to adopt euphemisms and to obscure offensive terms. Indeed, the spread of decency fed these lists. Words and ideas long considered acceptable gradually became tabooed, and were welcomed with open arms into the cant and slang dictionary tradition. The aura of naughtiness surrounding these works, must surely have helped sales.

It is clear that publishers were responding to market trends: after the publication of Egan's *Life in London*, for example, the inclusion of a slang glossary could boost the sales of any similar work. People bought them, largely, for entertainment, as we can see from the publishers' advertisements included in them: no one would advertise a book of dirty songs in a dictionary aimed at sombre moralists or disinterested linguists, for example. A glossary, especially a short one, is a very easily digestible format. From it, one could acquire vocabulary and information with which to entertain and impress one's friends. A reader or theatre-goer who had enjoyed the thrills of *Life in London*, could raise his status amongst his peers by casually employing the same flash terminology in everyday life. In effect, through their repeated appearance in books and periodicals, on stage, and in songs, these words became standing jokes. Like catchphrases from television and film, and from music-hall before them, they signalled one's right to belong: I am like you (and you will like me), because I not only use the word *out-and-outer* (for example), but also understand quite what is so great about that. It is crucial, too, to stop using these terms before they become outmoded and irritating.

A development new to this period is the historical approach to slang lexicography. This innovation can, without doubt, be attributed to Grose's coincident interest in all things antiquarian and all things vulgar. Many earlier slang lexicographers had turned to previously published lists in the construction of their glossaries, but most had not acknowledged their debt.[6] Grose, on the other hand, paraded his antiquarian sources, both in the introductory material

---

[6] Rowland's *Martin Mark-all* does make use of two sources, both acknowledged, but his intention is to discredit and update Dekker's glossary rather than to present a historical account.

and in the body of the dictionary. He used cited authorities and quotations within entries, far more commonly than usage labels, to indicate that terms were no longer current. Indeed, he implied that he had consulted a wider range of texts than he really had. Grose understood the difference between research and plagiarism, however, and prudently left his more recent sources unacknowledged.

Because of Grose's influence, at first direct and later through Egan, many dictionaries produced in this period contained the same core word-list. The continued listing of these terms does not indicate continued usage, but even the largely derivative dictionaries usually added a few recent innovations, which can only be identified by detailed comparison. Many of the independently produced shorter lists are actually better witnesses of current non-standard language than more regularly consulted works like the *Lexicon*.

While it is certain that some of the lists were aimed at slang-receivers (like Parker's glossary, which explains terms found in the text), others were undoubtedly used in slang production. Novelists and film-makers have used these glossaries in the perilous process of introducing unfamiliar terms into their fictional works. Without explanation, these may bewilder readers; with, the text may become frustratingly stilted. Many authors have chosen to negotiate this difficulty for the sake of the added interest and authenticity that specialized vocabulary can bestow. They tend to regard their dictionary sources with unqualified respect, and to rely on their contents implicitly. 'The dictionary', even a dictionary of disreputable language, and even one clearly compiled by an amateur, has an air of certainty that users seldom question. The makers of *Gangs of New York* were well aware that Asbury was not a reliable source, and presumably that Matsell was not above reproach, but a list of words in alphabetical order has an authority all of its own, as demonstrated by their unconvincing use by several of the authors discussed here.

I have been able to discuss only a sample of literature from this period employing cant and slang, and have concentrated on those writers whose dictionary sources can be identified with some confidence.[7] So common was the use of cant in literature for a time, that Thackeray incorporated a parody in *Vanity Fair*:

'Mofy! Is that your snum?' said a voice from the area. 'I'll gully the dag and bimbole the clinky in a snuffkin.'

---

[7] See Partridge, *Slang*, ch. iv & v, for a much fuller account of the use of slang and cant in literature during this period.

'Nuffle your clod, and beladle your glumbanions,' said Vizard, with a dreadful oath.

'This way, men: if they screak, out with your snickers and slick! Look to the pewter-room, Blowser. You, Mark, to the old gaff's mopus box! and I,' added he, in a lower but more horrible voice, 'I will look to Amelia!'[8]

No less impenetrable than some of the extracts quoted above, this passage employs partially fabricated cant to mock the gullibility of contemporary readers and the fashion for cant among writers of the period.

There are a number of pitfalls in using these dictionaries to study the history of non-standard English. In the first edition of his dictionary, for example, Grose marked the following terms for various types of thief, among others, as cant: *ark ruffian, badger, buttock and file, colt, dromedary, figger, high pad, ken cracker, mace, natty lad, rapparee, sneak,* and *tory.* Later compilers of specialized cant dictionaries certainly aimed to select these terms from Grose, but were also tempted by all the other terms for thieves not marked as cant. These include *amuser, budge, collector, dunaker, eriff, fagger, gentleman's master, hosteler, knight of the road, lift, napper, ostler, queer bird, rusher, varlet,* and *wiper drawer.* Naturally people other than thieves need terms referring to criminals: not all terms meaning 'thief' are necessarily cant, or even slang. However, neither Grose nor any of his successors was particularly careful with such distinctions.

Like the terms first recorded in Harman's *Caveat,* some of the words listed in these dictionaries appear to have had far more extensive usage than is really the case. Grose looked to writers like Shakespeare, Fielding, Swift, and Smollett for additions to his dictionary, and later lexicographers and writers looked to Grose and to dictionaries derived from his. Dickens was influenced by Egan's flash language, and his interest was to be returned by Hotten, who was to make extensive use of Dickens's novels, as well as Borrows' and Ainsworth's, in compiling his slang dictionary. These interrelationships between slang documenters and producers immeasurably complicate the study of the history of non-standard language and undermine much apparently independent evidence.

The cut-off date for this volume, 1858, is to some extent arbitrary. However, dictionaries after that point began to develop and specialize

---

[8] William Thackeray, *Vanity Fair* No. II, Feb. 1847, 43–4, quoted in Hollingsworth, *The Newgate Novel,* 207. Thackeray removed this passage in 1853, and it is not usually found in modern editions.

in different directions. Hotten followed very much in the mould of Grose, combining material from earlier lists and literature and from slang-speaking informants to produce an all-purpose dictionary of historical and contemporary non-standard language. Like Grose, he allowed the odd dialectal and jargon term to slip in, and like Grose, he modified the content of his dictionary in its several editions. Where he differed from Grose was in his aspirations. Grose had dictionaries by Johnson and Bailey to emulate; Hotten had the *OED*. Although no fascicles were published until after his death, the work of the Philological Society undoubtedly inspired Hotten to ask his readers for additional material. This encouraged him to greater efforts in definition, citation, and etymology, and in the provision of usage information. His ambitious and all-embracing approach was to be followed by Farmer and Henley and by Barrère.[9] Both of these dictionaries were to include synonyms in other European languages.[10]

As all-purpose slang dictionaries became ever more comprehensive and expensive, shorter glossaries became increasingly specialized. Lists of university and college slang still had a niche, but they were joined by lists of the vocabulary of public schools, trades, and other occupational and interest groups.[11] As new Englishes were being documented around the world, so too were their slangs.[12]

So what became of the cant glossary, a tradition stretching back to Harman's *Caveat*, in which the revelation of a secret language is intended to thwart those who seek to abuse society's charitable instincts and trusting nature? That tradition also continued, through Vaux, Haggart, and Tufts into the work of Frost, Willard, and Sullivan.[13] From having been at the very core of the non-standard English dictionary tradition, cant glossaries were to become increasingly marginal.

[9] Farmer and Henley, *Slang and its Analogues*; Albert Marie Victor Barrère, *Argot and Slang; a new French and English Dictionary of the Cant Words, Quaint Expressions, Slang Terms and Flash Phrases* . . . (London: The Ballantyne Press, 1889); Albert Marie Victor Barrère and Charles G. Leland, *A Dictionary of Slang, Jargon, and Cant* (Edinburgh: The Ballantyne Press, 1889/90).

[10] These dictionaries will be discussed in more detail in later volumes in this series.

[11] For example, *Guide to Eton* (London: Whittaker, 1861); Lyman Hotchkiss Bagg's *Four Years at Yale* (New Haven, CT: Charles C. Chatfield, 1871); Peter Lund Simmonds, *The Commercial Dictionary of Trade Products* (London: G. Routledge & Sons, 1872); H. G. Crickmore, *Dictionary or Glossary of Racing Terms and Slang* (New York: H. G. Crickmore, 1880).

[12] For example, Henry Yule and A. C. Burnell, *Hobson-Jobson; a Glossary of Colloquial Anglo-Indian Words and Phrases* (London: John Murray, 1886); James Maitland, *The American Slang Dictionary* (Chicago: Privately Printed, 1891); Karl Lentzner, *Dictionary of the Slang-English of Australia, and of Some Mixed Languages* (Leipzig: Ehrhardt Karras, 1892).

[13] For example, Thomas Frost, *Circus Life and Circus Celebrities* (London: Tinsley Brothers, 1875); Josiah Flynt Willard, *Tramping with Tramps* (London: T. Fisher Unwin, 1899); Joseph M. Sullivan, *Criminal Slang: a Dictionary of the Vernacular of the Under World* (Chicago: Detective Pub. Co., 1908).

Perhaps dictionary-buyers stopped believing in an underworld united across Britain or America by its secret language. Certainly by the end of this period, there were criminal centres in many major industrial towns. Despite the increasing size of cities like London and New York, glossaries of their cant would have had a falling market share. Who, in Chicago, would want to know how New York villains were talking? What use would an understanding of London cant be to a householder in Manchester?

The idea of a national criminal language lost credibility at the same time that, in London at least, law-abiding citizens stopped playing a major part in the implementation of the law. They no longer observed public whippings and executions; they no longer pelted criminals in the stocks and the pillories. The national embarrassment of transportation and the hulks was replaced by the contained, controlled, reforming efficiency of the prison service. Uniformed officers patrolled the streets, and fears of riot and revolution were replaced by dreams of industry and empire. England, its language, and its slang were stretching out and, for a time at least, taking over much of the rest of the world.

Appendix

In tables showing the semantic coverage of dictionaries, the totals are for comparison only, and do not represent the number of entries in the dictionary concerned. For an explanation of the methodology used in constructing these tables, see Volume I.[i] Where dictionaries are derived from Grose's, either directly or indirectly, the ordering of subject matter is determined by the order in Table 1.1, that is, semantic areas are ranked according to their relative size in the first edition of Grose's dictionary. This is to facilitate reference between tables. For dictionaries independent of Grose, ranking is determined by relative size. Where dictionaries include usage labels, it is not always clear whether they are intended to refer to all entries under a single headword. I have considered each case separately.

For tables showing sources, 'new entries' are those that are not from the dictionary sources identified in the text. 'Sources indistinguishable' indicates that the same or a similar entry is found in more than one of the dictionaries listed. Often the overlap between sources is so great that attribution to particular sources can only be made on the basis of minor differences in spelling or definition. Where a lexicographer's main source is obvious, I have attributed all possible entries to that source regardless of their co-occurrence in other lists. For example, Egan's main source is the *Lexicon Balatronicum*, but he also uses the *Flash Dictionary*, which is indirectly derived from Grose's. Thus I have attributed to the *Flash Dictionary* only those terms that are not found in the *Lexicon*, and I have attributed to the *Lexicon* all terms found in it, regardless of their occurrence in the *Flash Dictionary* or the other sources listed (see Table 5.2).

The cumulative effect of rounding each calculation up or down sometimes means that for tables showing usage labels (e.g. Table 1.3.1), the total percentage is not always the same as the sum of the percentages above it.

---

[i] Coleman, *Cant and Slang Dictionaries* i.193–5.

Table 1.1 Grose's sources

Source	Entries (% of Grose's entries)
B. E.	254 (6.5%)
Bailey	50 (1.3%)
Dekker	12 (0.3%)
New	12 (0.3%)
Carew	1[a] (0.0%)
Sources indistinguishable	1,803 (46.3%)
New entries	1,761 (45.2%)
Total	3,893

[a] Although the Carew word-list is derived entirely from the *New Canting Dictionary*, a variant form, *glim* or *glimmer* 'fire', is found in most versions of the Carew lists, and from there in Grose's dictionary.

Table 1.2 An outline of the subject matter of Grose's *Classical Dictionary of the Vulgar Tongue*

Semantic area	1785	1788	1796
Crime & dishonesty	554 (10.1%)	680 (9.8%)	688 (9.7%)
Emotion & temperament	460 (8.4%)	592 (8.5%)	601 (8.5%)
Body & health	395 (7.2%)	523 (7.5%)	531 (7.5%)
Food & drink	376 (6.8%)	479 (6.9%)	493 (6.9%)
Work	324 (5.9%)	390 (5.6%)	392 (5.5%)
Money	295 (5.4%)	363 (5.2%)	373 (5.3%)
Sex	280 (5.1%)	338 (4.9%)	344 (4.8%)
Pleasure & pastimes	267 (4.8%)	341 (4.9%)	300 (4.2%)
Domestic life	253 (4.6%)	330 (4.7%)	335 (4.7%)
War & violence	229 (4.2%)	284 (4.1%)	288 (4.1%)
Animals & nature	223 (4.0%)	283 (4.1%)	289 (4.1%)
Speech	220 (4.0%)	282 (4.0%)	284 (4.0%)
Law & order	219 (4.0%)	280 (4.0%)	291 (4.1%)
Clothes	200 (3.6%)	253 (3.6%)	263 (3.7%)
Fools & victims	193 (3.5%)	230 (3.3%)	233 (3.3%)
Looks	193 (3.5%)	241 (3.5%)	243 (3.4%)
People	193 (3.5%)	230 (3.3%)	235 (3.3%)
Artefacts	189 (3.4%)	247 (3.5%)	248 (3.5%)
Poverty	172 (3.1%)	187 (2.7%)	189 (2.7%)
Geography & travel	163 (3.0%)	214 (3.1%)	223 (3.1%)
Other	109 (2.0%)	201 (2.9%)	256 (3.6%)
Total	5,507	6,968	7,099

Table 1.2.1 An outline of the subject matter of additions to Grose's *Classical Dictionary*

Semantic area	Working copy	1788	1796
Crime & dishonesty	19 (7.0%)	117 (7.8%)	8 (6.1%)
Emotion & temperament	8 (2.9%)	156 (10.4%)	9 (6.9%)
Body & health	33 (12.1%)	135 (9.0%)	8 (6.1%)
Food & drink	29 (10.6%)	108 (7.2%)	14 (10.7%)
Work	20 (7.3%)	63 (4.2%)	2 (1.5%)
Money	11 (4.0%)	72 (4.8%)	10 (7.6%)
Sex	15 (5.5%)	73 (4.9%)	6 (4.6%)
Pleasure & pastimes	13 (4.8%)	81 (5.4%)	9 (6.9%)
Domestic life	10 (3.7%)	83 (5.5%)	5 (3.8%)
War & violence	11 (4.0%)	51 (3.4%)	4 (3.1%)
Animals & nature	13 (4.8%)	59 (3.9%)	6 (4.6%)
Speech	3 (1.1%)	65 (4.3%)	2 (1.5%)
Law & order	20 (7.3%)	56 (3.7%)	11 (8.4%)
Clothes	6 (2.2%)	56 (3.7%)	10 (7.6%)
Fools & victims	4 (1.5%)	39 (2.6%)	3 (2.3%)
Looks	8 (2.9%)	46 (3.1%)	2 (1.5%)
People	13 (4.8%)	49 (3.3%)	5 (3.8%)
Artefacts	12 (4.4%)	58 (3.9%)	1 (0.8%)
Poverty	4 (1.5%)	29 (1.9%)	2 (1.5%)
Geography & travel	14 (5.1%)	54 (3.6%)	9 (6.9%)
Other	7 (2.6%)	47 (3.1%)	5 (3.8%)
Total	273	1,497	131

Table 1.3 The usage labels of Grose's *Classical Dictionary*

Label	1785	1788	1796
Cant	394 (65.4%)	472 (62.1%)	469 (61.4%)
Naval & nautical	33 (5.5%)	59 (7.8%)	60 (7.9%)
Military	16 (2.7%)	16 (2.1%)	15 (2.0%)
Other jargons	25 (4.2%)	35 (4.6%)	38 (5.0%)
Slang	5 (0.8%)	11 (1.4%)	12 (1.6%)
Nursery & school	4 (0.7%)	6 (0.8%)	7 (0.9%)
University	19 (3.2%)	21 (2.8%)	21 (2.7%)
Irish	34 (5.6%)	39 (5.1%)	40 (5.2%)
Scots	9 (1.5%)	9 (1.2%)	9 (1.2%)
Welsh	2 (0.3%)	2 (0.3%)	2 (0.3%)
US	3 (0.5%)	4 (0.5%)	4 (0.5%)
Black	4 (0.7%)	5 (0.7%)	5 (0.7%)
Other dialects	13 (2.2%)	14 (1.8%)	14 (1.8%)
Colloquial	5 (0.8%)	10 (1.3%)	10 (1.3%)
Archaic & dated	11 (1.8%)	15 (2.0%)	15 (2.0%)

Table 1.3 (*Continued*)

Label	1785		1788		1796	
Derogatory	11	(1.8%)	13	(1.7%)	13	(1.7%)
Vulgar	1	(0.2%)	1	(0.1%)	1	(0.1%)
Jocular	7	(1.2%)	17	(2.2%)	17	(2.2%)
Euphemistic	5	(0.8%)	8	(1.1%)	9	(1.2%)
Figurative	1	(0.2%)	3	(0.4%)	3	(0.4%)
Total	602		760		764	

Table 1.3.1 A summary of the usage labels of Grose's *Classical Dictionary*

	1785 (% of labels)	[% of all entries]	1788 (% of labels)	[% of all entries]	1796 (% of labels)	[% of all entries]
Cant	394 (65.4%)	[10.1%]	472 (62.1%)	[9.4%]	469 (61.4%)	[9.2%]
Jargon	74 (12.3%)	[1.9%]	110 (14.5%)	[2.2%]	113 (14.8%)	[2.2%]
Slang	28 (4.7%)	[0.7%]	38 (5.0%)	[0.8%]	40 (5.2%)	[0.8%]
Dialect	65 (10.8%)	[1.7%]	73 (9.6%)	[1.5%]	74 (9.7%)	[1.5%]
Other	41 (6.8%)	[1.1%]	67 (8.8%)	[1.3%]	68 (8.9%)	[1.3%]
Total	602	[15.5%]	760	[15.2%]	764	[15.0%]

Table 1.3.2 Usage labels in additions to Grose's *Classical Dictionary*

Label	Working copy	1788	1796
Cant	26 (61.9%)	89 (54.6%)	0 (0.0%)
Naval & nautical	8 (19.0%)	21 (12.9%)	1 (16.7%)
Military	0 (0.0%)	1 (0.6%)	0 (0.0%)
Other jargons	2 (4.8%)	10 (6.1%)	3 (50.0%)
Slang	0 (0.0%)	7 (4.3%)	0 (0.0%)
Nursery & school	0 (0.0%)	2 (1.2%)	0 (0.0%)
University	1 (2.4%)	1 (0.6%)	0 (0.0%)
Dialect	1 (2.4%)	1 (0.6%)	1 (16.7%)
Irish	1 (2.4%)	4 (2.5%)	0 (0.0%)
US	0 (0.0%)	1 (0.6%)	0 (0.0%)
Black	0 (0.0%)	1 (0.6%)	0 (0.0%)
Colloquial	0 (0.0%)	5 (3.1%)	0 (0.0%)
Archaic & dated	0 (0.0%)	4 (2.5%)	0 (0.0%)
Derogatory	0 (0.0%)	1 (0.6%)	0 (0.0%)
Vulgar	2 (4.8%)	1 (0.6%)	0 (0.0%)
Jocular	0 (0.0%)	10 (6.1%)	0 (0.0%)
Euphemistic	1 (2.4%)	3 (1.8%)	1 (16.7%)
Figurative	0 (0.0%)	1 (0.6%)	0 (0.0%)
Total	42	163	6

Table 1.3.2.1 A summary of the usage labels in additions to Grose's *Classical Dictionary*

Label	Working copy	(% of labels)	[% of new entries]	1788	(% of labels)	[% of new entries]	1796	(% of labels)	[% of new entries]
Cant	26	(61.9%)	[13.8%]	89	(54.6%)	[7.9%]	0	(0.0%)	[0.0%]
Jargon	10	(23.8%)	[5.3%]	32	(19.6%)	[2.9%]	4	(66.7%)	[3.9%]
Slang	1	(2.4%)	[0.5%]	10	(6.1%)	[0.9%]	0	(0.0%)	[0.0%]
Dialect	2	(4.8%)	[1.1%]	7	(4.3%)	[0.6%]	1	(16.7%)	[1.0%]
Other	3	(7.1%)	[1.6%]	25	(15.3%)	[2.2%]	1	(16.7%)	[1.0%]
Total	42		[22.3%]	163		[14.6%]	6		[5.8%]

Table 1.4 Lexicographic features in Grose's *Classical Dictionary*

Entries including	1785	1788	1796
Citations	448 (11.5%)	600 (12.0%)	611 (12.0%)
Authorities	29 (0.7%)	39 (0.8%)	50 (1.0%)
Etymologies	476 (12.2%)	660 (13.2%)	657 (12.9%)
Cross-references	155 (4.0%)	189 (3.8%)	191 (3.7%)
Total no. of entries	3,893	4,997	5,097

Table 1.4.1 Lexicographic features in additions to Grose's *Classical Dictionary*

Entries including	Working copy	1788	1796
Citations	38 (20.2%)	150 (13.4%)	8 (7.8%)
Authorities	5 (2.7%)	19 (1.7%)	1 (1.0%)
Etymologies	17 (9.0%)	167 (14.9%)	8 (7.8%)
Cross-references	1 (0.5%)	37 (3.3%)	2 (1.9%)
Total no. of entries	188	1,120	103

Table 1.5 Etymological categories in the first edition of Grose's *Classical Dictionary* (1785)

Type of etymology	Entries
Figurative, metonymic, or metaphorical	193 (39.8%)
Proper name	98 (20.2%)
Foreign source	59 (12.2%)
Sound symbolic	10 (2.1%)
Other	125 (25.8%)
Total	485[a]

[a] This is higher than the total shown in Table 1.4 because some entries contain more than one etymology.

Table 2.1 An outline of the subject matter of the *Lexicon Balatronicum* and Matsell's debt to it

Semantic area	*Lexicon Balatronicum*		Matsell's *Vocabulum* entries from the *Lexicon*		
	Total	New entries	Main list	Addenda	Total
Crime & dishonesty	749 (10.0%)	78 (13.8%)	340 (17.4%)	2 (5.3%)	342 (17.2%)
Emotion & temperament	610 (8.1%)	32 (5.6%)	163 (8.4%)	4 (10.5%)	167 (8.4%)
Body & health	590 (7.9%)	56 (9.9%)	182 (9.3%)	15 (39.5%)	197 (9.9%)
Food & drink	508 (6.8%)	26 (4.6%)	100 (5.1%)	0 (0.0%)	100 (5.0%)
Work	426 (5.7%)	25 (4.4%)	92 (4.7%)	1 (2.6%)	93 (4.7%)
Money	390 (5.2%)	33 (5.8%)	131 (6.7%)	2 (5.3%)	133 (6.7%)
Sex	351 (4.7%)	27 (4.8%)	43 (2.2%)	0 (0.0%)	43 (2.2%)
Pleasure & pastimes	315 (4.2%)	24 (4.2%)	52 (2.7%)	3 (7.9%)	55 (2.8%)
Domestic life	357 (4.8%)	28 (4.9%)	85 (4.4%)	0 (0.0%)	85 (4.3%)
War & violence	298 (4.0%)	15 (2.6%)	65 (3.3%)	9 (23.7%)	74 (3.7%)
Animals & nature	303 (4.0%)	29 (5.1%)	64 (3.3%)	0 (0.0%)	64 (3.2%)
Speech	304 (4.1%)	20 (3.5%)	54 (2.8%)	0 (0.0%)	54 (2.7%)
Law & order	332 (4.4%)	48 (8.5%)	121 (6.2%)	0 (0.0%)	121 (6.1%)
Clothes	278 (3.7%)	22 (3.9%)	85 (4.4%)	0 (0.0%)	85 (4.3%)
Fools & victims	227 (3.0%)	13 (2.3%)	37 (1.9%)	1 (2.6%)	38 (1.9%)
Looks	246 (3.3%)	10 (1.8%)	36 (1.8%)	0 (0.0%)	36 (1.8%)
People	250 (3.3%)	14 (2.5%)	63 (3.2%)	0 (0.0%)	63 (3.2%)
Artefacts	276 (3.7%)	31 (5.5%)	101 (5.2%)	0 (0.0%)	101 (5.1%)
Poverty	193 (2.6%)	10 (1.8%)	39 (2.0%)	0 (0.0%)	39 (2.0%)
Geography & travel	237 (3.2%)	23 (4.1%)	44 (2.2%)	0 (0.0%)	44 (2.2%)
Other	261 (3.5%)	3 (0.5%)	54 (2.8%)	1 (2.6%)	55 (2.8%)
Total	7,501	567	1,951	38	1,989

Table 2.2 The usage labels of the *Lexicon Balatronicum* and Matsell's selection from them

Label	*Lexicon Balatronicum*		Matsell		
	Total	New entries	Main list	Addenda	[% of label from the Total *Lexicon*[a]]
Cant	469 (59.1%)	13 (27.1%)	249	4	253 [53.9%]
Naval & nautical	61 (7.7%)	2 (4.2%)	5	0	5 [8.2%]
Military	13 (1.6%)	0 (0.0%)	1	0	1 [7.7%]
Other jargons	40 (5.0%)	2 (4.2%)	5	3	8 [20.0%]
Slang	22 (2.8%)	9 (18.8%)	12	8	20 [90.9%]

Table 2.2 (*Continued*)

Label	*Lexicon Balatronicum* Total		New entries		Matsell Main list	Addenda	Total *Lexicon*[a]	[% of label from the
Nursery & school	7	(0.9%)	0	(0.0%)	1	0	1	[14.3%]
University	35	(4.4%)	15	(31.3%)	5	0	5	[14.3%]
Irish	42	(5.3%)	2	(4.2%)	5	1	6	[14.3%]
Scots	8	(1.0%)	0	(0.0%)	4	0	4	[50.0%]
Welsh	2	(0.3%)	0	(0.0%)	1	0	1	[50.0%]
US	4	(0.5%)	0	(0.0%)	0	0	0	[0.0%]
Black	5	(0.6%)	0	(0.0%)	3	0	3	[60.0%]
Other dialects	14	(1.8%)	0	(0.0%)	0	0	0	[0.0%]
Colloquial	10	(1.3%)	1	(2.1%)	5	0	5	[50.0%]
Archaic & dated	15	(1.9%)	0	(0.0%)	8	0	8	[53.3%]
Derogatory	14	(1.8%)	1	(2.1%)	0	0	0	[0.0%]
Vulgar	2	(0.3%)	1	(2.1%)	0	0	0	[0.0%]
Jocular	19	(2.4%)	2	(4.2%)	1	0	1	[5.3%]
Euphemistic	9	(1.1%)	0	(0.0%)	3	0	3	[33.3%]
Figurative	3	(0.4%)	0	(0.0%)	1	0	1	[33.3%]
Total	794		48		309	16	325	[40.9%]

[a] Note that Matsell does not include any usage labels within entries. The percentage indicates the proportion of *Lexicon* entries with each label that he adopts.

Table 2.2.1 A summary of the usage labels of the *Lexicon Balatronicum* and Matsell's selection from them

Label	*Lexicon Balatronicum* Total	(% of labels)	[% of entries]	New entries	(% of labels)	[% of new entries]	Matsell Main list	Addenda	Total [% of *Lexicon*]
Cant	469	(59.1%)	[8.7%]	13	(27.1%)	[3.2%]	249	4	253 [53.9%]
Jargon	114	(14.4%)	[2.1%]	4	(8.3%)	[1.0%]	11	3	14 [12.3%]
Slang	64	(8.1%)	[1.2%]	24	(50.0%)	[5.8%]	18	8	26 [40.6%]
Dialect	75	(9.4%)	[1.4%]	2	(4.2%)	[0.5%]	13	1	14 [18.7%]
Other	72	(9.1%)	[1.3%]	5	(10.4%)	[1.2%]	18	0	18 [25.0%]
Total	794		[14.8%]	48		[11.7%]	309	16	325 [40.9%]

Table 2.3 Lexicographic features of the *Lexicon Balatronicum* and Matsell's debt to it

Entries including	*Lexicon Balatronicum*		Matsell		
	Total	New entries	Main list	Addenda	Total
Citations	737 (13.7%)	135 (32.8%)	201 (14.0%)	1 (0.5%)	202 (12.3%)
Authorities	55 (1.0%)	11 (2.7%)	1 (0.1%)	0 (0.0%)	1 (0.1%)
Etymologies	647 (12.0%)	2 (0.5%)	9 (0.6%)	0 (0.0%)	9 (0.5%)
Cross-references	197 (3.7%)	7 (1.7%)	3 (0.2%)	0 (0.0%)	3 (0.2%)
Total no. of entries	5,381	411	1,439	206	1,645

Table 2.4 Matsell's sources

Source	Main list	Addenda	Total
Lexicon Balatronicum (1811)	1,409 (61.4%)	32 (15.5%)	1,441 (57.7%)
The Vulgar Tongue (1857)	188 (8.2%)	0 (0.0%)	188 (7.5%)
Vaux's *Memoirs* (1819)	30 (1.3%)	0 (0.3%)	30 (1.2%)
Flash Dictionary (1821)	15 (0.7%)	0 (0.0%)	15 (0.6%)
Kent (1835) or *Sinks of London* (1848)	13 (0.6%)	6 (2.9%)	19 (0.8%)
Sources indistinguishable	61 (2.7%)	3 (1.5%)	64 (2.6%)
New entries	577 (25.2%)	165 (80.1%)	742 (29.7%)
Total	2,293	206	2,499

Table 2.4.1 An outline of the subject matter of the Matsell lists

Semantic area	Matsell			Asbury (1927)	Scorsese (2002)
	Main list	Addenda	Total		
Crime & dishonesty	618 (19.2%)	179 (22.4%)	797 (19.8%)	45 (13.2%)	13 (25.0%)
Emotion & temperament	264 (8.2%)	74 (9.3%)	338 (8.4%)	13 (3.8%)	3 (5.8%)
Body & health	231 (7.2%)	28 (3.5%)	259 (6.4%)	30 (8.8%)	2 (3.8%)
Food & drink	143 (4.4%)	22 (2.8%)	165 (4.1%)	18 (5.3%)	0 (0.0%)
Work	166 (5.2%)	47 (5.9%)	213 (5.3%)	20 (5.9%)	1 (1.9%)
Money	252 (7.8%)	71 (8.9%)	323 (8.0%)	39 (11.4%)	3 (5.8%)
Sex	64 (2.0%)	18 (2.3%)	82 (2.0%)	20 (5.9%)	4 (7.7%)
Pleasure & pastimes	98 (3.0%)	36 (4.5%)	134 (3.3%)	6 (1.8%)	2 (3.8%)
Domestic life	139 (4.3%)	31 (3.9%)	170 (4.2%)	17 (5.0%)	2 (3.8%)
War & violence	102 (3.2%)	25 (3.1%)	127 (3.2%)	11 (3.2%)	3 (5.8%)

Table 2.4.1 (*Continued*)

Semantic area	Matsell						Asbury (1927)		Scorsese (2002)	
	Main list		Addenda		Total					
Animals & nature	101	(3.1%)	22	(2.8%)	123	(3.1%)	4	(1.2%)	0	(0.0%)
Speech	81	(2.5%)	17	(2.1%)	98	(2.4%)	7	(2.1%)	1	(1.9%)
Law & order	207	(6.4%)	56	(7.0%)	263	(6.5%)	24	(7.0%)	3	(5.8%)
Clothes	155	(4.8%)	33	(4.1%)	188	(4.7%)	13	(3.8%)	2	(3.8%)
Fools & victims	55	(1.7%)	12	(1.5%)	67	(1.7%)	7	(2.1%)	1	(1.9%)
Looks	44	(1.4%)	5	(0.6%)	49	(1.2%)	4	(1.2%)	2	(3.8%)
People	90	(2.8%)	17	(2.1%)	107	(2.7%)	17	(5.0%)	5	(9.6%)
Artefacts	161	(5.0%)	35	(4.4%)	196	(4.9%)	17	(5.0%)	2	(3.8%)
Poverty	50	(1.6%)	5	(0.6%)	55	(1.4%)	5	(1.5%)	0	(0.0%)
Geography & travel	99	(3.1%)	32	(4.0%)	131	(3.3%)	16	(4.7%)	1	(1.9%)
Other	98	(3.0%)	33	(4.1%)	131	(3.3%)	8	(2.3%)	2	(3.8%)
Total	3,218		798		4,016		341		52	

Table 2.4.1.1 An outline of the subject matter of Matsell's new entries

Semantic area	Main list		Addenda		Total	
Crime & dishonesty	22	(7.4%)	25	(9.6%)	47	(8.4%)
Emotion & temperament	15	(5.0%)	9	(3.5%)	24	(4.3%)
Body & health	27	(9.0%)	11	(4.2%)	38	(6.8%)
Food & drink	2	(0.7%)	2	(0.8%)	4	(0.7%)
Work	6	(2.0%)	4	(1.5%)	10	(1.8%)
Money	16	(5.4%)	14	(5.4%)	30	(5.4%)
Sex	0	(0.0%)	0	(0.0%)	0	(0.0%)
Pleasure & pastimes	109	(36.5%)	85	(32.7%)	194	(34.7%)
Domestic life	0	(0.0%)	2	(0.8%)	2	(0.4%)
War & violence	67	(22.4%)	54	(20.8%)	121	(21.6%)
Animals & nature	0	(0.0%)	1	(0.4%)	1	(0.2%)
Speech	1	(0.3%)	3	(1.2%)	4	(0.7%)
Law & order	1	(0.3%)	2	(0.8%)	3	(0.5%)
Clothes	2	(0.7%)	3	(1.2%)	5	(0.9%)
Fools & victims	27	(9.0%)	27	(10.4%)	54	(9.7%)
Looks	2	(0.7%)	1	(0.4%)	3	(0.5%)
People	1	(0.3%)	5	(1.9%)	6	(1.1%)
Artefacts	0	(0.0%)	1	(0.4%)	1	(0.2%)
Poverty	1	(0.3%)	0	(0.0%)	1	(0.2%)
Geography & travel	0	(0.0%)	0	(0.0%)	0	(0.0%)
Other	0	(0.0%)	11	(4.2%)	11	(2.0%)
Total	299		260		559	

Table 2.4.2 Lexicographic features in the Matsell lists

Entries including	Matsell			Asbury (1927)	Scorsese (2002)
	Main list	Addenda	Total		
Citations	275 (12.0%)	5 (2.4%)	280 (11.2%)	9 (3.7%)	1 (2.5%)
Authorities	3 (0.1%)	0 (0.0%)	3 (0.1%)	0 (0.0%)	0 (0.0%)
Etymologies	17 (0.7%)	3 (1.5%)	20 (0.8%)	1 (0.4%)	0 (0.0%)
Cross-references	5 (0.2%)	4 (1.9%)	9 (0.4%)	0 (0.0%)	0 (0.0%)
Total no. of entries	2,293	206	2,499	245	40

Table 3.1 Potter's sources

Source	Entries (% of Potter's entries)
Grose's *Classical Dictionary* (1788)	222 (18.2%)
Parker's *Life's Painter* (1789)	47 (3.9%)
New Canting Dictionary (1725)	45 (3.7%)
Poulter's *Discoveries* (1753)	16 (1.3%)
Carew	4 (0.3%)
Sources indistinguishable	667 (54.7%)
New entries	218 (17.9%)
Total	1,219

Table 3.1.1 Kent's sources

Source	Entries (% of Kent's entries)
Flash Dictionary	1,011 (61.7%)
Egan's dictionary	180 (11.0%)
Life in London[a]	62 (3.8%)
Sources indistinguishable	33 (2.0%)
New entries	353 (21.5%)
Total	1,639

[a] Where Egan lists terms in his dictionary also found in a similar form in *Life in London*, I have assumed that the dictionary is Kent's source.

Table 3.1.2 Duncombe's sources

Source	Entries (% of Duncombe's entries)
Kent	393 (31.4%)
Carew (1812b)	163 (13.0%)
Sources indistinguishable	130 (10.4%)
New entries	565 (45.2%)
Total	1,251

Table 3.2 An outline of the subject matter of the Potter-group dictionaries

Semantic area	Potter	Andrewes	*Flash*	Kent	*Sinks*	Duncombe
Crime & dishonesty	297 (17.7%)	302 (18.2%)	292 (16.4%)	335 (14.8%)	341 (15.3%)	269 (15.2%)
Emotion & temperament	80 (4.8%)	79 (4.8%)	86 (4.8%)	157 (7.0%)	155 (7.0%)	113 (6.4%)
Body & health	105 (6.2%)	89 (5.4%)	105 (5.9%)	173 (7.7%)	172 (7.7%)	139 (7.7%)
Food & drink	115 (6.8%)	115 (6.9%)	121 (6.8%)	175 (7.8%)	173 (7.8%)	134 (7.9%)
Work	99 (5.9%)	103 (6.2%)	123 (6.9%)	153 (6.8%)	145 (6.5%)	99 (5.6%)
Money	137 (8.1%)	159 (9.6%)	174 (9.8%)	200 (8.9%)	195 (8.8%)	128 (7.2%)
Sex	79 (4.7%)	26 (1.6%)	26 (1.5%)	39 (1.7%)	36 (1.6%)	31 (1.8%)
Pleasure & pastimes	38 (2.3%)	42 (2.5%)	48 (2.7%)	69 (3.1%)	68 (3.1%)	41 (2.3%)
Domestic life	43 (2.6%)	54 (3.3%)	69 (3.9%)	79 (3.5%)	69 (3.1%)	66 (3.7%)
War & violence	49 (2.9%)	52 (3.1%)	61 (3.4%)	71 (3.1%)	66 (3.0%)	45 (2.5%)
Animals & nature	49 (2.9%)	57 (3.4%)	58 (3.3%)	65 (2.9%)	63 (2.8%)	38 (2.1%)
Speech	61 (3.6%)	48 (2.9%)	58 (3.3%)	58 (2.8%)	57 (2.6%)	51 (2.9%)
Law & order	120 (7.1%)	103 (6.2%)	108 (6.1%)	117 (5.2%)	117 (5.3%)	176 (9.9%)
Clothes	81 (4.8%)	78 (4.7%)	77 (4.3%)	118 (5.2%)	104 (4.7%)	53 (3.0%)
Fools & victims	38 (2.3%)	38 (2.3%)	31 (1.7%)	48 (2.1%)	49 (2.2%)	25 (1.4%)
Looks	15 (0.9%)	29 (1.8%)	26 (1.5%)	24 (1.1%)	30 (1.3%)	20 (1.1%)
People	54 (3.2%)	61 (3.9%)	65 (3.7%)	76 (3.4%)	69 (3.1%)	78 (4.4%)
Artefacts	97 (5.8%)	107 (6.5%)	108 (6.1%)	89 (3.9%)	97 (4.4%)	80 (4.5%)
Poverty	54 (3.2%)	35 (2.1%)	47 (2.6%)	71 (3.1%)	73 (3.3%)	56 (3.2%)
Geography & travel	50 (3.0%)	41 (2.5%)	59 (3.3%)	80 (3.5%)	76 (3.4%)	66 (3.7%)
Other	21 (1.2%)	37 (2.2%)	35 (2.0%)	59 (2.6%)	69 (3.1%)	61 (3.4%)
Total	1,682	1,655	1,777	2,256	2,224	1,769

Table 3.3 Lexicographic features in the Potter-group dictionaries

Entries including	Potter		Andrewes	*Flash*	Kent	*Sinks*	Duncombe
Citations	4	(0.3%)	4 (0.3%)	2 (0.2%)	13 (0.8%)	9 (0.6%)	38 (3.0%)
Authorities	0	(0.0%)	2 (0.2%)	0 (0.0%)	1 (0.1%)	0 (0.0%)	0 (0.0%)
Etymologies	1	(0.1%)	2 (0.2%)	2 (0.2%)	4 (0.2%)	3 (0.2%)	7 (0.6%)
Cross-references	32	(2.6%)	15 (1.3%)	11 (0.9%)	4 (0.2%)	4 (0.2%)	10 (0.8%)
Total no. of entries	1,219		1,163	1,210	1,639	1,629	1,251

Table 4.1 An outline of the subject matter of the Vaux lists

Semantic area	Vaux's *Memoirs*		Vaux entries not in Potter or the *Lexicon*		Fink's selection	
Crime & dishonesty	187	(37.6%)	140	(39.0%)	10	(15.9%)
Emotion & temperament	58	(11.6%)	38	(10.6%)	7	(11.1%)
Money	41	(8.2%)	26	(7.2%)	2	(3.2%)
Speech	32	(6.4%)	24	(6.7%)	2	(3.2%)
Law & order	28	(5.6%)	20	(5.6%)	4	(6.3%)
Geography & travel	19	(3.8%)	18	(5.0%)	4	(6.3%)
Clothes	17	(3.4%)	10	(2.8%)	4	(6.3%)
Pleasure & pastimes	15	(3.0%)	12	(3.3%)	4	(6.3%)
Artefacts	14	(2.8%)	11	(3.1%)	5	(7.9%)
Body & health	10	(2.0%)	8	(2.2%)	5	(7.9%)
Domestic life	10	(2.0%)	7	(1.9%)	2	(3.2%)
Fools & victims	10	(2.0%)	6	(1.7%)	2	(3.2%)
People	10	(2.0%)	6	(1.7%)	4	(6.3%)
Work	9	(1.8%)	6	(1.7%)	2	(3.2%)
Food & drink	8	(1.6%)	6	(1.7%)	5	(7.9%)
War & violence	7	(1.4%)	5	(1.4%)	0	(0.0%)
Poverty	4	(0.8%)	4	(1.1%)	0	(0.0%)
Sex	3	(0.6%)	1	(0.3%)	0	(0.0%)
Animals & nature	2	(0.4%)	2	(0.6%)	0	(0.0%)
Other	14	(2.8%)	9	(2.5%)	1	(1.6%)
Total	498		359		63	

Table 4.2 Vaux's usage labels

Label	Entries	[% of entries]
Cant	12 (60.0%)	[1.5%]
Flash	1 (5.0%)	[0.1%]
Low	1 (5.0%)	[0.1%]
Obsolete	6 (30.0%)	[0.8%]
Total	20	[2.5%]

Table 4.3 Lexicographic features in the Vaux lists

Entries including	Vaux's *Memoirs*	Vaux's entries not in Potter or the *Lexicon*	Fink's selection
Citations	127 (38.3%)	80 (34.5%)	16 (35.6%)
Etymologies	3 (0.9%)	3 (1.3%)	0 (0.0%)
Cross-references	108 (32.5%)	82 (35.3%)	0 (0.0%)
Total no. of entries	332	232	45

Table 5.1 An outline of the subject matter of Egan's lexicological footnotes and the two *Tom and Jerry* glossaries (1822, *c.*1823)

Semantic area	*Life in London* footnotes	1822 glossary	*c.* 1823 glossary
Food & drink	25 (14.5%)	39 (9.3%)	7 (6.3%)
Work	16 (9.3%)	36 (8.6%)	10 (9.0%)
Pleasure & pastimes	15 (8.7%)	20 (4.8%)	7 (6.3%)
Body & health	14 (8.1%)	26 (6.2%)	5 (4.5%)
Law & order	14 (8.1%)	10 (2.4%)	2 (1.8%)
Crime & dishonesty	13 (7.6%)	45 (10.8%)	10 (9.0%)
Money	13 (7.6%)	33 (7.9%)	12 (10.8%)
Emotion & temperament	11 (6.4%)	40 (9.6%)	14 (12.6%)
Poverty	9 (5.2%)	25 (6.0%)	4 (3.6%)
Geography & travel	8 (4.7%)	21 (5.0%)	8 (7.2%)
Domestic life	8 (4.7%)	19 (4.5%)	5 (4.5%)
Clothes	6 (3.5%)	19 (4.5%)	7 (6.3%)
Sex	6 (3.5%)	17 (4.1%)	1 (0.9%)
Fools & victims	4 (2.3%)	12 (2.9%)	2 (1.8%)
Artefacts	3 (1.7%)	13 (3.1%)	3 (2.7%)
War & violence	0 (0.0%)	13 (3.1%)	5 (4.5%)
People	0 (0.0%)	12 (2.9%)	5 (4.5%)
Other	7 (4.1%)	18 (4.3%)	4 (3.6%)
Total	172	418	111

Table 5.2 Egan's sources

Source	Entries (% of Egan's entries)
Lexicon Balatronicum (1811)	4,972 (87.0%)
Vaux's *Memoirs* (1819)	386 (6.8%)
Life of David Haggart (1821)	46 (0.8%)
Flash Dictionary (1821)	35 (0.6%)
Burrowes's (1821)	22 (0.4%)
Sources indistinguishable	42 (0.7%)
New entries	211 (3.7%)
Total	5,714

Table 5.2.1 An outline of the subject matter of Egan's dictionary

Semantic area	Egan	New entries
Crime & dishonesty	921 (11.6%)	18 (6.6%)
Emotion & temperament	714 (9.0%)	18 (6.6%)
Body & health	576 (7.2%)	17 (6.3%)
Food & drink	522 (6.6%)	35 (12.9%)
Work	437 (5.5%)	8 (2.9%)
Money	446 (5.6%)	14 (5.1%)
Sex	346 (4.3%)	6 (2.2%)
Pleasure & pastimes	378 (4.8%)	33 (12.1%)
Domestic life	370 (4.6%)	20 (7.4%)
War & violence	314 (3.9%)	23 (8.5%)
Animals & nature	311 (3.9%)	5 (1.8%)
Speech	315 (4.0%)	6 (2.2%)
Law & order	356 (4.5%)	6 (2.2%)
Clothes	308 (3.9%)	8 (2.9%)
Fools & victims	228 (2.9%)	9 (3.3%)
Looks	238 (3.0%)	3 (1.1%)
People	249 (3.1%)	4 (1.5%)
Artefacts	291 (3.7%)	4 (1.5%)
Poverty	229 (2.9%)	14 (5.1%)
Geography & travel	256 (3.2%)	9 (3.3%)
Other	152 (1.9%)	12 (4.4%)
Total	7,957	272

Table 5.2.2 The usage labels of Egan's list

Label	Total	New entries
Cant	643 (58.3%)	56 (37.6%)
Naval & nautical	93 (8.4%)	25 (16.8%)
Military	9 (0.8%)	0 (0.0%)
Other jargons	55 (5.0%)	13 (8.7%)
Slang	35 (3.2%)	9 (6.0%)
Nursery & school	5 (0.5%)	0 (0.0%)
University	79 (7.2%)	41 (27.5%)
Irish	39 (3.5%)	3 (2.0%)
Scots	28 (2.5%)	0 (0.0%)
Welsh	2 (0.2%)	0 (0.0%)
US	4 (0.4%)	0 (0.0%)
Black	5 (0.5%)	0 (0.0%)
Other dialects	18 (1.6%)	0 (0.0%)
Colloquial	10 (0.9%)	0 (0.0%)
Archaic & dated	36 (3.3%)	0 (0.0%)
Derogatory	11 (1.0%)	0 (0.0%)
Vulgar	0 (0.0%)	0 (0.0%)
Jocular	19 (1.7%)	1 (0.7%)
Euphemistic	8 (0.7%)	0 (0.0%)
Figurative	3 (0.3%)	1 (0.7%)
Total	1,102	149

Table 5.2.2.1 A summary of the usage labels of Egan's list

Label	Entries	(% of labels)	% of all entries	New entries	(% of labels)	% of all new entries
Cant	643	(58.3%)	11.3%	56	(37.6%)	26.5%
Jargon	157	(14.2%)	2.7%	38	(25.5%)	18.0%
Slang	119	(10.8%)	2.1%	50	(33.6%)	23.7%
Dialect	96	(8.7%)	1.7%	3	(2.0%)	1.4%
Other	87	(7.9%)	1.5%	2	(1.3%)	0.9%
Total	1,102		19.3%	149		70.6%

Table 5.2.3 Lexicographic features in Egan's list

Entries that include	Total	New entries
Citations	903 (15.8%)	33 (15.6%)
Authorities	99 (1.7%)	15 (7.1%)
Etymologies	608 (10.6%)	7 (3.3%)
Cross-references	197 (3.4%)	2 (0.9%)
Total no. of entries	5,714	211

Table 6.1 Bee's sources

Source	Main list (% of main list)	Addenda (% of addenda)
Lexicon Balatronicum	484 (21.6%)	21 (14.5%)
Egan[a]	48 (2.1%)	4 (2.8%)
Vaux	11 (0.5%)	0 (0.0%)
Egan or Vaux	50 (2.2%)	3 (2.1%)
Perry	29 (1.3%)	1 (0.7%)
Potter	26 (1.2%)	0 (0.0%)
Sources indistinguishable	284 (12.7%)	21 (14.5%)
New entries[b]	1,305 (58.3%)	95 (65.5%)
Total	2,237	145

[a] Since Bee insists that he did not use (and could not have used) Egan's dictionary, and since none of the entries is identical, it might be more accurate to attribute all the Egan/Vaux terms to Vaux and to consider the overlap with Egan's dictionary mere coincidental co-recording of contemporary terms.

[b] Forty-six of these new entries were listed in B. E.'s *New Dictionary of the Terms Ancient and Modern of the Canting Crew* (*c.*1698) and not in the *Lexicon Balatronicum*. They are largely hunting terms, which Bee is more likely to have gathered from a modern specialist work or from his own extensive knowledge than from B. E., especially since the definitions are dissimilar.

Table 6.2 An outline of the subject matter of Bee's word-lists and of his debt to the *Lexicon*

Semantic area	Main listing	Addenda	Total	Entries from the *Lexicon* [% of field adopted[a]]	
Crime & dishonesty	286 (9.1%)	5 (2.5%)	291 (8.7%)	66 (8.7%)	[8.8%]
Emotion & temperament	238 (7.6%)	14 (7.0%)	252 (7.5%)	74 (9.8%)	[12.1%]
Body & health	135 (4.3%)	11 (5.5%)	146 (4.4%)	46 (6.1%)	[7.8%]
Food & drink	214 (6.8%)	14 (7.0%)	228 (6.8%)	117 (15.5%)	[23.0%]
Work	159 (5.1%)	12 (6.0%)	171 (5.1%)	36 (4.8%)	[8.5%]
Money	142 (4.5%)	14 (7.0%)	156 (4.7%)	36 (4.8%)	[9.2%]
Sex	84 (2.7%)	7 (3.5%)	91 (2.7%)	30 (4.0%)	[8.5%]
Pleasure & pastimes	404 (12.9%)	29 (14.6%)	433 (13.0%)	45 (5.9%)	[14.3%]

Table 6.2 (*Continued*)

Semantic area	Main listing		Addenda		Total		Entries from the *Lexicon* [% of field adopted[a]]		
Domestic life	107	(3.4%)	9	(4.5%)	116	(3.5%)	32	(4.2%)	[9.0%]
War & violence	147	(4.7%)	17	(8.5%)	164	(4.9%)	24	(3.2%)	[8.1%]
Animals & nature	224	(7.1%)	10	(5.0%)	234	(7.0%)	23	(3.0%)	[7.6%]
Speech	129	(4.1%)	7	(3.5%)	136	(4.1%)	33	(4.4%)	[10.9%]
Law & order	123	(3.9%)	6	(3.0%)	129	(3.9%)	16	(2.1%)	[4.8%]
Clothes	86	(2.7%)	6	(3.0%)	92	(2.8%)	27	(3.6%)	[9.7%]
Fools & victims	63	(2.0%)	3	(1.5%)	66	(2.0%)	15	(2.0%)	[6.6%]
Looks	59	(1.9%)	3	(1.5%)	62	(1.9%)	18	(2.4%)	[7.3%]
People	148	(4.7%)	6	(3.0%)	154	(4.6%)	31	(4.1%)	[12.4%]
Artefacts	104	(3.3%)	7	(3.5%)	111	(3.3%)	16	(2.1%)	[5.8%]
Poverty	78	(2.5%)	2	(1.0%)	80	(2.4%)	25	(3.3%)	[13.0%]
Geography & travel	117	(3.7%)	9	(4.5%)	126	(3.8%)	24	(3.2%)	[10.1%]
Other	94	(3.0%)	8	(4.0%)	102	(3.1%)	23	(3.0%)	[8.8%]
Total	3,141		199		3,340		757		[10.1%]

[a] See Table 2.1.

Table 6.3 Lexicographic features in Bee's dictionary

Entries including	Bee
Citations	560 (23.5%)
Authorities	125 (5.2%)
Etymologies	379 (15.9%)
Cross-references	209 (8.8%)
Total no. of entries	2,382

Table 7.1 An outline of the subject matter of Parker's word-list

Semantic area	1789 editions	1800 edition
Crime & dishonesty	33 (16.9%)	34 (23.0%)
Money	31 (15.9%)	18 (12.2%)
Body & health	25 (12.8%)	13 (8.8%)
Clothes	20 (10.3%)	9 (6.1%)
Law & order	13 (6.7%)	13 (8.8%)
Food & drink	10 (5.1%)	8 (5.4%)
Domestic life	8 (4.1%)	8 (5.4%)
Work	8 (4.1%)	8 (5.4%)
Artefacts	7 (3.6%)	3 (2.0%)

Table 7.1 (*Continued*)

Semantic area	1789 editions		1800 edition	
Speech	7	(3.6%)	7	(4.7%)
Emotion & temperament	6	(3.1%)	7	(4.7%)
People	6	(3.1%)	5	(3.4%)
Animals & nature	4	(2.1%)	1	(0.7%)
Geography & travel	4	(2.1%)	4	(2.7%)
Pleasure & pastimes	3	(1.5%)	4	(2.7%)
Looks	2	(1.0%)	0	(0.0%)
Sex	2	(1.0%)	2	(1.4%)
War & violence	2	(1.0%)	0	(0.0%)
Fools & victims	1	(0.5%)	1	(0.7%)
Poverty	1	(0.5%)	1	(0.7%)
Other	2	(1.0%)	2	(1.4%)
Total	195		148	

Table 7.2 An outline of the subject matter of T. B.'s glossary

Semantic area	Entries
Crime & dishonesty	24 (25.0%)
Law & order	15 (15.6%)
Money	14 (14.6%)
Poverty	11 (11.5%)
Emotion & temperament	8 (8.3%)
Other	24 (25.0%)
Total	96

Table 7.3 An outline of the subject matter of the 'Diary' glossary

Semantic area	Entries
Crime & dishonesty	6 (24.0%)
Food & drink	5 (20.0%)
Law & order	4 (16.0%)
Work	2 (8.0%)
Clothes	2 (8.0%)
Other	6 (24.0%)
Total	25

Table 7.4 An outline of the subject
matter of English's glossary

Semantic area	Entries
Work	12 (24.5%)
Clothes	7 (14.3%)
Poverty	6 (12.2%)
Body & health	4 (8.2%)
Sex	4 (8.2%)
Animals	3 (6.1%)
Looks	3 (6.1%)
Law & order	3 (6.1%)
Shopping	3 (6.1%)
Food & drink	2 (4.1%)
Money	1 (2.0%)
Geography & travel	1 (2.0%)
Total	49

Table 7.5 An outline of the subject
matter of the notebook glossary

Semantic area	Entries
Crime & dishonesty	34 (30.4%)
Law & order	11 (9.8%)
Clothes	9 (8.0%)
Money	8 (7.1%)
Artefacts	8 (7.1%)
Work	7 (6.3%)
Geography & travel	6 (5.4%)
Body & health	6 (5.4%)
War & violence	6 (5.4%)
Pleasure & pastimes	4 (3.6%)
Animals & nature	4 (3.6%)
Other	9 (8.0%)
Total	112

Table 7.6 An outline of the subject
matter of Perry's glossary

Semantic area	Entries
Crime & dishonesty	43 (30.1%)
Emotion & temperament	23 (16.1%)
Speech	10 (7.0%)

Table 7.6 (*Continued*)

Semantic area	Entries
Geography & travel	10 (7.0%)
Sex	9 (6.3%)
Body & health	9 (6.3%)
Law & order	6 (4.2%)
War & violence	4 (2.8%)
Fools & victims	4 (2.8%)
Other	25 (17.5%)
Total	143

Table 7.7 An outline of the subject matter of Reynolds's *Fancy* glossary

Semantic area	Entries
War & violence	11 (19.6%)
Food & drink	10 (17.9%)
Pleasure & pastimes	10 (17.9%)
Body & health	5 (8.9%)
Money	4 (7.1%)
Clothes	3 (5.4%)
Animals & nature	2 (3.6%)
Other	11 (19.6%)
Total	56

Table 7.8 An outline of the subject matter of Haggart's glossary

Semantic area	Entries
Money	28 (16.8%)
Clothes	23 (13.8%)
Crime & dishonesty	16 (9.6%)
Law & order	14 (8.4%)
Artefacts	12 (7.2%)
Work	10 (6.0%)
Animals & nature	9 (5.4%)
Speech	7 (4.2%)
Food & drink	7 (4.2%)
Pleasure & pastimes	6 (3.6%)
Emotion & temperament	6 (3.6%)
War & violence	5 (3.0%)
Other	24 (14.4%)
Total	167

Table 7.9 An outline of the subject
matter of Burrowes's glossary

Semantic area	Entries
Body & health	30 (14.1%)
Crime & dishonesty	26 (12.2%)
Emotion & temperament	25 (11.7%)
Money	23 (10.8%)
Artefacts	14 (6.6%)
Food & drink	13 (6.1%)
Pleasure & pastimes	11 (5.2%)
Work	10 (4.7%)
Geography & travel	10 (4.7%)
Domestic life	8 (3.8%)
Clothes	7 (3.3%)
Animals & nature	7 (3.3%)
Speech	6 (2.8%)
People	5 (2.3%)
Law & order	5 (2.3%)
Other	13 (6.1%)
Total	213

Table 7.10 An outline of the subject
matter of the *Vulgarities of Speech* cant list

Semantic area	Entries
Emotion & temperament	91 (22.2%)
Crime & dishonesty	47 (11.5%)
Speech	24 (5.9%)
Body & health	21 (5.1%)
Fools & victims	20 (4.9%)
Poverty	18 (4.4%)
Money	18 (4.4%)
Domestic life	17 (4.2%)
War & violence	15 (3.7%)
Animals & nature	15 (3.7%)
Food & drink	15 (3.7%)
Pleasure & pastimes	14 (3.4%)
Clothes	13 (3.2%)
Geography & travel	10 (2.4%)
Other	71 (17.4%)
Total	409

Table 7.11 An outline of the subject matter of the Brandon lists

Semantic area	Brandon	Ducange (1857b)	Archbold from Brandon	New entries	Total
Crime & dishonesty	88 (24.6%)	87 (24.5%)	60 (30.0%)	28 (41.2%)	88 (32.7%)
Money	68 (19.0%)	68 (19.2%)	32 (16.0%)	13 (19.1%)	45 (16.8%)
Clothes	48 (13.4%)	48 (13.5%)	26 (13.0%)	4 (5.9%)	30 (11.2%)
Artefacts	24 (6.7%)	24 (6.8%)	12 (6.0%)	4 (5.9%)	16 (6.0%)
Food & drink	15 (4.2%)	15 (4.2%)	8 (4.0%)	2 (2.9%)	10 (3.7%)
Domestic life	14 (3.9%)	14 (3.9%)	5 (2.5%)	2 (2.9%)	7 (2.6%)
Emotion & temperament	13 (3.6%)	13 (3.7%)	7 (3.5%)	3 (4.4%)	10 (3.7%)
People	13 (3.6%)	13 (3.7%)	6 (3.0%)	1 (1.5%)	7 (2.6%)
Work	13 (3.6%)	13 (3.7%)	8 (4.0%)	6 (8.8%)	14 (5.2%)
Poverty	12 (3.4%)	12 (3.4%)	4 (2.0%)	0 (0.0%)	4 (1.5%)
Geography & travel	9 (2.5%)	9 (2.5%)	8 (4.0%)	2 (2.9%)	10 (3.7%)
Pleasure & pastimes	8 (2.2%)	8 (2.3%)	3 (1.5%)	0 (0.0%)	3 (1.1%)
Body & health	7 (2.0%)	7 (2.0%)	3 (1.5%)	1 (1.5%)	4 (1.5%)
Law & order	7 (2.0%)	7 (2.0%)	7 (3.5%)	0 (0.0%)	7 (2.6%)
Speech	7 (2.0%)	6 (1.7%)	5 (2.5%)	0 (0.0%)	5 (1.9%)
Animals & nature	6 (1.7%)	6 (1.7%)	5 (2.5%)	0 (0.0%)	5 (1.9%)
Other	5 (1.4%)	5 (1.4%)	1 (0.5%)	2 (2.9%)	3 (1.1%)
Total	357	355	200	68	268

Table 7.11.1 Usage labels in Brandon's list, and Archbold's use of them

Label	Brandon	(% of labels)	[% of entries]	Archbold's selection	(% of labels)	[% of Archbold's entries from Brandon]
* (Scottish)	16	(66.7%)	[6.2%]	3	(18.8%)	[2.0%]
† (Gypsy)	4	(16.7%)	[1.6%]	0	(0.0%)	[0.0%]
‡ (Calmet's Buildings)	2	(8.3%)	[0.8%]	0	(0.0%)	[0.0%]
Dialect	2	(8.3%)	[0.8%]	0	(0.0%)	[0.0%]
Total	24		[9.3%]	3	(12.5%)	[2.0%]

Table 7.12 An outline of the subject
matter of Mayhew's glossaries

Semantic area	Entries
Money	22 (44.9%)
Crime & dishonesty	9 (18.4%)
Emotion & temperament	6 (12.2%)
Food & drink	4 (8.2%)
Work	2 (4.1%)
Other	6 (12.2%)
Total	49

Table 7.13 An outline of the subject
matter of the *Yokel's Preceptor* glossary

Semantic area	Entries
Money	18 (22.8%)
Crime & dishonesty	15 (19.0%)
Emotion & temperament	7 (8.9%)
Body & health	6 (7.6%)
Sex	5 (6.3%)
Geography & travel	5 (6.3%)
People	3 (3.8%)
Domestic life	3 (3.8%)
Artefacts	3 (3.8%)
Speech	2 (2.5%)
Food & drink	2 (2.5%)
Other	10 (12.7%)
Total	79

Table 7.14 An outline of the subject matter of the *Vulgar Tongue* lists

Semantic area	1857a	1857 total[a]	1859
Crime & dishonesty	94 (15.1%)	181 (18.5%)	193 (19.3%)
Money	75 (12.0%)	143 (14.6%)	133 (13.3%)
Food & drink	67 (10.8%)	82 (8.4%)	84 (8.4%)
Work	43 (6.9%)	56 (5.7%)	56 (5.6%)
Emotion & temperament	39 (6.3%)	52 (5.3%)	57 (5.7%)
Clothes	37 (5.9%)	85 (8.7%)	76 (7.6%)
Body & health	35 (5.6%)	42 (4.3%)	42 (4.2%)
Geography & travel	30 (4.8%)	39 (4.0%)	40 (4.0%)
Domestic life	24 (3.9%)	38 (3.9%)	36 (3.6%)
Law & order	21 (3.4%)	28 (2.9%)	29 (2.9%)

Table 7.14 (*Continued*)

Semantic area	1857a		1857 total[a]		1859	
People	21	(3.4%)	34	(3.5%)	35	(3.5%)
Pleasure & pastimes	21	(3.4%)	29	(3.0%)	31	(3.1%)
Artefacts	20	(3.2%)	44	(4.5%)	49	(4.9%)
War & violence	17	(2.7%)	17	(1.7%)	18	(1.8%)
Poverty	15	(2.4%)	27	(2.8%)	30	(3.0%)
Animals & nature	12	(1.9%)	18	(1.8%)	20	(2.0%)
Speech	12	(1.9%)	18	(1.8%)	22	(2.2%)
Fools & victims	8	(1.3%)	8	(0.8%)	10	(1.0%)
Looks	7	(1.1%)	7	(0.7%)	7	(0.7%)
Other	25	(4.0%)	30	(3.1%)	33	(3.3%)
Total	623		978		1,001	

[a] For details of the second *Vulgar Tongue* list see Table 7.11.

Table 7.14.1 Usage labels in the first word-list in the *Vulgar Tongue* (1857)

Label	Entries (% of labels)	[% of entries]
Thieves	220 (47.3%)	[45.7%]
General	208 (44.7%)	[43.2%]
Low life	16 (3.4%)	[3.3%]
Pugilists	9 (1.9%)	[1.9%]
Gamblers/turf	4 (0.9%)	[0.8%]
Sailors	3 (0.6%)	[0.6%]
Politics	2 (0.4%)	[0.4%]
Shopkeepers	1 (0.2%)	[0.2%]
Beggars	1 (0.2%)	[0.2%]
Commercial travellers	1 (0.2%)	[0.2%]
Total	465	[96.7%]

Table 7.14.1.1 A summary of the usage labels in the *Vulgar Tongue* lists (1857)

Label	First list entries	[% of all entries]	Second list entries	[% of all entries]	Total entries	[% of all entries]
Cant	221 (47.5%)	[45.9%]	2 (8.3%)	[0.8%]	223 (45.6%)	[30.2%]
Jargon	7 (1.5%)	[1.5%]	0 (0.0%)	[0.0%]	7 (1.4%)	[0.9%]
Slang	221 (47.5%)	[45.9%]	0 (0.0%)	[0.0%]	221 (45.2%)	[30.0%]
Dialect	16 (3.4%)	[3.3%]	22 (91.7%)	[8.6%]	38 (7.8%)	[5.1%]
Other	0 (0.0%)	[0.0%]	0 (0.0%)	[0.0%]	0 (0.0%)	[0.0%]
Total	465	[96.7%]	24	[9.3%]	489	[66.3%]
Total entries	481		257		738	

Table 7.14.2 A comparison between the grammatical make-up and labelling of the first word-list of the *Vulgar Tongue* (1857)[a]

Grammatical make-up	Entries	Grammatical labels	[% of category labelled]
Nouns and noun phrases	319 (66.3%)	293 (74.2%)	[91.8%]
Verbs and verb phrases	81 (16.8%)	61 (15.4%)	[75.3%]
Past participles	9 (1.9%)	9 (2.3%)	[100.0%]
Present participles	6 (1.2%)	5 (1.3%)	[83.3%]
Adjectives and adjectival phrases	23 (4.8%)	19 (4.8%)	[82.6%]
Adverbs and adverbial phrases	6 (1.2%)	3 (0.8%)	[50.0%]
Prepositional phrases, clauses, and sentences	36 (7.5%)	4 (1.0%)	[11.1%]
Interjections	1 (0.2%)	1 (0.3%)	[100.0%]
Total	481	395	[82.1%]

[a] Where the headword itself is not defined, but is followed by a phrase that is, I have categorized the entry according to the definition. I have made ad hoc judgements about what the grammatical label refers to where the definition and headword do not match.

Table 8.1 An outline of the subject matter of Tuft's list

Semantic area	Entries
Crime & dishonesty	15 (15.5%)
Artefacts	13 (13.4%)
Clothes	12 (12.4%)
Animals & nature	11 (11.3%)
Law & order	8 (8.2%)
Emotion & temperament	8 (8.2%)
Domestic life	7 (7.2%)
People	6 (6.2%)
Money	5 (5.2%)
War & violence	3 (3.1%)
Body & health	3 (3.1%)
Other	6 (6.2%)
Total	97

Table 8.2 An outline of the subject matter
of the 'Flash Language' list

Semantic area	Entries
Crime & dishonesty	72 (23.3%)
Money	28 (9.1%)
Emotion & temperament	26 (8.4%)
Work	23 (7.4%)
Domestic life	17 (5.5%)
Clothes	17 (5.5%)
Artefacts	17 (5.5%)
Speech	14 (4.5%)
People	14 (4.5%)
Body & health	13 (4.2%)
Animals & nature	13 (4.2%)
Law & order	12 (3.9%)
Food & drink	11 (3.6%)
Other	32 (10.4%)
Total	309

Table 8.3 An outline of the subject
matter of Judson's list

Semantic area	Entries
Crime & dishonesty	38 (23.5%)
Money	15 (9.3%)
Food & drink	12 (7.4%)
Emotion & temperament	11 (6.8%)
Domestic life	10 (6.2%)
Artefacts	10 (6.2%)
People	9 (5.6%)
Pleasure & pastimes	8 (4.9%)
Geography & travel	8 (4.9%)
Body & health	7 (4.3%)
Speech	6 (3.7%)
Law & order	6 (3.7%)
Other	22 (13.6%)
Total	162

Table 9.1 An outline of the subject matter of the *Gradus* lists

Semantic area	1803	1824 Total	New entries
Education	78 (31.1%)	154 (35.6%)	76 (42.5%)
Rank	31 (12.4%)	61 (14.1%)	31 (17.3%)
Emotion & temperament	19 (7.6%)	21 (4.9%)	2 (1.1%)
Food & drink	14 (5.6%)	23 (5.3%)	9 (5.0%)
Rules & penalties	13 (5.2%)	23 (5.3%)	10 (5.6%)
Speech	13 (5.2%)	15 (3.5%)	2 (1.1%)
Body & health	9 (3.6%)	12 (2.8%)	1 (0.6%)
Pleasure & pastimes	8 (3.2%)	12 (2.8%)	4 (2.2%)
Colleges	7 (2.8%)	10 (2.3%)	3 (1.7%)
Money	7 (2.8%)	11 (2.5%)	4 (2.2%)
Poverty	7 (2.8%)	7 (1.6%)	0 (0.0%)
Religion	7 (2.8%)	9 (2.1%)	2 (1.1%)
Work	7 (2.8%)	17 (3.9%)	10 (5.6%)
Geography & travel	6 (2.4%)	10 (2.3%)	4 (2.2%)
Clothes	5 (2.0%)	9 (2.1%)	4 (2.2%)
Sex	4 (1.6%)	4 (0.9%)	0 (0.0%)
Success	4 (1.6%)	9 (2.1%)	5 (2.8%)
Time	3 (1.2%)	8 (1.9%)	5 (2.8%)
Failure	2 (0.8%)	9 (2.1%)	7 (3.9%)
Other	7 (2.8%)	8 (1.9%)	0 (0.0%)
Total	251	432	179

Table 9.1.1 The usage labels of the *Gradus*

Label	1803	1824
Academic	1 (25.0%)	1 (20.0%)
Obsolete	2 (50.0%)	3 (60.0%)
Old	1 (25.0%)	1 (20.0%)
Total	4	5

Table 9.1.2 Lexicographic features of the *Gradus*

Feature	1803	1824 Total	New entries
Citations	253	310	37
Entries containing citations	151 (96.2%)	138 (53.7%)	22 (22.0%)
Authorities	243	296	35

Table 9.1.2 (*Continued*)

Feature	1803	1824 Total	New entries
Entries containing authorities	106 (67.5%)	126 (49.0%)	19 (19.0%)
Etymologies	37	54	11
Entries containing etymologies	30 (19.1%)	43 (16.7%)	10 (10.0%)
Dates	48	76	11
Entries containing dates	37 (23.6%)	45 (17.5%)	8 (8.0%)
Footnotes	29	80	25
Entries containing footnotes	22 (14.0%)	44 (17.1%)	7 (7.0%)
Entries including anecdotal or encyclopaedic information	53 (33.8%)	67 (26.1%)	13 (13.0%)
Entries including synonyms or other related terms	41 (26.1%)	59 (23.0%)	11 (11.0%)
Entries including proverbs	1 (0.6%)	1 (0.4%)	0 (0.0%)
Entries including cross-references	28 (17.8%)	55 (21.4%)	24 (24.0%)
Entries including Latin	62 (39.5%)	102 (39.7%)	35 (35.0%)
Entries including Greek	12 (7.6%)	20 (7.8%)	6 (6.0%)
Total entries	157	257	100

Table 9.2 An outline of the subject matter of Bristed's list

Semantic area	Entries
Education	18 (33.3%)
Emotion & temperament	8 (14.8%)
Rank	4 (7.4%)
Pleasure & pastimes	4 (7.4%)
Failure	3 (5.6%)
Speech	3 (5.6%)
Success	3 (5.6%)
Degree[a]	2 (3.7%)
Food	2 (3.7%)
Rules & regulations	2 (3.7%)
Work	2 (3.7%)
Other	3 (5.6%)
Total	54

[a] These are intensifiers, not terms referring to specific qualifications.

Bibliography

AINSWORTH, W. HARRISON, *Rookwood: A Romance in Three Volumes* (London: Richard Bentley, 1834)

ALSTON, R. C., *A Bibliography of the English Language from the Invention of Printing to the Year 1800. A Corrected Reprint of Volumes I–X.* (Ilkley: Janus Press, 1974)

American National Biography, ed. John C. Garraty and Mark C. Carnes (Oxford/New York: Oxford University Press, 1999)

ANDREWES, GEORGE, *The Stranger's Guide or Frauds of London Detected* (London/Glasgow: J. Bailey/Messrs. Lumsden, 1808)

——*Dictionary of the Slang and Cant Languages Ancient and Modern* (London: G. Smeeton, 1809)

ANGLICUS *see* Ducange Anglicus

ARCHBOLD, JOHN FREDERICK, *Archbold's Snowden's Magistrates Assistant, and Police Officers and Constables Guide*, 3rd edn. (London: Shaw and Sons, 1857)

——*Archbold's Snowden's Magistrates Assistant, and Police Officers and Constables Guide*, 3rd edn. (London: Shaw and Sons, 1859)

ASBURY, HERBERT, *The Gangs of New York. An Informal History of the Underworld* (1927) (New York: Garden City Publishing, 1928)

Australian Dictionary of Biography, ed. A. G. L. Shaw and C. M. H. Clark (London and New York: Cambridge University Press/Melbourne: Melbourne University Press, 1967)

AWDELAY, JOHN, *The Fraternitie of Vacabondes* (1561) (London: I. Awdeley, 1575)

B., T., *The Pettyfogger Dramatized; in Two Acts* (London: the Author, 1797)

BADCOCK, JOHN, *Letters from London. Observations of a Russian during a Residence in England of Ten Months* (London: no publisher's details, 1816)

——*Fancy-ana, or, A History of Pugilism* (London: W. Lewis for J. Walker, 1825)

——*A Living Picture of London* (London: W. Clarke, 1828)

see also John Bee

BAER, MARC, *Theatre and Disorder in Late Georgian England* (Oxford: Clarendon Press, 1992)

BAGG, LYMAN HOTCHKISS, *Four Years at Yale* (New Haven, CT: Charles C. Chatfield, 1871)

BAILEY, NATHAN, *Dictionarium Britannicum* (London: T. Cox, 1730)

Bang-up Dictionary, or, The Lounger and Sportsman's Vade Mecum (London: M. Jones, 1812)

BARRÈRE, ALBERT MARIE VICTOR, *Argot and Slang; a new French and English Dictionary of the Cant Words, Quaint Expressions, Slang Terms and Flash Phrases . . .* (London: The Ballantyne Press, 1889)

——and CHARLES G. LELAND, *A Dictionary of Slang, Jargon, and Cant* (Edinburgh: The Ballantyne Press, 1889/90)

BARTLETT, JOHN RUSSELL, *Dictionary of Americanisms. A Glossary of Words and Phrases Usually Regarded as Peculiar to the United States* (1848), 3rd edn. (London: John Camden Hotten, 1860)

BEATTIE, J. M., *Crime and the Courts in England 1660–1800* (Princeton, NJ: Princeton University Press, 1986)

BEE, JOHN, *Slang. A Dictionary of the Turf, the Ring, the Chase, the Pit, of Bon Ton, and the Varieties of Life* (London: T. Hughes, 1823)

——*Sportsman's Slang; A New Dictionary of Terms used in the Affairs of the Turf, the Ring, the Chase, and the Cock-pit; with those of Bon Ton, and the Varieties of Life* (London: For the Author, 1825)

see also John Badcock

BLAKE, N. F., *Non-standard Language in English Literature* (London: Andre Deutsch, 1981)

BORROW, GEORGE, *Lavengro; The Scholar—The Gypsy—The Priest* (London: John Murray, 1851)

BRACE OF CANTABS *see Gradus ad Cantabrigiam*

BRISTED, CHARLES ASTOR, *Five Years in an English University* (New York: G. P. Putnam, 1852)

BROCKETT, JOHN TROTTER, *A Glossary of North Country Words, in Use* (Newcastle upon Tyne: E. Charnley, 1825)

BUNTLINE *see* Judson

BURKE, WILLIAM JEREMIAH, *The Literature of Slang* (New York: New York Public Library, 1939)

BURNS, ROBERT, *The Poems and Songs of Robert Burns*, ed. James Kinsley (Oxford: Clarendon Press, 1968)

BURROWES, J., *Life in St. George's Fields or, The Rambles and Adventures of Disconsolate William, Esq. (From St. James's,) and his accomplished Surrey Friend, Flash Dick* (London: J. Smith, 1821)

[CAREW, BAMPFYLDE-MOORE], *The Life and Adventures of Bampfylde-Moore Carew* (London: J. Buckland, C. Bathurst, and T. Davies, 1793)

——*The Surprising Adventures of Bampfylde Moore Carew* (Tiverton: W. Salter, 1812)

CAULFIELD, JAMES, *Blackguardiana* (London: John Shepherd, 1795)

COCKBURN, J. S. (ed.), *Crime in England 1550–1800* (Princeton, NJ: Princeton University Press, 1977)

COLBY, J. M. and A. W. PURDUE, *The Civilisation of the Crowd. Popular Culture in England 1750–1900* (1984) (Stroud: Sutton, 1999)

COLEMAN, JULIE, *A History of Cant and Slang Dictionaries: Volume I 1567–1784* (Oxford: Oxford University Press, 2004)

——and ANNE MCDERMOTT (eds.), *Historical Dictionaries and Historical Dictionary Research* (Tübingen: Niemeyer, forthcoming)

——'The third edition of Grose's *Classical Dictionary of the Vulgar Tongue*: Bookseller's Hack-work or Posthumous Masterpiece?' in Coleman and McDermott (eds.), *Historical Dictionaries*, 71–81

COLES, ELISHA, *An English Dictionary* (London: Samuel Crouch, 1676)

CONSIDINE, JOHN, 'Du Cange: Lexicography and the Medieval Heritage', in Coleman and McDermott (eds.), *Historical Dictionaries*, 1–10

COOPER, DAVID D., *The Lesson of the Scaffold* (London: Allen Lane, 1974)

CORNWALL, BERNARD, *Gallows Thief* (London: HarperCollins, 2002)

CRAIG, JOHN, *The Mint. A History of the London Mint from A. D. 287 to 1948* (Cambridge: Cambridge University Press, 1953)

CRAIGIE, WILLIAM A. and JAMES R. HULBERT, *A Dictionary of American English on Historical Principles* (London: Oxford University Press, 1938–44)

CRICKMORE, H. G., *Dictionary or Glossary of Racing Terms and Slang* (New York: H. G. Crickmore, 1880)

CRITCHLEY, T. A., *A History of Police in England and Wales. 900–1966* (London: Constable & Co., 1967)

DAB: Dictionary of American Biography, ed. Allen Johnson, et al. (New York: Charles Scribner's Sons, 1927–)

DALTON, JAMES, *A Genuine Narrative of all the Street Robberies Committed since October last, by James Dalton, and his Accomplices* (London: J. Roberts, 1728)

DEKKER, THOMAS, *The Belman of London* (London: Nathaniel Butter, 1608)

'The Diary of a Celebrated Police Officer', *Rambler's Magazine*, New York, 1810, ii.65–8

DICKENS, CHARLES, *Oliver Twist; or, The Parish Boy's Progress* by "Boz" (London: Richard Bentley, 1838)

——*Oliver Twist*, ed. Peter Fairclough (1966) (Harmondsworth: Penguin, 1983)

DNB: Dictionary of National Biography (London: Smith, Elder & Co., 1885–1903)

DUCANGE ANGLICUS, *The Vulgar Tongue comprising Two Glossaries of Slang, Cant, and Flash Words and Phrases used in London at the Present Day* (London: Bernard Quaritch, 1857)

——*The Vulgar Tongue: A Glossary of Slang, Cant, and Flash Words and Phrases, Used in London, from 1839 to 1859 . . . Second edition, Improved and much Enlarged* (London: Bernard Quaritch, 1859)

Duncombe's New and Improved Flash Dictionary of the Cant Words, Queer Sayings, and Crack Terms, now in use in the Politer Circles, and the most Accomplished Flash Cribb Society (London: Edward Duncombe, *c.* 1850)

see also Kent

E., B., *A New Dictionary of the Terms Ancient and Modern of the Canting Crew* (London: W. Hawes, *c.* 1698)

EGAN, PIERCE, *Boxiana; or, Sketches of Antient and Modern Pugilism* (London: G. Smeeton, 1818–1824)

——*Life in London; or, the day and Night Scenes of Jerry Hawthorn, Esq. and his Elegant Friend Corinthian Tom, Accompanied by Bob Logic, The Oxonian, in their Rambles and Sprees through the Metropolis* (London: Sherwood, Neely, and Jones, 1821)

——*Grose's Classical Dictionary of the Vulgar Tongue. Revised and Corrected* (London: Printed for the Editor, 1823)

ELKINS, JAMES R., *Strangers to Us All. Lawyers and Poetry* [http://www.wvu.edu/~lawfac/jelkins/lp-2001/hall.html]

EMSLEY, CLIVE, *Policing and its Context 1750–1870* (London: Macmillan, 1983)

ENGLISH, JAMES, 'A New Vocabulary of Fashionable Phrases', 111–12, *European Magazine* 64 (1813)

FARMER, JOHN STEPHEN, and WILLIAM ERNEST HENLEY, *Slang and Its Analogues Past and Present* (London/Edinburgh: Privately published for subscribers only, 1890–4)

FIELDING, HENRY, *The History of Tom Jones. A Foundling*, ed. Martin C. Ballestin and Fredson Bowers (Oxford: Clarendon Press, 1974)

FINK, AVERIL F., 'James Hardy Vaux, Convict and Fatalist', in the *Royal Australian Historical Society Journal and Proceedings*, December 1962, 48.321–43

The Flash Dictionary (London: G. Smeeton, 1821)

'The Flash Language', in *The Ladies' Repository*, October, 1848, iii.315–17

FRANKLIN, JULIAN, *A Dictionary of Rhyming Slang* (London: Routledge & Kegan Paul, 1961)

FROST, THOMAS, *Circus Life and Circus Celebrities* (London: Tinsley Brothers, 1875)

FRYER, PETER, *Staying Power. The History of Black People in Britain* (1984) (London: Pluto Press, 1992)

GATRELL, V. A. C., *The Hanging Tree. Execution and the English People 1770–1868* (Oxford: Oxford University Press, 1996)

Gentleman's Magazine, July 1767, 340; September 1783, 728; November 1783, 928; December 1783, 1011–12, 1028; May 1784, 329; July 1784, 485; October 1788, 911; May 1791, 493–9; December 1794, 1084–5; January 1795, 18–20

GNEUSS, HELMUT, *English Language Scholarship: A Survey and Bibliography to the End of the Nineteenth Century* (Binghampton, NY: Medieval and Renaissance Texts and Studies, 1996)

GOLDIN, HYMAN E., FRANK O'LEARY, and MORRIS LIPSIUS, *Dictionary of American Underworld Lingo* (New York: Citadel Press, 1962)

GOTTI, MAURIZIO, *The Language of Thieves and Vagabonds* (Tübingen: Max Niemeyer Verlag, 1999)

Gradus ad Cantabrigiam, or, a Dictionary of Terms, Academical and Colloquial, or Cant, which are used at the University of Cambridge, by 'A Pembrochian' (London: Thomas Maiden for W. J. and J. Richardson, 1803)

Gradus ad Cantabrigiam; or New University Guide to the Academical Customs, and Colloquial or Cant Terms Peculiar to the University of Cambridge. Observing Wherein it Differs from Oxford, by 'A Brace of Cantabs' (London: John Hearne, 1824)

GREEN, DAVID R., *From Artisans to Paupers: Economic Change and Poverty in London, 1790–1870* (Aldershot: Scolar, 1995)

GREENE, ROBERT, *A Notable Discoverie of Coosnage* (London: John Wolfe for T.N., 1591)

GRIFFITHS, ARTHUR, *The Chronicles of Newgate* (London: Chapman and Hall Ltd., 1896)

GROSE, FRANCIS, *The Antiquities of England and Wales* (London: Hooper & Wigstead, 1773–87)

——British Library Additional MS 17398 [Notes and drawings by F. Grose, in counties of England and Wales 1775–1777]

——*A Classical Dictionary of the Vulgar Tongue* (London: S. Hooper, 1785)

——*A Treatise on Ancient Armour and Weapons* (London: S. Hooper, 1785–9)

——*Military Antiquities respecting a History of the English Army, from the Conquest to the Present Time* (London: S. Hooper, 1786)

——*A Provincial Glossary* (London: S. Hooper, 1787)

——*A Classical Dictionary of the Vulgar Tongue* (London: S. Hooper, 1788)

——*The Antiquities of Ireland* (London: S. Hooper, 1791–5)

——*The Olio* (London: S. Hooper, 1792)

——*A Classical Dictionary of the Vulgar Tongue. The Third Edition, Corrected and Enlarged* (London: Hooper & Co., 1796)

——*The Antiquities of Scotland* (London: Hooper & Wigstead, 1797)

see also Egan and Partridge

Guide to Eton (London: Whittaker, 1861)

GURR, TED ROBERT, *Rogues, Rebels, and Reformers. A Political History of Urban Crime and Conflict* (Beverly Hills/London: Sage Publications, 1976)

HAGGART, DAVID, *The Life of David Haggart, Alias John Wilson, Alias John Morison, Alias Barney McCoul, Alias John McColgan, Alias Daniel O'Brien, Alias the Switcher.* Written by himself, while under sentence of death (Edinburgh: James Ballantyne & Co., 1821)

—— *Life of David Haggart*, 2nd edn. (Edinburgh: James Ballantyne & Co., 1821)

HALL, BENJAMIN HOMER, *A Collection of College Words and Customs* (Cambridge, MA: John Bartlett, 1851)

HALL, JOHN, *Memoirs of the Right Villainous John Hall* (London: H. Hills, 1708)

HALLIWELL, JAMES ORCHARD, *A Dictionary of Archaic and Provincial Words* (London: J. R. Smith, 1847)

HARMAN, THOMAS, *Caveat or Warening for Commen Cursetors* (London: William Griffith, 1567)

HAY, DOUGLAS, et al., *Albion's Fatal Tree. Crime and Society in Eighteenth Century England* (London: Penguin, 1975)

—— 'Property, Authority and the Criminal Law', 17–63, in Hay et al. (1975)

HEAD, RICHARD, *The English Rogue described in the Life of Meriton Latroon* (London: Henry Marsh, 1665)

——*The Canting Academy, or the Devils Cabinet Opened* (London: F. Leach for Mat. Drew, 1673)

——*The Canting Academy or Villanies Discovered* . . . 2nd edn. (London: F. Leech for Mat. Drew, 1674)

Hell upon Earth: or the most Pleasant and Delectable History of Whittington's Colledge, Otherwise (vulgarly) called Newgate (London: no publisher's details, 1703)

HINDE, R. S. E., *The British Penal System 1773–1950* (London: Gerald Duckworth & Co. Ltd., 1951)

HINDLEY, CHARLES, *The True History of Tom and Jerry* (London: Reeves and Turner, 1888)

HITCHIN, CHARLES, *The Regulator or, a Discovery of the Thieves, Thief-Takers and Locks, alias Receivers of Stolen Goods in and about the City of London* (London: T. Warner, 1718)

HOLLINGSWORTH, KEITH, *The Newgate Novel, 1830–1847. Bulwer, Ainsworth, Dickens, & Thackeray* (Detroit: Wayne State University Press, 1963)

HOOPER, W. EDEN, *The History of Newgate and the Old Bailey* (London: Underwood Press Ltd., 1935)

HOTTEN, JOHN CAMDEN, *A Dictionary of Modern Slang, Cant, and Vulgar Words* (London: John Camden Hotten, 1859)

HUGHES, ROBERT, *The Fatal Shore. A History of the Transportation of Convicts to Australia, 1787–1868* (London: Collins Harvill, 1987)

JAMIESON, JOHN, *An Etymological Dictionary of the Scottish Language* (Edinburgh: Printed at the University Press for W. Creech, 1808)

JOHANNSEN, ALBERT, *The House of Beadle & Adams and its Dime and Nickel Novels: The Story of a Vanished Literature* (University of Oklahoma Press: http://www.niulib.niu.edu/badndp/judson_edward.html, 1999–2003)

JOHNSON, SAMUEL, *A Dictionary of the English Language* (London: W. Stratham for J. & P. Knapton, etc., 1755; repr. Hildesheim: Georg Olms Verlagsbuchhandlung, 1968)

JUDSON, EDWARD Z. C., *The Mysteries and Miseries of New York: A Story of Real Life, By Ned Buntline* (New York: Burgess & Garrett, 1848)

KEATING, NEAL, 'Henry Tufts, Land Pirate' [http://www.charm.net/~claustro/outlaw/land_pirate/default.htm]

KENT, GEORGE, *Modern Flash Dictionary; by George Kent, Historian to the Prize Ring* (London: J. Duncombe, 1835)
see also Duncombe

KILLINGRAY, DAVID (ed.), *Africans in Britain* (Ilford: Frank Cass, 1994)

KING, MOLL, *The Life and Character of Moll King, Late Mistress of King's Coffee-house in Covent Garden* (London: W. Price, 1747)

LANDAU, SIDNEY I., *Dictionaries. The Art and Craft of Lexicography* (1984) (Cambridge: Cambridge University Press, 1993)

LANE, JOAN, *Apprenticeship in England 1600–1914* (London: University College London Press, 1996)

LENTZNER, KARL, *Dictionary of the Slang-English of Australia, and of Some Mixed Languages* (Leipzig: Ehrhardt Karras, 1892)

Lexicon Balatronicum. A Dictionary of Buckish Slang, University Wit, and Pickpocket Eloquence (London: Printed for C. Chapel, Pall-Mall, 1811)

LIGHTER, J. E. (ed.), *Random House Historical Dictionary of American Slang* (New York: Random House, 1994, 1997)

LINEBAUGH, PETER, *The London Hanged. Crime and Civil Society in the Eighteenth Century* (London: Penguin, 1991)

LONGMATE, NORMAN, *The Waterdrinkers. A History of Temperance* (London: Hamish Hamilton, 1968)

LORIMER, DOUGLAS, *Colour, Class and the Victorians* (Leicester: Leicester University Press, 1978)

LOW, DONALD A., *Thieves' Kitchen. The Regency Underworld* (London: J.M. Dent & Sons Ltd, 1982)

MAITLAND, JAMES, *The American Slang Dictionary* (Chicago: Privately Printed, 1891)

MATSELL, GEORGE, *Vocabulum, or, the Rogue's Lexicon. Compiled from the most Authentic Sources* (New York: George W. Matsell & Co., 1859)

MAYHEW, HENRY, *London Labour and the London Poor; A Cyclopaedia of the Condition and Earnings of Those that will Work, Those that cannot Work, and Those that will not Work* (London: George Woodfall and Son, 1851)

MCMULLAN, JOHN L., *The Canting Crew. London's Criminal Underworld 1550–1700* (New Brunswick, NJ: Rutgers University Press, 1984)

MENCKEN, H. L., *The American Language*, 4th edn. (New York: Alfred A. Knopf, 1937)

MILES, W. A., *Poverty, Mendicity and Crime; or, the facts, examinations, &c. upon which the Report was founded, Presented to the House of Lords . . . to which is added a Dictionary of the Flash or Cant Language, Known to Every Thief and Beggar edited by H. Brandon, esq.* (London: Shaw and Sons, 1839)

MILLER, WILBUR R., *Cops and Bobbies. Police Authority in New York and London, 1830–1870* (Chicago/London: University of Chicago Press, 1977)

[MOORE, THOMAS], *Tom Crib's Memorial to Congress . . . by one of the fancy* (London: Longman et al., 1819)

MUGGLESTONE, LYNDA, *'Talking Proper'. The Rise of Accent as Social Symbol* (Oxford: Clarendon Press, 1995)

N., W. W., 'Cant and Thieves' Jargon', *Journal of American Folk-Lore* III. Boston 1890, 314–15

New Canting Dictionary (London: The Booksellers of London and Westminster, 1725)

OED: Oxford English Dictionary, 3rd edn., ed. John Simpson. *OED Online.* (Oxford: Oxford University Press, 2000–) [http://dictionary.oed.com/cgi/entry/00299451]

OSSELTON, N. E., 'Dialect Words in General Dictionaries,' 34–45 in *Chosen Words. Past and Present Problems for Dictionary Makers* (Exeter: University of Exeter Press, 1995)

OUSBY, IAN, *Bloodhounds of Heaven. The Detective in English Fiction from Godwin to Doyle* (Cambridge, MA/London: Harvard University Press, 1976)

——(ed.), *The Cambridge Guide to Literature in English* (Cambridge and New York: Cambridge University Press, 1993)

PARKER, GEORGE, *A View of Society and Manners in High and Low Life* (London: Printed for the Author, 1781)

—— *Life's Painter of Variegated Characters* (London: R. Bassam, 1789)

PARTRIDGE, ERIC, *A Classical Dictionary of the Vulgar Tongue by Captain Francis Grose* (1931) (London: Routledge & Kegan Paul, 1963)

——*Slang Today and Yesterday* (1933) (London: Routledge & Kegan Paul, 1950)

——*A Dictionary of Slang and Unconventional English* (1938) 8th edn., ed. Paul Beale (London: Routledge, 2002)

PEARSON, EDMUND (ed.), *The Autobiography of a Criminal. Henry Tufts* (London: Jarrolds, 1931)

A PEMBROCHIAN see *Gradus*

PERRY, WILLIAM, *The London Guide, and Stranger's Safeguard* (London/Liverpool: J. Bumpus, W. Sharpe/T. Hughes et al., 1818)

PLAYFAIR, GILES, *The Punitive Obsession. An Unvarnished History of the English Prison System* (London: Victor Gollancz, 1971)

PORTER, DENNIS, *The Pursuit of Crime. Art and Ideology in Detective Fiction* (New Haven, CT/London: Yale University Press, 1981)

PORTER, ROY, *Disease, Medicine and Society in England 1550–1860* (London: Macmillan, 1987)

POTTER, HUMPHRY TRISTRAM, *A New Dictionary of all the Cant and Flash Languages*, 3rd edn. (London: B. Crosby, 1797)

——*A New Dictionary of all the Cant and Flash Languages* (London: W. Mackintosh, sold by J. Downes, c.1797)

——*A New Dictionary of all the Cant and Flash Languages*, 3rd edn., corrected (London: J. Downes, 1800)

POULTER, JOHN, *The Discoveries of John Poulter*, 5th edn. (Sherbourne: R. Goadby, 1753)

QUARITCH *see* Ducange Anglicus

Jack Randall's Diary of Proceedings at the House of Call for Genius, ed. Mr. Breakwindow (London: W. Simpkin and R. Marshall, 1820)

RAWLINGS, PHILIP, *Crime and Power. A History of Criminal Justice 1688–1998* (London and New York: Longman, 1999)

RAY, JOHN, *A Collection of English Words not Generally used . . .* (London: H. Bruges for Tho. Burrell, 1674)

Real Life in London; or, the Rambles and Adventures of Bob Tallyho, Esq. and his cousin, The Hon. Tom Dashall, through the Metropolis; exhibiting a living picture of fashionable characters, manners, and amusements in high and low life. By an Amateur (London: Jones & Co., 1821)

REID, J. C., *Bucks and Bruisers. Pierce Egan and Regency England* (London: Routledge & Kegan Paul, 1971)

[REYNOLDS, JOHN HAMILTON], *The Fancy: A Selection from the Poetical Remains of the late Peter Corcoran* (London: Taylor and Hessey, 1820)

RICHARDSON, JAMES F., *The New York Police. Colonial Times to 1901* (New York: Oxford University Press, 1970)

ROSE, LIONEL, *Rogues and Vagabonds. Vagrant Underworld in Britain 1815–1985* (London & New York: Routledge, 1988)

R[OWLANDS], S[AMUEL], *Martin Mark-all, Beadle of Bridewell* (London: John Budge & Richard Bonian, 1610)

THE ROYAL HUMANE SOCIETY website: http://www.royalhumane.org/history/history.htm

SCHORSCH, ANITA, *Images of Childhood: An Illustrated Social History* (New York: Mayflower Books Inc., 1979)

SCORSESE, MARTIN, *Gangs of New York* (Los Angeles, CA: Miramax, 2003)

Scoundrel's Dictionary (London: J. Brownnell, 1754)

SHADWELL, THOMAS, *The Squire of Alsatia* (London: James Knapton, 1688)

SHAKESPEARE, WILLIAM, *All's Well That Ends Well*, The Arden Shakespeare, ed. G. K. Hunter (London: Methuen & Co. Ltd., 1959)

——*Much Ado About Nothing*, The Arden Shakespeare, ed. A. R. Humphreys (London/New York: Routledge, 1981)

——*Timon of Athens*, The Arden Shakespeare, ed. H. J. Oliver (1959) London/Cambridge, MA: Methuen/Harvard University Press, 1963)

SILVESTER, JOHN, British Library Additional MS 47466, British Library Egerton MS 3710 [Notebooks concerning London criminals c.1812, 1816]

SIMMONDS, PETER LUND, *The Commercial Dictionary of Trade Products* (London: G. Routledge & Sons, 1872)

Sinks of London Laid Open: A Pocket Companion for the Uninitiated (London: J. Duncombe, 1848)

'SLANG', *Household Words*, Saturday, 24 September, 1853, 73–8

SMEETON, GEORGE, *Life and Death in London, or, The Kaleidoscope of Villainy* (London: G. Smeeton, 1817)

——*Account of the dreadful murder of the unfortunate Mary Minting, on Saturday, February 14, 1818, at Union-Street, Mary-le-bone: with the particulars of the suicide of W. Haitch, her murderer: Also, the trial of David Evans, for the wilful murder of his wife. Unfolding another melancholy instance of the horrid effects of drunkeness!* (London: G. Smeeton, 1818)

——*An Account of a most shocking murder committed by Charlotte Lawson on her mistress, by beating her brains out with a brick-bat, and afterwards cutting her to pieces* (London: Smeeton, c.1832–1839)

——*Doings in London* (London: Smeeton, 1828)

SMITH, ALEXANDER, *The Thieves New Canting Dictionary* (London: Sam Briscoe, 1719)

SMOLLETT, TOBIAS, *The Adventures of Roderick Random*, ed. Paul-Gabriel Boucé (Oxford: Oxford University Press, 1979)

SNOWDEN *see* Archbold

Songs, Duets, Choruses, &c. see *Tom and Jerry*

STARNES, DE WITT T., and GERTRUDE E. NOYES, *The English Dictionary from Cawdrey to Johnson, 1604–1755* (Chapel Hill: University of North Carolina Press, 1946)

STRAY, CHRISTOPHER, *English Slang in the Nineteenth Century* (Bristol: Thoemmes Press, 2002)

SULLIVAN, JOSEPH M., *Criminal Slang: a Dictionary of the Vernacular of the Under World* (Chicago: Detective Pub. Co., 1908)

SWIFT, JONATHON, *Polite Conversation* (1738), ed. Herbert Davis with Louis Landa, *A Proposal for Correcting the English Tongue, Polite Conversation, &c.* (Oxford: Basil Blackwell, 1957)

THOMAS, J. E., *House of Care. Prisons and Prisoners in England 1500–1800* (Nottingham: University of Nottingham, Dept of Adult Education, 1988)

The Times, December the 5th, 1857, 12: 'The Ellesmere Jewel Robbery'

TOBIAS, J. J., *Crime and Police in England 1700–1900* (Dublin: Gill & Macmillan, 1979)

Tom and Jerry; or Life in London. A Musical Extravaganza in Three Acts. To Which is affixed, the most Copious Vocabulary of Flash and Cant yet published. Founded on Pierce Egan's popular work of "Life in London" (Dublin: The Bookseller, 1822)

——*Songs, Duets, Choruses, &c. in Tom and Jerry. As Sung at the Newcastle Theatre for Several Successive Nights, With Unbounded Applause. With a Glossary of all the Cant and Flash Phrases* (Newcastle: J. Marshall, c.1823)

TUFTS, HENRY, *A Narrative of the Life, Adventures, Travels and Sufferings of Henry Tufts* (Dover, NH: Samuel Bragg, jun., 1807)

The Universal Songster, or, Museum of Mirth, Vol. II (London: John Fairburn, 1826)

VAUX, JAMES HARDY, *Memoirs of James Hardy Vaux. Written by Himself* . . . (London: W. Clowes, 1819)

The Vulgarities of Speech Corrected; with Elegant Expressions for Provincial and Vulgar English, Scots, and Irish (London: James Bulcock, 1826)

WALKER, GILBERT, *A Manifest Detection of the Most Vyle and Detestable Use of Diceplay* . . . (London: Abraham Uele, 1552)

WEBSTER, NOAH, *An American Dictionary of the English Language* (New York: S. Converse, 1828)

The Whole Art of Thieving and Defrauding Discovered (London: Printed for the Booksellers, 1786)

WILDE, WILLIAM CUMMING, 'Notes on Thief Talk', *Journal of American Folk-Lore*, 1890 III, 303–10

WILLARD, JOSIAH FLYNT, *Tramping with Tramps* (London: T. Fisher Unwin, 1899)

Yokel's Preceptor: or, More Sprees in London! . . . *To which is added A Joskin's Vocabulary of the various Slang Words now in constant use* . . . (London: H. Smith, *c.*1855)

YULE, HENRY and A. C. BURNELL, *Hobson-Jobson; a Glossary of Colloquial Anglo-Indian Words and Phrases* (London: John Murray, 1886)

Word Index

Included here are all the cant and slang terms mentioned in the text, and all terms cited or quoted from the dictionaries studied here. Brief definitions are given to aid in the identification of the reference required. Where it was impossible to define a term with any brevity, or where a detailed definition would have duplicated material in the text unnecessarily, an indication of meaning is given in square brackets. Where terms are cited only in specific phrases, such as proverbs, the phrase is given in italics. Page numbers in bold refer to terms included in illustrations. Indentation is intended to help in the location of terms, and not to indicate relationships between them.

scamp "a highwayman" 116
  the scamp "highway robbery" 86
  flash scamp "a thief" 151
  scamp-foot (*for* foot-scamp) "a highwayman"
    116, 133
  scampsman "a highwayman" 202
scandal-broth "tea" 37
scapegallows "one who deserves to be
  hanged" 37
scapegrace "a dissolute man" 37
scarce: to make oneself scarce **vb** "to slip
  away" 37
scarper **vb** "to run away" 225, 226
scavey "sense; knowledge" 26
schism-shop "a dissenters' meeting-house" 58
schofel "forged money" 226
scold's cure "a coffin" 86
sconce **vb** "to fine" 4, 248
  [*to build a large sconce*] **vb** "to run up a large
  debt" 24
Scotch warming-pan "a female bedfellow; a
  fart" 61
scout "a college servant" 82, 247
  "a watch" 213
scrag "the neck" 199
scran "food" 37
scrapper "a boxer" 99
scratch "a mark in a boxing ring at which the
  fight begins" 211, 212
screen *also* skreen "a banknote" 80, **206**, 207
screeve *also* screave "a banknote" 234
screw "a skeleton key" 77
  screwsman "a burglar who uses skeleton
  keys" 94
scrip "subscription" 38
scuddick *also* (*erron*) scurrick "a halfpenny"
  167, 216
scum "the mob" 76
scurfed "arrested" 164
scurrick *see* scuddick
scuttle (a nob) **vb** "to break (a head)" 169, 173
seedy "poor" 200, 218, 234
septzambecs "seven" 135
septzyams "seventy" 135
serve **vb** "to sentence" 86
  serve (out) **vb** "to beat" 85, 86
set to "a fight" 216
  vb "to begin a fight" 212
sevenpence "seven years transportation" 126
shag "a sexual partner" 58
shake **vb** "to rob" 77, 139, 146
shakester *see* shickster
shallow [a type of hat] 37, 38
  go on the shallows **vb** "to be half naked" 220

sham **vb** "to pretend" 176
shank: [*to ride Shank's naggy*] 26
sharp "a sharper; a cheat; a gambler" 37, 194,
  196, **206**
  "knowing; alert" 183
sheep-walk "prison" 151
Sheila "a girl; a woman" 139
shelf: laid on the shelf "pawned" 37
sheriff's journeyman 83
sherry **vb** "to run away" 94, 243
shicer "a worthless person" 139
shicker "bad; a worthless person" 226
shickster *also* chickster, shakester "a woman; a
  prostitute" 101, 127, 220, 226
shift: shifting ballast "a passenger on board
  ship" 24
  for shift one's bob *see* bob
shimmy *also* chimmy "a chemise" 127
shindy "a dance" 89
  "a riot" 191
ship: ship-shape "in order" 24
  shipped "expelled" 254
shirt: to have one's shirt out "to lose one's
  temper" 235
shoe-string "a small stake" 100
short "an undiluted shot of spirits" 173, 212
  "hard up" 158
  short stuff "a glass of liquor" 158
shoulder-tapper "a bailiff" 37
shove: shove the moon **vb** "to leave lodgings by
  night" 166
  shove in the mouth "a drink" 89
  shove my trunk **vb** "to leave" 195
  shove the tumbler **vb** "to be whipped
  publicly" 207
shy-cock "a debtor who evades the bailiff" 201
sideboards "shirt collars" 230
siesta *also* siester, (*erron*) sigster "an afternoon
  nap" 131
sigher "a methodist's criminal accomplice" 117
sign: sign of five shillings [a public house called
  'The Crown'] 42
  sign of fifteen shillings [a public house called
  'The Three Crowns'] 42
  sign of a house to let "mourning clothes worn
  by a widow" 35
sigster *see* siesta
silence: [*silence in court, the cat is pissing*] 172
silversmith "a pawnbroker" 158
Simeonite "a follower of Simeon" 251
sing **vb** "to call out" 89
  sing dummy **vb** "to say nothing" 243
single peeper *see* peeper
sir reverence "a human turd" 32

Subject Index

Page references in bold refer to illustrations. Dictionaries are listed under the names of their editors, except where they are usually referred to by their title.